GUIDE TO WRITING EMPIRICAL PAPERS, THESES, and DISSERTATIONS

GUIDE TO WRITING EMPIRICAL PAPERS, THESES, and DISSERTATIONS

G. David Garson
North Carolina State University
Raleigh, North Carolina

CRC Press is an imprint of the
Taylor & Francis Group, an **informa** business

CRC Press
Taylor & Francis Group
6000 Broken Sound Parkway NW, Suite 300
Boca Raton, FL 33487-2742

First issued in paperback 2019

ISBN-13: 978-0-8247-0605-0 (hbk)
ISBN-13: 978-0-367-39668-8 (pbk)

Visit the Taylor & Francis Web site at
http://www.taylorandfrancis.com

and the CRC Press Web site at
http://www.crcpress.com

Preface

The inspiration for this book was both the foundation of a new doctoral program in my department, and also my memories of what little guidance I received when writing my dissertation at a famed Ivy League institution. While every paper, thesis, and dissertation is different, it is my hope that this volume will be helpful to writers starting on the path to publication. Other books have been written on this subject, but I have sought to make this one of particular relevance to those engaged in empirical research, in which the writing process is inextricably bound to research design and statistical methodology.

This volume is intended to enrich students' comprehension of the structure and execution of the written research project. Toward this end, each chapter contains an overview, a checklist of writing considerations, and bibliographic guidance to further understanding of the topic. Special attention has been given to computer-based research tools, not just in statistical matters, but in brainstorming one's topic, locating data and information, managing a bibliography, and all the other elements of the research process.

An attempt has been made in this book to treat the entire quantitative research process in its writing aspects, including brainstorming, framing an analytic question, developing a comprehensive outline, and providing a roadmap for the reader. Electronic search resources and bibliographic software get particular attention as a prelude to meta-analysis of prior research and development of the literature review. The student is urged to think in terms of modeling as well as operationalizing variables. Selection of research designs and appropriate statistical methodology are treated, as are the basics of writing fundamentals, validity, and data visualization. The work concludes with emphasis on research ethics and issues associated with drawing inferences and making generalizations. Dealing with one's thesis or dissertation committee is not forgotten, and final chapters make explicit the special characteristics of quantitative research writing in the humanities and in the natural sciences. Last, but not least, funding sources for dissertation research are inventoried, with Web links and other contact information.

I wish to thank all those who have helped with the preparation of this book, especially my students and Paige Force, production editor at Marcel Dekker, Inc. Errors and omissions, of course, are my own and should this volume prove of some use and see another edition, I would thank dear readers who are kind enough to send their reactions and suggestions. In the meantime, additional information on quantitative research is found at my website, http://www2.chass.ncsu.edu/garson/PA765/.

G. David Garson

Contents

1

Brainstorming

I. CHOOSING A SUBJECT

Selecting a subject seems like an easy task, but it is entirely possible to make critical mistakes at this early stage, sabotaging the ultimate outcome. Many students make bad choices at the outset—choices that, in the case of a dissertation, can literally waste years of effort. A good choice will not only be better from a scholarly point of view, but it will also provide a more do-able, fun, and satisfying creative activity for the writer. A good subject has five attributes:

1. *A good subject is important.* The subject must be important in terms of substantive policy, theory construction/validation, or both. Beware, for example, of case studies that have no clear implications for public policy and no particular relation to theories in the field. Even in historical studies, it is best to pick a topic that transcends mere description. For instance, although a history of Wyatt Earp's life might be acceptable, it might be more interesting to write on theories about the role of the American frontier in forming the political culture of the country using Wyatt Earp's life to illustrate.

2. *A good subject is focused.* The subject must be limited in scope. It is tempting to state that the purpose of the researcher's essay or dissertation "is to describe . . . ," "is to explore . . . ," "is to inventory . . . ," "is to set forth the dimensions of . . . ," or "is to discuss . . . ." Such starts may lead into perfectly fine theses, but more often, they are a sign the writer has not focused his or her research question, which results in a "look at this, look at that" tour guide of the subject rather than a clear story line.

3. *A good subject is organized.* The subject must be organized to tell a clear story, and the reader should be given a road map that tells where the story will be going. In general, if there is no story to tell or if it is told in a disorganized way, readers will not give the writer the "benefit of the doubt." Many will put the piece of writing down well before the end or skip to the concluding section for a summary. Writers know that to hold the reader's attention, there must be a beginning, a middle, and an end to any story. The beginning must grab the reader's attention by showing there is a point to what has been written, it discusses something that at least in principle could be viewed in different ways, and it shows what difference the author's way makes. The middle builds the evidence, drawing the reader into the plot, whether the subject is scientific, sociopolitical, psychological, or something else. The ending brings the story to a climax.

4. *A good subject is informative.* There must be new information, qualitative or quantitative, that is credible and convincing. Even in a review essay, the review must forge a new sort of synthesis, providing new insights. Having original data is the typical method of satisfying this requirement, but other strategies could include new ways of categorizing data, new ways of comparing data across types of settings, or new ways of relating data to theories in the field.

5. *Finally, a good subject is readable.* Writing style should be professional but not jargon-laden, lively but not emotional, and committed but not biased. Sometimes professional editors are even brought in to improve writing style, but most writers are on their own. At a minimum, the author must think explicitly about writing style and obtain feedback from readers who have experience with a diversity of styles and have a basis for providing feedback to the author.

Choosing a subject can sometimes be a real obstacle for writers, particularly beginning authors. The conventional advice, apart from asking one's advisor for ideas, is to write about something that is of interest to you personally. If you are in a position to conduct personal interviews related to a topic, this, too, will help you understand your topic better and may generate ideas to refine your topic. Other common prewriting activities include outlining, talking with others, reading, field trips, doodling, creating lists, writing journals, and creating story boards. The prewriting book by McKay (1989) contains no fewer than 70 types of prewriting exercises!

Searching the world wide web can be a useful way of generating a topic. At least one web site, "Filamentality" at http://www.kn.pacbell.com/wired/fil/, is designed as a fill-in-the-blank interactive web site that guides novice users through using the web to pick a writing topic. There are also web sites such as "Hot Sheets" (http://www.hotsheet.com) and "Research Paper Help" (http://www.researchpaper.com) that categorize topics and provide Internet links to help prospective writers explore possible topics. The former includes links to dozens of web search engines. The latter includes an "Idea Directory" that generates research ideas with Internet links based on user input. For instance, inputting ''pollution'' as an area of interest generated these research topics, each with appropriate web links:

Science-Biology: Plants as indicators of pollution
Science-Oceans and Seas: Current levels of ocean pollution
Society-Government & Law: Recent legislation on air pollution
Science-Geography: American air pollution levels.
Science-Oceans and Seas: Recent proposals to prevent ocean pollution and contamination
Society-Population: Exponential growth's relationship to resource usage, population, and pollution
Science-Energy: The pros and cons of wood stoves as alternative energy sources
Science-Technology: Stone buildings and monuments all over the world are suffering severe weather and pollution damage. What is being done to control this situation?
Science-Architecture: Can the Acropolis be saved from pollution, decay, and erosion?

Internet research is becoming more important every day and is not to be neglected, though it is now a vast sea of knowledge with both reliable and unreliable sources that must be carefully evaluated by the writer.

A more useful brainstorming approach is to browse scholarly journals or current periodicals in one's area of writing, being open to finding topics that spark interest. Supporting or contradicting an article can be a good starting point for writing term papers, theses, or even dissertations. For any given article, one can ask such questions as: Does the author of the article seem to have a bias or conflict of interest? Does the writer have experiences that seem to contradict the article? What different conclusion might the article come to if it centered on a different population, location, or time period? What different conclusions might occur if certain other variables were included in the study? Is the article based on some theory and if so are there other implications of that theory not discussed by the article, or if the article is devoid of theory, have the authors failed to consider relevant theories in their field?

In summary, choosing a good topic is a major determinant of your success as a writer. By picking a subject that interests you, you will be able to sustain the energy required for a significant writing effort. Moreover, displaying a certain degree of enthusiasm for your topic will be contagious to your peers, teachers, dissertation committee, and readers. If you cannot make the topic compelling, you may have chosen unwisely. For course-related papers, of course, it is essential to make the paper fit the themes of the course. For all writing efforts, you must pick a researchable topic, not so broad as to prevent gathering convincing evidence and not so narrow as to limit information and evidence.

A. Brainstorming

Brainstorming is the name for a set of techniques that may help you select an initial subject. It is often used during a meeting to encourage the spontaneous contribution of ideas from all members of the group, but it can also be used by the individual researcher. Some may be tempted to skip brainstorming and go directly to the next chapter, formulating an analytic question, but it is advisable to take the creative brainstorming phase seriously before proceeding. Brainstorming should not be considered an optional exercise. In almost all cases, a serious effort at brainstorming will generate significant improvements in the writer's research concept. Brainstorming is a worthwhile effort.

1. Brainstorming Described

Brainstorming was invented in the late 1930s and early 1940s by Alex F. Osborne, arising in the context of the advertising industry. Starting in the 1930s, Osborne and others brought together groups of decision-makers to address specific problems with as many ideas as possible. Osborne believed that generation of ideas was a skill anyone could acquire through use of various creative thought techniques. The core of his vision was ''deferred judgment,'' that is, by suppressing criticism and evaluation of ideas during the brainstorming process, the capacity to synthesize is increased by releasing the writer's or decision-maker's mind from the analysis mode of thinking.

(a) Brainstorming as a Group Process. Usually brainstorming will generate more ideas if it is done on a group rather than individual basis. Consider whether you could get other students, perhaps ones who also need writing topics or who have similar interests (such as class members or fellow doctoral students), to participate in a brainstorming group. You may want to do this at a set of lunches during which each person's topic gets brainstormed by the group.

There is no exact size for a brainstorming group. Some prefer groups of 5 to 7 people as optimal, whereas others recommend up to 10 or 12. However, there is unanimous agreement that the benefits of brainstorming decline when this technique is attempted in large groups. There is also agreement that more ideas are generated if the participants have a few days' advance notice, giving time to let some ideas form beforehand.

How the brainstorming process works. You, as leader, start the brainstorming session by outlining the objective (for example, to generate interesting topics in the area of criminal justice). Keep the atmosphere relaxed and emphasize that the purpose is to generate as many ideas as possible, not to evaluate the ideas.

Encourage active participation of all members of the group, trying to develop an enthusiastic atmosphere.

As group leader, you should try to discourage any evaluation or even discussion during the brainstorming process, including any criticisms or compliments. It is often helpful to start with a warm-up practice on an unrelated topic, such as, "How can we attract more squirrels to the campus?" With any luck, participants will have fun, understand the brainstorming process better, and be impressed with how it stimulates creativity.

Go on to the main topic and encourage everyone to participate. Set a time limit, perhaps 25 minutes. One method is to go around the room, having every member suggest an idea off the top of their head. Emphasize that every idea is welcome, because even "crazy" ones may lead to good ideas later in the process. Also let people know that it is okay to build on one another's ideas. One may use a blackboard, flip chart, or sticky notes to write down and post every idea as it is generated. Having another person volunteer for this task will be helpful, perhaps even using two volunteer recorders to speed things up. Also, tolerate periods of silence as people think about the topic.

After a long list of ideas is generated, a second step in the group process is to cluster the ideas in categories. This can be done by rearranging the sticky notes, if that method was used. Another method is drawing conceptual maps on the blackboard or flip chart. In such conceptual charts, circles are used to represent variables of concepts or ideas and arrows are used to depict causal effects or relationships. One may generate such maps on a blackboard based on group consensus, or it may be valuable to have group members individually create such maps, then discuss differences among them and hold a group discussion about reconciling and synthesizing differences in models.

Ask someone to identify the most important central idea, then write it on the board and circle it. Add other ideas as additional circles one at a time. As each circle is added, get group discussion on its relation to circled concepts already on the board and draw appropriate connecting arrows. Or, you may wish to attach a verb to each arrow, clarifying the meaning of the connection (for example, causes, must precede, must accompany, etc.). Getting clarification of the meaning of each suggested item is appropriate in this stage.

A final step is evaluation. Often this is best done after a break, though that timing is not essential. In the evaluative discussion, remove ideas that the group feels would not be workable. Discuss various criteria for prioritizing the remaining ideas: importance, interest, and feasibility.

(b) Brainstorming as an Individual Process. It is possible to brainstorm on your own (see the "Example" subsection below). Before doing so, consider some of the approaches in the "Checklist" subsection later in this chapter. Individual-level brainstorming is not a one-shot process. You may find it useful to keep an idea notebook or its index card or database equivalent, in which you jot down ideas, inspirations, tangents, and other bits and pieces that may one day become parts of your study.

Freewriting is a well-established approach to individual brainstorming. Freewriting is allowing yourself to write freely, without restrictions, without worrying about grammar or writing style, even without worrying if what you write is coherent. You may find this easier to do as stream-of-consciousness dictation into a tape recorder. Regardless, the concept of freewriting is to encourage free association of ideas, not stopping for at least 15 minutes. Later on, at the end of the freewriting process, the writer sifts through the ideas that he or she has written, editing some, deleting others, highlighting sentences or phrases that seem particularly evocative, then organizing the sifted version of one's writing into an outline for a paper.

(c) The Delphi Technique. Delphi is an approach to brainstorming that can be conducted without the need for face-to-face meetings. Frequently it is implemented through mail. Now that e-mail is common, vastly speeding things up, the Delphi technique promises to become much more popular. Delphi is sometimes used to generate ideas among a group of experts but it could be used to generate topic ideas for writing. There are many variations, but in general Delphi is a five-step process.

How Delphi works. A group of experts or other respondents is approached, and the general nature of Delphi is explained to them. Their willingness to participate is secured. In the case of dissertation writing, the group of experts might be fellow students who agree to participate by e-mail.

A questionnaire is developed that calls on respondents to list topic ideas related to a subject, such as that on which the writer has chosen to focus. The instrument is mailed or faxed to appropriate respondents who complete and return it.

The researcher summarizes results from the first wave of returns and sends back a second questionnaire that asks the respondents to prioritize items previously submitted according to one or more criteria, such as substantive importance, theoretical importance, and feasibility. The authorship of items remains anonymous.

The process is repeated until there is convergence and the researcher concludes additional iterations would not change results.

All participants get a final summary of the group's consensus. Final feedback is solicited from respondents, who may further change their opinions in view of the collective group opinion.

(d) The Nominal Group Process. The nominal group process is an alternative face-to-face technique very similar to brainstorming, except that an attempt is made to reach consensus in the end. This is done by having each person assign priorities by silent ballot, tallying the ballots, and discussing the group priorities that have received the highest votes.

2. Brainstorming Checklist

Here are some specific activities and concepts to consider when doing brainstorming:

Develop a ''quick and dirty'' reading list (not your literature review, which is a later topic of this book) and read a wide variety of perspectives.

Consider whether your brainstorming benefited from your prior research of the literature.

Many political think tanks have their working papers online on the Internet, often providing good background. Ask you advisor for names of think tanks and research institutes in your area of specialization.

It can be a good idea to look at some of the debate in the Congressional Record. Although not research material, it helps develop the issues pertaining to your topic. For a keyword search of the Congressional Record as well as bills before Congress, go to the ''Thomas'' web site of the Library of Congress at http://thomas.loc.gov/home/thomas2.html.

Do a search of the Library of Congress by going to http://lcweb2.loc.gov/ammem/booksquery.html. You won't be able to read text online, but after you have entered your keywords and gotten some hits, click the ''Browse Shelves'' button to see titles related to the ones you found. Browsing the electronic shelves can generate more subject ideas.

Of course, do a search of the web with a good search engine, such as Altavista (http://www.altavista.com) or All the Web (http://www.alltheweb.com).

For doctoral research, have you consulted with experts for their ideas on suitable topics or feasibility of topics already identified?

Keep a notebook of ideas as you seek to select your subject.

Consider putting a twist on an existing concept or investigating hypotheses contrary to conventional wisdom.

Avoid topics in which you have a personal stake, emotional involvement, or other conflict of interest.

Write out a formal definition of your key subject terms.

Consider if your subject can be divided into different types, and create a typology.

Create an inventory of the alleged causes of your subject.

List the alleged consequences of your subject.

List several subjects similar to your subject, ones that would be interesting to compare, and then make lists of similarities and differences in these analogies.

Write each key element in your thesis and supporting hypotheses out as exact opposites. Consider whether these negations also contain interesting ideas you should explore.

Create a time line that shows the historical development of your subject.

List types of actors affected by your subject and write a paragraph giving the typical views of each type.

List public policy controversies and issues related to your subject.

If you have a dissertation or thesis committee of faculty members, write out a preliminary paper with some leading bibliography to describe general orienting questions for your area of interest and obtain feedback on these questions for your dissertation, thesis, or paper.

Don't let brainstorming be a one-time thing at the beginning of your writing project. Instead, look for opportunities over the entire course of your writing to exchange and develop ideas with others.

3. Brainstorming Examples

Suppose you are considering writing about something in the area of environmental regulation. Compose a list of everything you can think of related to this topic, freely associating and omitting nothing, continuing until you run out of ideas. Don't stop to evaluate your ideas, edit them, or even be grammatical. An example of such a list might be this:

Subject: Environmental Regulation
Air pollution.
Noise pollution.
Water pollution.
Chemical pollution/hazardous waste.
Endangered species.
Is it effective?
Cost/benefit analysis.
EPA agency.
EPA regulations versus property rights.
Conservatives versus liberals on environmental regulation.
Al Gore.
Politician's platforms on environment.
Federal funding for environment.
State funding.
Private costs/funding.
Private sector ads on environmental issues.
Public opinion on environment, causes of.
Smokey the Bear.
Conservation.
Conservation/environment in 1900s versus 1990s.

Once you have generated a list, reconsider your topic. Drop ideas that do not seem as important, interesting, or feasible to investigate. The next step is to look at this list with a view toward forming an analytic topic. One needs to find testable propositions, usually ones positing a causal relationship. Such relationships often take such forms as these:

The more the one, the less the other (or vice versa): the better organized the conservation/environmental movements in a given decade, the more the conservation/environmental legislation in that decade.

First one, then the other: chemical pollution led to more species being endangered.

Two (or more) things operating jointly create a third thing. There is an interaction effect whereby joint federal and state funding of environmental objectives can achieve results that can accomplish neither operating alone.

Such relationships, of course, are not known to be true beforehand. Indeed, if they are self-evident or commonly accepted by all, motivation for research is undermined. The best testable propositions are plausible but not indisputable, leaving the researcher room to compare the posited relationships with other plausible alternatives.

4. Brainstorming software

A variety of software exists to assist the writer with brainstorming. An example is *IdeaFisher* and its ''light'' version, *Writer's Edge* (*http://www.ideafisher.com/*), described by Fisher (1995). This software functions like a superthesaurus. When the writer enters a keyword from his or her theme, *IdeaFisher* or *Writer's Edge* will generate hundreds of words and concepts related to the topic, not only synonyms, but all kinds of associated concepts and words in a variety of categories: people, things, places, processes, verbs, descriptors, abstractions, and other categories of words and phrases associated with the keyword. *IdeaFisher* also has specialized sets of dialogues that lead a writer through his or her topic, exploring ramifications. Although somewhat weighted toward business applications, this software has add-on modules for such topics as strategic planning, evaluation, general problem solving, or conflict resolution, to name a few specialty areas. The dialogues in conflict resolution, for instance, contain questions for the author such as ''List five ways in which conflict can be described positively (e.g; challenging, enlightening, constructive, barrier-breaking, fostering innovation), or list five ways that describe conflict negatively (e.g., disruptive, unsettling, fragmenting, self-perpetuating, stressful).''

Brainstorming Toolbox and *Innovation Toolbox* are also examples of brainstorming software (*http://www.infiniteinnovations.co.uk/*). The *Innovations Toolbox* creates interactive exercises implementing a variety of brainstorming techniques, including:

1. *Random word.* A random word generator electronically implements the brainstorming technique of free association. A random picture variant is also supported, based on the thought that visuals generate group brainstorming discussion.
2. *Innovation.* A list of innovation-related questions is posed to the user, encouraging the writer to examine his or her concepts from a variety of perspectives.
3. *Problem identification.* Questions force the writer to spell out the exact problem being addressed and related assumptions.
4. *False rules.* Rules from other fields of knowledge are presented so the author can consider the extent to which they do or do not apply to the writer's subject.
5. *Thesaurus.* A synonym technique to consider variants on one's key ideas.
6. *Random phrases.* A word and phrase manipulator creates ad lib-type variations on one's original statements.
7. *Analogies.* A technique that prompts the writer to consider other processes and relationships to spell out similarities and differences between one's subject and the analogy.

Drawn from the field of creative writing, these software tools are available in a free 30-day trial version from the Infinite Innovations, Ltd. web site above.

ParaMind (http://www.paramind.net/) is another type of brainstorming software. It works by generating new text from your writing, thereby expanding on any idea based on one of hundreds of built-in related word chains, to which the writer can add. As such, it goes beyond common ''writer's helper'' software that may ask the writer questions related to his or her subject, flow charting the writer's concepts or generating random word combinations that provide idea variations typed in by the author. In *ParaMind*, a single sentence or paragraph can be expanded and permuted into up to 100 pages of related statements. In simple ''merge'' mode, *ParaMind* operates as a sort of thesaurus, suggesting substitutes for words the writer highlights in the text. However, in ''large merge'' mode, many pages of new, reworded relationships are generated, providing feedback on hundreds of new relationships and associations relevant to the concepts contained in the author's original text.

Yet another example of brainstorming software is *Solutions*, which grows out of process brainstorming in business decision-making. *Solutions* provides a structured model for project definition, identification of potential areas for improvement, analysis of causes, development and selection of solutions, action plan development, and evaluation of results. *Solutions* is built around the four steps of definition, analysis, action, and evaluation. Built-in group tools consist of brainstorming with optional group voting and force field analysis for selection of ideas; diagramming techniques for root cause identification and analysis; and flow charting and process mapping. These tools are integrated. Brainstorming session ideas can be dragged and dropped into the module for diagramming causes. The root causes or identified steps in the flow charting module can be dragged and dropped to another brainstorming session. The software can be used on an individual or group basis to generate ideas. A free demo version is available at http://www.dssinfotech.com/Solutions.shtml.

Other software includes *Brainstorming 101*, available for free downloading in demo format at http://www.brainstorming.org/. Likewise, a 30-day evaluation copy of the software *Brainstormer* is available for free at *http://www.jpb.com/creative/brainstormer.html.*

BIBLIOGRAPHY

Clark, C. H. (1989). *Brainstorming: How to Create Successful Ideas*. Wilshire Book Co. [A popular general text on the subject.]

Delbecq, A., Van de Ven, D. (1975). Group Techniques for Program Planning: A Guide to Nominal Group and Delphi Processes. Glenview, IL: Scott-Foresman.

Fisher, M. (1995). The IdeaFisher: How to Land That Big Idea—and Other Secrets of Creativity in Business. Princeton, NJ: Peterson's. [Covers *IdeaFisher* brainstorming software.]

Fligor, M. (1990). Brainstorming: The Book of Topics. Creative Learning Press.

Lamm, K. (1998). 10,000 Ideas for Term Papers, Projects, Reports and Speeches: Intriguing, Original Research Topics for Every Student's Need. New York: IDG Books Worldwide. [Covers 30 subject areas.]

McKay, T. (1989). Writing Warm Ups : Seventy Activities for Prewriting/Teachers Edition. San Francisco: Alemany Press.

Michalko, M. (1994). Thinkpak: A Brainstorming Card Deck/Cards. Berkeley, CA: Ten Speed Press. [Not a book but a set of color-coded cards divided into nine key groups, boxed with instruction booklet, designed to facilitate brainstorming.]

Nadler, G., Shozo H. (1996). Breakthrough Thinking: The Seven Principles of Creative Problem Solving. 2nd ed. Roseville, CA: Prima Publishing. [A book on the creative process, broadly conceived, with an emphasis on how creative people generate ideas in nonacademic settings.]

Rawlinson, J.G. (1981; 1970). Creative thinking and brainstorming. New York: Wiley.

Wujec, T. (1995). Five Star Mind: Games and Exercises to Stimulate Your Creativity and Imagination. New York: Doubleday/Main Street Books. [Provides variations on brainstorming processes using puzzles, tips, thought association, relaxation techniques, and games.]

2

Framing an Analytic Question

I. INTRODUCTION

The difference between analyzing a subject and merely writing about it is the heart of what distinguishes the research paper from journalistic writing. Research papers revolve around clear analytic topics. Good topics are narrow enough to be "doable" yet broad enough to avoid a "who cares?" reaction from readers. Good topics are ambitious enough to be challenging but not so overly ambitious that their scope may prevent realistic completion of the research project. Analytic questions are empirical puzzles that cannot be answered merely by describing the history and present circumstances of the object of investigation. Rather, qualitative or quantitative data about that object must be analyzed. If your paper can be completed merely by giving a history or description, you do not have an analytic topic.

What is analysis? In contrast to descriptive or speculative writing, research papers pose one or more hypotheses, assemble evidence, and come to conclusions. For dissertations, these conclusions should make an original contribution to one's discipline. A good research topic can be said to be analytic when four conditions are met:

1. *A dependent variable is identified.* At least one thing must be being explained. Moreover, this one thing must vary so that we can investigate what other things (independent variables) vary with it.
2. *A plausible explanation is posed.* There must be at least one idea of how one or more independent variables relate to the dependent vari-

able. This is the hypothesis, or a set of hypotheses, constituting a theory.

3. *Counterhypotheses are examined.* Analysis can show some explanatory models that are consistent with the data, but the same data may be consistent with many alternative models. Analysis must include investigation of alternative hypotheses and theories.
4. *Operationalization of all variables makes analysis concrete and specific.* All the terms appearing in the hypotheses must have a meaning that is defined well enough to allow us to gather evidence.

Note that the analytic questions associated with one's thesis are *not* usually the same as questions asked of respondents in an opinion survey (Steeves et al., 1996). Rather, the analytic questions associated with the thesis are ones the researcher poses based on theories in the discipline or scientific constructs. For instance, in a study in which the central analytic question revolves around whether additional years of education lead to greater job satisfaction controlling for differences in salary level, one would *not* ask respondents if they felt more satisfied on their jobs as a result of their education, disregarding differences in salary level. Rather, one would have separate items about degree of job satisfaction, level of income, and years of education. The researcher would use statistical inference to assess the validity of the analytic question's central hypothesis.

Under some circumstances, the researcher may want the respondent in a survey to consider the analytic question itself. This may be useful, for instance, in understanding differences among subjects in their perceptions of key terms. Respondents in the foregoing example might be asked to define ''job satisfaction,'' for instance. Such a question may reveal intersubjective differences of perception, but the researcher should be very aware that respondents' answers may reflect not only their own experience but also popular, cultural, political, social, religious, and other types of influences. Moreover, the researcher must consider whether the very act of asking direct questions about the analytic query may contaminate the results. For example, does forcing respondents to clarify in their minds what job satisfaction is lead to changes in their thinking about something that, in truth, was much more ambiguous or otherwise different in respondents' minds before they were interviewed?

II. FRAMING AN ANALYTIC QUESTION

A. Dimensions of Analysis

Framing a good analytic topic is the key to success in research writing. The analytic process revolves around four dimensions:

1. *Having a clear dependent variable.* Decide specifically what you wish to explain. This involves identifying one or more dependent variables whose

variance the researcher wishes to explain it may also be helpful to be explicit about related phenomena for which the researcher will not try to account. If the researcher is writing about the effectiveness of a crime control program, for example, he or she will need to clarify what types of crimes are to be considered. It may be that homicides are very different causally from robberies. It may be that homicides of men differ causally from homicides of women. Refining the dependent variable is part of the analytic process, but eventually the researcher must stake out what it is he or she will be explaining and differentiate what is beyond the scope of the research effort. Less can be more. That is, it is best to have a limited scope that involves feasible research.

2. *Having clear hypotheses.* Based on literature review and brainstorming, the researcher should develop a list of all variables thought to affect the dependent variable(s) that has been selected. The researcher then identifies causal relationships among sets of variables. The literature review is essential and must not be skipped because, ideally, hypotheses arise from theory. Be specific. It is not enough, for instance, to say that A and B cause X, because this could mean several things: (1) that A causes B, which in turn causes X; (2) that A causes X, and B independently also causes X; or (3) that the joint interaction of A and B causes X. Specifying the direct, indirect, and interaction effects in the model can be clarified by diagrams in which variables become circles, effects become arrows, directions are plus and minus signs, and size of effect is shown by size of arrow or by a coefficient from 0 to 1.0 attached to the arrow. As the number of variables in the researcher's model exceeds three, such diagrams are almost a necessity.

3. *Having alternative hypotheses.* The default assumption in research writing is that more than one hypothesis or model will fit any given set of data. It is not enough to demonstrate that the data fit the hypotheses the researcher has advanced. Other theories may fit the data too. Ultimately, the researcher will never be able to prove his or her hypotheses to be "true," although it may be possible to disprove them. The best the researcher can do, and should do, is to compare the fit of the data to his or her model with the fit of the data to plausible alternative models, particularly those implied by the professional literature. In doing so, the researcher develops a list of hypotheses and alternative hypotheses to be investigated.

4. *Operationalization of variables.* Operationalization involves making a list of all variables mentioned anywhere in any of the hypotheses or alternative hypotheses for models to be investigated. All the items on the list must be translated into operational terms. For every term (e.g., *effectiveness*) the researcher must have at least one and ideally four or more indicators (such as favorable client response to evaluation items, differential cost of service compared with a reference, objective progress measures). Operationalization of variables is discussed more fully in a later section of this guide. Operationalization, of course,

will feed into later research processes, such as selection and application of appropriate methodologic procedures, also discussed in later sections.

If an analytic question involves hypotheses that cannot be confirmed or disproved by empirical means, then these are *metaphysical* propositions inappropriate for scientific and social scientific analysis. The philosopher Popper's ''Falsifiability Criterion'' should apply to quantitative analyses: propositions must be falsifiable at least in principle if they are to be investigated empirically. The empirical researcher must be agnostic on metaphysical propositions (the term ''agnostic'' has a root meaning of ''unknown'' or ''unknowable''). For instance, the explanation that a set of labor riots occurred because of the Marxian process of synthesis and antithesis is not falsifiable and is, therefore, a metaphysical proposition. As a theory, synthesis/antithesis may give the researcher some insights, but ultimately it explains everything and is merely a vocabulary that can be used like similar vocabularies (such as systems theory) in the process of explaining something empirically by other means. Those other means must involve empirically falsifiable propositions.

Of course, difficulty in obtaining evidence is not a reason to consider a proposition metaphysical. For instance, once-untestable propositions in astronomy have become testable with the Hubble space telescope, but these were never metaphysical propositions. It was only that measurement technology had not been developed. Still, for practical purposes, whereas the theorist has more latitude, the empirical researcher must be content with propositions testable by today's available methods and techniques.

Empirical accuracy of a theory is not enough. The researcher should bear in mind the common observation that for any set of data, there will be two or more competing explanations that explain the data satisfactorily, sometimes to an equal degree. How then to decide among theories? The scientific method puts forward three additional criteria for good theory: (1) deductive fertility (the theory is best that generates the largest number of interesting, testable hypotheses); (2) generality (the theory is best that explains the largest range of phenomena); and (3) parsimony (the theory is best that explains the data using the smallest number of assumptions and axioms). A parsimonious, generalizable, fertile theory is the nirvana of empirical research.

In summary, a good analytic topic is one that centers on an empirical puzzle. Two or more strategies (theories) may unlock the puzzle. Each engenders at least one empirically testable proposition, allowing the researcher to see which better fits the data that may be collected. The puzzle is interesting. The solution is nonobvious. Usually the hypotheses involved in proposed solutions grow out of significant strands in the literature of the discipline, When the puzzle is solved, the solution will have many implications for theory and practice. If all this is true, one has selected an analytic topic very wisely.

B. Analytic Topic Checklist

1. Have you selected a topic capable of sustaining your interest over the length of time (usually twice as long as you initially expect!) needed to complete your paper, thesis, or dissertation?
2. Is your topic interesting enough to motivate you for the long run, but resistible enough that it does not consume you to the neglect of obligations in your studies or career?
3. Did you choose a topic early and plan your research and writing in a framework that enables you to meet deadlines, avoiding a last-minute writing crisis?
4. Have you selected a topic your audience will deem to be substantive? For dissertations, have you identified a topic that can be considered an original contribution to your field (because it confirms/refutes/amends a theory pertinent to your discipline, fills a gap in your discipline's literature, exemplifies new research methodologies, or establishes new baseline or trend data important to questions in your discipline)?
5. Have you carefully examined your central question, considering each key word for possible multiple meanings, and the differences between it and its various common synonyms?
6. Have you identified your dependent variable(s)?
7. Have you considered if your dependent variable is actually of two or more types, each requiring a separate causal explanation?
8. Have you consulted the professional literature to develop a list of relevant independent variables?
9. Have you avoided taking notes on everything related to your topic, instead taking notes in a format closely tied to the specific testable propositions you are analyzing?
10. In taking notes, have you kept an accurate record of full references so you will not have to go back (e.g., page numbers for direct quotations)? Do you know the exact reference requirements of the format (the APA format from the American Psychological Association is common) you will be using?
11. Have you related your dependent and independent variables to each other, possibly in the form of a diagrammatic model?
12. For each pair of variables that would be connected by an arrow in a diagrammatic model, have you considered whether there is a third variable that might intervene or be common anteceding causes of both?
13. Have you researched and developed possible alternative models for the same data?

14. Have you identified outliers (cases that deviate greatly from what your theories and propositions would lead you to predict) and whether they call for a second (or more) separate theory from the one you are investigating primarily?
15. Have you looked at other dissertations or journal articles in this area with a view to refining your model and its alternatives?
16. Have you considered interdisciplinary perspectives (economic, psychological, social, cultural, and political)?
17. Have you written out a formal research statement that summarizes your research objectives?
18. Are you prepared to have your dissertation or paper evaluated in terms of whether you have accomplished the purposes contained in your research statement?
19. Are you sure your research statement does not duplicate work already published?
20. Have you given particular care to selection of your title, which will play a significant role in what readers expect you to accomplish in your dissertation, thesis, or paper? Could a reader interested in your topic find your work doing an electronic search based on keywords in your title? Does your title refrain from implying a higher level of generalization of your findings than your data warrant?
21. Have you avoided subjects in which you have a personal stake or "axe to grind?" These are conflicts of interest to be avoided for their own sake and because your research must both be and have the appearance of being objective.

C. Analytic Research Examples

In pursuing an analytic topic, the researcher asks common sense questions that often arise from his or her review of the literature. These questions include: What relationships are discussed in this article and how do they relate to the propositions I am studying? What are the influences, constraints, and linkages among variables and agents in the model underlying the article, and how do they relate to my model? Which variables or information are left out, either in the article or in the researcher's model, that would make an important difference? What evidence is presented, and by what methods, and did the method of measurement influence the findings? What alternative theories are mentioned and do they apply to the researcher's model as well? Is there any discernible bias by the writer of the article, and has the researcher considered such possible biases in his or her own work? What assumptions are made in the article, and would other assumptions be plausible and lead to different conclusions?

Example 1: Electing Nixon. In specifying a subject as an analytic topic, it is common in undergraduate social science writing to write about something without ever having an analytic topic. For example, a student may select the subject, ''Why Richard Nixon was Elected President,'' then present historical information related to this topic. The essay may be well-organized, informative, and deserving of an ''A.'' However, when framed this loosely, the reader is very likely to be left without the basis for a well-supported conclusion about more specific topics, such as ''Was the margin of Electoral College votes resulting in Nixon's election accounted for by popular reaction against the Vietnam War under President Johnson, and not to Johnson's ''Great Society'' liberal agenda, civil rights, or his handling of the economy?'' This more specific question meets the four necessary conditions of an analytic topic.

1. There is a dependent variable: Nixon's margin of votes.
2. There is a plausible explanation: a popular reaction against the Vietnam War in the time leading up to Nixon's election, and it is possible this was a dominant factor.
3. There are plausible counterhypotheses: popular reaction against Johnson's ''Great Society'' liberal agenda, civil rights, or his handling of the economy.
4. The variables can be operationalized: all the terms that appear in the hypotheses can be given concrete meaning in terms of such indicators as Electoral College votes on the one hand and public opinion poll items on the other.

Example 2: Environmental regulation. A second example is environmental regulation. The section on ''Brainstorming'' included an example of writing on the subject of ''Environmental Regulation.'' Brainstorming resulted in this list of subjects:

Air pollution.
Noise pollution.
Water pollution.
Chemical pollution/hazardous waste.
Endangered species.
Is it effective?
Cost/benefit analysis.
EPA agency.
EPA regulations versus property rights.
Conservatives vs. liberals on environmental regulation.
Al Gore.
Politician's platforms on environment.
Federal funding for environment.
State funding.
Private costs/funding.
Private sector ads on environmental issues.

Public opinion on environment, causes of.
Smokey the Bear.
Conservation.
Conservation/environment in 1900s versus 1990s.

The next step would be to specify possible analytic topics derived from this list of subjects. This is a creative process with no specific right answer. However, good answers will meet the four criteria: (1) a dependent variable or set of dependent variables; (2) a hypothesis or theory relating one or more independent variables to the dependent variable(s); (3) plausible alternative explanatory models; and (4) variables that can be measured operationally.

Are corporate issue ads more effective than environmental group issue ads in impacting public opinion? One could create a small group experiment that exposed subjects to corporate and environmental group ads and measured reactions.

Was the Forest Service's "Smokey the Bear" campaign effective? If evidence could be obtained on variations in school systems' use of "Smokey the Bear" materials (based on Forest Service records for the order of such material) and on trends in forest fires before and since the "Smokey" campaign in the districts selected, then the effect of the campaign over and beyond district fire trends could be assessed.

Is the environmental movement of the 1990s less partisan than the conservation movement of the early 1900s? The political party affiliations and activities of board members of leading conservation/environmental groups in the two periods could be investigated to determine if connections to political parties (Progressive, Democratic, Republican) have the same pattern now as then. Explaining why would be the focus for yet another analytic topic.

Does federal funding of water quality supplement or displace state funding? Data could be obtained on state funding on municipal sewage treatment, then on selected areas, showing historical trends and variations, examining the extent to which federal funding in the same area seems supplementary (raising the total funding trend line but not affecting the state funding trend line) or displacing (causing reversals in the state trend line), or combinations of both.

Example 3: Comparative research. In a course on comparative politics, an analytic paper would go beyond merely describing chronological facts and events based on information from encyclopedias and newspaper articles. The typical analytic paper would pick at least two countries that have something in common (this will be the control variable) but that have one other variable that varies (this is the independent variable) and is thought to affect some dependent variable of interest such as regime stability, the status of women, or economic development policy. Typically, the dependent variable(s) vary among the nations being studied. For instance, one might study the impact of high oil prices in the 1970s on the domestic political stability of African nations. To do so, it would be important to include at least one country where the oil crisis had destabilizing effects and one where it did not. The writer is then in a position to identify and assess one or more independent variables that explain the difference, with the control being that all countries in the study were similarly affected by the worldwide oil crisis (this might lead to excluding a nation with its own internal oil reserves).

In comparative research, one is looking at questions in which two countries have similar control factors but differ in outcomes because of some independent variables that the researcher is trying to analyze. For instance two countries like Taiwan and Singapore share the control variable of having a large middle class, yet in terms of an outcome dependent variable, such as type of government, the former country is more democratic and the latter more autocratic. The analytic question is why, and this question cannot be answered merely be describing the history of each. Rather, independent variables must be analyzed (e.g., differences in economic structure) comparing the nations. Of course, the more nations compared by the same methodology, the more confidence the researcher will have in the generalizability of his or her findings.

BIBLIOGRAPHY

Brown, A., Dowling, P. (1998). Reading Research/Doing Research. Philadelphia, PA: Falmer Press. [A book for doctoral students in education who are considering their dissertation. Includes practical guidance on the development of a research question as well as related topics, such as doing literature reviews.]

Krathwohl, D. R. (1988). How to Prepare a Research Proposal : Guidelines for Funding and Dissertations in the Social and Behavioral Sciences. Syracuse, NY: Syracuse University Press. [A bit dated but still helpful.]

Levine, S. J. (1998). Guide for Writing a Funding Proposal. Available online at the website http://www.canr.msu.edu/aee/dissthes/propint.htm.

Seltzer, R. A. (1996). Mistakes That Social Scientists Make: Error and Redemption in the Research Process. New York: St. Martin's Press. [A collection of short, true anecdotes by leading social scientists about mistakes they have made. Not limited to issues pertaining to framing analytic questions, this work is nonetheless an excellent one to read early in one's research process, particularly for doctoral students.]

Silverman, D. (1999). Doing Qualitative Research: A Practical Handbook. Thousand Oaks, Ca: Sage Publications. [Covers narrowing down a topic, keeping a research diary, writing research reports, and presentation of research to different audiences.]

Steeves, R. H., Kahn, D. L., Cohen, M. Z. (1996). Technical notes: Asking substantive theory questions of naturalistically derived data. Western J Nurs Res 18(2): 209–212.

Stern, P. C., Kalof, L. (1996). Evaluating Social Science Research. 2nd ed. New York: Oxford University Press. [Generally relevant, but see especially chapter 1, "Scientific and Nonscientific Statements of Fact."]

3

Typical Outlines

I. FORMING AN OUTLINE

Forming a workable paper, thesis, or dissertation outline is half the battle of writing. An outline is part of the roadmap that tells the reader where you will go with your story. It is also an important tool in your own reasoning process for establishing the foundation for your research and eventual written work. A bad outline will lead you down endless mazes and yield an unreadable final product. A good outline will ease and encourage you along the path to victory in your chosen project.

Of course, it is difficult to write an effective outline without having a clear idea about the content of your writing project. Often your outline will include much of the generic sample below. Be prepared to write a paragraph or so about each point. It is often advisable to leave the introduction and the conclusion to last. By writing a paragraph or more under each outline topic, the researcher is carrying forward into the outline the results of the brainstorming process discussed in Chapter 1 and efforts to frame an analytic topic discussed in Chapter 2.

A. Sample Outline

Title page
Acknowledgments page
Abstract page, with keyword list
Table of contents
Table of figures

- Introduction
  - Statement of the research problem
    - Contextual background
    - Theoretical relevance
    - Policy relevance
  - Research statement
    - Research questions
    - Hypotheses
    - Definition of terms
- Body
  - Literature review
  - Differentiation of planned research from existing literature
  - Methodology to be used
    - Research design
    - Population, sampling, and data acquisition
    - Instrumentation, including assessment of validity and reliability
    - Qualitative and/or statistical procedures
  - Hypotheses
    - Hypotheses related to theories and models
    - Operationalization of variables
  - Preliminary evidence on relationships
  - Evidence with use of control variables
  - Consideration of alternative models
- Conclusion/Discussion
  - Scope of generalization, limitations, delimitations, and threats to validity
  - Summary of findings, related to previous research/theory
  - Implications for theory and/or practice
  - Future research agenda
- Endnotes
- References

The sample outline above is a *standard outline*. It flows in a logical order from introduction to evidence to conclusions. However, it should be noted that on rare occasions the researcher may require a *hierarchical outline*. The hierarchical outline has a tree-like structure that branches into finer and finer categories, ultimately ending up with ''leaves'' that contain conclusions pertinent to that path along the tree. Such an outline might be appropriate, for instance, when the purpose is taxonomic (placing observed phenomena into an exhaustive set of categories). Field guides to identification of plants, rocks, or celestial phenomena are often arranged hierarchically, based on empirical but nonstatistical observation. A statistical methodology that organizes data into hierarchical trees is inductive expert systems, which rely on such algorithms as ID3 from information theory.

In general, however, hierarchical outlines are rare in quantitative writing, and the researcher is well advised to stick to the standard outline unless there are compelling reasons not to.

II. STANDARD OUTLINES

Each of the elements of the typical standard outline just described will now be explained in more detail. Keep in mind, however, that the format discussed below is a template, not an iron code of scientific investigation. Some sections may be inappropriate for some types of research and, in other cases, sections not included below may be needed. Moreover, the outlining process is often best undertaken when not conceived as a before-the-fact initial writing effort but as an ongoing process wherein the researcher continually goes back and reconsiders the logic and storyline of his or her writing and redrafts the outline accordingly.

A. Standard Outline Elements

1. *Title page.* Your title should include critical key words (e.g., your dependent variable). The words in your title have an important function in electronic reference retrieval and may influence the impact of your work on your discipline. Strip off unnecessary words like ''A study of'' and any redundant words. If your work is later published in book form, *then* you may entertain a ''sexier'' title that is more catchy and cryptic, but avoid this temptation in academic work. Your academic department or publisher may supply rigid guidelines, but in general, the title page typically includes the full title of your dissertation, thesis, or paper; your full name; the degree, course, or publication for which the work is submitted; and the date of submission. If contact information is not on the title page, it should be on a subsequent separate page: name, address, telephone, e-mail, fax, and web address, if any.

2. *Acknowledgment page.* Be sure to acknowledge explicitly anyone who has helped you with the substance or mechanics of the research. This will include your advisor and members of your committee. If you have benefitted from the ideas of one or more persons, acknowledge this. Acknowledge everyone who read your drafts and gave you feedback. It is better to err on the side of having a lengthy acknowledgment page than to exclude anyone.

3. *Abstract page, with keyword list.* This page is more important than it may seem. It sets the tone for and expectations of your readers. Moreover, in this era of electronic indexing, what you put here will be widely incorporated by various search and bibliographic services and, in the case of dissertations, in *Dissertation Abstracts*. Your work may even be cited by others on the basis of the abstract alone. Supply a keyword list of your choosing to prevent clerical people in reference service organizations from choosing your descriptors for you.

About 150 to 300 words is typical. It need not be limited to a single paragraph (though that is common) but may extend to two or three, if necessary. Do include your actual main findings, not just a description of the areas your research covers. It is customary to put verbs in the past tense, to reflect research already completed, in contrast to abstracts in the proposal stage of writing.

4. *Table of contents.* The table of contents will follow in a standard outline. Of course, the outline discussed here, although typical, is only one of a great many variations on a theme. Whatever variation you choose, do include page numbers. Hint: learn how to get your word processor to compute these for you automatically. To do so, you will have to enter markers as you type in chapter, section, and subsection titles, so learn this before you start typing.

5. *Table of figures.* Have separate listings for figures, charts, and tables. As with the table of contents, learn before you start to write how to get your word processor to generate these listings automatically.

6. *Introduction.* The introduction gets disproportionate reader attention and deserves polishing and repolishing by the writer. Keep in mind that what you say at the beginning is apt to be the standard by which you are judged at the end. Typically, the introduction contains a statement of the research problem, discusses the problem's context in terms of practical policy, academic theory, or both, and sets forth a statement of the proposed research to be elaborated on in subsequent sections. The introduction is also the place where the writer clearly identifies the audience for the writing and indicates whether it is assumed that this audience is already cognizant of certain knowledge pertinent to the research at hand, information which, for a different audience, might otherwise have to be set forth in the paper, thesis, or dissertation.

7. *Statement of research problem.* The statement of the research problem is where the researcher sets forth the subject and makes the case that it merits the reader's interest. The statement of the research problem should indicate the general nature of the hypotheses to be investigated. It should also demonstrate that these raise questions about which researchers might disagree, that there are policy and theoretical issues involved. That is, the statement of the research problem defines the scope and general direction of the proposed research and presents the motivation for interest.

8. *Contextual background.* The section on the context of research is not the literature review section, although they are directly related. Without reviewing the literature in detail, in the contextual background section, the researcher makes a fuller presentation of the objectives mentioned in the problem statement. That is, here there is a fuller presentation of the theoretical and practical importance of the research. However, the presentation is still a summary and not the full literature review. Often, after completing the literature review, the researcher may be in a better position to refine the contextual background section.

9. *Theoretical relevance.* Purely policy-oriented writing is common and important; however, if at all possible, the researcher should relate the proposed research to theory reflected in the literature of the field. This prefigures and, frankly, is a little redundant with the literature review, but in the section on theoretical context, the researcher is only hitting the highlights and main points. If there is no such theory, of course, the researcher is well advised not to force an inappropriate framework onto his or her topic simply for the sake of "being theoretical." However, there is also an opportunity here to set forth personal, original typologies, frameworks, and theories.

10. *Policy relevance.* Purely theoretical writing is acceptable, but if the research has policy implications, these should be highlighted here. This prefigures and is somewhat redundant with the findings and conclusion sections. However, in the section on policy context, the researcher is only suggesting how findings of the research at hand may relate to existing policy debates or existing or proposed legislation. If there are no policy implications, the researcher should not force an inappropriate framework onto his or her topic simply for the sake of "being relevant."

11. *Research statement.* The research statement is a relatively short concluding section to the introduction in which the researcher recapitulates the research problem and its theoretical and policy importance, then summarizes where the rest of the dissertation or article is going, including the general nature of the literature review, types of hypotheses, data collection strategy, and methodological procedures to be invoked. Key terms are also defined at this point. In essence, the research statement is an extended abstract of the entire body: some redundancy is expected, but comprehensive treatment is avoided in the research statement.

12. *Body.* A good introduction has given the reader a beginning-to-end overview of the entire work. The body goes back and starts at the beginning again but presents each element in much greater detail. In writing the portion of the outline that forms the body, the researcher may find it helpful to write out one sentence (not just a heading) for each of his or her main points. Although headings are the type of outline many used in their high school days, outlining using full sentences is much less ambiguous and makes for clearer argumentation.

13. *Literature review.* It is easy and common to write bad literature reviews. Bad reviews lose the reader in details and irrelevancies, give the impression the writer is meandering, and tempt the reader simply to skip ahead to the section on methodology. Good reviews relate the literature to the hypotheses section that will follow and keep the "story line" of the work in the forefront. This requires omitting much perfectly fine and hard-gotten literature research which, although interesting and important in other contexts, is simply not very relevant to the research questions at hand. In general, it is a bad idea to arrange

the literature review in chronological or journalistic order (the inverted pyramid from most important to least important). Reading the literature will help the researcher refine his or her hypotheses, which in turn points deeper into the literature, and so on in an interative process. After a few iterations, the researcher should know what hypotheses are to be investigated, and the literature should be organized according to clusters of hypotheses. Formal hypotheses are not presented in the literature review, but it is still possible to organize in parallel. For instance, one set of hypotheses may deal with economic independent variables and another set with educational variables, so the literature review would have sections paralleling this.

14. *Differentiation of planned research from existing literature.* In this section, the researcher makes explicit how his or her proposed research confirms, disproves, qualifies, extends, or is an original addition to the literature of the discipline. These are not mutually exclusive categories as, obviously, the research may confirm one set of theories, disprove others, or provide the basis for synthesis of seemingly contrary findings in the existing literature.

15. *Methodology to be used.* The methodology section is particularly crucial in doctoral dissertations. Often, this section is the one most thoroughly discussed with one's doctoral advisor and committee. The researcher does not want to invest substantial research time when he or she lacks agreement on the methodology to be used. There is no one perfect methodology. Strong consideration should be given to a multitrait, multimethod approach supplemented with qualitative research. That is, use multiple indicators for each variable, confirm the results of one method (crosstabulations based on survey research, for instance) with those of another (e.g., regression models based on archival data), then increase the validity of one's findings by supplementing with qualitative research examples (such as case studies).

16. *Research design.* This section sets out the research design, whether experimental or observational. Analysis of variance alone has dozens of research designs, but the objective of all designs is to come as close as possible to controlling for all variables that might reasonably be thought to influence the dependent variables being investigated. For this reason, the research design section must highlight the treatment of potential control and modifier variables that may affect the main relationships of interest.

17. *Sampling and data acquisition.* In this section the researcher describes the types of data to be collected. Often, random sampling protocols are discussed here. Response rates should be reported, along with a demographic profile of one's sample and, if available, of known characteristics of the population. Nonresponse should be analyzed, as by wave projection methods. One should also describe quality control procedures such as tests of interrater reliability, triangulation of respondents, recoding of recorded interviews, and others.

18. *Instrumentation, including assessment of validity and reliability.* Of-

ten, previous researchers have examined the same variables that are the focus of the proposed research. Sometimes, scales have been developed to measure a concept, have been validated in large populations, and are accepted instruments in the profession. In this section, the researcher discusses past measures and tests of their reliability and validity. If using original measures, the researcher should discuss validity and reliability concerns and tests related to them. If there is a separate section on operationalization of variables, as in this example outline, specific items are not discussed in this section.

19. *Qualitative and/or statistical procedures.* Whatever statistical procedures are invoked, all of the assumptions of the selected procedure should be evaluated in relation to the proposed research. Where appropriate, tests of assumptions (e.g., tests of multivariate normality, homogeneity of variances) should be reported. Nearly all research reports significance levels of findings, but in doctoral research it is also important to discuss statistical power and alpha (significance level) reduction procedures when, as is usual, multiple tests are conducted. In addition to assessment of significance of relationships, the effect size (magnitude) of relationships should also always be reported.

20. *Hypotheses.* This section is the kingpin of the entire dissertation or article structure. Care should be taken to make sure there is parallelism between the hypotheses section and the earlier introduction section's research statement, with the literature review, and with the conclusion.

21. *Hypotheses related to theories and models.* In this section, one formally lists the research hypotheses, grouping and introducing them in relation to the theoretical model being tested. "Formal" means that hypotheses are expressed in terms of their statistical test, which is often a null hypothesis (e.g., introduction of community policing in a police district will not affect the burglary rate). One should also state the alpha (significance) level that will be used for testing hypotheses (e.g., .05). Although optional, it is desirable to state the expected direction and general strength of association (weak, moderate, strong) expected on the basis of one's theory or model.

22. *Operationalization of variables.* The list of hypotheses gives the list of variables involved in the research. All should be listed and formally defined. Ideally, each variable should be measured by multiple (such as >3) indicators. The researcher should discuss each indicator in terms of whether it is an item with intrinsic high reliability and validity (e.g., gender); a component of an accepted, validated instrument (as discussed in the instrumentation section above); an indicator whose reliability and validity has been confirmed by the author (discuss how); or an indicator whose reliability and validity have not been tested. Actual instruments containing all items, along with full coding instructions, should be reproduced in an appendix.

23. *Preliminary evidence on relationships.* The first task of the researcher is to determine if any relationship exists that connects the primary independent

and dependent variables of interest. In graphical terms, the researcher asks for each arrow in the model, "Is the relationship significant, in the expected direction, and of the general level of magnitude predicted?" Some authors separate a "Results" section from a subsequent "Findings" section, with data in the one and conclusions in the other. Unless required by one's department or journal of publication, however, this practice tends to confuse the reader and is deprecated here.

24. *Evidence with use of control variables.* If the originally posited relationships are upheld by the evidence, the researcher must then consider for each relationship in the model whether there are additional variables (hopefully ones that have been anticipated and for which measures have been taken!) that modify the relationship because they are intervening or common anteceding variables. Even relationships that are statistically insignificant overall may have a significant relationship for some ranges of a modifier variable.

25. *Consideration of alternative models.* The researcher must assume that his or her data will support more than one model. Plausible alternative models should be investigated to determine if they fit the data as well as or better than the initial model. These alternatives may be suggested by the literature, by the researcher's original judgment, and by statistical coefficients based on the original model (e.g., modification indexes in structural equation models). The researcher must also balance tests of model fit against the preference for model parsimony. Simpler models may be preferred to more complex ones, unless the fit of the latter is substantially better.

26. *Conclusion/discussion.* The conclusion should be fully consistent with the introduction and should flow from the presentation of evidence. The central purpose of the conclusion is to show how the researcher has completed the tasks set forth in the introduction. There is a tendency among researchers to feel that on completing writing of the body, the conclusion is a minor effort to be tacked on. Avoid this viewpoint, as the concluding section is apt to be the most-read, most-influential section of the work. Moreover, the evaluation of the work will have much to do with the consistency of the concluding section with the introductory, methods, and literature review sections that came at the beginning of the work. Writing the conclusion is a major effort to which the researcher must allocate significant time. Note that this section is usually labeled "Conclusion" or "Discussion," not "Summary."

27. *Scope of generalization, limitations, delimitations, and threats to validity.* The most common error in writing the conclusion is making generalizations not supported by the data. The researcher should remind readers, and him- or herself, of the exact boundaries of generalization. Delimitations are boundaries set by the researcher for reasons of scope, whereas limitations are boundaries inherent in the nature of the data. For instance, if one has random sample data on Arizona city managers, one does not want to generalize to American city

managers unless one has demonstrated that those in Arizona are similar in important respects to national averages for city managers. In fact, all limitations and threats to validity should be recapitulated at this point. The limits may be extensive enough that the researcher should label findings as exploratory or preliminary results. One should err on the side of humility.

28. *Summary of findings related to previous research and theory.* This section is the culmination of the article, thesis, or dissertation. It is an extended summary of the work's story line, relating each main point to the evidence presented in the body of the work, with brief mention of relevance to previous research and theory discussed in the introduction and literature review. Overall, the discussion section summary need not be comprehensive of all findings in the body of the study. Rather, its purpose is to highlight and consolidate the story line of the thesis. No new findings should be presented here—all such analysis should have been in earlier sections. The researcher should address whether findings support the thesis in effect size as well as in significance and direction. The researcher should also discuss findings inconsistent with or that only partially support his or her thesis.

It is important in this section to "stick to the facts," avoiding the often strong temptation to generalize beyond what is actually proved by data in earlier sections. In this discussion section summary, the researcher should keep in mind that the findings have already been presented in the body of the paper, thesis, or dissertation. Therefore, whereas a summary in the discussion section is needed and appropriate, it should not be unnecessarily redundant. Instead, the discussion section summary is just that—discussion—and leads directly into the next section on implications for theory and practice.

29. *Implications for theory and practice.* In this section, the researcher discusses at greater length the significance of the work's findings for confirmation, modification, or rejection of current theories and practice related to the subject at hand. The researcher will hark back to the review of the literature section, showing how his or her study supports, extends, revises, or refutes earlier literature in the profession. The more applied the thesis, the more this section will focus on implications for professional practice in the domain studied.

30. *Future related research agenda.* It is common to end the conclusion with a discussion outlining the main elements of a future research agenda growing out of the present research. These are suggestions directed toward the discipline and are not necessarily commitments of the author for future work. Such a section is most effective if it elaborates on one, two, or three research agenda elements most strongly associated with the researcher's own work. Such elements are typically logical and direct next steps rather than long-range research needs. However, a rationale should be apparent why such next steps were not incorporated into the researcher's own work in the current paper, thesis, or dissertation. At the same time, a laundry list of a large number of possibilities for future research

should be avoided, as it distracts from the "story" of the current work and diffuses the actual helpfulness of the future research section as a whole.

31. *Endnotes.* The Endnotes section is not for citations, which go in the References section. Rather, Endnotes is used for elucidating comments and providing relevant supplementary information whose insertion into the body of the text would be distracting to the story line. Endnotes are listed automatically by number by most word processing programs, which will automatically renumber when additional endnotes are inserted in the middle.

32. *References.* A References section lists only references cited in the work, as opposed to a Bibliography, which lists all references consulted. Most publishers and academic departments do not want a bibliography. Your publisher or academic department will very likely specify the reference format style to use. One of many advantages of using bibliographic software, discussed in a separate section of this guide, is that with almost no effort you can generate the references in one format for your academic department and in any number of other formats according to publishers' specifications. As a default, the APA reference style used by the American Psychological Association is probably the most widely used.

Bypassing the outlining process may well lead to a disorganized paper, thesis, or dissertation. Outlining forces the researcher to clarify things in her or his own mind. It forces the researcher to consider the logical order of his or her argument and whether there are portions that are missing, redundant, or irrelevant to the arguments being made. The outlining process may prompt the researcher to conduct additional investigation to fill holes in the outline or may prompt the researcher to discard left over material left over that has no proper place in the outline.

1. Outlining Checklist

1. Have you examined some examples of outlines for similar dissertations, theses, or articles to determine what seems most applicable to your own context? Hint: look at *Dissertation Abstracts Online*, available on Dialog Information Services through most reference libraries (http://library.dialog.com/bluesheets/html/bl0035.html).
2. Have you obtained guidelines from your academic department or publisher to assure your outline conforms to stylistic requirements that vary from discipline to discipline?
3. Does your title contain key words that form a "miniabstract" of your paper, thesis, or dissertation, and that make clear what your dependent variable is?
4. Do you avoid abbreviations in your title?
5. Does your abstract include all relevant key words for electronic search purposes?

6. Does your abstract include your main findings, not just an indication of the area you are studying?
7. Does your outline start with a description of a problem to be studied and a clear explanation of why the problem is important in the profession, in theory or in policy terms?
8. Have you clearly identified your target audience (such as, practitioners, theorists, agency policymakers)?
9. Have you avoided giving equal weight to main and supporting ideas in your outline?
10. Have you outlined the methodology you propose to use to investigate the issues you have selected, and have you demonstrated how triangulation (a multimethod approach) might enhance your research design?
11. Is your outline arranged in a way that the story line stays in the forefront, and the story builds to a climax in the conclusion?
12. Would an impartial reader understand the logic of your research from your outline? (Give it to some friends and test this out!)
13. Do you follow familiar organizing principles, such as arranging your coverage in subsections from general to specific or from abstract to concrete?
14. Does the content correspond to your heading levels in your outline, so that the higher the heading level, the more important the topic? Or are important, key parts of your story line hidden away in obscure subsections of your outline?
15. In associating content with heading levels, have you observed the principle of coordination (that similar levels of generality should have similar heading levels). For instance, if outline level ''A'' is ''Reproductive System'' and ''B'' is ''Nervous System,'' it would be a violation of coordination to let ''C'' be ''The Heart.'' Rather, ''C'' would be ''Circulatory System'' and ''The Heart'' would have to be a subtopic of ''C.''
16. Does your outline serve as a summary of your work?
17. Will your conclusion correspond to your introduction?
18. Have you let the evidence speak for itself, using a professional tone that avoids normative or dramatic adjectives like ''unprecedented,'' ''obvious,'' ''overwhelming,'' or ''striking?''
19. Have you given space to discuss contrary, partially supportive, and negative findings, as well as findings in support of your thesis?
20. Have you arranged for peer review feedback for your outline?
21. In terms of the sheer format of the headings in your outline, have you observed parallelism? That is, are headings at the same level expressed similarly in similar terms. You might use terms like ''campaigning'', ''voting'', and ''electing''; or you might use ''to cam-

paign,'' ''to vote,'' or ''to elect'', or you might use these terms as adjectives, but you would violate parallelism if you ''mixed and matched'' types of grammatical form.

2. Outlining Examples

Numerous sites on the world wide web provide examples of good outlining. For instance, Purdue University has such a site at *http://owl.english.purdue.edu/Files/64.html.* However, as content on the web changes so rapidly, one may be better off simply entering terms like ''writing/outlining,'' ''outlining skills,'' ''standard outline,'' or ''hierarchical outline'' into a web search engine such as *http://www.altavista.com* or *http://www.alltheweb.com.*

Past award-winning dissertation titles provide good examples of outlines that may be worth examining. Abstracts are provided through *Dissertation Abstracts Online*, a service of Dialog and other vendors, available through most research library reference departments (http://library.dialog.com/bluesheets/html/bl0035.html). The dissertations themselves are available free in many cases through your research library's interlibrary loan department and are almost always available for a fee through University Microfilm International (UMI; http://www.umi.com/), which also has an online dissertation search service, Proquest (http://wwwlib.umi.com/dissertations/). University Microfilm International supplies full text of dissertations in Postscript Document Format (.pdf), which one can download online, for a typical cost (at present) of about $20/dissertation, depending on length. The .pdf format will require you to have Acrobat Reader, a browsing utility available for free download at the website http://www.adobe.com/supportservice/custsupport/download.html.

The professional association for your discipline also gives awards for best dissertations. For instance, the Leonard D. White Award is given annually by the American Political Science Association for the best doctoral dissertation completed in that year or the previous year in the general field of public administration, including broadly related problems of policy formation and administrative theory. See *http://www.apsanet.org/Awards/whitepast.html.* Check with your own discipline's professional association for a similar list of award-winning dissertations that may provide guidance in your outline-formation efforts.

BIBLIOGRAPHY

Davis, G. B., Parker, C. A. (1997). Writing the Doctoral Dissertation: A Systematic Approach. Haupage, NY: Barrons Educational Series. [Focuses on the mechanics of dissertation writing. One author is a professor of management.]

Gelfand, H., Walker, C. J. (1990). Mastering APA style: Student's Workbook and Training Guide. Washington, D.C.: American Psychological Association.

4

The Roadmap Concept

I. INTRODUCTION

The author's familiarity with a topic can create a form of myopia. The author may be so familiar with the subject that he or she forgets that readers need a "roadmap" so that they, too, can see how the information presented reaches a final conclusion. Creating a roadmap for your dissertation or paper not only helps your readers, it helps *you* by forcing you to be explicit about your plan of work, clarifying your thoughts. Just as an hour spent outlining can save the writer many times that in writing time, so an hour spent designing a good road map for the reader will help avoid the frustrations of wandering and wondering about what it is you are trying to say—frustrations that will be held against the writer/researcher. The roadmap concept is simple, involving four elements:

1. Stick to your outline, articulated in your table of contents. The outline should reflect your *framework*, discussed below. Logically arrange section and subsection headings. It is better to err on the side of having an abundance of these "signpost" headings.

2. Start every chapter with a summary of where your story has been and where it will go in the current chapter. Your topic sentence should reinforce the focus of the study as a whole, elaborating on it and building toward the conclusion.

3. Use transitional paragraphs to start each chapter section and subsection, tying the immediately preceding section to the current one. Use transitional paragraphs at the end of each chapter section and subsection, tying the current section to the one ahead. The lead sentence of your paragraph should state con-

cisely the connection of the immediately prior section to that which follows, and it or a second sentence should, as appropriate, recall and reinforce the theme of your writing effort. The overall structure of each chapter should be well-paced, not mired in unnecessary side points but rather maintaining the progression of ideas in a logical manner that builds toward a solution of the empirical puzzle that is the focus of your research.

4. End every chapter with a summary of your story thus far, recapitulating how it has advanced in the current chapter and pointing out the segment to come.

The roadmap concept is simple and basic, but it is often ignored. Roadmapping involves some redundancy, but clarity is preferable to ambiguity. Maps serve four functions: they orient the user, present the big picture, give direction, and show how one gets from the beginning to the end. The same four functions are served by good roadmapping when creating one's writing project outline. Remember, if your readers become confused along the path, they are more apt to blame you for your organization and direction rather than blame themselves for not understanding.

II. THE ROADMAP CONCEPT

Having a framework for analysis is the single most important part of the roadmap concept. A framework is a set of concepts that helps organize findings related to the empirical puzzle the researcher is investigating. The three most common forms of framework are typologies, metaphors, and theories.

A. Typologies

A typology is simply a set of categories into which one may class the cases that comprise the research data. For instance, biologists class types of insects into species, subspecies, and finer classifications of families of insects. Typologies may be simple categories, tabulations, trees, or expert systems.

1. Simple Categories

Simple categories class cases along a single dimension of meaning, such as gender, age group, or latitude. Types of moss might be categorized by the altitude at which they are found, for instance. Automobile models might be classed by their average price. Such categorical frameworks are the simplest type, but they do provide some basis for orderly consideration of the data. Ideally, the categorical dimension used is germane to the research purpose. For instance, in a study of human safety in car crashes, car color would be a poor framework choice, price range would be better, and weight range might be better still.

2. Tabulations

Tabulations are typologies that reflect two or more dimensions. Typically, two or three dimensions are involved because, as additional dimensions are added, the number of classes formed can escalate beyond the available data. Consider the case of dimensions with four classes each (location: east, west, north, south). A two-dimensional tabulation will have 16 classes (4 × 4). A three-dimensional tabulation will have 64 classes (4^4). A four-dimensional classification will have 256 classes. When the number of classes approaches the number of cases in the dataset, the utility of the framework is practically zero, as each case may then be classified on an arbitrary basis. As a rule of thumb, a tabular framework should have no more than 20% the number of classes as there are data cases, and usually many fewer. Two-by-two tabular frameworks are the most common. For instance, a study of a type of crime might class cases by offender along two offender dimensions: above and below the poverty line in income, and under or over age 21. Such a tabular framework implies, of course, that age and income are determinants of crime, and offenders lying in each of the four quadrants will differ, on average, in important respects.

3. Trees

Trees are hierarchical tabulations involving two or more dimensions ordered by precedence. If you have played the game of "Twenty Questions" you are familiar with the concept. In correctly identifying an unknown about which one player is thinking, the most important dimension is put first: "animal, mineral, or vegetable." Then the next player tries to explore the second most important dimension, then the third, and so on. In Twenty Questions, the precedence of the dimensions is unclear because, initially, there is no knowledge of the data and there is only one case. In actual research, many cases are known to the researcher, and the dimensions may be chosen on an informed basis.

The classic tree structure is that common in biology and botany, as reflected in familiar "field guides." A field guide to trees, for instance, may first class trees by those with needles versus those with leaves. Within needles, one may then class by type of cone. Within leaves, one may class by those with alternative leaves versus those with opposite leaves, and so on. Note that in a hierarchical structure, different dimensions may be examined, depending on which path down the decision tree one takes. If one takes the leaves path, for instance, one will never encounter the cone dimension. Hierarchical structures are appropriate when the researcher is able to establish a clear precedence among the dimensions for purposes of prediction or of causal explanation (not the same thing, nor necessarily involving the same dimensions). Thus, a tree typology requires a predictive or causal model and is closer to being a theoretical framework (discussed below) than is simple categorization or tabulation.

4. Expert Systems

Expert systems are hierarchical typologies in which the dimensions and their cutting points are determined either inductively on the basis of the data or on the basis of how actual experts in the field classify cases. An inductive expert system uses information theory algorithms (such as the ID3 algorithm) to determine the precedence of dimensions (using variables in the dataset), and then sets optimal cutting points to maximize the correct classification of cases. The result of an inductive expert system for the dependent variable of how a person voted, Republican or Democrat, might first use income above or below $48,347, then use education above or below 13 years, then use political identification of parents, and so on. The cutting points (such as $48,347) are determined empirically to best classify the cases (here, to best explain why someone voted Republican or Democratic). The danger, of course, is that such cutting points or even selection and ordering of explanatory variables may be arbitrary, even to the point of fitting noise in the data. Procedures exist in inductive expert systems to "trim" the branches in the hierarchical structure into simpler forms that, hopefully, are less arbitrary and more generalizable to other datasets. Using human experts to create the tree structure rather than relying on empirical induction, or to use human experts to refine an induced tree, is one approach to increasing the reliability and generalizability of expert systems trees.

B. Metaphors

A metaphor, for purposes of a framework, is a sustained set of analogies that help the reader understand a difficult subject by relating it to a familiar one. The metaphor also suggests interesting hypotheses, drawing the researcher to investigate whether what is true in the familiar context is also true in the complex one being studied. An example of metaphor from the field of sociology is Erving Goffman's *Presentation of the Self in Everyday Life.* In this book, Goffman used the theater as a metaphor for studying the behavior of people at work and in other settings. Just as behavior backstage and onstage differs in theater, so Goffman found people may have an onstage presentation of themselves and a backstage persona that differs. Just as the leading actor has supporting actors in theater, Goffman found that people are their own leading actors and surround themselves with associates who will best support them in the role they are trying to play. He also found that people use "scripts," seek "applause," and display other theatrical similarities. The effectiveness of a metaphor as a framework depends on the richness of the similarities between the phenomenon under study and the source of the metaphor, as well as on the ability of the researcher to discern these similarities without forcing analogies on unwilling data.

C. Theories

Theories are sets of general propositions supported by more specific hypotheses that may be tested empirically. Theories may be deductive or inductive. Deductive theories put forward axioms, which are basic assumptions, then derive corollaries, which are implied hypotheses. For instance, "economic man" theories of rational choice posit that people make decisions based on their own economic advantage. A corollary is that a person will vote for the candidate who seems to promise the most economic advantage in terms of tax, social welfare, education, and other policies. Another corollary is that adults with children will vote differently from adults without children on local school bond issues.

Inductive theories have the same format of general theoretical propositions and supporting specific hypotheses. However, they are formulated based on inference, not from axioms but from the actual distribution of data as well as actual findings of other researchers. This means that new research must be well founded on a review of the literature, which is the subject of a later chapter in this volume. In reviewing related literature, the researcher will find that previous authors have used their own frameworks and this, too, will help the researcher construct his or her own, building on what has gone before.

After a framework for analysis has been established, style must be considered. The four stylistic elements of roadmapping are simple: (1) stick to your outline (which should reflect your framework); (2) start chapters with summaries; (3) use transitional paragraphs at the start and end of every section and subsection; and (4) end every chapter with a summary.

Nonlinear writing. The tendency is to insert the roadmapping elements as one goes along, writing in a linear fashion by starting at the beginning of the outline and working toward the end in one pass. However, a nonlinear approach to writing and rewriting will result in a better finished product. Even before collecting evidence, try to write at least the bare bones of your chapter summaries and key transitional section paragraphs. Doing so may prompt you to think about your data collecting needs. It will almost certainly help you maintain your storyline in the forefront of every section of your dissertation or paper, where it belongs.

Reader-centered writing. In this day and age, everyone, your readers included, suffers from information overload. A 1997 *Newsweek* article quoted experts saying that the typical professional sends and receives an average of 177 messages a day. "Infostress" is a neologism that has worked its way into everyday language. The consequence is that there is an increased burden on the writer to keep focused on the readers' needs in terms of the "three Es": effective, efficient, and engaging writing.

1. Effective. In addition to roadmap principles and sound methodology, make a judgment about who your readers are and try to anticipate what they will want to know and what questions they are apt to have.

2. Efficient. The dissertation should have as much information as needed to sustain the story and conclusions, but it should not wander into related fields and carry excess baggage. Understand that there is a difference between spoken and written English, so avoid slang, colloquialism, jargon, and other "professionalese," acronymns, overly complex sentence structure, foreign phrases, and cli-

chés in favor of clarity and precision. Stick to your storyline and operate on the assumption that if a section of your writing does not pertain to your central theme, you should probably put it in an appendix or leave it out altogether.

3. Engaging. Writing style should seek to stimulate interest by highlighting what issues may be involved, de-emphasizing sheer description. Statistical and other general forms of evidence should be illustrated with short case portraits that give a human face to the evidence. Use the active rather than passive voice where appropriate. Format does matter: avoid uninterrupted series of dense paragraphs, use bulleted lists, have enough section and subsection headings, and keep paragraphs relatively short. Avoid unnecessary formalism on the one hand and inappropriate personalization of writing on the other.

In overall impression, what should come through is that the researcher is committed to the topic and wants to communicate his or her enthusiasm for solving the empirical puzzle. The tone of the writing should be neither stilted nor casual. Ideally, the writing is precise, interesting, and naturally flowing. The choice of words is accurate, and strong words that are neither "padding" nor "overblown," but that compel the reader's attention, are used. Always proofread and revise. Reading aloud can help the revision process to see if the objectives mentioned here are close to being met.

D. Roadmap Checklist

1. Do you have an organizing framework?
2. Is your framework well-founded in a review of the literature?
3. Have you written out at least the bare bones of your chapter summaries and key section transitional paragraphs at four points in the process of writing your dissertation or article: (1) at the outset; (2) after data collection; (3) in your first draft, after quantitative analysis of the data; and (4) in your subsequent major drafts?
4. Have you pulled out your roadmap summaries and paragraphs and read them as if they were a standalone essay? Assess whether they flow logically and tell your story well.
5. Have you tried reading the essay aloud, listening to the rhythm of its wording? Get others to read the essay and give you feedback. Then get feedback from your dissertation advisors or others who will receive your completed work.
6. Does your title also accurately reflect the roadmap?
7. Do you have an abstract, and have you made sure it reflects your roadmap components?
8. Is your narrative well-paced and not "lumpy?" That is, will the reader find each chapter a "good read," or will he or she feel some sections are too abbreviated, needing elaboration and well-placed details, whereas other sections ramble on too long?

9. Does each chapter and each major section have a clear order, with a definite beginning and a definite ending?

10. Have you avoided talking down to your readers by not including too-obvious transitional forms such as "My subject is . . . " or "These are the causes that influence . . . ").

11. Have you avoided overwhelming the reader with details in your introduction and literature review at the expense of highlighting your main themes and the story line.

12. Do you know the one provocative thought you would like to leave with your readers, and is this well placed in your storyline?

13. Have you remembered that not all your information belongs in your dissertation or paper? The body should contain your main "storyline." Put secondary but important information in appendices. Material that does not back up points in your storyline should be left out.

14. Did you strive to find the right balance between eliminating repetitious text and redundant words on the one hand, still taking advantage of parallel construction on the other? For instance, Abraham Lincoln masterfully used parallel construction to express parallel ideas, as in his second inaugural address:

> With malice toward none; with charity for all; with firmness in the right, as God gives us to see the right, let us strive on to finish the work we are in: to bind up the nation's wounds; to care for him who shall have borne the battle, and for his widow and his orphan, to do all which may achieve and cherish a just and lasting peace among ourselves, and with all nations."

15. Although it is desirable to give evidence of organization in your writing, have you avoided being formulaic? That is, often one's organizing framework creates a set of categories, each of which is discussed in turn. Do you find yourself with empty categories, straining to force out an example to fit, or do you have cases that don't fit well into one and just one category? These are signs the organizing categories must be rethought.

16. Have you avoided wordiness and used energetic sentences? Do your readers find your writing style to be natural and interesting? If you are prone to awkward sentence structure, consider paying for the services of an editor, if only once for its tutorial benefit.

17. Have you avoided monotonous wording, instead making a conscious effort to select words that are engaging, not jargon-laden, and that are precise, avoiding slang, and colorful but not overdone, avoiding cliches?

18. Have you used paragraph breaks in a way that reinforces your organizational structure? Too many short paragraphs may indicate you are listing ideas without developing them sufficiently. Too-long paragraphs may indicate you are

not sufficiently differentiating your concepts and discussing separately the relation among them.

19. Do you have any doubt at all about your grammar? If so, use the services of an editor, or at least use grammar-checking software (now built-in to leading word processing packages).

20. Have you written in a ''voice'' appropriate for your audience and subject? Each discipline has its own style, perhaps best picked up by reading a variety of journal articles in that field. The researcher wishes to avoid jargon but also to adopt the professional writing tone of his or her field. Finding this balance is one of the greatest challenges of professional writing, as the researcher may easily be criticized for too much jargon *or* for failure to use the normal terms of discourse in his or her field. Be aware, it is *not* true that the more integration of specialized terminology, the better: true professionals dislike unnecessary jargon but insist on specialized terminology when it is necessary to be exact in meaning.

21. Does your organization fit your topic? The less familiar the subject to the audience, the more the need for background sections. The more the audience is expected to implement or act on the research, the more detailed it will have to be.

22. Is your wording unambiguous? Try to find a willing friend to read a chapter or section of what you have written, then summarize it in his or her own words. If the resulting summary misrepresents your ideas, probably you are not communicating clearly enough.

E. Chapter Summaries, Transitional Paragraphs, and Abstracts in Your Roadmap

Chapter summaries. A chapter summary should capture the essence of what you have written, helping the reader understand what you are doing and why. It should use your framework as its organizing focus. It should tie together the main ideas of each of your sections and subsections, but in condensed form. All major chapter concepts should be reflected in the summary, which should also allude to previous chapters and point toward ones ahead.

Transitional paragraphs. Transitional paragraphs make heavy use of constructs such as:

Conclusion: in conclusion, therefore, as a result, so, consequently, in summary
Contradiction: but, though, although, however, still, anyway, nevertheless, yet
Dating: during the last 20 years, in the 1920s, over the last decade
Emphasis: indeed, in fact, even
Enumeration: first, second, last, finally
Illustration: as illustration, for example, for instance, that is

Logic: consequently, it follows that, therefore, thus
Modifiers: in California, among African-Americans, under these conditions
Reinforcement: furthermore, in addition, moreover, similarly, and, also, likewise, too

Abstracts. In considering the art of summary writing, you may find it instructive to study abstracts of articles that have appeared in the the leading journals of your discipline, found in such references as *Econlit*, *Psychological Abstracts*, *Sociology Abstracts*, *U.S. Political Science Documents*, and *Dissertation Abstracts*. Even better, study journal articles related to your topic and focus on their summary abstracts, and even more on their introductory sections and the frameworks they introduce to organize the research they present.

BIBLIOGRAPHY

Alred, G. J., Brusaw, C. T., Olin, W. E. (1991). The Professional Writer: A Guide for Advanced Technical Writing. New York: St Martins Press.

Barzun, J., Graff H. F. (1992). The Modern Researcher. 5th ed. New York: Harcourt, Brace, Jovanovich.

Cone, J. D., Foster, S. L. (1993). Dissertations and Theses from Start to Finish: Psychology and Related Fields. Washington, D.C.: American Psychological Association.

Mulkerne, D. J. D. Jr. (1988). The Perfect Term Paper: Step by Step. New York: Doubleday.

Steffens, H. J., Dickerson, M. J., Fulwiler, T. (1987). Writer's Guide: History. New York: D C Heath & Co.

5

Reference Search Resources

I. RESOURCES FOR REVIEWING THE LITERATURE

Researchers often write the literature review even before the introduction, because only by a thorough review of the literature is it possible to put the research question in proper context. Readers will expect the researcher to relate classic studies to his or her subject, know what other research has already been done for each relationship in the researcher's model, and show awareness of the work of experts in the subfield. The researcher should be sure that professional journals related to the research subject are identified and have been examined to identify relevant studies. Even if there is little other research bearing on the research model, the researcher will want to discuss the two or three most-related studies, if only to highlight that a gap in the literature exists and that the researcher's proposal is, indeed, innovative.

The number of bibliographic search software tools and resources has mushroomed in the last 10 years. Some of these are discussed below. Fortunately, there is some standardization in the format for entry of search terms as discussed in the Checklist section below, and this standardization facilitates the work of search software.

Contrary to what you might have been told, you will not be able to do adequate professional bibliographic research solely on the basis of free, public resources on the Internet (unless your university or employer has made fee-based services ''free'' to you by paying for the needed online information resources). A great deal is free, but many of the most important online databases require payment of fees. By and large, one will not be able to get abstracts, much less full text, for specialized professional bibliographic databases without payment of fees to such vendors as Dialog (the nation's largest), Lexis/Nexis, ABI/Inform, and others. You may need to consult with your academic department or research library about getting an account giving access to key databases. Be aware also that sometimes, such libraries make limited access available, as through dated CD-ROM access to databases, but up-to-date citations require online access at an additional fee.

The search process is usually best conceptualized in terms of overlapping Venn diagrams. That is, if the researcher is interested, for example, in performance measurement in urban police departments, it would be common to approach this by creating three sets: (1) performance measurement (performance measurement, performance indicators, productivity measurement, productivity indicators, etc.); (2) urban (city, municipal, urban, metropolitan, etc.); and (3) police (police, policing, crime control, public safety, etc.). After search services such as Dialog return the separate sets, the researcher then requests their intersection. For instance, given sets 1, 2, and 3 above, the Dialog search command for the intersection is "s s1 and s2 and s3," where the initial "s" means "search," and "s1," "s2," and "s3" are the three concept sets. Dialog searching is discussed further below.

Narrowing the search is necessary when many hits (many abstracts or index listings) are found. Common methods of narrowing include restriction by date (e.g., only publications since 1995), by requiring one or more key terms be in the title, and use of exclusion terms (such as, excluding hits with "military" from the police example above). Broadening the search may also be appropriate at times. Common methods include expanding (using descriptor fields of existing good hits as additional search terms); drilling (searching for other hits by the same author(s) as existing good hits); and chaining (using citations of existing good hits to find additional hits, then using their citations to find others, and so on).

II. SEARCH RESOURCES

There are several types of search software and resources, some free, some fee-based, most now provided on the Internet. However, before leaping into discussion of electronic search resources, you will be wise to take the time to undertake some preliminary, more traditional steps that will help you understand what you are looking for and recognize it when you see it in search output.

1. Do not to start with computer searches. Doing so may lead to your being inundated with large numbers of references, called "hits," while you are still ill-prepared to evaluate their significance.

2. Start instead with one or more recent articles or conference papers, perhaps recommended to you by your faculty advisor. If your advisor or depart-

ment is associated with work in the area you are studying, start with reports and articles emanating from your own department.

3. In your starting articles, notice which other articles and books seem to be cited most frequently and are most central. You may wish to consult relevant textbook chapters as an additional way of identifying classic or central works germane to your topic. Read these other articles and books too, noting what relevant works they cite. You may wish to continue down this road until you stop uncovering new, directly relevant references.

4. Use the *Social Science Citation Index*, the *Science Citation Index*, or the *Web of Science* database to find out which later papers have cited the articles you are starting with, and read the more promising of these as well.

After you have undertaken these four steps, you are prepared to use electronic search engines to conduct an electronic bibliographic search. Make sure to look up abstracts of recent and forthcoming conference papers, as this will give you the most up-to-date information.

A. Literature Search Resources

1. *Bibliographic Searching with Dialog.* Dialog, from Knight-Ridder Information Services, is the nation's largest provider of online bibliographic databases. It covers most bibliographic databases used by scholars of all disciplines, including *Dissertations Abstracts, National Technical Information Service (NTIS), Books in Print*, and many others. These databases are described in the Dialog "bluesheets," available online. Note, however, that you will have to have an account and password for this fee-based commercial service. Sometimes these can be obtained from one's research library reference department. Dialog bluesheets, which explain the content and coding of each Dialog database, are found at http://library.dialog.com/bluesheets/. A tutorial on Dialog searching is found at the website http://www2.chass.ncsu.edu/garson/pa540/dialog.htm.

2. *ERIC: Educational Resources Information Center.* ERIC is a free, general-purpose online bibliographic database sponsored by the United States Department of Education. Although it has some special emphasis on educational coverage, it also has good general coverage of the social sciences, humanities, and general topics. ERIC is also on Dialog, but can be accessed directly for free.

The ERIC bibliographic database itself is found at http://ericir.syr.edu/Eric/. The ERIC FAQ sheet on frequently asked questions is found at http://ericir.syr.edu/Eric/plweb_faq.html.

In certain circumstances, one may also want to search the corresponding U.K. resources: the BEI (British Education Index) and BETI (British Education Theses Index), although these are more narrowly focused on educational issues.

3. *Searching for Book Titles.* Dialog and ERIC mostly provide access to journal abstracts. Dialog also provides access to *Books in Print*, which indexes

almost 2 million books still in print, on all subjects, as well as the *Out of Print-Out of Stock Index.* These databases are updated bimonthly. Searching for book titles also can be accomplished through a number of routes, one of which is your own research library's online card catalog. Other major possibilities are listed below.

Library of Congress. Not only can you enter keywords but after you find a hit, click on ''Browse Stacks'' to view books adjacent to the ones you found. The Library of Congress web address is http://lcweb2.loc.gov/ammem/booksquery.html.

Amazon.com. The world's largest online bookseller provides keyword access to books in print and, where available, related book reviews. It can be found on the web at http://www.amazon.com/. A similar site is Barnes and Noble at http://www.barnesandnoble.com.

The Center for Research Libraries (CRL). CRL provides access to 5 million volumes not commonly held in one's local research library. Not all access is online, and some requires your local research library to be affiliated with the CRL. Its web address is http://wwwcrl.uchicago.edu/.

ProCite. ProCite and some other bibliographic software are capable of retrieving card catalog information from the Library of Congress and most college research libraries. *BookWhere?* is built into the software *Reference Manager* or may be purchased on a standalone basis. This is discussed further in the next chapter on ''Bibliographic Software.''

4. *Legal and Legislative Searching with Lexis-Nexis.* Lexis-Nexis, from Mead Data Central, is the nation's largest provider of online legal and legislative information, including state and federal case precedents, legislation past and proposed, and various Washington-related databases.

The Lexis-Nexis Home Page is at http://www.lexis.com/.

Lexis-Nexis Instructions (NCSU) (.pdf document) are at http://wally.rit.edu/pubs/starts/wml/lexis.html, among other sites.

Academic Universe is the scaled-down version of Lexis-Nexis. You must be on a subscribing campus to access AU.

5. *The NTIS: National Technical Information Service.* NTIS is the government's clearinghouse for all federally funded research. Particularly relevant to policy analysis and public administration, NTIS provides online searching of government reports, publications, proposals, data tapes, and many other document types. Information returned includes the citation and usually a summary or abstract. Most items can be ordered online, but the format of the items themselves is usually paper or microfiche, not downloadable electronic format. The NTIS Search Page is at http://www.ntis.gov/search.htm.

6. *Proquest Dissertation Search.* University Microfilm International (UMI) provides online searching for relevant doctoral dissertations. Abstracts are avail-

able free, with full text (in .pdf format) available for download for a fee. The ProQuest Dissertation Search site is at http://wwwlib.umi.com/dissertations/.

7. *General online web search engines.* There are dozens of general purpose web search engines that operate through keyword entry. By examining their options in their ''Help'' sections, one can refine one's search by use of Boolean logic, wildcards, domain conditions, and other tricks of the trade. Some of the leading web search engines are:

www.alltheweb.com help: http://www.ussc.alltheweb.com/
www.altavista.com help: http://www.altavista.com/av/content/help.htm
www.excite.com help: http://www.excite.com/Info/searching.html
www.infoseek.com help: http://www.infoseek.com/Help?pg=HomeHelp.html
www.lycos.com help: http://www.lycos.com/help/
www.yahoo.com help: http://howto.yahoo.com/

8. *Government Documents through GPO Access.* The U. S. Government Printing Office provides GPO access to search federal information. One website is http://www.lib.ncsu.edu/stacks/gpo/, but your library may also provide a link. The general gateway is at http://www.access.gpo.gov.

9. *Statistical Data Sources.* The are many sources of data on the web. One gateway, by the author, is at http://www2.chass.ncsu.edu/garson/pa765/links.htm.

10. *General Purpose and Social Science Bibliographic Databases.* A wide variety of databases, mostly now available online, exist to aid the researcher. Here those of a general or social science nature are discussed alphabetically, whereas similar resources for the humanities and the natural sciences are discussed in the final chapters of this book. In most cases, these will be available in an electronic format from one's major research university reference library.

Academic Index (Expanded). Indexes and abstracts on 1,500 general and scholarly periodicals in the humanities and social sciences; with selected coverage in science and technology. Started in 1992, it is updated biweekly.

Africa News Service. Files 606 and 806 on Dialog, this international news agency covers political, economic, and social developments in Africa. Coverage from 1996, with more than 75,000 records, updated daily.

Ageline. File 163 on Dialog, this database from the American Association of Retired Persons (AARP) covers the study of aging in social, psychological, health-related, and economic contexts. There is no print equivalent of the database. Coverage from 1978, with selected coverage back to 1966. More than 50,000 records, updated bimonthly.

API News. File 258 on Dialog, the Associated Press newswire serves some 15,000 newspapers and broadcast outlets in 115 countries, based on reports from more than 1,100 journalists in 141 United States and 83 oversearch news bureaus, with additional access to news from 1,500 newspaper members and 6,000 radio-television members in the United States. Coverage is from 1984, with more than 3.3 million records, updated daily.

Applied Social Sciences Index and Abstracts (ASSIA). File 232 on Dialog, ASSIA covers law, economics, business, politics, race relations, health, education, and local government. With almost equal representation from U.S. and U.K. publications, with 15% from the rest of the world, it draws from about 680 worldwide English-based journals and newspapers. Coverage is from 1987, with more than 200,000 records, updated monthly by about 1,700 records.

Asia-Pacific News. File 728 on Dialog, this full-text database covers general circulation newspapers and news journals of the Asia-Pacific region. More than half a million records, updated daily.

Asia Intelligence Wire. File 619 on Dialog, this database covers news and business information from 200 sources, including Cambodia, China, India, Hong Kong, Indochina, Indonesia, Japan, Korea, Malaysia, Myanmar, Philippines, Singapore, Taiwan, Thailand, and Vietnam. Coverage from 1995, with more than 410,000 records, updated daily.

Bibliography of Asian Studies. An online database of over 410,000 records on East, Southeast, and South Asia published world-wide since 1971. Focus is on the most important 100+ periodicals in Asian Studies. Updated quarterly.

Biography Master Index (BMI). File 287 on Dialog, this provides biographical information on some 4 million people in all fields of endeavor. It incorporates listings from more than 700 biographical dictionaries, such as *Who's Who in America.* The print version is Gale Research's eight-volume publication, *Biography and Genealogy Master Index* (2nd ed, 1980), and its annual updates and a similar microfiche product, *Bio-Base.* Updated annually.

BNA Daily News From Washington. File 655 on Dialog, this service from the Bureau of National Affairs, Inc. provides daily comprehensive news coverage of national and international government and private sector activities with a focus on topics like business law and regulation, international trade, environmental issues, product liability, occupational health and safety, retirement and benefit plans, and more. Coverage from 1990, with more than 350,000 records, updated daily.

Book Review Index. File 137 on Dialog, this database has more than 3 million reviews of more than 1 million books and periodical titles. Coverage since 1969 based on nearly 500 periodicals and newspapers. Updated about three times a year.

Books in Print. File 470 in Dialog, this venerable reference covers some 1.9 million titles that are currently in print, declared out of print, or soon to be published in all subjects. The print versions of this resource are *Books in Print, Subject Guide to Books in Print, Forthcoming Books, Books in Print Supplement,* and the *Out of Print-Out of Stock Index.* Online since 1994, it is updated bimonthly.

Bowker Biographical Directory. File 236 in Dialog, this database corresponds to the print versions of *American Men & Women of Science* (AMWS), *Who's Who in American Politics* (WWAP), and *Who's Who in American Art* (WWAA). More than 160,000 records, updated on a 3-year cycle.

Britannica Online. Available in many reference libraries, this service can also be accessed directly on the web at http://www.britannica.com/. The site not only features articles by world-renowned experts but also leads to expert-selected book citations and Internet links.

British Books in Print. File 430 on Dialog, this database covers U.K. books including ones up to 9 months in advance of publication. Has 2 million records, updated monthly.

British Education Index (BEI). A counterpart to ERIC but more narrowly focused on education. See also the *British Education Theses Index (BETI)*

British Humanities Index (BHI). Contrary to its title, this U.K. database covers journal articles in the social sciences, economics, and political science as well as the humanities.

Business and Industry. File 9 on Dialog, this database covers facts, figures, and key events dealing with public and private companies, industries, markets, and products for all manufacturing and service industries at an international level. Coverage since 1994, with 1.5 million records, updated daily.

Business and Management Practices. File 13 on Dialog, this service provides abstracts covering processes, methods, and strategies of managing a business. Coverage since 1995, with 125,000 records, updated weekly.

Business Dateline. File 635 on Dialog, this service provides the full text of major news and feature stories from 550 regional business publications from throughout the United States and Canada. Coverage since 1985, with more than 1 million records, updated daily.

Business Index. Provides indexes and abstracts for more than 850 business, management, and trade journals, plus selected citations to an additional 3,000 publications. Updated monthly.

Business Source Elite. Indexes and abstracts of more than 1,400 popular business publications and scholarly journals. Includes full text from 850 periodicals. Coverage since 1984 with full text since 1990. Updated daily.

Business Wire. Files 610 and 810 on Dialog, this service provides the full text of news releases issued by approximately 10,000 corporations, universities, research institutes, hospitals, and other organizations.

ComAbstracts. Abstracts of more than 40 journals in the field of communications. Updated regularly.

Congressional Universe. Legislative resources, including hearing transcripts, committee reports, bills, public laws, selected committee prints, congressional documents, the *Congressional Record*, the *Federal Register*, the current *Code of Federal Regulations*, and the current *U.S. Code*. Updated regularly.

Much of this is also available from Congress itself at http://thomas.loc.gov/ and at http://www.house.gov/.

Contemporary Women's Issues. This database gives worldwide full-text access to journals, newsletters, and research reports pertaining to topics such as development, human rights, the workplace, violence and exploitation of women, education, politics, family life, pay equity, legal status of women, lesbian concerns, women's health, gender equity, and reproductive rights. Started in 1992. Updated weekly.

ContentsFirst. A service of FirstSearch started in 1990, it provides the table of contents of approximately 12,500 journals across many disciplines. Updated daily.

Criminal Justice Periodicals Index. File 171 on Dialog, this database covers more than 100 journals, newsletters, and law reporters. Covers from 1975, more than 300,000 records, updated monthly.

Current Contents Search. This weekly service, which is file 440 on Dialog, transmits tables of contents from current issues of 6,500 leading science, social science, and arts and humanities periodicals. It is composed of seven subsets: *Clinical Medicine*; *Life Sciences*; *Engineering, Technology, and Applied Sciences*; *Agriculture, Biology, and Environmental Sciences*; *Physical, Chemical, and Earth Sciences*; *Social and Behavioral Sciences*; and *Arts and Humanities*. In addition to providing tables of contents, it also provides a complete bibliographic record for each article, review, letter, note, and editorial. *Current Contents Search* records also appear in Scisearch (Dialog files 34 and 432–434), Social Scisearch (Dialog file 7), and Arts and Humanities Search (Dialog file 439). Coverage from 1990, with more than 8 million records, updated weekly.

Current Research in Britain (CRIB). This is a national register of U.K. research at universities and other research institutions.

DIALINDEX. File 411 on Dialog, DIALINDEX is the online master index to Dialog databases. The researcher can use it to identify automatically how many hits each of hundreds of Dialog databases contain for given search requests.

Dissertation Abstracts. File 35 on Dialog, this is a "must use" resource. *Dissertation Abstracts* indexes and abstracts doctoral dissertations from most American, Canadian, and selected foreign institutions of higher learning. Since 1988, it has also provided coverage of masters' theses. Coverage from 1861, with 1.6 million records, it is updated monthly.

Dunn and Bradstreet Who Owns Whom. File 522 on Dialog, this worldwide company directory file shows the size of the corporate structure, family hierarchy, and key information on the parent company, headquarters, branches, and subsidiaries world-wide for any company. More than 6 million records, updated quarterly.

EconBase. File 565 on Dialog, this database contains time series on economics, business conditions, finance, manufacturing, household income distribution, and demographics. Coverage from 1948, with more than 10,000 records, reloaded monthly.

EconLit. File 139 on Dialog, this database indexes and selectively abstracts more than 300 economic journals worldwide, based on the American Economic Association's *Journal of Economic Literature.* Coverage since 1969, with 500,000 records, updated monthly.

Education Abstracts. File 437 on Dialog, this database indexes and abstracts articles from more than 400 education journals. Coverage since 1983 with abstracting since 1994. Updated monthly.

Electronic Collections Online (ECO). Indexes about 1,300 popular, trade, and other periodicals available electronically, with coverage across many disciplines since 1965.

Encyclopedia of Associations. File 114 on Dialog, this database provides data on more than 80,000 nonprofit membership organizations world-wide. The print versions are the *National Organizations of the U.S.*; *International Organizations*; and *Regional, State, and Local Organizations.* More than 110,000 records, updated annually.

ERIC. File 1 on Dialog, this educational and general database was discussed in a previous section of this chapter.

Ethnic NewsWatch. This service is a full-text database of more than 200 newspapers, magazines, and periodicals constituting the ethnic, minority, and native press. It has about a half million full-text articles. Coverage since 1992.

FactSearch. This service is a guide to statistical statements on current social, economic, political, environmental, and health issues, based on newspapers, periodicals, and government documents. Started in 1984.

FastDoc. This service indexes approximately 1,000 periodicals on a variety of topics. Started in 1990 .

Federal News Service (FNS). File 660 on Dialog, FNS provides transcripts of press briefings, speeches, conferences, and interviews on official U.S. policy. Often it is the only source for information discussed at federal government briefings, which are often not covered by the media. Also covers transcripts for major Russian policy statements. Coverage from 1991, with more than 100,000 records, updated daily.

Federal Register. File 180 on Dialog, the *Federal Register* is an online full-text version of the daily print publication of the U.S. Government that serves as the official medium for notifying the public of agency actions. Updated every federal workday. Coverage from 1985, with over half a million records.

Funk & Wagnal's New World Encyclopedia. An electronic encyclopedia with more than 25,000 entries.

Gale Database of Publications and Broadcast Media. File 469 on Dialog, this database lets one search for publications on narrow research topics. More than 60,000 newspapers, magazines, journals, periodicals, directories, newsletters and radio, television, and cable stations and systems are covered. The print versions are the *Gale Directory of Publications and Broadcast Media*, *Directories In Print*, *City and State Directories In Print*, and *Newsletters In Print*. Current coverage only, updated semiannually.

Gale Directory of Online, Portable, and Internet Databases. File 230 on Dialog, this covers publicly available databases and database products accessible through an online vendor, Internet, or batch processor, or available for direct lease, license, or purchase as a CD-ROM, diskette, magnetic tape, or handheld product. Over 20,000 records, updated semiannually.

Gale Group Business A.R.T.S. File 88 on Dialog, this abstract and full text database on ''Applied Research, Theory, and Scholarship'' covers current research and expert opinion in business, management, science, the humanities, and social sciences. Covers from 1976, with more than 3 million records drawn from over 1,550 periodicals, updated daily.

Gale Group Legal Resource Index. File 250 on Dialog, LRI claims to be the most comprehensive index to legal literature in English, drawing from more than 7000 journals from all major nations. Topics include legal aspects of mergers and acquisitions, taxation, environmental hazards, legal ethics, and criminal justice. Coverage from 1980, with more than 750,000 records, updated daily.

Gale Group Management Contents. File 75 on Dialog, this abstract database (with selected full text) covers business management techniques from key management journals. There is a focus on theoretical background as well as practical how-to topics in management. Coverage from 1986, with more than 100,000 records, updated weekly.

The Gale Group National Newspaper Index. File 111 on Dialog, this database indexes the full *Christian Science Monitor*, *The New York Times*, *Los Angeles Times*, *Washington Post*, and *The Wall Street Journal*. Coverage since 1979 (1982 for *Los Angeles Times* and *Washington Post*), with more than 4.5 million records, updated weekly.

Gale Group Newswire ASAP. File 649 on Dialog, this database covers the United Press International and several other selected newswire services worldwide. Coverage from 1983, with 1.4 million records, updated daily.

GPO Access. The gateway provided by the U.S. Government Printing Office (GPO) for all types of federal information. Many databases are available, including ones on federal legislation, laws and regulations, the U.S. Congress, economic indicators, historical documents, presidential papers, Supreme Court decisions, and much more. The direct web address is http://www.access.gpo.gov.

GPO Monthly Catalog. File 68 on Dialog, this lists all federal government publications in all disciplines. The print version is the *Monthly Catalog of United States Government Publications*. Coverage since 1976, with more than half a million records, updated monthly.

GPO Publications Reference File. File 166 on Dialog, this indexes public documents currently for sale by the Superintendent of Documents of the legislative and executive branches of the U.S. Federal Government. Coverage from 1971. With more than 10,000 records, updated biweekly.

Info Latino America. File 466 on Dialog, this database covers economic, political, and social issues in Latin America. Based on two daily newspapers and one news journal for each Latin American country. Coverage from 1988, with more than 100,000 records, updated weekly.

Index to Legal Periodicals and Books. Indexes some 620 legal journals and other periodicals from the United States, Canada, Great Britain, Ireland, Australia, and New Zealand. Started in 1981, it is updated monthly.

Inside Conferences. File 65 on Dialog, this U.K. database covers all papers given at every congress, symposium, conference, exposition, workshop, and meeting received at the British Library Document Supply Centre. Coverage since 1993, with more than 2.5 million records (.5 million added annually), updated weekly.

Latin American News. File 749 on Dialog, this database includes full-text stories from *El Norte* and *Reforma* (leading Mexican Spanish-language daily newspapers), as well as indexed coverage of other Latin American newspapers. Coverage from 1994, with more than 400,000 records, updated daily.

LC MARC-Books. File 426 on Dialog, this is the definitive card catalog database from the Library of Congress. Coverage of books since 1968, with more than 5 million records, updated weekly.

Marquis Who's Who. File 239 on Dialog, this database provides biographical information on outstanding individuals in all areas. Coverage from 1985, with more than 800,000 records, updated semiannually.

MasterFILE Premier. Indexes and abstracts more than 2,700 periodicals with full text for 1,800. Coverage of many fields. Started in 1984, with full text since 1990. Updated daily.

Mental Health Abstracts. File 86 on Dialog, this database abstracts mental health literature world-wide based on more than 1,200 journals. Not available in print. Coverage from 1967, with more than .5 million records, updated monthly.

Mental Measurements Yearbook. Covers reviews and full-text of articles on standardized tests dealing with educational skills, personality, vocational aptitude, psychology, and other topics. Started in 1963, it is updated quarterly.

National Criminal Justice Reference Service Abstracts (NCJRS). This service covers more than 140,000 publications on criminal justice, including federal, state, and local government reports, books, research reports, journal articles, and unpublished research. Subject areas include corrections, courts, drugs and crime, law enforcement, juvenile justice, crime statistics, and victims of crime. Started in the 1970s, it is updated regularly.

National Trade Data Bank. Covers more than 70,000 government publications related to exports, imports, and economic conditions in foreign countries, chapters of the CIA's *World Fact Book*, embassy reports on foreign industries, and export/import statistics on individual products. Updated monthly.

NetFirst. A guide to Internet resources.

New York Times. The nation's leading newspaper. Also available through Dialog. Full text usually available for the most recent 90 days.

Newspaper Abstracts Daily. File 483 on Dialog, this database provides lengthy article summaries for more than 25 newspapers including the *New York Times* and the *Wall Street Journal.* Also covers a unique collection of African-American newspapers. From 1989, with more than 5 million records, updated daily.

Newspaper Abstracts. File 603 on Dialog, this service from Bell & Howell Information and Learning covers more than 20 major newspapers, including: *Atlanta Constitution*; *Boston Globe*, *Chicago Tribune*, *Christian Science Monitor*, *Guardian and Guardian Weekly* (London), *Los Angeles Times*; *The New York Times*, *Pravda* (English-language edition), *San Francisco Chronicle*, *USA Today*, *The Wall Street Journal*, *Washington Times*, and the *Black Newspaper Collection*. Coverage from 1984–1988, closed file.

Newspaper Source. Abstracts and indexes the *New York Times*, *Wall Street Journal* (Eastern and Western editions), *Christian Science Monitor*, *USA Today*, and selected other newspapers. No coverage of obituaries (unless famous), sports tables, ads/classifieds, stock prices, and weather. Started in 1995. See also Dialog's PAPERS coverage.

New York Times–Fulltext. Files 471 and 472 on Dialog, this covers the full text of *The New York Times*. Coverage from 1981, with about 2 million records, updated daily. *New York Times Abstracts* (File 474) covers from 1969.

NTIS. File 6 on Dialog, the National Technical Information Service indexes and abstracts unclassified U.S. government-sponsored research and worldwide scientific, technical, engineering, and business-related information. Started in 1964, it has more than 2 million records. Updated weekly.

PAIS International. File 49 on Dialog, this database indexes and abstracts periodical literature on public administration, public policy, law, finance, international relations, political science, and related topics. Coverage from 1972, with about .5 million records, updated monthly.

PapersFirst. Indexes conference papers from world-wide congresses, conferences, expositions, workshops, and symposiums. Started in 1993.

Periodical Abstracts (Periodical Abstracts PlusText). File 484 on Dialog, this database indexes and abstracts more than 1,800 general periodicals covering the social sciences, humanities, general sciences, economics, environmental issues, government, history, politics, women's studies, ethnic studies, including 635 periodicals in the social sciences, 396 in humanities, 169 in general sciences,

212 in business, and 239 general-interest publications. Some scholarly journals are covered, including *American Sociological Review* and *American Political Science Review*. Full text is available for 600 journals. Coverage since 1971 with images since 1987 and full text since 1991.

Population Demographics. File on Dialog, this database provides statistical data on U.S. population, households, income, education, and occupations, often with breakdowns by sex, age groups, and race. Based on most recent U.S. census, with current year estimates and 5-year-out projections. It has over 50,000 records, updated annually.

Primary Search. Indexes children's periodicals. Coverage since 1984.

ProceedingsFirst. Indexes papers from congresses, conferences, expositions, workshops, and symposiums. Coverage since 1993.

PsycInfo. File 11 on Dialog, this is the American Psychological Association database covering world-wide literature in psychology, psychiatry, sociology, anthropology, education, linguistics, and pharmacology. Covers dissertations, journal articles, and technical reports and book chapters. Coverage since 1887, with more than 1.5 million records, updated monthly.

Public Opinion Online (POLL). File 468 on Dialog, this is the largest database of public opinion survey items for U. S. polls, covering all topics. Each record in the file corresponds to a single question of a single survey. Contributing polling organizations include Gallup, Harris, Roper, Hart, Teeter, Yankelovich, Market Opinion Research, Associated Press, Research & Forecasts Opinion Research Corporation, National Opinion Research Center, ABC, CBS, NBC, CNN, *The New York Times*, *The Washington Post*, *The Wall Street Journal*, *USA Today*, *Los Angeles Times*, *Newsweek*, *Time*, and *U.S. News and World Report*. Coverage from 1936, with more than 275,000 records, updated biweekly.

Readers Guide Abstracts Full Text. File 141 on Dialog, this database indexes the 240 popular general interest serials indexed in *Readers Guide to Periodical Literature*. There is full text for more than 120 of these. Coverage from 1983, with more than 1 million records, updated monthly.

Reference USA. Information on some 10 million U. S. companies.

Research Centers and Services Directory. File 115 on Dialog, this database covers more than 27,500 research organizations world-wide. The print version is the *Research Centers Directory*. Current coverage only, reloaded semiannually.

Science. File 370 on Dialog, Science, this database from the American Association for the Advancement of Science (AAAS) covers the advancement of science, especially governmental policy and social aspects of science and technology. Does cover social science also. Coverage from 1996, about 4,000 records, updated weekly.

Social Sciences Abstracts. Indexes and abstracts world periodicals in sociology, anthropology, geography, economics, political science, and law. Started in 1983 with abstracts since 1994, updated monthly.

Social Sciences Citation Index (Social SciSearch). File 7 on Dialog, this database indexes some 1,400 journals in 50 disciplines. This service lets the researcher track a chain of citations, see who cites whom, and count citations as an impact measure. Coverage from 1972, with more than 3 million records, updated weekly.

Social Work Abstracts. Provides coverage of social work, human services, homelessness, AIDS, child and family welfare, aging, substance abuse, legislation, community organization, and more. Has some 26,000 records. Started in 1994 with selected coverage since 1977.

Sociological Abstracts (SocioFile). File 37 on Dialog, this database indexes and abstracts sociology and related disciplines. The print versions are the *Sociological Abstracts* and *Social Planning/Policy & Development Abstracts* (SOPODA). Includes dissertation citations from *Dissertation Abstracts International.* Coverage from 1963, with over half a million records, updated five times a year.

Standard and Poor's Company Profiles. Information on mostly large U.S. companies, with brief biographical data on executives. Updated monthly.

Standard and Poor's Stock Reports. This service provides detailed financial investment reports for about 6,300 public companies traded on major American exchanges. Updated bimonthly.

STAT-USA. The Commerce Department's data bank on business, trade, and economic information from more than 50 federal agencies.

Statistical Universe. Indexes statistical data produced by the federal government, important international intergovernmental organizations, and others. Print versions are the *American Statistics Index* (1973-), the *Statistical Reference Index* (1980-), and the *Index to International Statistics* (1983-).

TV and Radio Transcripts Daily. File 648 on Dialog, this database contains complete verbatim transcripts of programming from ABC News and CNBC/Dow Jones Desktop Video, as well as other selected sources. Coverage from 1997, with more than 30,000 records, updated daily.

Ulrich's International Periodicals Directory. File 480 on Dialog, produced by R.R. Bowker, this reference provides publisher contact and other data on more than 200,000 periodicals world-wide. Although not providing bibliographic citations directly, it is useful in identifying if specialized periodicals exist for a topic of research interest.

UnCover. File 420 on Dialog, this alert service from the Colorado Alliance of Research Libraries delivers the table of contents of 17,000 user-selected periodicals directly to one's e-mail box. It is also possible to receive weekly alerts on the latest articles published on the specified topics, delivered to the user's e-mail address. Coverage since 1988, with more than 7 million records, updated daily.

UPI News. Files 261 (recent) and 861 (from 1996) on Dialog, this is a full-text database of United Press International wire stories. About half a million records, updated daily.

USA Today. File 703 on Dialog, this is the electronic version of the national newspaper of the same name. Coverage from 1989, updated daily.

U. S. Newswire. Files 605 (current) and 665 (from 1995) on Dialog. This database has full-text news releases from the White House, Cabinet, federal agencies, Congressional offices, political parties, trade associations, interest groups, and labor unions. Coverage from 1995, with more than 30,000 records, updated daily.

Wall Street Journal Abstracts. File 475 on Dialog, this covers the nation's leading financial newspaper. Coverage from 1973, updated daily.

Washington Post Online. File 146 on Dialog. Coverage from 1983.

Washington Times Online. File 717 on Dialog. Coverage from 1989.

Wilson Business Abstracts Fulltext. File 553 on Dialog, this database abstracts more than 400 periodicals and provides full text for more than 150, including the *Wall Street Journal* and the *New York Times*. Coverage from 1983, with more than 1.2 million records, updated monthly.

Wilson Social Sciences Abstracts. File 142 on Dialog, this database abstracts more than 415 social science periodicals. Coverage from 1988, with more than 600,000 records, updated monthly.

World Almanac. General reference data, now available online.

World Book Encyclopedia. An online encyclopedia with more than 17,500 subject entries.

WorldCat. A union catalog of world-wide library holdings.

Xinhua News. Files 618 (current) and 818 (from 1996) on Dialog, this database provides reports from 135 world-wide bureaus of the state news agency of the People's Republic of China. More than a quarter million records, updated daily.

B. Search Resources Checklist

1. Remember, do not rely just on electronic searching or the Internet. In addition to traditional library research, be sure to ask faculty and staff at your institution about your analytic topic; ask especially if they think it is original and what work they know of that may be related.

2. For larger writing projects, like dissertations, it is a good idea to try to write a conference paper or working paper to see if members of the audience, referees, discussants, or other colleagues give you feedback about related prior work.

3. Although some warn against sharing your ideas with more advanced scholars who may purloin them, you are better advised to seek as early and as extensive an entry into the network of specialists in your field as possible. Al-

though some relevant specialists will prove too busy or simply unfriendly, do persist. It is more likely that you will encounter specialists who view aiding younger scholars as an enjoyable part of their job.

4. Have you taken advantage of the advice and services of your research university's reference librarians? They are trained professionals, expert in information searching, paid to help you with your research tasks, including literature reviews. Do not be afraid to explain your goals and ask for help.

5. Be aware that even online bibliographic resources may be as much as a year behind actual publication in the field. Always look through recent journal issues for relevant articles and follow-up on pertinent citations they contain. You may want to subscribe to key journals, because recent articles on related subjects may cross-fertilize into your own research.

6. For doctoral dissertations, you will want to search the online databases of funding agencies, such as the National Science Foundations, to identify projects that relate to yours but that have not yet reached the stage of publication and are not to be found in the usual online reference databases. For U.K. research, see the "Current Research in Britain" database.

7. Use the *Social Science Citation Index* or the *Science Citation Index* to find out who has been citing articles recently that you have found to be the most related to your research. Follow-up on these by obtaining copies through your research library's document delivery service. Also, use these indexes to understand which of your hits is most cited and most central to your research, then make sure you read these articles or books in their original, full versions.

8. For your more central hits, have you looked for more recent articles by the same author (using the author's name as a search term)?

9. For your more central hits that are books, have you used the *Book Review Index* and other search methods to locate book reviews to help you evaluate these references?

10. Have you given greater credence to well-reviewed books or to articles that appear in peer-reviewed journals than to sources of unknown professional standing?

11. For your more central hits, have you read them in full and carefully evaluated their methods, including whether the results of analysis justify the statements in the abstract and the conclusion? You may be surprised to find how often even published articles are susceptible to methodological critique and misrepresentation of data.

12. Know your terms. After pulling up some hits through electronic searches, look carefully at the "Descriptors" field. Here, you will find terms used in the relevant profession to catalogue the article you have found. These terms may be different from the ones you used in your search and may not have appeared in the article itself, but the descriptors do apply to the article in the professional judgment of a human coder trained in the terminology of the disci-

pline. By using such descriptors in subsequent searches, you may find additional pertinent bibliography that would not come to light by using your initial search terms.

13. For research involving sources outside the United States, one must be aware of language differences in using search terms, even when all sources are in English. In educational research, for instance, American ''elementary schools'' correspond in England to ''primary schools.'' Likewise, ''learning disabilities'' in the United States are ''learning difficulties'' in the United Kingdom.

14. Enter keywords in lower case. Altavista and most search engines will then find hits in either case. By the same token, entering keywords in uppercase requires an exact match by case on most search engines.

15. In Altavista and most search engines, enclose phrases in quotation marks to force the phrase to be considered a single term for hit purposes.

16. Enter a plus sign before a word to stipulate that all hits must have that word, enter a minus sign before a word to stipulate that no hit may have this word, in Altavista and most search engines.

17. Do wildcard searching by adding an asterisk at the end of a keyword, to get multiple endings: e.g., presiden* for president, presidents, presidential, presidency, etc., in Altavista and most search engines.

18. Enter domain:gov in Altavista and some other search engines to limit your search to governmental agencies, domain:com just to search for firms, or domain:edu just to search for educational institutions.

19. Altavista and many search engines support piping: use the pipe (|) to search within a certain set of results. For instance, ''public administration''|theory, looks for the subset of ''theory'' hits within the set of ''public administration'' hits.

20. Note that Dialog and many other search engines allow you to save complex searches involving many search terms and conditions. Do save your search requests so you may easily rerun them later or on different databases.

C. Search Engines

Try using one of these search engines of the web: enter keywords and then compare the hits found.

www.alltheweb.com
www.altavista.com
www.boggle.com
www.excite.com
www.hotbot.com
www.infoseek.com
www.lycos.com
www.netfind.com

www.netguide.com
www.webcrawler.com
www.yahoo.com

Search newsgroups at www.google.com. Search online discussion lists at www.topica.com.

BIBLIOGRAPHY

Allan, G., Skinner, C. (1991). Handbook for Research Students in the Social Sciences. London: The Falmer Press.

Maykut, P., Morehouse, R. (1994). Beginning Qualitative Research. London: Falmer Press.

McKenzie, G., Powell, J., Usher, R. (1997). Understanding Social Research: Perspectives on Methodology and Practice. Philadelphia: Falmer Press.

Pfaffenberger, B. (1996). *Web Search Strategies*. New York: IDG Books Worldwide. A bit dated; written by a social scientist. General strategies still pertinent.

6

Bibliographic Software

I. INTRODUCTION

Several bibliographic software packages are available to aid serious research. Bibliographic software can save the researcher enormous amounts of time and is strongly recommended for doctoral dissertation writing. Better bibliographic software is closely integrated with digital literature search resources discussed in the previous chapter. Online bibliographic databases and online libraries, such as the Library of Congress, can be searched from within bibliographic software. The citations found (the "hits") can be archived automatically in the database function of such software, to be used later to "cite while you write" in your word processor and to create reference lists automatically in any standard citation format, at the click of a button.

II. BIBLIOGRAPHIC SOFTWARE

By far, the leading vendor of bibliographic software is ISI Research, which, having bought out its competitors, now publishes four products: *Reference Manager*, *ProCite*, *EndNote*, and *Reference Web Poster*. The first three software packages perform similar bibliographic functions and, as new versions come out, each is more full-featured. Each could support doctoral dissertation research. Nonetheless, as a generalization, *ProCite* and *Reference Manager* are a bit more powerful and full-featured than *EndNote*. Products from other vendors are mentioned at the end of this chapter.

A. How *ProCite* Works

To take *ProCite* as an example, its ''Cite While You Write'' feature means that *ProCite* installs itself on your recent-version WordPerfect or Word toolbar. Highlight any author or subject and you can find the proper citation in your *ProCite* database without leaving your word processor. Later, you can generate references or footnotes in American Psychological Association (APA), Modern Language Association (MLA), or any of dozens of other styles, all automatically. *Biblio-Link II* is a companion software utility that takes raw bibliographic downloads from Dialog or from bibliographic CD-ROMs like Sociofile, which your library may have available, and neatly places the authors, titles, abstracts, and other information in the database. *ProCite* can go out over the Internet to connect to the Library of Congress and any of dozens of university libraries to retrieve library catalog citations and put them, automatically, into a *ProCite* database. (*Bookwhere?* was a separate Internet search package for this purpose but has been integrated into *ProCite* from version 5 up).

ProCite automatically detects your computer's Internet hookup, then goes out over the Internet to retrieve book citations from libraries you designate, using keywords you enter. It can also search CD-ROM bibliographies and results downloaded from online bibliographic searches, such as Dialog. Figure 1 shows the *ProCite* interface with Internet search features active.

To create a database of citations using the Internet, first the researcher using *ProCite* would click on File, New, to create the (still empty) file, which *ProCite* will end in .pdt. For instance, in research on neural networks, one might create a file called neural.pdt. Then one would select Tools, Internet Search, causing the Internet Search dialog box to appear. One would enter one's search parameters, here the keyword ''neural network,'' as shown in Figure 1. Then, still in the Internet Search dialog box, one would click on the Select Hosts icon (the world) on the left to check off which Internet-accessible libraries and databases one wanted, then click on the Search icon (the binoculars) to actually initiate the search.

At the end of the Internet search, the results would be displayed, as in Figure 1. Note that at this point the found records (hits) will *not* be in the neural.pdt database but rather in a temporary database. The researcher then decides which records to save to the temporary database. This can be done by scrolling down and using the mouse to click on the mark box that starts each record/citation/line. If the researcher wants to know more before deciding whether to mark a record, double-clicking on that record line will bring up the full record with all the available information. There is also an option to mark all records automatically. After marking the records to be saved to neural.pdt, the actual transfer is accomplished by clicking on the Copy Marked icon (a record with an ''x'') and selecting the target database, here neural.pdt.

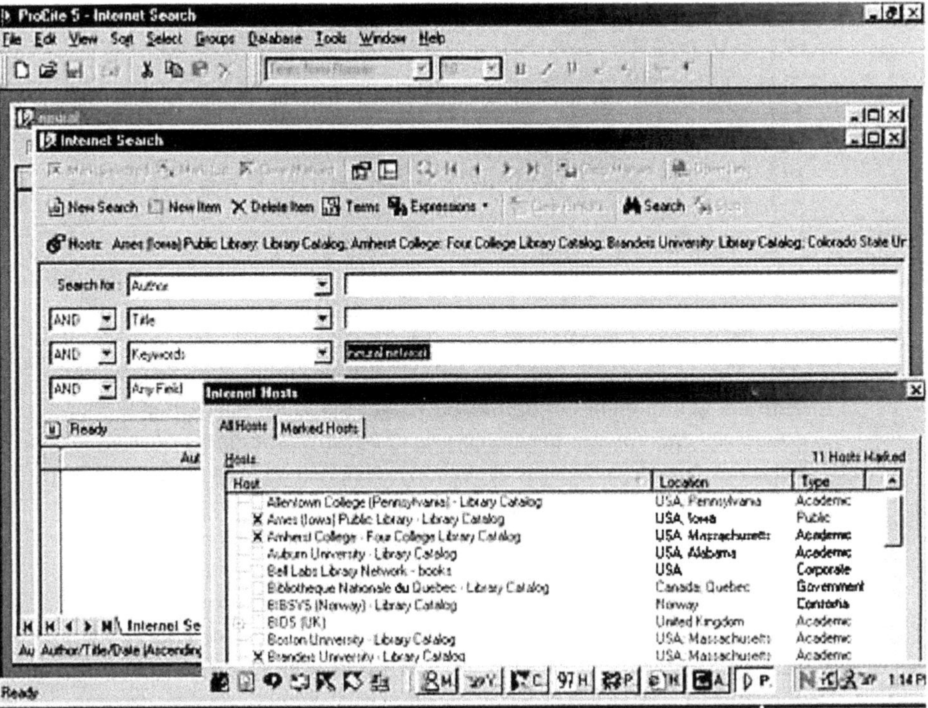

FIGURE 1 *ProCite* Internet search features.

It is also possible to retrieve into *ProCite* the raw bibliographic downloads one might obtain from a CD-ROM or online bibliographic sources, such as Dialog Information Services. Such searches yield records that look like this, if "tagged" format output is requested:

5/5/8 (Item 7 from file: 7)
FN- DIALOG(R)File 7:Social SciSearch(R)|
CZ- (c) 2000 Inst for Sci Info. All rts. reserv.|
AZ- <DIALOG> 03158391|
GA- ZB364|
NR- <NR1> 22|
TI- Unionization in a comparative neural network model: A trade union membership prediction in 12 states|
AU- Aprile D|
CS- SEME RES CTR,/ROME//ITALY/ (REPRINT)|
SO- <JN> SUBSTANCE USE & MISUSE|

SO- <PY> 1998|
SO- <VO> 33|
SO- <IS1> N3|
SO- <PG> 819–836|
PU- MARCEL DEKKER INC|
PU- <ADDRESS> 270 MADISON AVE, NEW YORK, NY 10016|
SN- 1082–6084|
LA- English|
DT- Article|
SF- CC SOCS Current Contents, Social & Behavioral Sciences|
SC- SUBSTANCE ABUSE|
AB- The sociometric and theoretical models traditionally associated with the determinants of unionization and based on international comparisons, generally use linear analysis of a restricted number of complex variables. The effectiveness of such models often have an unsatisfactory result. In this study, a different theoretical and methodological approach has been used. It is based on an integrated scheme made by transposing the principles of the ''Squashing Theory'' (Buscema, 1994) into the social field, by the connectionist paradigm, and by the Artificial Neural Networks (ANN). This has permitted the carrying out of a larger data base (49 variables, 12 nations, 12 years maximum time interval), the adjusting of a model that has an elevated explanatory capacity (in terms of open variance), an ulterior capacity of generalization (in terms of a one-year span) and of metageneralization (in terms of generalization to nonprocessed nations). What emerges is surely the need for more and greater in-depth study of socializing facts which follow such aspects.|
DE- Author Keywords:_unionization; comparisons; Neural Networks|
CR- <CR1> ASHENFELTER O, 1969, V83, Q J EC|BAIN GS, 1982, V20, BRIT J IND
RELATIONS|BAIN GS, 1992, IND RELATIONS|BAIN GS, 1980, PROFILES
UNION GROWT|BAIN GS, 1976, UNION GROWTH
LAV|VISSER J, 1993, V9, INT J COMP LAW IND R|VISSER
J, 1992, PROSPETTIVE OCSE OCC|VISSER J, 1990, SEARCH INCLUSIVE UNI|

Note that Dialog has been asked for tagged output (e.g., TI- precedes the title, AU- precedes the author(s), and so on). It is also possible to import other formats, such as text delimited files, in which a comma, tab, or other character separates fields. It is the job of *ProCite* to import such searches from plain text (also known as ASCII, DOS) files into *ProCite* .pdt data files. Formerly this was done with a separate companion product, *BiblioLink*.

To import records from a tagged text file, in the Tools menu select Import Text File to display an Open File dialog. Locate and open the text file that contains the tagged records you want to import into *ProCite*. Note: The file must end in .txt, so you may have to rename it. *ProCite* will display the file onscreen as shown in Figure 2. In the File Type drop-down list, select Tagged. In the File Format drop-down list, select Dialog as the format (there is a pull-down list of many other services). In the Target Database drop-down list, select the *ProCite* database to receive the records, here neural.pdt. Click on the Transfer button to begin importing records. Click the ''close'' box to return to the database record list. Note that the imported records are marked. To see only those records you just transferred, select Marked Records for viewing when you are back in the neural.pdt *ProCite* database in this example.

At this point, the collected citations are in a *ProCite* database, neural.pdt, as shown in Figure 3. In *ProCite*, you can quickly scan records in a one-record-per-row view; generate bibliography in APA, MLA, Turabian, or any other for-

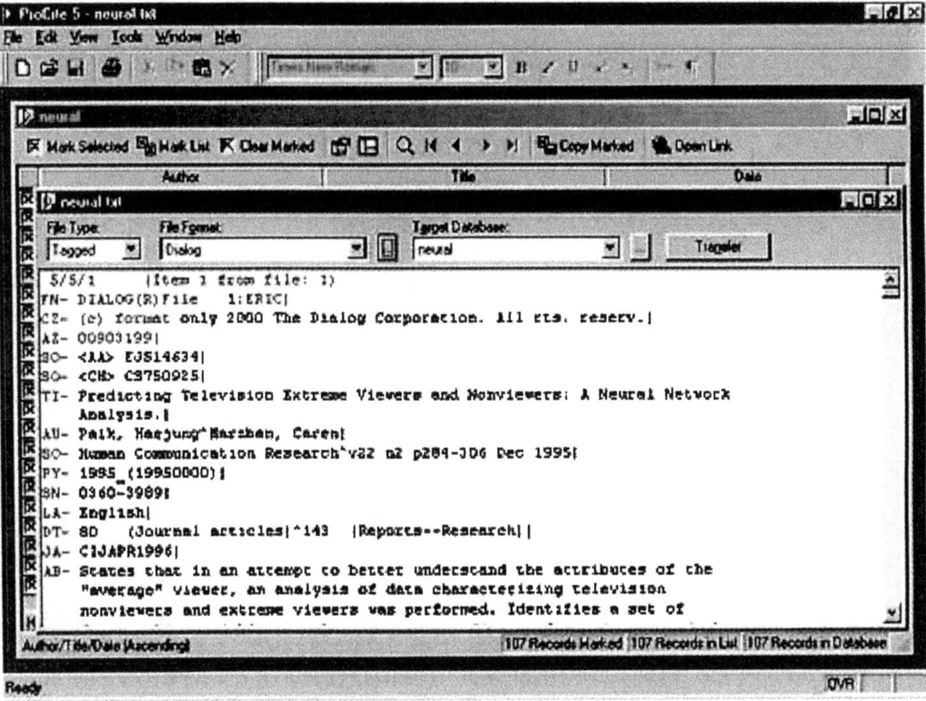

FIGURE 2 Text file import screen.

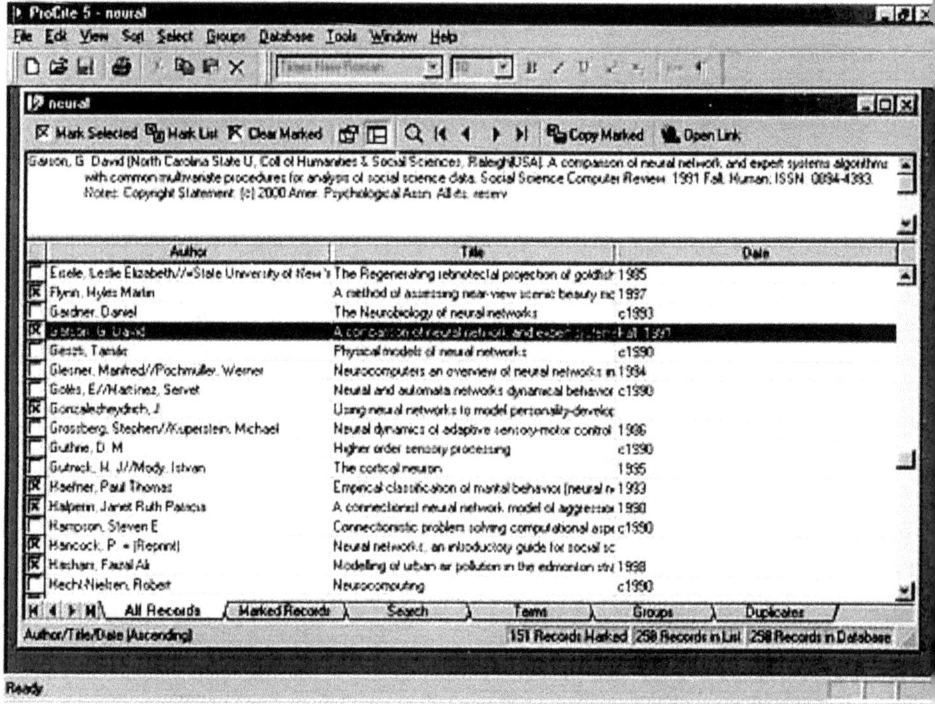

Figure 3 *ProCite* user interface, with Preview pane.

mat; copy any citation into the Windows clipboard for pasting in other applications; click on the Terms tab at the bottom to view a list of automatically compiled keywords, as shown in Figure 4. Figure 4 shows the Terms Window, pointing to the 23 citations for ''artificial intelligence'' in the keyword list for the neural.pdt database, highlighting the citation for a particular author. After selecting a term, the researcher can view all related citations; look up citations by author or title; sort citations by type (book, journal article, dissertation, and others); mark a subset of records, and more.

It should be noted that the importation process is not as smooth and flawless as one might wish. This is not the fault of the software but rather because each database contains unique fields and, often, dirty data. The result is that the researcher will want to edit records to clean them up. This can be done by double-clicking on a record in *ProCite* to view it, as shown in Figure 5. In this individual record view, the fields can be edited at will. In Figure 5, for instance, the author field was imported as ''<Author> Woelfel, Joseph'' rather than as ''Woelfel,

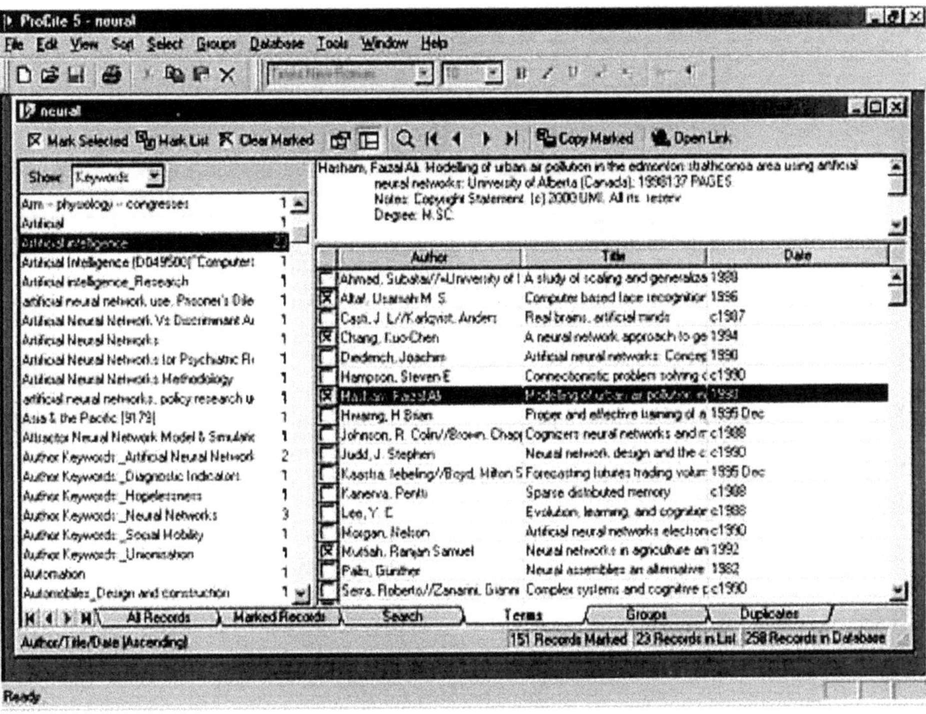

Figure 4 *ProCite* terms window.

Joseph,’’ causing the listing of this record not to appear alphabetically in the Ws as it should. After editing out ‘‘<Author>’’ the record will automatically appear in the proper place.

ProCite has many other features. One of particular interest is the NetCite feature. If the user has Netscape or Internet Explorer open to a web page of interest, then in *ProCite*, he or she can select Tools, Import Web Page to capture a citation of the current web page to one’s ProCite database, as shown in Figure 6. The capture will include the text contents of the page as well as the URL. Later, the user can highlight a URL record in *ProCite,* then select Database, Open URL, and the browser will be opened to that location. In this way, ProCite can be used as a superior alternative to your browser’s built-in bookmarks feature, as well as to add URLs to one’s bibliographical citations.

In the network version of *ProCite*, bibliographic databases can be shared by multiple users simultaneously. It handles large records, allowing up to 32,000 characters per field and unlimited records per database. Cite-while-you-write will,

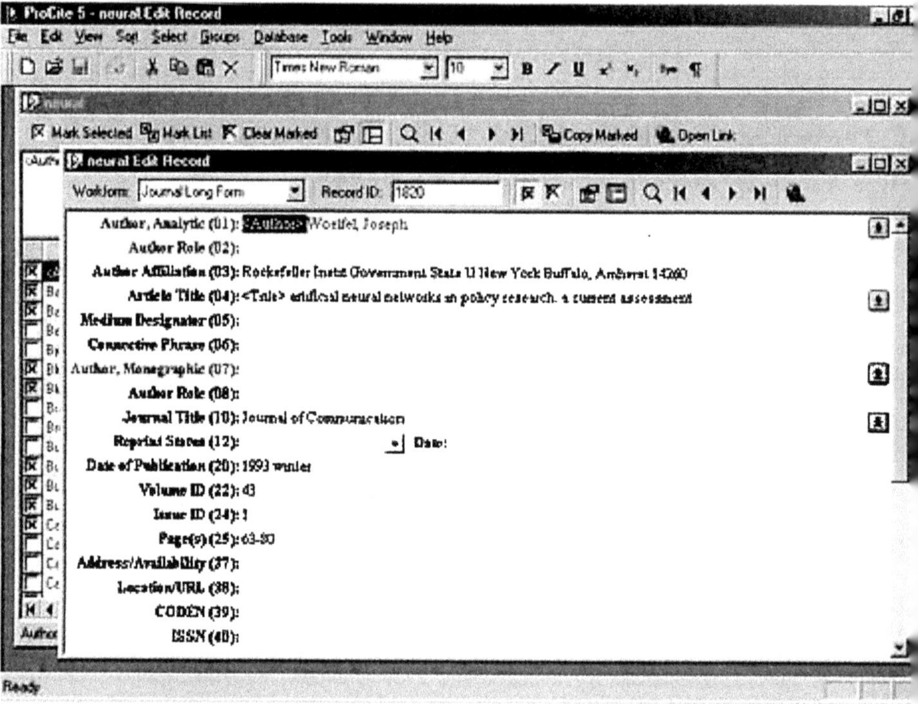

FIGURE 5 Editing a record in *ProCite.*

no doubt, be the bottom-line payoff for many scholars. Figure 7 shows this working inside WordPerfect. As can be seen, *ProCite* has installed itself automatically as a tool under the WordPerfect Tools menu.

Highlight an author name or subject keyword, then click Tools, ProCite, Insert Citation, and *ProCite* will be launched, retrieving the relevant record or records and inserting the citation at that location. In *WordPerfect*, click on Tools, ProCite, Generate Bibliography, and a dialog box will open, allowing you to select the desired format for automatic compilation of your references or endnotes. If you need to resubmit the manuscript in a different format, only a few keystrokes accomplishes reformatting. Cite-while-you-write works the same way in Microsoft Word.

In summary, *ProCite* provides a research aid closely integrated with the word processing tools almost all social scientists already use. It multiplies the bibliographic research capabilities available to researchers at universities that provide Internet access or bibliographic downloading. Moreover, the NetCite feature provides an excellent tool for making the Internet a manageable research environ-

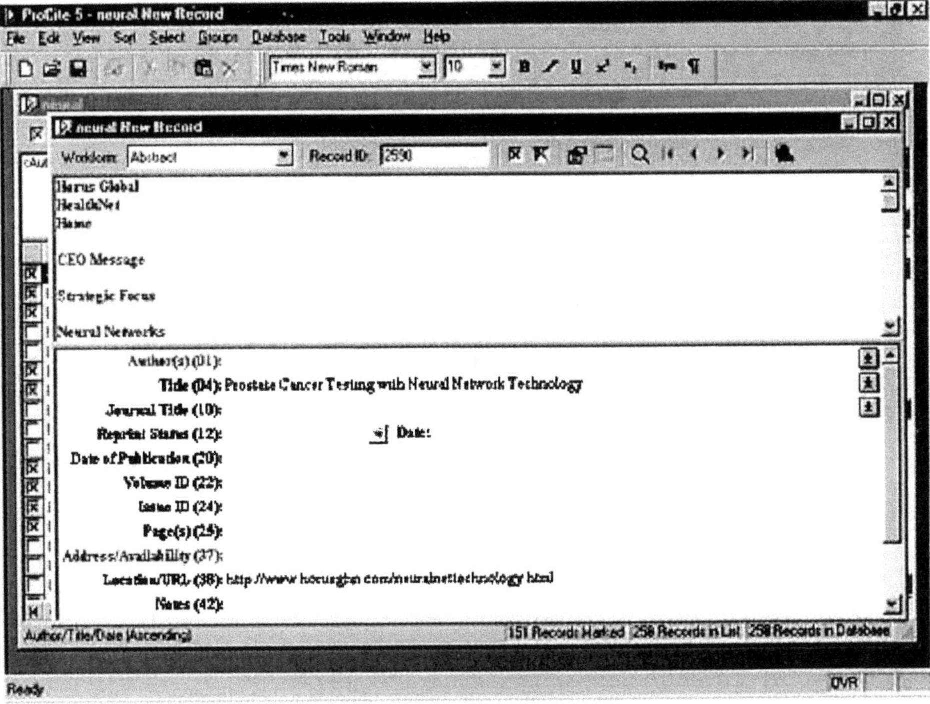

FIGURE 6 Web page capture in *ProCite*.

ment. Researchers who try a set of packages such as this will not want to be without them in any future research project.

B. How *Reference Manager* Works

Reference Manager is another bibliographic database program from ISI Research. Among the functions it supports are instant preparation of formatted in-text citations and bibliographies for manuscripts; creating and maintaining research databases; and collecting bibliographic references from a variety of online, CD-ROM, or Internet data services. Limited only by your system's resources, you can create bibliographic databases, each filled with references. Information in a bibliographic database is kept in up to 33 text fields of variable lengths that can include almost any type of information.

It is simple to use *Reference Manager*. One opens a bibliographic database in the usual Windows manner: select File from the menu bar, then either New Database or Open Database from the pull-down menu. If you choose New Data-

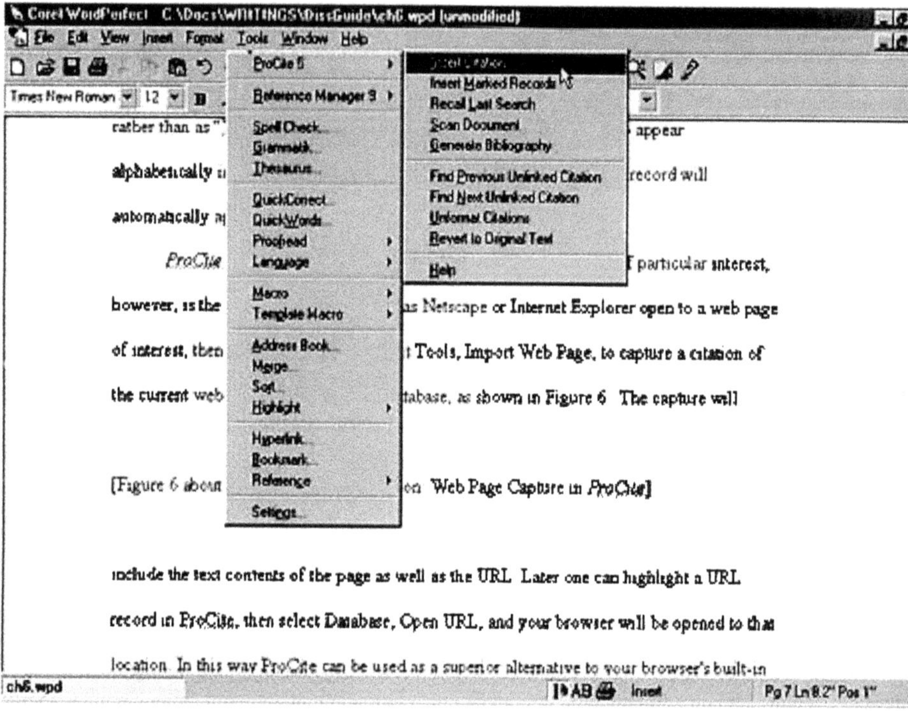

FIGURE 7 Using *ProCite* within *WordPerfect.*

base, then you will see a screen such as that shown in Figure 8, where the example is a research database on the topic of this book, ''writing.''

Had you instead selected Open Database, you could have navigated to where one of your previously saved bibliographic databases was stored, to edit or add to it. Either way, the screen has two panes: the pane at the top will present the highlighted reference in the abbreviated reference list in the lower portion. The default list shows the Reference ID, Author, and Title fields, although this view can be customized to show any fields.

A menu bar at the top has choices such as File, Edit, View, and References. Below that is a toolbar, with the tools New, Open, Save, Cut, Copy, and so on. The status bar at the bottom of the window shows a one-line prompt if your move you cursor over a tool. The status bar also has an indicator for the number of records you have marked for selection for some purpose, and the reference location as it relates to the total number of references in the list. In Figure 8 the number marked and the reference location are both 0 because Figure 8 shows a new, empty database with no records as yet.

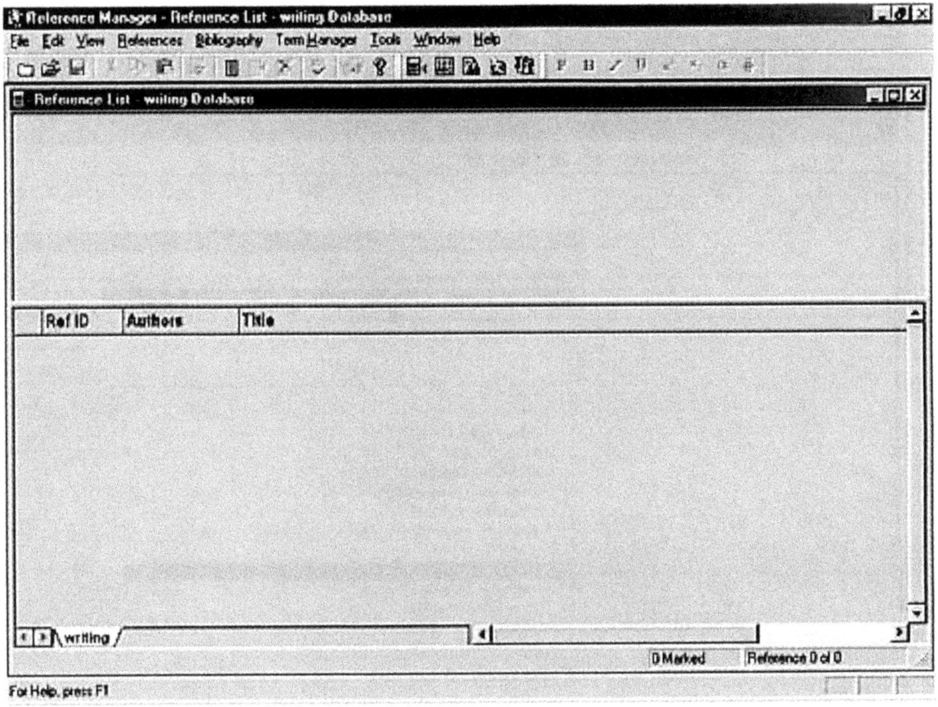

FIGURE 8 *Reference Manager* new database screen.

To retrieve records into a new database, one may search the Internet, search CD-ROM bibliographies, or use results downloaded from such commercial bibliographic database vendors as Dialog Information Services, the nation's largest. In the case of searching the Internet, in *Reference Manager* one chooses References, Internet Search from the menu bar. This brings up a ''Retrieval Window,'' shown in Figure 9.

To enter your search terms in the Retrieval Window, move the cursor to the first box under the Field column. Strike any key and a list of searchable fields pops up automatically. In Figure 9, ''Any'' has been selected, indicating any field, but one could specify a particular field. Then under the Subject heading, a term is entered (''empirical,'' in Figure 9). Tab to the Connector field to add additional terms: ''A'' for AND, ''O'' for OR, or ''N'' for NOT. These connector terms can also be selected by clicking on their icons in the toolbar. Other parameters are entered the same way.

Next one must specify which Internet sites to search. In the Retrieval Window, first select ''Z39.50 sites'' in the pull-down databases list in the upper left.

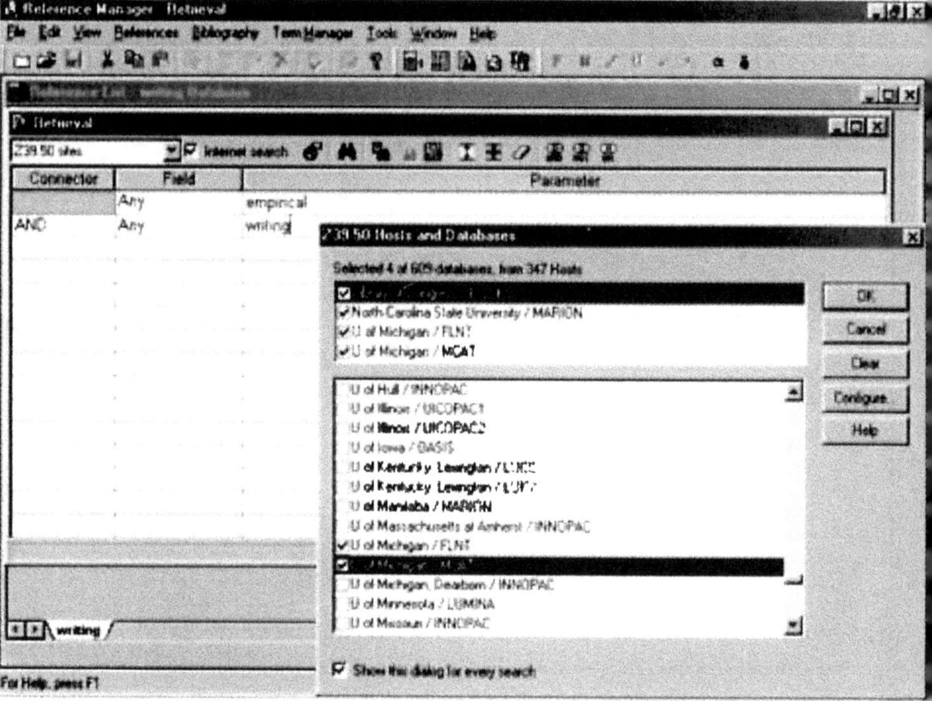

Figure 9 *Reference Manager* Retrieval window and Z39.50 site list.

Z39.50 refers to a communication standard used to put certain databases on line, including the holdings of hundreds of libraries.[1] Also make sure the Internet Search box is checked. Clicking on the tool immediately after the words Internet Search causes the list of Z39.50 sites to appear as a drop-down list, as shown in Figure 9. This window is also activated by clicking on the Begin Search icon, which depicts a pair of binoculars. Figure 9 shows four library sites selected, including the Library of Congress and North Carolina State University, from a list of more than 300.

Note that the search criteria hits one receives will change from search to search as libraries on the Internet are updated. Thus, if you replicate the search shown in Figure 10, your hits may be different. Figure 10 shows the *Reference Manager* interface after the example ''writing'' database has been loaded with hits from searching four libraries. Hit number 9 is highlighted, causing the corresponding record to display in the top pane of the display (Mary MacNealey, *Strategies for Empirical Research in Writing*). In the bottom pane, which lists the hits, one row per hit, clicking on the Authors heading will alphabetize by

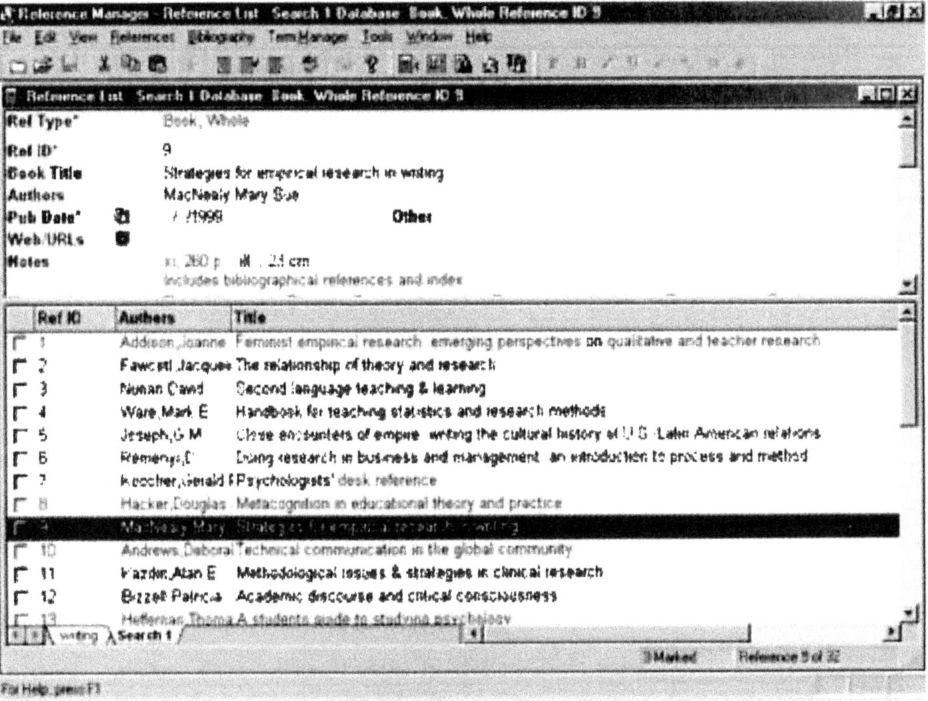

FIGURE 10 *Reference Manager* database.

authors, ''Title'' alphabetizes by title, and so on. One can customize to cause other fields to show than these defaults.

When you do a search, it is inevitable that many of the hits will not be ones you want. *Reference Manager* provides a convenient way to save only the hits you need, usually a minority of selections. Notice near the bottom of Figure 9, there are two tabs, ''Search 1'' and ''Writing.'' Search 1 is the Internet search just described above. Actually, there are no records yet in the Writing bibliographic database. To populate this database, just use the mouse to drag citations from the Search 1 list onto the tab for Writing. As you scroll through the list of citations in the bottom pane of the *Reference Manager* interface, you can mark the records you want by mouse-clicking in the checkbox for that line/record, or you may use the down-arrow key to scroll down and the spacebar to cause the current line/record to be marked. Then select References, Copy between Databases, check Marked References, and copy the marked references from the temporary Search 1 database to the permanent Writing database, in this example.

To search and select records from either a temporary bibliographic database like Search 1 or a permanent one like Writing, *Reference Manager*'s Term Manager option on the menu bar may be clicked, which causes the corresponding window to pop up as shown in Figure 11.

The Term Manager lists words from the Keywords field of all of the records. It also lists all journal titles and all author names. By highlighting a keyword ("written communication" in Figure 11) and clicking on the Search icon (the binoculars), *Reference Manager* will put that selection into a new temporary database (shown as Retrieved in the tab at the bottom of Figure 11). One can move any or all retrieved records to the permanent database (Writing in this example) simply by dragging them to that tab using one's mouse. If you want to move all the retrieved records, highlight the first one and then shift-click on the last one, thereby highlighting them all, then drag the set to the Writing database tab and click on Yes to All when prompted. To move all records from one database such as Search 1 to another such as Writing, select References from the menu bar, then select Copy Between Databases.

Once a database has been assembled, you can "cite while you write."

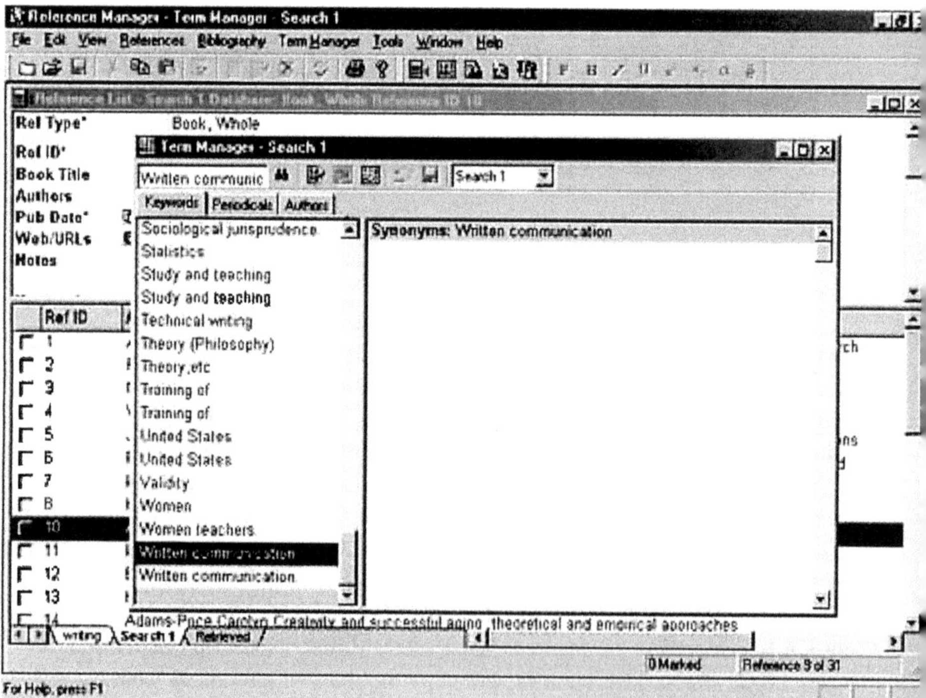

FIGURE 11 *Reference Manager* Term Manager window.

Reference Manager installs itself on the Tools menu of *WordPerfect* or *Microsoft Word*, two leading word processing packages. Thus, if while you are writing you feel a citation is called for at some point, inside your word processor you can select Tools, Reference Manager, Insert Citation, and a search dialog box will pop up. In this box one may enter search terms (in the field "Identifying Text")

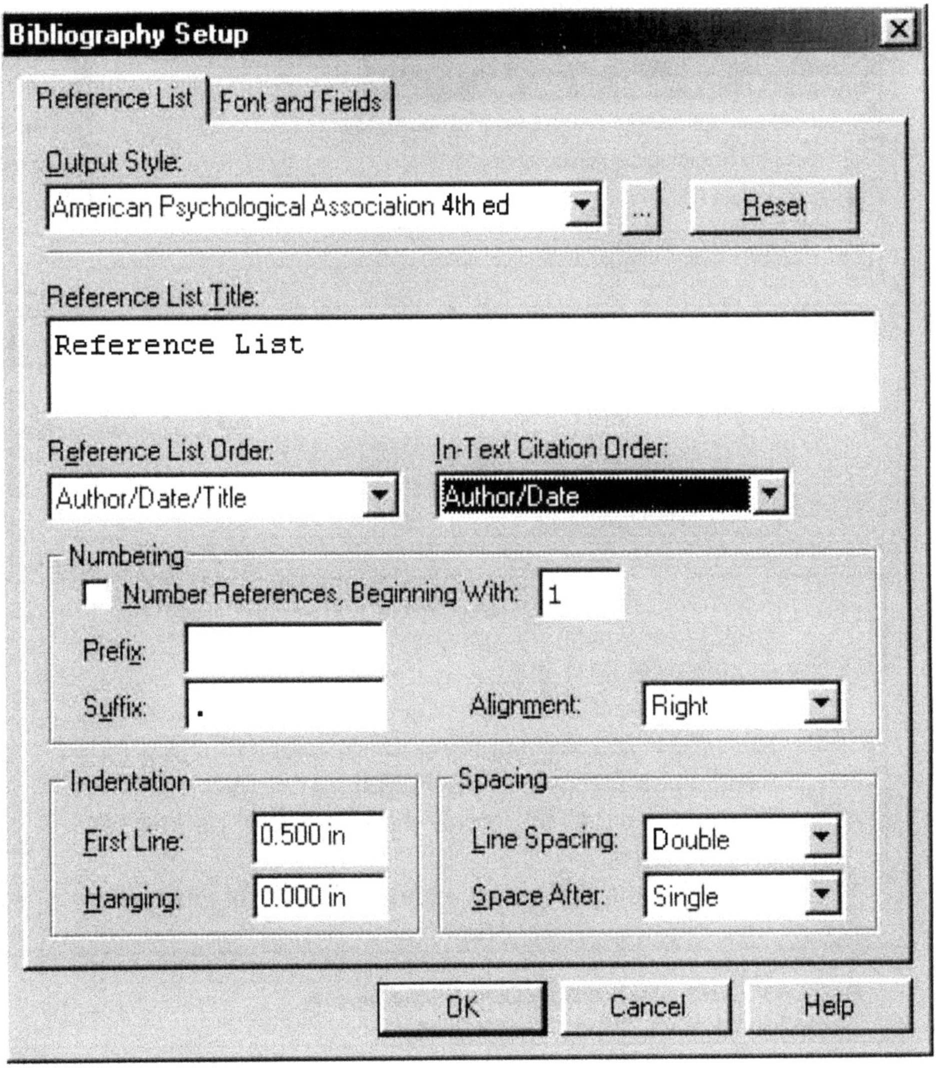

FIGURE 12 *Reference Manager* Bibliography Setup window.

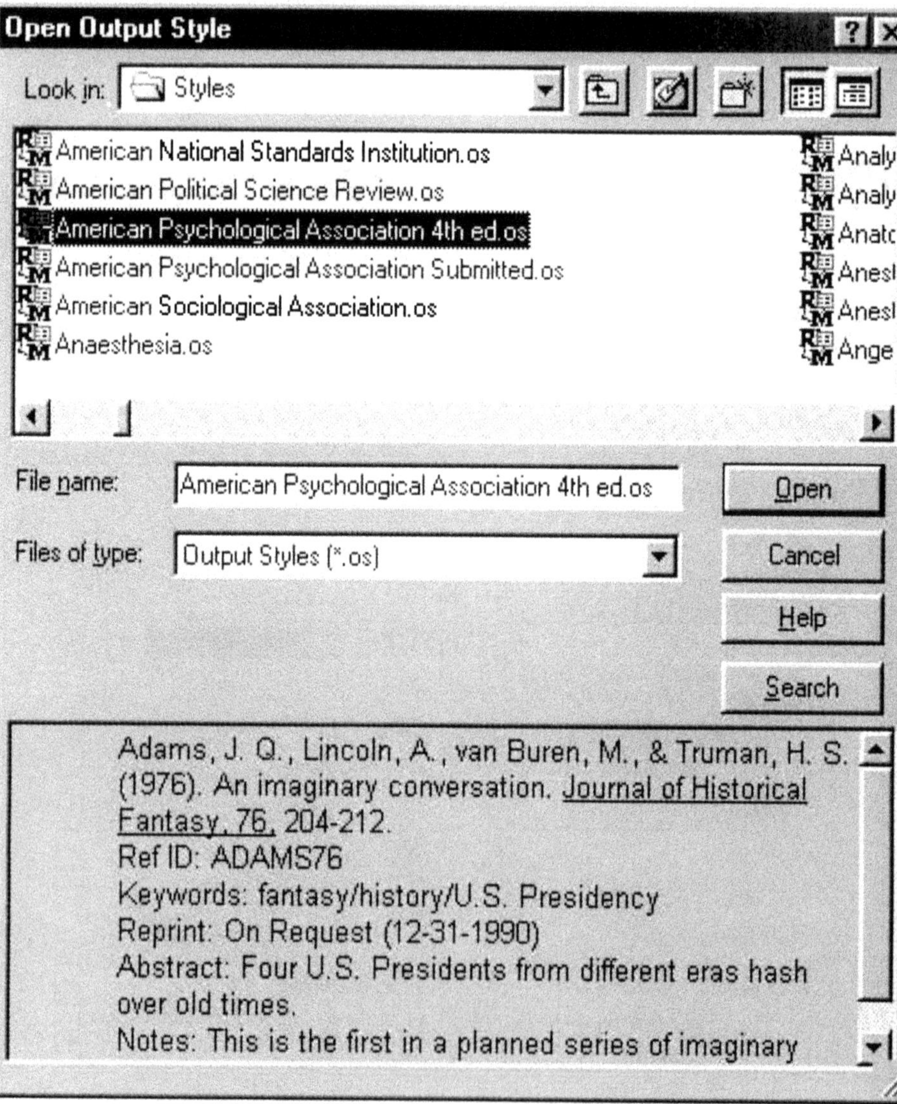

FIGURE 13 *Reference Manager* Output Style window.

and select which *Reference Manager* databases to search. If there is only one match, that citation will be placed in the text automatically, (e.g., Smith, 1999) and added to the reference list. If there are multiple matches, another window will pop up. From this the writer may select the desired citation from among the possibilities in the bibliographic database that has been assembled.

To output bibliography for the reference list, within one's word processor one selects Tools, Reference Manager, Generate Bibliography. Figure 12 shows the Bibliography Setup window that appears. In this window, one can select the citation style to be used, the ordering of the citations (such as alphabetical), how the citation list is to be titled (e.g., ''Reference List''), and other formatting parameters. Figure 13 shows the window that appears when the writer clicks within the Bibliography Setup Window to select the output style (such as APA style, which is perhaps the most widely used). It is here, by simply choosing, that the writer can cause all citations to be rewritten to the specifications of one or another journal as needed.

There is, of course, much more to *Reference Manager* software, but the basic operations are as described above. With *Reference Manager*, one can search up to 10 bibliographic databases simultaneously, each with unlimited records and up to 33 fields of up to 32K characters; use 35 predefined reference styles; detect duplicates; search multiple Internet libraries simultaneously; save search strategies; import data from CD-ROM and online bibliographic services, and much more. It should be noted that *Reference Manager* and *EndNote*, in their versions at this writing, cannot automatically create subject bibliographies, whereas *ProCite* can. *Reference Manager* supports selection of records by subject using only the keyword field (or author or journal) in the Term Manager, whereas *ProCite* supports subject searching on the main screen. On the other hand, *Reference Manager* can search multiple databases simultaneously, whereas *ProCite* searches one at a time. Note, though, that the relative features of each package vary as new versions appear. All three packages would suffice for nearly all types of doctoral writing.

C. Bibliographic Software Checklist

1. Review alternative brands of bibliographic software. It is worth trying out the demo/trial versions before purchase, to assure they will meet your needs.
2. Check with your academic department regarding support for one or another brand of bibliographic software. Such support may be a major selection consideration.
3. If expense is a consideration, it may be possible to get by with shareware such as *RefMaker*, particularly for smaller projects.
4. When downloading Dialog bibliography, remember to invoke the TAG

format (e.g., T s6/5/all TAG). (Dialog is discussed in the previous chapter on search software).

5. Remember, automated construction of bibliographic databases cannot substitute for traditional strategies such as reading leading articles, following up on citations of leading articles, and communication with experts in the field.

BIBLIOGRAPHY

ProCite, *Reference Manager*, or *Endnote*. Publisher: Research Information Systems, 800 Jones Street, Berkeley, CA 94710; Phone: (510) 559–8592; Sales: (800) 554–3049; Fax: (510) 559–8683; http://www.isiresearchsoft.com/. Trial versions are available for download at the website.

Citation, *Ibidem*, and *Nota Bene*. Oberon Development Ltd., 147 E. Oakland Avenue, Columbus OH 43201; Phone (800) 243–3833 (sales); Fax (212) 334–0845; http://www.oberon-res.com/. Trial version available for download.

RefMaker. Shareware available at *http://www.geocities.com/Broadway/6858/*.

ENDNOTES

1. Access to Z39.50 sites can vary. They may be down for updating, restricted to certain communication ports, require a paid subscription, or will prompt for a username and password.

BIBLIOGRAPHIC SOFTWARE BIBLIOGRAPHY

Biggs, D. R. ed. (1995). ProCite in libraries: Applications in Bibliographic Database Management. Washington, DC: Information Today, Inc.

Walker, G., Janes, J., Tenopir, C., eds. (1999). Online Retrieval: A Dialogue of Theory and Practice. Englewood, CA: Libraries Unlimited.

7

Meta-Analysis

I. WRITING THE REVIEW

Literature reviews are always part of dissertations and master's theses. They are required as part of articles in most social science journals. A literature review establishes the importance of the topic and assures that the researcher's contribution will not be redundant with past work in the field. The purpose of the literature review is to identify which previous work is directly relevant to the hypotheses and theories the researcher will be investigating. It follows that an efficient and effective literature review cannot be accomplished without a firm grasp of one's theories and hypotheses.

A literature review provides evidence of what has and has not worked in past research, and it also helps reshape hypotheses and theories. This means that the researcher must approach the literature review as a circular process, cycling between review of the literature and refinement of hypotheses and theories and more literature review. Effective literature review is the opposite of "finding out everything about a topic" and then going on to the methodology section of one's work. Rather, it is formulating hypotheses, gathering literature on these hypotheses, refining the hypotheses and adding more, gathering more literature, and doing this through several cycles until one settles on a final set of hypotheses backed by relevant literature. During this cyclical process, much irrelevant literature will be uncovered that, in spite of the work involved in collecting it, should be jettisoned for the sake of maintaining clarity of investigation and presentation.

A. Meta-Analysis

"Meta-analysis" is simply the concept that the literature review is research on research. Put another way, meta-analysis is the systematic study of past research articles with a view to coming to an overall conclusion about the relationship of one or more independent (causal) variables to a dependent (effect) variable of interest. In empirical research, meta-analysis seeks to reconcile and make comparable diverse studies based on differing methodologies, samples, levels of aggregation, and statistical procedures. Thus, at times, meta-analysis may use special statistical techniques designed to handle data at different levels of aggregation. Likewise special meta-analysis statistical software may be used to arrive at an overall statistical estimate of the relation of an independent variable to a dependent variable, based on findings in individual studies. However, meta-analysis also may be a purely systematic review of studies of a given phenomenon, without use of specialized statistical techniques. There are a variety of ways of accomplishing meta-analysis, but certain dimensions have all approaches in common:

1. Inventory, definition, clarification, and operationalization of a dependent variable
2. Inventory, definition, clarification, and operationalization of potential independent variables
3. Inventory, definition, clarification, and operationalization of control or modifier variables, and interaction effects
4. The modeling of relationships among modifier, independent, and dependent variables
5. Outlining methodologies for testing the models

Meta-analysis is relevant to qualitative research as well as quantitative, helping to clarify pertinent questions to ask, possible answers to be evaluated, and selection of appropriate qualitative methodologies.

Meta-analysis is a form of research that advances scientific understanding in its own right, and results of meta-analysis are routinely published in scientific journals. By combining the results of many similar studies, often with small sample sizes, it may be possible to come to stronger conclusions about the relationships under study than can be done through any one existing study. Comparison of studies can also highlight the full set of relevant control variables and interaction effects needed to properly model the phenomenon at hand. Meta-analysis helps highlight gaps in the literature. It also helps identify which studies may be considered outliers, meriting closer examination because of their exceptional nature. Overall, because of its systematic nature, meta-analysis is a more effective form of literature review than the traditional literary approach.

In some approaches, meta-analysis refers to specific statistical procedures for combining the effect sizes found in a set of studies. Statistical meta-analysis is discussed in a separate section below. However, there is a broader definition of meta-analysis, that meta-analysis revolves around establishing a system for organizing the literature you are reviewing. It could be as simple as assigning code numbers to topics you encounter, then entering the citation and corresponding code numbers into a bibliographic database. Then, all citations pertaining to given topic could be easily retrieved. However, a more rigorous form of meta-analysis is to make your cataloging process hypothesis-centered, as described in the following section. The hypothesis-centered approach allows you to retrieve citations by topic, by hypothesis, or even by variable.

Not every study the researcher encounters belongs in a literature review, particularly a review built around meta-analysis. A good literature review is apt to unearth a very large number of studies related in some way to the selected topic. Filtering criteria are necessary to select only those studies most pertinent to one's purpose. Common filtering rules involve selecting studies with these attributes:

1. Empirical data are reported, at least giving means and standard deviations or other measures of central tendency and variance
2. The order of data type preference is: enumeration data (full data on the entire population of interest), randomized experiment data, random sample data, quasiexperimental data, representative case studies, anecdotal examples. The researcher must determine where to draw the line, if at all, and how to evaluate other data types, such as nonrandom samples or random samples with very small sample size.
3. Year of study is often a criterion for selection of studies, particularly for the study of phenomena (such as women's career preferences) that have changed qualitatively over time.

In general, the researcher wants to include in the meta-analysis all studies of sound design, based on useful samples, and that focus on as many variables as possible that form the relationship model being investigated.

1. Meta-Analysis Schedule

The *meta-analysis schedule* is the researcher's main tool for systematic review of the literature. It may be implemented as a form to be filled out on paper, but it is better implemented as an electronic database with fields. This can be done from within bibliographic software simply by adding user-defined fields. Assuming one is using a database capable of freefield text search, it is not necessary to create a large number of structured fields and complicated codes to implement the meta-analytic schedule. If you are consistent in use of labels and terms, you will be able to recall the citations you want simply through keyword searching for any set of record attributes. The schedule database may have these fields:

1. *The citation.* This set of fields is normally used for bibliographic citations (author, data, article title, journal title, etc.). If bibliographic software is used, these will be built into the database template.

2. *The dependent variable(s).* The dependent variable(s) are listed, along with operational definitions and references to any standard measures or scales used and their reliability and validity. For retrieval purposes, the researcher may also wish to enter synonyms or, better, use an accepted dictionary of descriptors (these are associated with existing online bibliographic databases, such as Socio-File).

3. *The independent variable(s).* The independent variable(s) are listed, along with operational definitions and references to any standard measures or scales used and their reliability and validity. For retrieval purposes, the researcher may also wish to enter synonyms or, better, use an accepted dictionary of descriptors.

4. *The control and modifier variable(s).* The control or modifier variable(s) are listed, along with operational definitions and references to any standard measures or scales used, their reliability and validity, and notation of their control role vis-à-vis other independents and the dependent(s). For retrieval purposes, the researcher may also wish to enter synonyms or, better, use an accepted dictionary of descriptors.

5. *The sample and/or population.* These fields list sample size, sample description, the population to which generalization is made, sample type (e.g., enumeration, random, availability, archival), and response rate. There may also be methodological notes, such as on analysis of nonresponse and type of data collection.

6. *Methodological procedures.* This section presents information about research design in relation to statistical procedures. At a minimum, there should be some information about research design (such as two-group comparison with repeated measures), statistical procedure (such as MANOVA), and alpha significance level (e.g., .05).

7. *The relationship model.* Hypotheses about relationships among variables are listed here. Normally, the researcher will list only those to be examined in his or her dissertation or work. For retrieval purposes, it is helpful to assign a code to each hypothesis. If the article at hand does not test any of the same hypotheses, then it may be omitted entirely. However, some writers will list hypotheses not to be investigated in their own research but that merely present other hypotheses of the authors using one or more of the same variables as the researcher. This broader net can be useful in presenting background information in a literature review, but care must be taken to prevent such coverage from distracting the reader from the dissertation or work's story line, not to mention stalling the research project with undue workload in the review process.

8. *Findings*. For each numbered hypothesis, there should be an indication of the direction of the relationship found and whether the null hypothesis was rejected, the significance level, and the association level. Be aware that findings of ''no significance'' may be the result of small sample size rather than actual lack of relationship. Utts (1991) gives the example of a meta-analysis of parapsychology, where the dependent is the proportion of correct hits guessed through apparent extrasensory perception (ESP). More than half of 24 comparable studies found no significant relationship, but when actual trials of the 13 nonsignificant experiments were combined to form a larger sample, the ESP effect was significant.

9. *Discussion*. The discussion field is a residual field that may contain the abstract of the article or other summary information desired by the researcher. If articles are included that do not test hypotheses also to be investigated by the researcher, for these articles the researcher may wish to fill out only the discussion and citation fields.

The *meta-analytic table* is an optional way of summarizing the results of the review of the literature. In this table, the columns are the hypothesis code (e.g., H8), if the null hypothesis was rejected (Y or N), followed by text fields for control variables, sampling issues, and validity issues. The rows are the citations as in-text references (e.g., Jones and Smith, 1989b), grouped by hypothesis. If a citation relates to more than one hypothesis, it is listed once for each. Table 1 below illustrates a simple implementation of a meta-analytic table.

Table 1 reflects the simplest sort of meta-analytic table. As you read the literature in your review, it is a good idea to take careful notes whenever a study reports that a variable has an impact on the dependent variable you are studying. A better meta-analytic table than that in Table 1 would have each impact factor (independent variable) as a separate column. Individual studies would still compose the rows, of course. In each factor cell, the reviewer would enter an indication of whether that factor was present in the particular study and if so, what the effect size estimate (e.g., beta weight in OLS regression) was, if reported. Where a study omits a given causal factor, the reviewer must consider if this was a variable not measured in the study or if it was a variable not present in the population. Studies that may be used to assess overall effect are those comparable on all factors that might impact the dependent variable.

In a more elaborate, team-based form of meta-analysis, more than one researcher reviews each study and enters the appropriate information for that row of the meta-analytic table. Before actual entry, however, the rows are reconciled by a consensus meeting. Reviewers may even undergo formal training to ''calibrate'' their ratings for greater consensus. Sometimes studies are fed to the reviewers ''blind'' to remove the bias present when the reviewer knows the author's name and institution.

TABLE 1 Meta-Analytic Table: Research Determinants of Party Vote

Hypothesis	Citation	Null rejected	Controls	Sample	Discussion
H1 religion as independent	Smith, 1984	Y	Yrs education	Availability sample of SMU students n = 78	Sample from a religious college
H1	Brenner, 1992	N (moderate strength of relationship)	Family income	Random sample, five New England states n = 282	Sampled during presidential election year
H1	Axelrod, 1999	N (moderate strength of relationship)	None	Self-selected national web-based sample n = 2,010	Required recall of 1996 presidential vote
H1	Black, 1999	Y	Individual income, years education, parental party id	Random sample of registered Boston voters n = 609	Mail survey with response rate of 38%
H2 race as independent	Andres, 1992	N	None	Self-selected national sample based on mail-in newspaper questionnaire n = −955	Year of Perot's independent candidacy
H2	etc.				

It is not enough that the literature you cite in your review be carefully organized to bear directly on the relationships posited by your model (in graphical terms, to the arrows in the diagram of your model). In addition, it must be a *critical* review. You cannot be content just to summarize the findings of various authors. Instead, at least for the key pieces of research bearing on your own project, you must methodologically critique the work that you cite. This requires that you have mastered understanding of the principles of validity. It is possible that you will encounter statistical errors (such as authors who confuse a finding of statistical significance with a finding of substantive significance; authors who report findings of significance when their sample is not random). However, it is far more common to find studies that suffer one or another shortcoming in validity, such as generalizing findings beyond the limitations of the sample studied, reliance on poorly operationalized variables, or failing to establish the reliability of scales used to measure important variables. You may be surprised how very common it is for published articles to suffer serious statistical and validity problems, which is why uncritically reporting findings (perhaps based only on reading abstracts, not the works themselves) can mislead readers and the researcher as well. Validity is discussed further in Chapter 14.

2. Statistical Aspects of Meta-Analysis

Integrating research findings across disparate studies presents formidable statistical challenges, sometimes requiring complex quantitative procedures outside the scope of this book. The researcher should be aware, however, that one form of meta-analysis is expressed in a set of statistical procedures designed to combine data from several studies to produce a single estimate. An introduction to such procedures is found in Wolf (1986) and in Hunter and Schmidt (1990). These procedures seek to convert the significance or effect coefficients, or both found in different studies into a common statistic that is weighted by the relative sample sizes of the studies surveyed and may also adjust for range restriction and sampling and measurement error. Statistical meta-analysis might seek a summary coefficient of either overall significance or overall effect size across studies. However, the latter has become more popular in contemporary meta-analytic studies.

Statistical meta-analysis makes certain assumptions:

1. The studies all focus on the same independent and dependent variables. As different studies typically used different control variables, there is a tendency to focus on the first-order correlation of a given independent variable with the dependent variable of interest, ignoring control and interaction effects because there are not enough studies in one's review that use the same additional mediating variables or study the same interaction effects.

2. The literature survey includes all relevant studies. Study selection can have a very profound effect on the conclusions of a meta-analysis. Because stud-

ies that find a significant relationship are more likely to be published than studies that fail to find a relationship, there is a possible selection bias inherent in meta-analysis based on literature review.

3. Meta-analysis assumes that the effect size estimates in the studies surveyed are all estimates of the same global population effect size for the variables studied. That is, the researcher must assume there is one universal level of relationship between the independent and dependent variables, across all the samples in all the studies, and the individual studies yield estimates of that universal level. As a corollary, the researcher is assuming that it is not necessary to build different relationship models for different populations. As Wolf (1986) notes, ''One of the greatest dangers [in meta-analysis] is conducting a quantitative review when the collection of available studies for a particular research domain are few in number and their results heterogenous.''

4. It is true that the meta-analytic process lumps together studies whose methodological quality ranges from questionable to excellent, this can and should be dealt with by coding research design quality and statistical inference quality as explicit variables to be analyzed empirically. Failure to do so leaves the meta-analytic study open to the charge of whitewashing studies of lower methodological merit.

5. When the literature review includes multiple studies based on the same study data, the results are not independent. Consequently, there is a danger of inflating the effective significance cut-off (the researcher may think he or she is using the nominal .05 significance cutoff, but the actual effective cutoff may be, say, .12). Statistical adjustments must be made when combining data results that are not independent.

6. Some meta-analytic procedures assume randomized experimental data. Thus, statistical meta-analysis has been most prominent in fields such as medicine, public health, psychology, and education

There are two general approaches to statistical meta-analysis: fixed effects models and random effects models. Fixed effects models look (only) at within-study variability, assume that otherwise similar studies should produce identical results, and that any difference in the dependent variable is the result of the levels of the independent variable(s). The Mantel-Haenszel odds ratio is an example of a statistic assuming a fixed effects model. Random effects models look both at between-study and within-study variability and assume that the studies in the review are a random sample from the universe of all possible studies. The DerSimonian Laird statistic is an example of a measure based on a random effects model. Most of the time, fixed effects and random effects models will give the same interpretation to a set of studies in a meta-analysis, but not always. In general, random effects models are more conservative (less likely to conclude that the independent variable has an effect on the dependent).

B. Meta-Analysis Software

1. Commercial Software for Statistical Meta-Analysis

1. *ES*. http://141.225.14.75/wshadish/es.htm or *http://www.assess.com/ES.html*. W. R. Shadish, L. Robinson, and C. Lu. Computes effect size as standardized mean difference over 40 different methods.
2. *Fast*Pro*. Uses Bayesian statistics to calculate posterior probability distributions and yields dichotomous, categorical, and continuous effect measures, including odds ratios. http://www.stata.com.
3. *MetaWin*. M. Rosenberg, D.C. Adams, and J. Gurevitch. (1997). http://www.sinauer.com. Implements fixed and random effects models on up to 500 studies. Uses resampling to test for between-group homogeneity among classes of studies using a randomization test.
4. *Power and Precision*. http://www.PowerAndPrecision.com. Or meta-analysis, not effect size calculation.
5. *Practical Meta-Analysis*. M. W. Lipsey and D. B. Wilson. A book from Sage Publications (Newbury Park, CA, 1996) that discusses SPSS macros implementing meta-analysis, available for free download from http://www.wam.umd.edu/~wilsondb/ma.html.
6. *STATA*. A comprehensive statistical package containing a meta-analysis command that calculates fixed-effects and random-effects estimates, together with a standard test for heterogeneity between studies and estimate of between-study variance. http://www.stat.com.

2. Freeware and Shareware for Statistical Meta-Analysis

1. *EasyMA*. http://hiru.mcmaster.ca/cochrane www.spc.univ-lyon1.fr/citccf/easyma or http://www.spc.univ-lyon1.fr/~mcu/easyma.
2. *MACALC.EXE*. Larry Lyons. http://www.mnsinc.com/solomon/MetaAnalysis.html.
3. *Meta-Analysis Easy To Answer (META)*. David Kenny. http://w3.nai.net/~dakenny/meta.htm.
4. *Meta.exe*. Ralf Schwarzer. http://www.yorku.ca/faculty/academic/schwarze/meta_e.htm.

C. Meta-Analysis Checklist

1. Does your review start with a discussion of your review methodology and strategies? Have your formally articulated your criteria for the inclusion or exclusion of studies in the set reported in the literature review?
2. Have you included proper discussion of qualitative studies and empir-

ical studies that are interesting but do not lend themselves to direct comparison by effect size with other studies in your review?

3. Have you articulated how you will deal with differences in the quality of research design and differences in the degree to which studies violate statistical assumptions?
4. Have you explained how you will deal with differences among studies in response rates and missing data?
5. Have you organized your literature review around and related directly to the hypotheses and theories you are investigating (not chronologically, alphabetically, or otherwise arbitrarily)?
6. Have you developed a meta-analytic schedule for classifying the literature in your review? Does your schedule provide for all important variables as well as for sample characteristics, research design characteristics, statistical quality, date of study, and source of study (especially peer-reviewed)?
7. Have you compared your review to the hypotheses and theories you are investigating, with a view toward making sure you have not left any gaps?
8. If gaps in your literature review are forced by absence of literature, have you stated this and provided credible evidence that the desired literature is, indeed, absent?
9. Have you made a systematic effort to search out unpublished studies to avoid publication bias (the bias that positive results are more often published)?
10. Have you relied, wherever possible, on original source material rather than on quotations from secondary authors who are citing original material?
11. Have you avoided the temptation to report all the literature you have encountered to show how widely read you are?
12. Have you highlighted controversies in the literature in relation to variables and relationships embedded in your hypotheses and theories, and have you indicated toward which side of the controversies they lean?
13. Do you have enough similar studies to explore first-order relationships between an independent and dependent variable of interest, as well as important control and interaction effects as reported in the literature?
14. Have you highlighted areas of consensus in the literature in relation to variables and relationships embedded in your hypotheses and theories, and indicated if they support that consensus or not?
15. Have you evaluated the quality of the literature you are examining

TABLE 2 Literature Review Table

Reference	Hypothesis	Upheld?	Controls	Sample	Validity issues
Johnson, 1991	H1	N	None	Birmingham, AL	1988–1989 first year of program
Harriman and Swain, 1998	H1	Y	Duration of training of community policing officers is shown to be a partial control	Five mid-sized midwestern cities, 1992–1997	Effect size was weak
No studies found	H1A				
Johnson, 1991	H2	Y	None	Birmingham, AL	1988–89 first year of program
Etc.					

(in terms of methodology, validity, reliability), not just the purported findings?

16. Have you considered interdisciplinary sources?
17. Have you fairly and fully discussed studies contrary to your perspectives?
18. Have you reread your draft literature review and revised it to assure that it is readable, interesting, and keeps your story line in the forefront?
19. Have you considered summarizing results in a meta-analytic table?
20. Have you considered graphing effect sizes of studies, identifying outliers for special examination?
21. Have you focused on effect size, not just significance?
22. Have you used APA or other standard citations in the reference section?

D. Meta-Analysis Example

As a brief example of meta-analysis, one might have a table of hypotheses and a corresponding literature review table. Taking the topic of community policing as an example, simple versions of meta-analytic tables are shown below.

Table of Hypotheses

Hypotheses on Crime and Community Policing

H1 Communities that have implemented community policing will have lower burglary rates than would be projected based on trends prior to implementation.

H1A The higher the percentage of full-time police involved in community policing, the greater the depressing effect on the burglary rate.

H2 Communities that have implemented community policing will *not* have lower murder rates than would be projected based on trends prior to implementation

It is common for dissertations to investigate one or two dozen hypotheses, not illustrated here.

Taking analysis of voting by party, other hypotheses might be developed, and the corresponding meta-analytic literature review table would look something like Table 2.

BIBLIOGRAPHY

Cook, T., Cooper, H., Cordray, D. S. (1992). Meta-Analysis for Explanation: A Casebook. New York: Russell Sage Foundation.

Cooper, H. M., Hedges, L. V., eds. (1994). The Handbook of Research Synthesis. New York: Russell Sage Foundation.

Cooper, H. M. (1998). Synthesizing Research: A Guide for Literature Reviews. 3rd ed. Newbury Park, CA: Sage Publications. [Has a psychology orientation.]

Cordray, D. S. (1990). An assessment from the policy perspective. In: Wachter, K. W., Straf, M. L., eds. The Future of Meta-Analysis New York: Russell Sage Foundation. [Extensively treats issues in meta-analysis as used in public policy analysis.]

Fink, A. (1998). Conducting Research Literature Reviews: From Paper to the Internet. Newbury Park, CA: Sage Publications. [Fink, who comes from the field of public health, covers selecting and stating questions; electronic searches; justifying a method for identifying and reviewing only the highest quality literature; preparing a structured literature abstraction form; synthesizing and reporting results; conducting and evaluating descriptive literature reviews; and how to understand and evaluate the principles of meta-analysis.]

Hunt, M. (1999). How Science Takes Stock: The Story of Meta-Analysis. New York: Russell Sage Foundation. [Covers the history, techniques, achievements, and controversies surrounding statistical meta-analysis in support of social policy makers and health professionals. An appendix covers in detail the mechanics of conducting a statistical meta-analytic investigation. Attempts to interpret technical aspects of meta-analysis to a more general audience.]

Hunter, J. E., Schmidt, F. L. (1990). Methods of Meta-Analysis. Newbury Park, CA: Sage Publications. [Covers statistical aspects of integrating findings across independent studies.]

Hunter, J. E. (1995). Methods of Meta-Analysis : Correcting Error and Bias in Research Findings. Newbury Park, CA: Sage Publications.

Rosenthal, R. (1984). Meta-Analytic Procedures for Social Research. Applied Social Research Methods Series. Vol. 6. Thousand Oaks, CA: Sage Publications. [Toward the quantitative end of the spectrum but still a good outline of a systematic approach to generalizing from multiple research papers.]

Utts, J. (1991). Replication and meta-analysis in parapsychology. Statistical Science 6(4): 363–403. Available at http://anson.ucdavis.edu/~utts/91rmp.html. [An interesting discussion of issues surrounding meta-analysis.]

Wolf, F. M. (1986). Meta-analysis: Quantitative methods for research synthesis. Quantitative Applications in the Social Sciences. Vol. 59. Newbury Park, CA: Sage Publications. [Covers statistical issues in integrating findings across disparate studies.]

8

Format of Your Literature Review

I. INTRODUCTION

There are many types of literature review, each with its own customary format. Bruce (1994) has identified six major types of literature review: list, search, survey, vehicle for learning, report, and research facilitator. As we are dealing with empirical research writing, we will focus on the format of reviews that are the last of Bruce's six types. The literature review in research writing is not a list, search results, a survey, an educational overview, or a report. Rather it is a careful mobilization of previous studies in support of the research being proposed by the author in his or her paper, thesis, or dissertation.

The researcher's meta-analysis, discussed in the previous chapter, largely determines the format of the review of the literature section. That is, the meta-analytic process will allow the researcher to group citations in the literature by dependent variable; then within this by independent variables; then within this by control variables. Of course, actual studies will be cross-cutting, looking at multiple dependents, independents, and controls. However, the objective of the researcher is to focus on one dependent variable at a time (often there will be only one), then systematically to discuss literature related to it.

A given reference may well require discussion at multiple points in the literature review section. It is more important to maintain the integrity of the discussion of variables than the unity of discussion of citations. Keep in mind that the literature review is really not about the literature—rather, it is about the variables and relations among them. For this reason, it is better to keep the discussion of a given variable or a given relationship between variables together in one's writing than it is to discuss in one place each author's writing in its aspects.

II. FORMAT OF YOUR LITERATURE REVIEW

Parsimony is a fundamental principle of all research writing, including the literature review. The literature review should keep the researcher's story line in the forefront as much as possible. That is, at every point in the literature review, the reader should be pointed ahead toward the hypotheses, theories, and models that will be tested in the dissertation, thesis, or article.

This is not to deny that background information has a place in the literature review. The bulk of the literature review should focus on the story line, but it is helpful and appropriate to place the story line in a broader context. Readers will expect major related studies to be discussed, even if they are ultimately different from what is to be investigated and tested in the study. However, care must be taken to delimit the background information section, labeling it for what it is, keeping it brief, and being explicit that it deals with things not to be tested. Much background information is best placed in an appendix, with only high points actually appearing in the body of the literature review.

Literature uncovered in your review should be subject to a triage. The most important set, and the only set cited in your review, are those citations that bear on the hypotheses in your study (i.e., the relationships in your model, the arrows in your diagram). The second set is composed of pertinent background material, which should be put in an appendix where it will not distract from the story line of your literature review section or chapter. The third set is neither hypothesis-related nor significant background to hypotheses in the model. This set should not be reported at all, however much work you have undertaken to obtain these citations.

A. Literature Review Format

As Bourner (1996) discusses, there are several reasons for undertaking a review of the literature:

- To understand the theoretical perspectives associated with studies in your area
- To understand opposing schools of thought as they apply to your area
- To become aware of variables relevant to your topic of interest
- To understand which are the seminal studies widely cited in your area
- To understand the application of appropriate methodological procedures to problems in your area
- To identify gaps in the literature
- To not duplicate prior research

To avoid the past research mistakes of others
To identify the community of scholars in your area

Moreover, as your final paper, thesis, or dissertation is required and as it aids in decisions about all other aspects of the research, the literature review is usually written early in the dissertation process, often at the proposal stage.

The format of a typical literature review section might be as follows.

1. Introduction

   The introduction provides the roadmap to the literature review section. It works from the general topic to the specific, reminding readers what hypotheses, theories, and models are to be investigated in the study. It explains the organization of the literature review section. The introduction defines the scope of the literature review, enunciating the criteria used to include or exclude studies from the review. The introduction also indicates how the literature review will uncover hypotheses to be tested in the body of the work, briefly identifies the opposing schools of thought (on substance, methodology, or theory) on the thesis being investigated, and indicates if there are overall trends in research in this area.

2. Background

   The background section describes the setting of the research. A relatively brief section, the background discusses in substantive terms why the issues to be investigated became important. It also discusses the historical response of the academic community as these issues emerged. Milestone studies are often described. The background section must conclude with a "focus" subsection, in which the particular hypotheses, theories, and models to be investigated are related to this substantive and academic history. Literature that defines the empirical problem being investigated, but that does not provide new data bearing on the controversy, is cited in this background section.

3. Review Methodology

   This section explains how you went about finding the studies included in your literature review. For electronic searches, you should be specific about what databases you examined and what your exact search strategies were (remember to save this information so you can report it here!), including what keywords and Boolean combinations you used in your search requests, and when the search was done. For example: "A search for *toxic** produced 2,444 references, which reduced to 742 when the search was limited to articles with *waste* in the title, and further reduced to 82 references with *policy* anywhere in the record. These 82 references were checked in the *Web of Science* citation databases and the 40 most-cited articles were read in full. Of these, 28 proved to be empirical studies, and this is the set included in the literature review which follows.'' Of course, in full-scale research, your literature search will not be limited to electronic searches but will also include literature uncovered from consultation with experts, from chains of citations, from directories of funded research, and other sources. You should describe and justify your criteria for inclusion and exclusion in each of your search strategies.

4. Research on the (First) Dependent Variable

   The body of the literature review will be focused around the dependent variables of concern to the researcher, and within this, the hypotheses related to the dependent variables. Often there will be only one dependent variable, in which case the main sections of the body will deal with the hypotheses. If there are multiple dependents, then the hypotheses will be treated in subsections. Conceptual cross-cutting makes this sound easier than it is, but the goal of the researcher is to segment the discussion of the literature into the same clusters that will appear later in the body of the work where evidence is presented.

   Avoid the temptation to review the literature not by dependent variable but by some other criterion, such as chronologically, alphabetically, methodology (e.g., qualitative vs. quantitative), school of thought, or valence of conclusion. Such other criteria may be used to order studies *within* sections that are organized by dependent variable, then by control variable within dependent variable, and only then by other criteria such as school of thought. Grouping primarily by criteria such as school of thought inappropriately makes that, not your dependent variable(s), the story line of your literature review.

   Research on (Second) Dependent Variable

   There may be a second or additional dependent variable, each discussed similarly in its turn.

5. Summary

   The summary section recapitulates the most relevant studies in relation to the hypotheses to be investigated, ideally tying them into a coherent model focused on one or more dependent variables, as well as summarizing for readers how each component relates to the existing literature. Alternative models suggested by the literature are also summarized. Thus, the summary provides an overview of the different positions researchers have taken on the empirical puzzle selected by the author, and explains how the author's current paper or thesis contributes to understanding. The summary is a precursor to a possibly separate concluding section in which the theoretical importance of the researcher's findings are discussed.

Although sometimes this is a separate conclusion section, the literature review's summary section may also differentiate the proposed research from the existing literature. There are several ways to differentiate your study from what has gone before: seeking evidence on hypotheses in dispute, confirming hypotheses advanced in the literature but only weakly confirmed, if at all, examining control or modifier variables for relationships established in the literature or introducing new variables into the models implied by the literature, and comparing the fit of alternative models to new data. At the end of the conclusion section, the author typically reminds the reader of the empirical puzzle being investigated, explains why it is important to solve it, and shows how his or her research is the key to the solution

B. Literature Review Format Checklist

1. Did you start the literature review before starting to collect data?
2. Are the studies in your review primary sources or original scholarship? Do not rely on summaries and citations by secondary authors.
3. Did you go back and forth in an iterative process between your literature review and your formulation of the hypotheses, theories, or models you will be investigating?
4. Is the outline of your literature review organized around the hypotheses, theories, or models you will be investigating? Do not organize the literature review chronologically or alphabetically.
5. Does your literature review explain how your study ties in to prevailing theories and larger themes in your discipline?
6. In each section of your review, before discussing specific studies, have you used topic sentences that clearly hark back to the theories and hypotheses you are investigating? Such a topic sentence might be "Some researchers argued that _____," which, if true, would support _____ theory because _____." This would be followed by discussion of a group of studies whose authors take a particular position.
7. If you have too many studies to structure your review in terms of one topic sentence per set of studies per paragraph, and instead need multiple paragraphs to discuss a set of studies, have you used explicit subsection headings to guide the reader along?
8. Did you draw connections between topics, providing a logical flow from one to the next?

9. Have you considered using circle-and-arrow figures to graphically illustrate the connections among your topics as well as among the variables being investigated?
10. Do your topic sentences remind the reader of what has gone before, and how the current topic relates to that? For instance, ''In addition to studies that suggest [what has just been discussed], other research indicates a further relationship involving [the topic about to be discussed].''
11. Is your literature review a piece of continuous prose with a beginning, middle, and end, and not simply a list of who has done what?
12. Is the outline of your literature review also consistent with your meta-analytic framework, discussed in a previous section of this guide?
13. Have you kept in mind any practical rules imposed by thesis committees or publishers, who from time to time may simply dictate a length limit on the literature review?
14. Have you labeled background information as such in a separate section, carefully indicating that it is presented to place your study in a broader context, but that you are not investigating various background topics?
15. In the body of the literature review, where you are discussing literature related to dependent variables and their associated hypotheses, is it clear to the reader which citations are the most important? Have you given more space and emphasis to the more important citations?
16. Also in the body of the literature review, have you made an effort to evaluate the methodological merits of the works you cite, avoiding an exclusive focus on their findings? Have you clearly indicated which citations have small samples or other validity problems?
17. Does the summary section of your literature review synopsize the hypotheses or models you will be investigating, as well as relating this to major citations in the body of the literature review?
18. Have you clearly indicated which related topics you will not be investigating, thereby carefully delimiting your study?
19. Have you considered using a concept map (a model presented in circle-and-arrow format) to make your summary more graphic?
20. Have you reread your literature review, evaluating whether it demonstrates adequately that you are aware of the range of debate in your selected area? Try to get others to read it from this perspective also.
21. In reviewing the literature, have you been on the lookout for especially fascinating quotes and have you incorporated them in your review?
22. Does the conclusion of your literature review clearly indicate the nature of your original contribution to your discipline through this study

(e.g., seeks to confirm/test an existing theory, fills a gap in the literature, develops a better model of the dependent variable, establishes a baseline for future studies, demonstrates the utility of a research procedure or tool).

C. Literature Review Format Example

Robson and Single (1995) provide this exemplary table of contents to their "Literature Review of Studies on the Economic Costs of Substance Abuse":

Other Drug Studies Outside of Canada
Canadian Drug Studies
Comparison of Estimates for All Substances
Summary And Conclusions
References

Many other literature review examples can be found on the web:

Literature Review Example: Economics-http://lime.weeg.uiowa.edu/~resmeth/lit-review.html
Literature Review Example: Geography-http://www.nene.ac.uk/aps/env/geodiss/litreveg.html
Literature Review Example: Public Administration-http://www.mgmt.dal.ca/ipac/Newsletters/N031998.htm#Literature Review
Literature Review Example: Political Science-http://socsci.colorado.edu/~davenpc/papers/move.html
Literature Review Example: Communications/Sociologyhttp://cotton.uamont.edu/roiger/write/litrev.html
Literature Review Example: Social Work-http://www.indiana.edu/~socwork/s371/litexample.html

D. Reference Style

In addition to formatting your review format, one must format one's actual citations and references properly. There are many correct styles, so you must consult with your academic department or publisher to determine which style is required in your situation. The most common style manuals include the *MLA Handbook for Writers of Research Papers* (Modern Language Association; see http://www.english.uiuc.edu/cws/wworkshop/bibliography/mla/mlamenu.htm); the *Publication Manual of the American Psychological Association* (APA; see http://www.english.uiuc.edu/cws/wworkshop/bibliography/apa/apamenu.htm); the *Chicago Manual of Style*; the *CBE Style Manual* (Council of Biology Editors); and *Information for IEEE Transactions* (engineering). Some, such as the American Psychological Association, also have information specific to citing online sources (see http://www.apa.org/journals/webref.html). Special issues pertaining to citing government documents are treated at http://www.lib.memphis.edu/gpo/citeweb.htm. Also, virtually all journals and publishers will either refer the writer to a style manual such as one of these or, more likely, will have an online style guide for their particular auspices.

Because reference styles vary widely and because there are so many variations within any given style (e.g., how to cite music; how to cite when the author is unknown; how to cite when there are corporate authors; etc.), style manuals are often full-book length. It is strongly recommended that the writer purchase the style manual appropriate to his or her discipline, as it is impossible here to outline all the possibilities.

To give just one illustration from a common format, a typical book citation in APA format would appear as follows:

> Smith, R. (2000). *Form and function in modern architecture.* Berkeley, CA: University of California Press.

Note in this style, only the first word of the title and the first word of any subtitle is capitalized (and all proper names, of course). Although not reflected in the example above, additional necessary information such as ''2nd ed.'' or ''Vol. 2'' may be added in parentheses immediately after the title. A typical APA article citation would appear as follows:

> Smith, D. (1999). Entropy in chaos theory. *International Review of Mathematical Modeling*, 22, 15–36.

Note that in APA style, authors are listed using only the initial(s) of their first names. If there are multiple authors, they are separated by commas, with an ampersand before the last author. The article title has neither underlining or quotation marks, and only the first word of the title is capitalized. The journal title, however, uses initial capitals throughout (except prepositions and articles, of course). The number following the comma after the journal title is the volume number: ''Vol.'' is not used, and issue numbers are not reported unless the journal begins with page 1 in each issue. The abbreviation ''pp.'' is used for pagination of newspapers and magazines, but is omitted for journal articles.

BIBLIOGRAPHY

Afolabi, M. (1992). The review of related literature in research. International Journal of Information and Library Research 4(1):59–66.

Bolker, J. (1998). Write Your Dissertation in Fifteen Minutes a Day: A Guide to Starting, Revising, and Finishing your Doctoral Thesis. Toronto: Owl Books. [Written by a clinical psychologist who cofounded the Harvard Writing Center. Covers the literature review as well as other dissertation processes.]

Bourner, T. (1996). The research process: Four steps to success. In: Greenfield, T. (ed). Research Methods: Guidance for Postgraduates. London: Arnold, 1996.

Bruce, C. S. (1994). Research student's early experiences of the dissertation literature review. Studies in Higher Education 19(2):217–229.

Friedman, B. (1998). The Research Tool Kit. Pacific Grove, CA: Brooks/Cole Publishing. [Chapter 3 deals with literature reviews.]

Garrard, J. (1999). Health Sciences Literature Review Made Easy: The Matrix Method. Gaithersburg, MD: Aspen Publishers.

Good, C. E. (1996). Citing and Typing the Law: A Guide to Legal Citation and Style:

Based on the Bluebook, a Uniform System of Citation. 16th ed. Washington: Word Store Publications.

Hart, C. (1999). Doing a literature review : Releasing the Social Science Research Imagination. Walnut Creek, CA: Altamira Press. [Does not use meta-analysis but does clearly explain qualitative aspects of reviewing the literature, particularly in social science.]

Levinson, D., ed. (1977). A Guide to Social Theory: Worldwide Cross-Cultural Tests, Volume I—Introduction. New Haven, CT, Human Relations Area Files. [This is the first of a 5-volume set, constituting an analytical propositional inventory of theories of human behavior, based on a review of the literature of worldwide cross-cultural studies. Unlike anthropology, equivalent propositional inventories are hard to come by in other disciplines, but this work provides insight into systematic and scientific literature review.]

Li, X., Crane, N. B. (1996). Electronic Styles: A Handbook for Citing Electronic Information. Medford, MA: Information Today.

Libutti, P., Kopala, M. (1995). The doctoral student, the dissertation, and the library: A review of the literature. Reference Librarian 48(5):5–25.

Robson, L., Single, E. (1995). Literature review of studies on the economic costs of substance abuse. http://www.ccsa.ca/costslit.htm. [Format example cited in this chapter.]

University of Chicago Press (1993). The Chicago Manual of Style: The Essential Guide for Writers, Editors and Publishers. Chicago: University of Chicago Press.

9

Thinking About Models

I. SPECIFYING YOUR MODELS

What is a theory? All theories rest on the assumptions of *axioms*, which are postulates accepted as self-evident statements (e.g., Alcohol impairs motor ability). *Theories* describe the elements of the model and their interrelationship to form the structure of a system of explanation (e.g., Alcohol use imposes substantial costs on communities in terms of public health, safety, and welfare, with negative impacts in each of these three areas, creating negative multiplier effects in the other two). *Hypotheses* are logical, testable inferences from theories, usually statements of covariation (e.g., When alcohol consumption in a community rises, traffic accidents rise) or temporal sequence (e.g., When a person consumes alcohol to a given blood alcohol level and then drives, the probability of a traffic accident increases). A *model* is composed of axioms, theories, and hypotheses applied to a particular empirical puzzle. This system of explanation includes, of course, the variables thought to bring about the state of some dependent variable(s) of interest and the relationships among these variables.

An explanatory model is the core of analysis. For instance, in the area of labor relations, the research model would go beyond mere discussion of a topic such as labor strikes. It would instead identify in detail how strikes come about, under what conditions, at what times, and what accounts for their variation in frequency or intensity. Nor would it be enough simply to list all variables (unemployment, downsizing, unionism, legislation, company profits) that in one way or another affect the topic. Rather, the researcher must explain how each variable relates to the others in a pattern of interrelationships.

The components of a model include a research question, subsidiary theories related to the question, and hypotheses related to each theory, as well as assumptions that may underlie the analysis. For instance, a research question might be, "Why have third parties been unsuccessful in American politics?" One of multiple theories about this question might be, "American political structure creates prohibitive social costs to the potential third-party voter." Some of the hypotheses subsidiary to this particular theory might be:

H1. In winner-take-all electoral districts, the voter will perceive voting for third party candidates as "throwing away" one's vote.
H2. The more leading political parties are candidate-centered rather than platform-centered, the more leading party candidates will be able to adopt policy positions which co-opt potential third-party voters.
H3. The more heterogenous the society in ethnic and racial terms, the greater the importance attached to leading parties as cultural unifiers and the more third party affiliation is seen as deviant behavior.

A minimum condition for a model is that its relationships are spelled out in ways that indicate at least the direction of the relationship. In empirical research the relationships must contain variables that can be measured so that the relationship can be tested. The minimum condition for an empirical model calls for associated hypotheses of the type, "The more the x, the more the y," or "The more the x, the less the y," as in the example above. A stronger form of modeling requires the researcher to posit the expected general magnitude of the effects to be observed; for instance, "Y increases exponentially as x increases," or "X will correlate with y at least moderately ($r >= .4$) when Z is present."

How does the researcher go about creating a model? The two general methods are *induction* and *deduction*. Induction is the process of examining cases and imagining generalizations that explain the variation in what is observed. Sometimes called "grounded theory," this case-oriented approach can be traced back to John Stuart Mill. Deduction, on the other hand, is the classic method of scientific investigation, traceable back to Aristotle and ancient philosophy. Deduction is the assertion of certain givens (axioms) and the inference of implied theorems from these axioms. Deduction also encompasses the inference of corollaries from theorems. Even today some researchers regard deductive theory formation as the only "pure" scientific form, claiming it avoids the possible biases that may occur when researchers induce generalizations from cases. In practice, this is not an either-or choice and most researchers go through several cycles of both induction and deduction in arriving at their models.

Not all models must be complex. Good research studies have been published that involve only bivariate relationships or just establish descriptive statistics about a single variable. In general, such narrowly defined studies are appropriate for topics new to a discipline, when little is known. In most areas the researcher may select, much will already be known. Undergraduate students, unfamiliar with searching the professional literature, may be surprised to find out just how much research has gone before them.

It is rarely interesting or even appropriate to focus on a single independent and single dependent variable (the A causes B model), or even on a series of such binary models. Almost always, the introduction of a third variable is what makes a model more interesting. For instance, it is mildly interesting to research whether gender is a factor in selecting/not selecting a major in computer science. It is only mildly interesting because one is mainly establishing or refuting an alleged fact. It is more interesting to research whether the relation of gender to majoring in computer science is affected by the proportion of gender role models on the computer science faculty, or if it is affected by differential perceptions of corporate employment prospects by gender.

We may find that such third variables have a *mediating* effect (it is an intervening variable between the causal or independent variable and the effect or dependent variable) or *moderating* effect (it is another independent variable affecting the independent or dependent variable, or it is an anteceding variable affecting both) on the original bivariate relationship of gender to majoring in computer science; we may also find relationships among these third variables themselves. For instance, women's perceptions of employment prospects in industry may be affected by proportion of female role models on the faculty. In summary, by introducing third variables we construct an interesting model that seeks to explain the conditions under which a fact (such as the fact that women tend not to major in computer science) may or may not exist. Modeling takes us out of the much less interesting realm of merely establishing whether a fact is or is not true.

II. THINKING ABOUT MODELS

The model-building process starts with selection of one or more dependent variables, then proceeds to literature review and brainstorming to uncover causal paths leading to the dependent(s), then uses deduction to arrive at other model implications and predictions, then evaluates the predictions in the light of data, and finally revises the model and begins the cycle over.

Transforming literature review into models is fundamental to model-building. Virtually all writing contains implicit if not explicit models. By drawing a diagrammatic model implicit in any written explanation, the researcher is in a better position to compare one explanation with another, to consider which variables are included and which are not, and to evaluate the extent to which evidence is cited to support the relationships represented by arrows in the diagram. This procedure is particularly useful when it is necessary to compare a large number of explanations of the same phenomenon, and when explanations are complex, involving many possible variables and relationships.

Consider as an example a model of the causes of the Civil War, reflected in the second inaugural address of March 4, 1865, by Abraham Lincoln.

> Fellow-Countrymen: At this second appearing to take the oath of the Presidential office there is less occasion for an extended address than there was at the first. Then a statement somewhat in detail of a course to be pursued seemed fitting and proper. Now, at the expiration of four years, during which public declarations have been constantly called forth on every point and phase of the great contest which still absorbs the attention and engrosses the energies of the nation, little that is new could be presented. The progress of our arms, upon which all else chiefly depends, is as well known to the public as to myself, and it is, I trust, reasonably satisfactory and encouraging to all. With high hope for the future, no prediction in regard to it is ventured.
>
> On the occasion corresponding to this four years ago all thoughts were anxiously directed to an impending civil war. All dreaded it, all sought to avert it. While the inaugural address was being delivered from this place, devoted altogether to saving the Union without war, urgent agents were in the city seeking to destroy it without war—seeking to dissolve the Union and divide effects by negotiation. Both parties deprecated war, but one of them would make war rather than let the nation survive, and the other would accept war rather than let it perish, and the war came.
>
> One-eighth of the whole population were colored slaves, not distributed generally over the Union, but localized in the southern part of it. These slaves constituted a peculiar and powerful interest. All knew that this interest was somehow the cause of the war. To strengthen, perpetuate, and extend this interest was the object for which the insurgents would rend the Union even by war, while the Government claimed no right to do more than to restrict the territorial enlargement of it. Neither party expected for the war the magnitude or the duration which it has already attained. Neither anticipated that the cause of the conflict might cease with or even before the conflict itself should cease. Each looked for an easier triumph, and a result less fundamental and astounding. Both read the same Bible and pray to the same God, and each invokes His aid against the other. It may seem strange that any men should dare to ask a just God's assistance in wringing their bread from the sweat of other men's faces, but let us judge not, that we be not judged. The prayers of both could not be answered. That of neither has been answered

> fully. The Almighty has His own purposes. "Woe unto the world because of offenses; for it must needs be that offenses come, but woe to that man by whom the offense cometh." If we shall suppose that American slavery is one of those offenses which, in the providence of God, must needs come, but which, having continued through His appointed time, He now wills to remove, and that He gives to both North and South this terrible war as the woe due to those by whom the offense came, shall we discern therein any departure from those divine attributes which the believers in a living God always ascribe to Him? Fondly do we hope, fervently do we pray, that this mighty scourge of war may speedily pass away. Yet, if God wills that it continue until all the wealth piled by the bondsman's two hundred and fifty years of unrequited toil shall be sunk, and until every drop of blood drawn with the lash shall be paid by another drawn with the sword, as was said three thousand years ago, so still it must be said "the judgments of the Lord are true and righteous altogether."
>
> With malice toward none, with charity for all, with firmness in the right as God gives us to see the right, let us strive on to finish the work we are in, to bind up the nation's wounds, to care for him who shall have borne the battle and for his widow and his orphan, to do all which may achieve and cherish a just and lasting peace among ourselves and with all nations.

Here Lincoln implies a model of the Civil War:

Research question: Why did the Civil War occur?

Theory 1: The Civil War occurred primarily because of factors rooted in slavery.

Variables mentioned:

Civil War ("all thoughts were anxiously directed to an impending civil war")

Negotiations ("seeking to dissolve the Union and divide effects by negotiation")

Distribution of slavery ("One-eighth of the whole population were colored slaves, not distributed generally over the Union, but localized in the southern part of it")

(Economic) interests in slavery ("These slaves constituted a peculiar and powerful interest")

Victory expectations ("Each looked for an easier triumph")

Religion ("Both read the same Bible and pray to the same God, and each invokes His aid")

Subsidiary hypotheses relating the variables:

H1. The failure of (Congressional) negotiations led directly to Civil War.

H2. An (economic) interest in slavery, combined with the concentration of slaves in the South, led to the failure of negotiations.

H3. Expectations of easy victory (low anticipated costs) led to Civil War, given the failure of negotiations.

H4 Null hypothesis. Religion was not a factor (it was a constant for both sides in the Civil War).

In moving from a literature review to a model, the researcher must take care to note that the implied model may not be a complete representation of the author's (here, Lincoln's) views on the research question, but may only be a representation of what is inferred directly from a particular piece of writing. In the real world, actual authors' views are complex, ambiguous, and self-contradictory in many cases. The researcher needs to emphasize that his or her research purpose is not to establish what particular authors believed based on the corpus of their life's work, but rather to generate alternative models associated with particular writings found in a search of relevant literature. Other literature by the same author may yield other models, which should be acknowledged. Even if this point is just made in a footnote, the researcher may spare himself or herself unnecessary criticism. Keep the focus on models, not on intellectual biographies of authors. In this case, for example, it would be better to refer not to "Lincoln's theory of the Civil War," but instead to "a theory of the Civil War associated with Lincoln's second inaugural address." Figure 1 shows the diagrammatic version of this model.

A. Conceptual Mapping

Some forms of conceptual diagramming or mapping may be part of the early brainstorming stage of theory development, discussed in Chapter 1. Used as brainstorming, conceptual mapping works like this: first the central concept is written on a sheet or blackboard. Arrows are drawn to it, or from it to other related concepts. Each newly added concept is considered a new hub, and the process is repeated to create new branches to or from additional concepts. An attempt is made to generate the concepts quickly, without analysis. After the brainstorming phase, the researcher considers patterns and groupings in the conceptual map, trying to render it as parsimoniously and logically as possible.

At the model-building stage, conceptual mapping has a more specific meaning, centered on translating systems of hypotheses into diagrammatic form. Assuming the researcher has already identified a dependent variable of interest and has developed a list of independent variables, he or she places the variables in diagram form, with circles representing variables, arrows representing relationships, and pluses or minuses above the arrows representing the direction of the relationship. The size of the lines or path coefficients above the lines may represent strength of relationship. Double-headed arrows may represent mutual causation or unexamined correlation. Arrows from a construct (also called conceptual variable, latent variable) to indicator variables depict operational definitions.

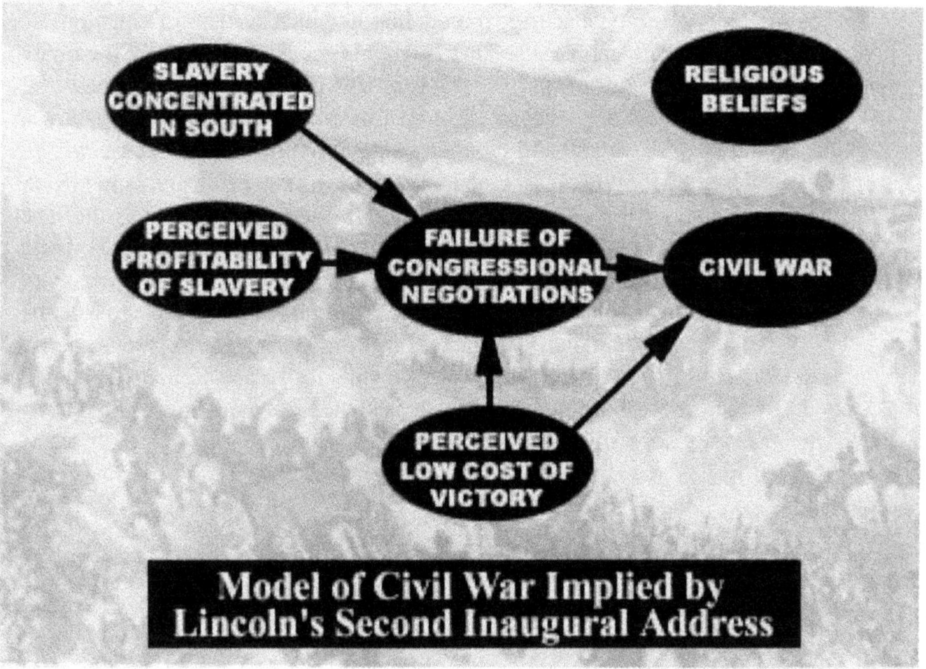

FIGURE 1 Model of Civil War implied by Lincoln's second inaugural address.

Overall, the process of conceptual mapping of causal diagrams forces the researcher to be explicit about which variables are in the model and what all the relationships are. Forcing such explicitness is helpful to the research process.

B. Formal Modeling

It is possible to move beyond diagrammatic modeling to formal models, where the arrows in a model diagram are represented as formulas. Modeling software, such as *STELLA* (High Performance Systems, Dartmouth, NH) allows one to enter graphical circle-and-arrow models, relate the arrows to formulas and spreadsheet data, and run the model's formulas on test data to simulate results. *STELLA* has been used extensively, for instance, to model forces in economics. A number of the citations in the bibliography for this chapter provide an introduction to mathematical modeling, systems dynamics simulation, and formal empirical theory. Most empirical writing uses modeling in the more general sense discussed above, but in some instances the researcher may wish to investigate the extent to which formal systems of equations can adequately model the variance found in some topic of interest.

Simulation is a type of formal modeling in which systems of equations are run iteratively to project results. That is, running a set of equations for time 1 generates new estimates of the model's variables in time 2, and these new estimates can be entered in a second iteration to estimate the state of variables in time 3, and so on. *Dynamo* and its microcomputer version, *Micro-Dynamo*, are software designed for this causal loop and flow-diagram type of simulation (Richardson and Pugh, 1981; Richardson, 1991). "Systems dynamics" is the label associated with this tradition of simulation and modeling, in which Jay Forrester (1968) and others at MIT and elsewhere developed models of animal ecology, urban growth, drug use, and many other topics (Goodman, 1974; Edward Roberts, 1978), including the famous "Club of Rome" model of world resource crisis (Meadows et al., 1973). Modeling project codirector Nancy Roberts has developed teaching materials that make systems dynamics modeling using *Micro-Dynamo* readily accessible (Roberts, et al., 1983).

II. THINKING ABOUT MODELS CHECKLIST

1. Have you brainstormed and reviewed the literature for possible causes of the dependent variable(s) in which you are interested?
2. In your literature review, have you made an effort to inventory theoretical perspectives on which each piece of empirical research is based?
3. For each relevant variable you have encountered, have you made an effort to specify its definition? Have you considered if an apparent single variable is, in fact, a multidimensional set of variables? Have you considered conceptual mapping (graphically linking circled concepts) as an aid to unfolding relationships among your variables?
4. For each causal generalization, have you thought about its scope of applicability (for example, by gender; by locality, region, or nation; by age; etc.)? Aim for the highest plausible level of generalization. The more generalized the theory, the more interesting it will be, because it can be applied in many contexts and thus is more useful for purposes of explanation.
5. For each intermediate variable in a causal sequence, have you thought about what other things it may cause, and whether these provide other indirect paths to your dependent variable(s)?
6. Have you considered whether causal links in your model are apt to be different for some ranges of an independent variable than others?
7. Have you used deductive reasoning to spell out the corollaries of your theorems?
8. Is your model *parsimonious*? A general rule of thumb in scientific investigation is the rule of parsimony, by which simpler models are to be preferred to more complex models when the power of explanation is substantially similar.

9. Have you tried contrarian thinking about each of your causal sequences (that is, considering the opposite of conventional wisdom)? Don't accept hypotheses from the literature without considering if there might be alternatives. Do consider the possibility of paradoxes.

10. Have you searched for counterexamples and alternative hypotheses?

11. Have you explored the value of metaphors for your subject?

12. For each actor or organization that figures in your model, have you considered the structure of motivation? Does your model encompass the sufficient and necessary motivations for action? Consider such motivational dimensions as remuneration, career development, symbolic reward, normative sanction, professionalism, governmental requirements, and market forces. More broadly, have you considered if you want a utility-maximization model, or one with a different basis, such as inertia or diffusion? If based on utility, have you considered marginal utility theory as well as raw utility-maximization?

13. Have you considered each of the major social science dimensions of explanation: economic, social, cultural, political, and psychological? You may find it fruitful to brainstorm these dimensions in terms of particular theorists (e.g., for economic, what would Marx say? For psychological, what would Freud say?)

14. Have you considered each of the major levels of explanation: individual, organizational, regional, national, and international?

15. Have you avoided ecological fallacy (the fallacy of composition), remembering that a relationship that is true, say, at the regional level is not necessarily true at the individual level? (For example, percent African American and illiteracy correlate at the state level but not well at the individual level, because southern states have high percent African American and have high illiteracy for both minorities and whites).

16. Have you avoided the post hoc fallacy by understanding that association does not necessarily mean causation? Two variables may be associated, for instance, if they have a common ancestor, even though there is not relation between them other (ex., ice cream sales are associated with fires, but only because both share a common prior variable – heat of the day). Have you looked for possible prior variables as an alternative explanation?

17. Have you looked at your dataset for outliers and considered if they need to be modeled on a separate basis?

18. If you know how, consider using inductive expert systems (such as the ID3 algorithm implemented by expert systems software) in your data matrix to induce an explanatory tree of the variables in your model, then consider which branches are plausible and deserve inclusion in your model.

19. After delineating your model to your satisfaction, have you identified clearly the portion(s) of the model you will investigate, particularly for larger models whose scope transcends what may reasonably be accomplished in a single study?

III. EXAMPLES

One way to think about models is to ask "What if?" For the example of research on the hypothesis that Internet addiction impedes students' rate of educational progress, we could simply seek to operationalize "Internet addiction," then see if it correlates with educational achievement. Better, we could obtain measures of both addiction and achievement over time to see if the correlation seems to have the expected chronological cause and effect sequence. However, our model would be better yet if we ask "What if?" questions. What if the level of parental control over Internet use is high compared to low? What if Internet use is distributed across multiple targets rather than concentrated in one area (e.g., not just on Internet gaming)? What if the student has been an "A" and "B" student in the past, compared with more marginal "C" and "D" students? No doubt many other "What if's" could be posed. Framing a "What if?" question is the same as introducing a third (or more) mediating or moderating variable into the model and, as explained above, that is what usually makes a model of greater interest—and of greater theoretical importance from the viewpoint of contribution to the discipline.

Once the model has been framed, the researcher can then use deductive reasoning to see if all the logical implications of the model have been spelled out. That is, deductive reasoning based on one's model can be used to generate many more testable propositions that make the model more comprehensive. Donal Muir, the late sociologist and author of the software "Theorem Generator," gave an example showing how his software could generate more than 50 logically implied theorems based on the input of 19 given model axioms.

A. Original Model Axioms

- A1. The greater a subject's environmental information, the greater subject's power.
- A2. The greater a subject's model adequacy, the greater subject's power.
- A3. The greater a subject's behavioral appropriateness, the greater subject's power.
- A4. The greater a subject's resources, the greater subject's power.
- A5. The greater a subject's power, the less subject's resources used for output.
- A6. The greater a subject's power, the greater subject's output gain.
- A7. The greater a subject's environmental supply of resources, the greater subject's output gain.
- A8. The greater a subject's output gain, the greater subject's stored resources.
- A9. The greater a subject's capacity for storing resources, the greater subject's stored resources.

A10. The greater a subject's resources used for output, the less subject's stored resources.
A11. The greater a subject's resources used internally, the less subject's stored resources.
A12. The greater a subject's stored resources, the greater subject's resources.
A13. The greater a subject's stored resources, the greater subject's resources available for internal use.
A14. The greater a subject's resources required for satisfaction, the greater subject's resources used internally.
A15. The greater a subject's resources available for internal use, the greater subject's satisfaction.
A16. The greater a subject's satisfaction, the less subject's attempt to increase satisfaction.
A17. The greater a subject's power, the less a second subject's power.
A18. The greater a subject's power, the greater subject's metasystem's power.
A19. The greater a subject's metasystem's power, the greater subject's power.

B. Additional Implied Theorems

T1. The greater a subject's attempt to increase power, the greater subject's attempt to increase environmental information.
T2. The greater a subject's attempt to increase power, the greater subject's attempt to increase model adequacy.
T3. The greater a subject's attempt to increase power, the greater subject's attempt to increase behavioral appropriateness.
T4. The greater a subject's attempt to increase power, the greater subject's attempt to increase resources.
T5. The greater a subject's attempt to decrease resources used for output, the greater subject's attempt to increase power.
T6. The greater a subject's attempt to increase output gain, the greater subject's attempt to increase power.
T7. The greater a subject's attempt to increase output gain, the greater subject's attempt to increase environmental supply of resources.
T8. The greater a subject's attempt to increase stored resources, the greater subject's attempt to increase output gain.
T9. The greater a subject's attempt to increase stored resources, the greater subject's attempt to increase capacity for storing resources.
T10. The greater a subject's attempt to increase stored resources, the greater subject's attempt to decrease resources used for output.

T11. The greater a subject's attempt to increase stored resources, the greater subject's attempt to decrease resources used internally.
T12. The greater a subject's attempt to increase resources, the greater subject's attempt to increase stored resources.
T13. The greater a subject's attempt to increase resources available for internal use, the greater subject's attempt to increase stored resources.
T14. The greater a subject's attempt to decrease resources used internally, the greater subject's attempt to decrease resources required for satisfaction.
T15. The greater a subject's attempt to increase satisfaction, the greater subject's attempt to increase resources available for internal use.
T16. The greater a subject's metasystem's environmental information, the greater subject's metasystem's power.
T17. The greater a subject's metasystem's model adequacy, the greater subject's metasystem's power.
T18. The greater a subject's metasystem's behavioral appropriateness, the greater subject's metasystem's power.
T19. The greater a subject's metasystem's resources, the greater subject's metasystem's power.
T20. The greater a subject's metasystem's power, the less subject's metasystem's resources used for output.
T21. The greater a subject's metasystem's power, the greater subject's metasystem's output gain.
T22. The greater a subject's metasystem's environmental supply of resources, the greater subject's metasystem's output gain.
T23. The greater a subject's metasystem's output gain, the greater subject's metasystem's stored resources.
T24. The greater a subject's metasystem's capacity for storing resources, the greater subject's metasystem's stored resources.
T25. The greater a subject's metasystem's resources used for output, the less subject's metasystem's stored resources.
T26. The greater a subject's metasystem's resources used internally, the less subject's metasystem's stored resources.
T27. The greater a subject's metasystem's stored resources, the greater subject's metasystem's resources.
T28. The greater a subject's metasystem's stored resources, the greater subject's metasystem's resources available for internal use.
T29. The greater a subject's metasystem's resources required for satisfaction, the greater subject's metasystem's resources used internally.
T30. The greater a subject's metasystem's resources available for internal use, the greater subject's metasystem's satisfaction.
T31. The greater a subject's metasystem's satisfaction, the less subject's metasystem's attempt to increase satisfaction.

T32. The greater a subject's metasystem's attempt to increase power, the greater subject's metasystem's attempt to increase environmental information.

T33. The greater a subject's metasystem's attempt to increase power, the greater subject's metasystem's attempt to increase model adequacy.

T34. The greater a subject's metasystem's attempt to increase power, the greater subject's metasystem's attempt to increase behavioral appropriateness.

T35. The greater a subject's metasystem's attempt to increase power, the greater subject's metasystem's attempt to increase resources.

T36. The greater a subject's metasystem's attempt to decrease resources used for output, the greater subject's metasystem's attempt to increase power.

T37. The greater a subject's metasystem's attempt to increase output gain, the greater subject's metasystem's attempt to increase power.

T38. The greater a subject's metasystem's attempt to increase output gain, the greater subject's metasystem's attempt to increase environmental supply of resources.

T39. The greater a subject's metasystem's attempt to increase stored resources, the greater subject's metasystem's attempt to increase output gain.

T40. The greater a subject's metasystem's attempt to increase stored resources, the greater subject's metasystem's attempt to increase capacity for storing resources.

T41. The greater a subject's metasystem's attempt to increase stored resources, the greater subject's metasystem's attempt to decrease resources used for output.

T42. The greater a subject's metasystem's attempt to increase stored resources, the greater subject's metasystem's attempt to decrease resources used internally.

T43. The greater a subject's metasystem's attempt to increase resources, the greater subject's metasystem's attempt to increase stored resources.

T44. The greater a subject's metasystem's attempt to increase resources available for internal use, the greater subject's metasystem's attempt to increase stored resources.

T45. The greater a subject's metasystem's attempt to decrease resources used internally, the greater subject's metasystem's attempt to decrease resources required for satisfaction.

T46. The greater a subject's metasystem's attempt to increase satisfaction, the greater subject's metasystem's attempt to increase resources available for internal use.

T47. The greater a subject's metasystem's power, the less a second subject's metasystem's power.

T48. The greater a subject's environmental information, the less subject's resources used for output.
T49. The greater a subject's environmental information, the greater subject's output gain.
T50. The greater a subject's environmental information, the less a second subject's power.
T51. The greater a subject's environmental information, the greater subject's metasystem's power.
T52. The greater a subject's environmental information, the greater subject's stored resources.
T53. The greater a subject's environmental information, the greater subject's power.

As the 53 corollaries of the 19 axioms in Muir's model suggest, there may well be a difference between spelling out one's model and identifying just which relationships within it are to be studied in a given paper, thesis, or dissertation. The researcher must be careful when setting forth the model(s) in the introductory sections not to imply that he or she is going to test every relationship associated with the model. In fact, identifying the specific relationships to be tested and not to be tested is an important part of the presentation of the research task. A work of research is normally assessed in terms of the tasks it sets for itself, and the importance of clearly delineating one's research tasks cannot be understated.

BIBLIOGRAPHY

Ader, H. J., and Mellenbergh, G. J. (2000). Research methodology on the social, behavioral, and life sciences: Designs, models, and methods. Sage Publications. [A text on research design and methodology which also includes extensive discussion of models.]

Axelrod, R. M. (1997). The complexity of cooperation: Agent-based models of competition and collaboration. Princeton, NJ: Princeton University Press. A formal mathematical approach.

Basmadjian, D. (1999). Art of modeling in science and engineering. CRC Press. Written to aid scientists and engineers in selecting appropriate models for various classes of problems involving mass, energy, momentum, thermodynamics, chemical kinetics, and other areas of applied physics, chemistry, and math.

Brandon, R. J., and Westcott, K., eds. (2000). Practical Applications of GIS for Archaeologists: A Predictive Modeling Kit. Book and CD-ROM. New York: Taylor & Francis Publishers. Spatial modeling using archaeological examples.

Cast, J. L. (1989). Alternate Realities: Mathematical Models of Nature and Man. New York: John Wiley and Sons. Although a textbook for undergraduate students, this is a more advanced work that covers topics in biology, cognitive processes, ecological and natural resource systems, fluid flow, evolution, artistic forms and games of chance, and relates them to the mathematical theories of chaos, bifurcation, and complexity.

Cowan, G., Pines, D., and Meltzer, D., eds. (1999). NY: Perseus Books.

Deaton, M. L., and Winebrake, J. J. (1999). Dynamic modeling of environmental systems. New York: Springer Verlag. Focus on environmental models using *Stella* modeling software.

Doty, D. H., and Glick, W. H. (1994). Typologies as a unique form of theory building: Toward improved understanding and modeling. Academy of Management Review 19:230–251.

Forrester, J. W. (1968). Principles of systems. Cambridge, MA: MIT Press.

Goodman, M. R. (1974). Study notes in system dynamics. Cambridge, MA: MIT Press.

Gershenfeld, N. A. (1999). The nature of mathematical modeling. New York: Cambridge University Press. For formal mathematical models.

Gioia, D. A., and Pitre, E. (1990). Multiparadigm perspectives on theory building. Academy of Management Review 15:584–602.

Kohler, T. A., and Gumerman, G. J. eds. (2000). Dynamics in Human and Primate Societies: Agent-Based Modeling of Social and Spatial Processes. New York: Oxford University Press.

Krieger, M. H. (1998). Constitutions of Matter: Mathematically Modeling the Most Everyday of Physical Phenomena. Reprint edition. Chicago: University of Chicago Press. Focuses on mathematical models in physics, including proofs that ordinary matter is stable and solutions to the Ising model of a phase transition.

Lave, J. G. March (1993). An Introduction to Models in the Social Sciences. Reprint edition. Lanham, MD: University Press of America. Originally published in 1975 by Harper and Row. Still the best social science introduction to thinking about model construction. Gives examples from exchange theory, adaptation theory, diffusion theory, and choice (decision-making) theory.

Matthias, R., and Hannon, B. (1997). Modeling Dynamic Economic Systems. New York: Springer Verlag Publishers.

Mavor, A. S., and Pew, R. W., eds. (1999). Modeling Human and Organizational Behavior: Application to Military Simulations. New York: National Academy Press.

Meadows, D. H., Meadows, D. L., Randers, J., and Behrens, W. W. (1973). The Limits to Growth. New York: Universe Books.

Morecroft, J. D. W., and Bodek, N. (1994). Modeling for learning organizations. New York: Productivity Press, Inc. Focuses on how to use modeling to simulate the actual performance of systems.

Morgan, M. S. (2000). Models As Mediators: Perspectives on Natural and Social Science. New York: Cambridge University Press. Contains 11 case studies of modeling in physics and in economics, where models are mathematical, diagrammatic, or actual physical models used to understand reality.

Morton, R. B. (1999). Methods and Models: A Guide to the Empirical Analysis of Formal Models in Political Science. New York: Cambridge University Press. Formal mathematical models in politics.

Muir, D. E. (1987). THEGEN: A Computer Algorithm for Axiomatic Analysis. Social Science Computer Review 5:207–210. Describes the software program used in the example for this section.

Pearl, J. (2000). Causality: Models, Reasoning, and Inference. New York: Cambridge University Press.

Preston, S. H., Heuveline P., and Michelle Guillon (2000). Demography: Measuring and Modeling Population Processes. New York: Blackwell Publishers. Covers basic demographic models of human population change (population projection, equilibrium models, measurement of fertility and mortality, modeling age patterns of vital events).

Prietula, M., Gasser, K., Gasser, L., and Carley, K. eds. (1998). Simulating Organizations: Computational Models of Institutions and Groups. Cambridge, MA: MIT Press.

Resnick, M. (1997). Turtles, Termites, and Traffic Jams: Explorations in Massively Parallel Microworlds. Cambridge, MA: MIT Press.

Richardson, G. P., and Pugh, A. L. (1981). Introduction to System Dynamics Modeling with DYNAMO. Cambridge, MA: MIT Press.

Richardson, G. P. (1991). Feedback Thought in Social Science and Systems Theory. Philadelphia, PA: University of Pennsylvania Press.

Roberts, E. B., ed. (1978). Managerial Applications of System Dynamics. Cambridge, MA: MIT Press.

Roberts, N., Andersen, D., Deal, R., Garet, M., and Shaffer, W. (1983). Introduction to Computer Simulation: A System Dynamics Modeling Approach. Reading, MA: Addison-Wesley.

Shier, D. R., and Wallenius, K. T. (1999). Applied Mathematical Modeling: A Multidisciplinary Approach. CRC Press. Case studies from a mathematical viewpoint of such phenomena as traffic, AIDS, cryptology, and networks with varying arrival times.

Shubik, M. (1985). Game Theory in the Social Sciences: Concepts and Solutions. Reprint edition. Cambridge, MA: MIT Press. Classic work on interpreting political and social phenomena as mathematically modeled games.

Sutton, R. I., and Staw, B. M. (1995). What theory is not. Administrative Science Quarterly, 40:371–384.

Thompson, J. R. (1989). Empirical Model Building. Wiley Series in Probability and Mathematical Statistics. John Wiley and Sons. A hands-on approach to the basic principles of empirical model building, incorporating 20 case studies, including examples of model building for growth and decay and for systems centered on competition and interaction.

Varian, H. R., ed. (1992). Economic and Financial Modeling with Mathematica. Book and Disk. New York: Springer Verlag. Uses Mathematica equation-solving software to construct economic models.

Vu, H. V., and Esfandiari, R. S. (1996). Dynamic Systems: Modeling and Analysis. New York: McGraw Hill. Standard textbook in system dynamics, with many primarily engineering examples.

Weick, K. E. (1989). Theory construction as disciplined imagination. Academy of Management Review 14:496–515.

Woods, R. L., and Lawrence, K. L. (1997). Modeling and Simulation of Dynamic Systems. New York: Prentice-Hall Publishers. Focuses on engineering models using differential equations for linear and nonlinear systems.

10

Operationalizing Variables

I. INTRODUCTION

Once the researcher has conceptualized a model, perhaps graphically representing it in a circle-and-arrows diagram, he or she then faces the task of measuring each of the variables in the model. This process is called operationalizing variables. For every variable in the model (''concept'' or ''construct''), there must be at least one and preferably multiple specific measures (''indicators''). Thus, operationalization is the associating of indicator variables with conceptual variables. Many issues arise in this process. Even the seemingly trivial challenge of operationalizing the conceptual variable ''Subject's gender'' can run into problems. A seemingly sound survey item that calls for self-reporting by checking ''male'' or ''female'' will normally suffice, but in a large population, such an item will yield results different from the operational item, ''Were you born a genetic female?'' To take a second example, the conceptual variable ''income'' may be operationalized in terms of family income or individual income, and in terms of cash income versus total value of benefits received in cash or in kind. The number of people below the poverty line will change significantly when in-kind goods and services such as food stamps or subsidized daycare are included in the measurement of ''income.''

In general, it is almost never possible to perfectly operationalize conceptual variables. Consider the variable ''alcoholism.'' In the General Social Survey, a leading database for the analysis of social phenomena, one will find three different operational measures: daily alcohol consumption, professional treatment for alcoholism, and self-reporting as an alcoholic. Even leaving aside such measurement problems as honesty in answering survey items attached to social stigmas, choices made in operationalizing alcoholism will strongly affect the outcome of research. An operationalization that requires meeting all three operational measures will involve one set of respondents (self-reported alcoholics under treatment, still drinking above a certain number of ounces of alcohol), whereas any one of the individual indicators will yield a different population (e.g., using persons under professional treatment will include substantial numbers of individuals who no longer consume alcohol). When considering any conceptual definition, the researcher must try to determine how many dimensions there are and what the best operational indicators would be for each dimension.

II. OPERATIONALIZING VARIABLES

Operational definition can be thought of as the process of specifying specific indicators for each dimension of a concept. Indicators are the concrete measures that are thought to reflect these dimensions, as a set of arithmetic problems may measure "addition/subtraction competency" and a set of survey items may measure "client satisfaction." How well the researcher operationalizes his or her variables will have a great deal to do with the outcome of findings later on and with the extent to which peer reviewers accept the validity of these findings. Criticism of operational definitions is the most frequent type of criticism researchers receive.

A. Considerations in Operationalization of Variables

Conceptual definitions describe constructs in broad terms. For instance, a conceptual definition of arithmetic skill might be, "Arithmetic skill is the ability to manipulate interval data to solve problems in which all variables are knowns." As a second instance, a conceptual definition of organizational effectiveness might be, "Organizational effectiveness is the extent to which an organization achieves its goals."

Dimensions are the set of scales applicable to a given conceptual definition. For instance, it might be found that "arithmetic skill" reflects two scalable dimensions: addition/subtraction and multiplication/division. "Organizational effectiveness" may reflect three scalable dimensions: client satisfaction/dissatisfaction, conformity/nonconformity of outcomes of the organization as agent with goals of its principal, and the cost/benefit ratio of its outputs. Of course, empirical investigation may determine that there are more or fewer dimensions for either of these concepts. Dimensions cannot be predefined but must be induced from the scalability of corresponding indicators.

Scalability is the extent to which indicators "belong together." There are several statistical definitions of and tests for scalability, including Likert scaling,

Guttman scaling, Mokken scaling, cluster analysis, discriminant analysis, and factor analysis. It is incumbent on the researcher to select one of these definitions of scalability and to demonstrate that by that definition, the indicator items for a concept do scale.

Benchmarks are target values on quantitative measures composed of one or more items that have been accepted formally or at least informally by a profession. Some benchmarks are formally endorsed by professional associations. Observed values are compared with benchmark target values to assess performance.

Indexes are sets of items that are thought to measure a latent variable. Items in an index will normally be more intercorrelated with each other than with other items (that is, items representing the same latent variable should be more interrelated with each other than with items representing other latent variables).

Scales are ordinal indexes that are thought to measure a latent variable. Guttman and Mokken scales meet a test of ordinality between items, but Likert scales may only be ordinal within an item. Indexes are ordinal when items stand in an ordinal relation to one another, such that the observed value on one item predicts all lower-ordered items. For the Guttman model, prediction is determinate, whereas for Mokken scales prediction is probabilistic.

Likert scales are by far the most common type of scale, and the usual response categories are "strongly agree," "agree," "don't know," "disagree," and "strongly disagree." Likert scales assure that a given answer on a given item can be judged to be more or less than another given answer on the same item, but Likert scales give no assurance that a set of indicators have an ordinal (or any other) relationship to each other, or even belong together. Statistical measures sometimes used with Likert scale items (but not limited to them) are discussed below.

Guttman scales are ones in which the items constitute a unidimensional series such that an answer to a given item predicts the answers to all previous items in the series (for example, in an arithmetic scale, correctly answering a subtraction item predicts correctly answering a prior item on addition but not necessarily a later item on multiplication). That is, a respondent who answers an item in a positive way must also answer less difficult items in a positive way. Note that Guttman scales have been criticized as too stringent and deterministic, leading to the rise in popularity of Mokken scales, discussed below.

The Coefficient of Scalability, Cs is the standard method for assessing whether a set of items form a Guttman scale. By arbitrary convention, Cs should be .60 or higher to consider a set of items Guttman scalable. Cs = 1–(E/X), where E is the number of Guttman errors and X is the number of errors expected by chance. A Guttman error is an interior blank or an exterior X in a Guttman table, which in turn is a table in which the X axis is the items arranged by increasing difficulty and the Y axis is the subjects arranged in order (from the origin) of descending number of correct answers. It is permissible to rearrange rows and columns to minimize the number of errors. For a perfect Guttman scale with no errors, the Guttman table will form a triangle of Xs (X indicating a correct answer to the item) with no interior blanks and no exterior Xs (which would indicate passing a more difficult item but missing a less difficult one). In the preceding formula, X, the number of errors expected by chance, equals p(n–Tn), where p is the probability of getting any item right by chance alone (.5 if there are two response categories), n is the number of choices of any type, and Tn is the number of choices in the most numerous category for each item. Tn relates to how many errors are expected by chance because, for instance, if there are 15 subjects and 13 responded a given way to item 1, then there cannot possibly be more than (15–13) = 2 errors for that item, and similarly for all other items.

The Coefficient of Reproducibility, Cr is an alternative measure for assessing whether a set of items form a Guttman scale. Cr = 1 − (E/N), where E = the number of Guttman errors and N equals the number of scale choices (which is the number of items times the number of subjects). The Cr should be more than .90 for the set of items to be considered scalable by Guttman criteria.

Stouffer's H technique is a variant that gives greater stability to Guttman scales by basing each Guttman scale position on three or more items, rather than just one. If three items are used per position, then passing either two or three of the items will be entered as passing that position in the Guttman scale. This is not to be confused with Loevinger's H, which is used in conjunction with Mokken scaling.

Mokken scales are similar to Guttman scales, but they are probabilistic in the sense that a respondent answering an item positively will have a significantly greater probability than null to answer a less difficult item in a positive way as well. All items in a Mokken scale have different difficulties, as reflected in different proportions of positive responses. The graphic representation (called a trace line) of the probability of a positive response to an item should increase monotonically as the latent trait increases along the x axis (and where the y axis, of course, is the probability). Double monotony must not exist (that is, trace lines of items in a scale should not intersect). Also, trace lines must be steep enough to produce only a limited number of Guttman errors (exceptions to the rule that a positive answer to an item implies a positive answer to all easier items). Loevinger's H measures the conformity of a set of items to Mokken's criteria and validates their use together as a scale of a unidimensional latent variable.

Loevinger's H is based on the ratio of observed Guttman errors to total errors expected under the null assumption that items are totally unrelated. Hij is this ratio for a given pair of items, i and j. Hij will be 0 when items are unrelated and Hij will be 1 when there are no Guttman errors for any given pair of items i and j. Hi is the mean Hij for all pairs involving item i. H is the mean Hij for all pairs, which is equal to 1–E/Eo, when E and Eo are summed across all item pairs.

The arbitrary but customary criterion for validating a set of items such as a Mokken scale is that H and all Hi must be .30. A rule of thumb is to speak of a ''strong scale'' for values exceeding 0.50, a ''moderate scale'' for values from .40 to .50, and a ''weak scale'' for values from .30 to .40. H is a better approximation to the classic reliability coefficient Rho than Cronbach's alpha, which has been widely used to measure the internal consistency of a scale. Specifically, alpha strongly underestimates Rho when there is large variation in item difficulties.

1. Measures of Internal Consistency

Internal consistency measures estimate how consistently individuals respond to the items within a scale. Note that measures of internal consistency are not tests of the unidimensionality of items in a scale. For example, if the first half of an instrument is educational items that correlate highly among themselves and the second is political items that correlate highly among themselves, the instrument would have a high Cronbach's Alpha anyway, even though two distinct dimensions were present. Note that measures of internal consistency are often called measures of ''internal consistency reliability'' or even ''reliability,'' but this merges the distinct concepts of internal consistency and reliability, which do not necessarily go together.

Interitem correlation is used to spot reverse-coded items. Scale items should correlate positively with one another. A negative correlation may well indicate, for instance, that an item was coded such that ''1'' meant the opposite direction (e.g., low) from the meaning of ''1'' (e.g., high) for the other items in the scale.

Cronbach's Alpha (a.k.a., ''the reliability coefficient''), originated by Cronbach in 1951, is the most common estimate of internal consistency of items in a scale. Alpha measures the extent to which item responses obtained at the same time correlate highly with each other. In addition to estimating internal consistency (''reliability'') from the average correlation, the formula for alpha also takes into account the number of items on the theory that the more items, the more reliable a scale will be. That is, when the number of items in a scale is higher, alpha will be higher even when the estimated average correlations are equal. Also, the more consistent within-subject responses are and the greater the variability among subjects in the sample, the higher will be Cronbach's Alpha. The widely accepted social science cutoff is that alpha should be .70 or higher for a set of items to be considered a scale, but some use .75 or .80. That .70 is as low as one should go is reflected in the fact that when alpha is .70, the standard error of measurement will be more than half (0.55) a standard deviation.

Computer programs like SPSS report ''Alpha if Item Deleted,'' which is an aid in refining a scale with many items (that is, one drops those where alpha increases significantly). In SPSS, From the Analyze menu, select Descriptives for Item, Descriptives for Scale, Descriptives for Scale if Item Deleted, Interitem Correlations. Alpha makes no assumptions about what one would obtain at a different time (the latter is reliability, discussed below). Alpha = (# of items/(# of items − 1)) * (1 − (sum of the variances of the items/variance of the total score)). (Miller, 1995).

Kuder-Richardson Formula 20, KR20, is a special case of Cronbach's Alpha for ordinal dichotomies. That is, Alpha = KR20 when the pair of items are both dichotomous. KR20 = (# of items/(# of items − 1)) * (1 − ((sum of p*q)/variance of the total score)), where p = proportion correct and q = proportion incorrect.

(a) Congeneric versus tau-equivalent v. parallel indicators. The psychometric literature sorts indicator sets for latent variables into three types. Congeneric sets are those presumed to have passed some test of convergent validity, such as Cronbach's Alpha, discussed above. Tau-equivalent sets also have equal variances for the indicators. Parallel sets are tau-equivalent sets in which the items have equal reliability coefficients. In structural equation modeling (SEM), tau-equivalence is tested by comparing an unconstrained model with one in which the factor loadings of the indicator variables on the factor are all set to 1.0, then seeing if the chi-square difference is insignificant. If the indicator model for the factor is found to be tau-equivalent, then the original model is compared with one in which measurement error variances are all constrained to be equal, and another chi-square difference test is conducted.

(b) Measures of Reliability. Test-retest and split halves reliability measure the probability that a given individual, responding to the same instrument two times, will produce essentially the same responses on both occasions. In the case of interrater reliability, reliability measures the probability that a given instrument, taken by two individuals, will produce essentially the same responses for both individuals. Reliability is a necessary but not sufficient condition for validity. For more information on measures of reliability.

Test-retest reliability is the correlation of the items for the same subjects on two time-separated administrations of the instrument.

Split halves reliability is the random allocation of items supposedly measuring the same thing into two separate instruments, to test whether the same individuals will score similarly on both, as would be expected if the items measure the same construct.

Interrater reliability is the correlation of the scores on the same instrument for two different subjects, typically when the instrument is one assessing some subjective phenomenon (such as ascribing content label codes to newspaper editorials) and the subjects are the raters or data gatherers in the research project. (Note that such individuals should be as blind as possible to expected outcomes of the study and should be randomly assigned). Interrater reliability is typically measured by Pearsonian correlation, with a *t*-test for significance of r. Pearson's r makes no assumptions about rater means. The *t*-test reveals if interrater means differ. If they do not, then intraclass correlation may be used instead of Pearson's r.

B. Checklist

1. Have you attempted to get multiple indicators (ideally, four or more) for each variable?
2. Are your measures, such as survey items, exhaustive of all possible responses?
3. Are your measures, such as survey items, mutually exclusive?
4. Have you avoided multidimensional items (e.g., double-barreled survey items such as "Do you approve of the way the president and the Federal Reserve Board have handled the economy in the last 12 months?")
5. Have you eliminated all forms of bias from your indicators (such as selection from only one source; placement of the "favorable" position always first on a scale, or always the "yes" response; use of actual bias words, as in "Do you favor the liberal policy of . . . ")?
6. Have you attempted to reduce bias, as by framing items in the form "Some people favor x while others favor y. Which do you favor?"
7. Have you included filter items, such as those that test if a respondent possesses enough information to make a knowledgeable response?
8. Have you avoided ambiguous language? Example: "Are you currently single, married, divorced, separated, or widowed?" seems acceptable, but pretesting will reveal that many divorced, separated, and widowed persons consider themselves to be "single."
9. Have you included validation items, so that responses on one item can be cross-checked for consistency with another item?
10. Have you tested your items (e.g., through translation and back-translation during pretesting) to assure they are culturally sensitive in regard to the populations you will be studying?
11. Have you indicated the measurement mode (e.g., "as measured by self-administered computer questionnaire") as part of the operational definition?
12. Have you defined all categories of each independent variable?
13. Have you indicated the time frame for all relevant variables (e.g., seconds, days, years)?
14. Have you indicated the mode of response used by respondents (e.g., recall of a story, pen-based circling of multiple choices on a written questionnaire)?

C. Examples

Example 1: A Multicultural Awareness-Knowledge-Skills Survey

Below are 30 items proposed by a doctoral student at the author's institution in relation to a dissertation on cultural diversity training of public employees and their supervisors. The proposed items are listed along with the author's observations.

1. Culture is not external but is within the person.

1	2	3	4
Strongly Disagree	Disagree	Agree	Strongly Agree

COMMENTS: Many will answer as intended. However, if one has had a cultural anthropology course, culture can be interpreted as artifacts, which are external. For example, statues are culture, the media is culture, etc. Consider substituting ''Cultural identity is . . . .'' Also, one should force choices, as is done here by leaving out ''don't know,'' ''not sure,'' and ''both'' answers, only when one has theoretical reason for thinking all such middle choices are false masking the true, listed choices.

2. One potentially negative consequence about gaining information concerning specific cultures is that people might stereotype members of those groups according to the information they have gained.

1	2	3	4
Strongly Disagree	Disagree	Agree	Strongly Agree

COMMENTS: Sentence structure is complex for a survey item (assumes high literacy). The item can be construed as tautological: if stereotyping occurs, isn't it always on the basis of information (however misguided) received by the respondent? Maybe what one wants to get at would be better reflected in an item like, ''If an agency provides cultural awareness information, it is more likely that cultural stereotyping by employees will increase rather than decrease.''

3. At this point in your life, rate your understanding of how your cultural background has influenced the way you think and act.

1	2	3	4
Very Limited	Limited	Fairly Aware	Very Aware

COMMENTS: Poorly worded. It is not clear if one is to rate one's understanding or to rate degree of influence. Better: ''How much do you feel your cultural background . . . ''The outcome (''think and act'') is vague, which is all right in this instance, but the response to this item masks multidimensionality. That is, responses from the same individual may differ depending on what specifier is added at the end

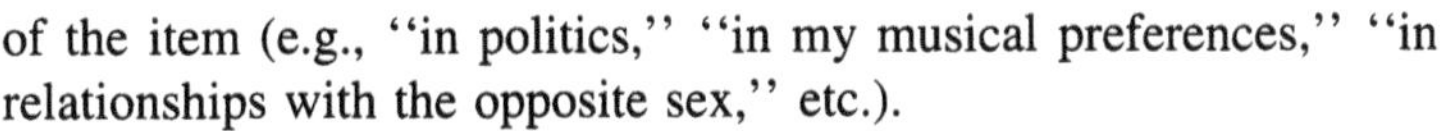

of the item (e.g., "in politics," "in my musical preferences," "in relationships with the opposite sex," etc.).

4. In general, rate your level of awareness regarding different cultural institutions and systems?

1	2	3	4
Very Limited	Limited	Fairly Aware	Very Aware

COMMENTS: Not a bad item, but it also masks multidimensionality based on a specifier (e.g., substitute "African American," "Hispanic," or "Thai" for "different" and one will get different responses from the same individual).

5. At present, how would you rate yourself in terms of being able to accurately compare your own culture perspective with that of a person from another culture?

1	2	3	4
Very Limited	Limited	Good	Very Good

COMMENT: Presumably one wants "cultural," not "Culture." Also, "cultural perspective" is a loaded term. Many will argue that the assumption that a given ethnic group is associated with a given "cultural perspective" is empirically wrong because diversity is the rule.

6. At the present time, how would you rate your own understanding of the following terms:
Managing Diversity

1	2	3	4
Very Limited	Limited	Good	Very Good

COMMENT: Labels are probably biased because respondents will want to see themselves as "good" rather than "limited" in understanding. Consider the prompt, "In terms of your own present understanding, please rate the following terms on the basis of their clarity of meaning to you." Then let the values be "Very clear, somewhat clear, somewhat unclear, very unclear." The same comments apply to items 7–16, which present additional terms.

17. How would you rate your ability to effectively supervise a person from a cultural background significantly different from your own?

1	2	3	4
Very Limited	Limited	Good	Very Good

COMMENT: Other than splitting an infinitive, this item seems acceptable.

18. How would you rate your ability to effectively provide services to a

person from a cultural background significantly different from your own?

1	2	3	4
Very Limited	Limited	Good	Very Good

COMMENT: This is multidimensional. Ability to provide services may be due to (1) one's own personal intercultural abilities or (2) the service resources actually available in one's agency or other setting, limiting what the respondent can do.

19. How would you rate your ability to work effectively with a coworker from a cultural background significantly different from your own?

1	2	3	4
Very Limited	Limited	Good	Very Good

COMMENTS: This item could be multidimensional also. A response of "Limited" might indicate an individual sensitive to his own need for intercultural training and experience, or it could indicate an individual with prejudices and stereotypes about the difficulties posed by employees from other cultures. Further, in the case of Hispanics or other speakers of foreign languages, "effectiveness" may have an objective, language-based component. Therefore, this item needs a follow-up item or two for those who answer "Limited" or "Very Limited" to determine just what they perceive the limitations to be, particularly if they see need for growth in themselves or if they simply blame others.

22. In general, how would you rate yourself in terms of being able to effectively identify biases, prejudices and discrimination in workplace/service delivery settings?

1	2	3	4
Very Limited	Limited	Good	Very Good

COMMENTS: This seems acceptable, except start, "In general, how would you rate your ability to identify effectively . . . "

23. How would you rate your ability to effectively conduct personal self-assessment related to your cultural values, biases, and assumptions?

1	2	3	4
Very Limited	Limited	Good	Very Good

COMMENTS: "Personal self-assessment" is vague. Some will be thinking in terms of a formal personnel assessment that goes in one's file, whereas others will be thinking of a brief mental thought to oneself. Start with a defining sentence such as "A personal self-assessment involves . . . .", then follow with this item.

24. How would you rate your ability to effectively conduct an organizational cultural audit?

1	2	3	4
Very Limited	Limited	Good	Very Good

COMMENTS: Same comments as previous item.

25. How would you rate your ability to interpret/explain the results of an organizational cultural audit to agency staff?

1	2	3	4
Very Limited	Limited	Good	Very Good

COMMENTS: Same comments as previous two items. In addition, this item is multidimensional, referring both to (1) the respondent's assessment of their ability to interpret and explain, and (2) the respondent's understanding of organizational cultural audits. These two dimensions need to be separated into two items.

26. How would you rate your ability to explain how cultural differences can affect individual and organizational outcomes?

1	2	3	4
Very Limited	Limited	Good	Very Good

COMMENTS: Same comments as previous item. The researcher needs a separate item to gauge the respondent's self-perception of their ability to explain things in general to others. This separate item should then be used as a control on items such as 26.

27. How would you rate your ability to understand the unique needs/perspectives of staff of color?

1	2	3	4
Very Limited	Limited	Good	Very Good

COMMENTS: The term ''of color'' is vague. It may refer specifically to African-Americans, or it may include Hispanics (a very diverse group), Asians, and other non-Caucasians. Ordinarily the different possibilities are dealt with in separate items.

28. How would you rate your ability to understand the unique needs/perspectives of female staff?

1	2	3	4
Very Limited	Limited	Good	Very Good

COMMENTS: Insert ''job-related'' after ''unique'' to provide the needed specificity.

Example 2: Census Bureau Measurement of Poverty

Five rules pertaining to the operational definition of poverty as followed by the Census Bureau have had an important effect on the actual count of the number of people in poverty: (1) poverty status was determined for unrelated individuals only if they were 15 years of age or older; (2) the count was only of poor families and individuals, not of poor households; (3) annual income was used; therefore no month-to-month profile of poverty was available; (4) before-tax cash income, not post-tax disposable income, was used in judging whether a family was poor; and (5) noncash benefits were not counted in determining poverty status.

Example 3: Office of Management and Budget Information Technology Investment Guide

Below is a governmental example of operational definition, from the U. S. Department of Energy, based on Office of Management and Budget guidelines for assessing information technology investment:

One approach to devising a ranked listing of projects is to use a scoring mechanism that provides a range of values associated with project strengths and weaknesses for risk and return issues. Table 1 shows an example of how individ-

TABLE 1 Example of Decision Criteria and Scoring Process Used to Rank IT Projects

IT Project (1 thru n) Weight
DECISION CRITERIA SCORING % Overall Risk Factors
Weights for Risks = 100%
Investment Size—How large is the proposed technology investment, especially in comparison to the overall IT budget?
1__________5__________10
Large Small
Project Longevity—Do projects adopt a modular approach that combines controlled systems development with rapid prototyping techniques? Are projects as narrow in scope and brief in duration as possible to reduce risk by identifying problems early and focusing on projected versus realized results.
1__________5__________10
Nonmodular Modular 30
Technical Risk—How will proposed technology be integrated into existing systems? Will proposed investment take advantage of Commercial Off-The-Shelf (COTS) software and systems? How will the complexity of the systems architecture and software design affect the development of the project?
1__________5__________10
Experimental Established
Custom Industry Standard 30
Overall Return Factors
Weights for Returns = 100%

Table 1 Continued

Business Impact or Mission Effectiveness—How will the technology investment contribute toward improvement in organizational performance in specific outcome-oriented terms?

1_____________5_____________10

Low High

25

Customer Needs—How well does the technology investment address identified internal and/or external customer needs and demands for increased service quality and timeliness or reductions in costs?

1_____________5_____________10

Low High

15

Return on Investment—Are the return on investment figures using benefit-cost analysis thresholds reliable and technically sound?

1_____________5_____________10

Risky Known

estimates benefit

20

Organizational Impact—How broadly will the technology investment affect the organization (i.e., the number of offices, users, work processes, and other systems)?

1_____________5_____________10

Low High

25

Expected Improvement—Is the proposed investment being used to support, maintain, or enhance existing operational systems and processes (tactical) or designed to improve future capability (strategic)? Are any projects required by law, court ruling, Presidential directive, etc.? Is the project required to maintain critical operations—payroll, beneficiary checks, human safety, etc.—at a minimal operating level? What is the expected magnitude of the performance improvement expected from the technology investment?

1_____________5_____________10

Tactical Strategic

Tactical: Improves existing process

Strategic: Provides new capability

15

Total Risk Adjusted Score = Weighted Sum of Overall Risk Factors + Weighted Sum of Overall Return Factors

Source: http://www-it.hr.doe.gov/implan/reference/ombitinv.htm

ual risk and return factors might be scored. This example is a hybrid table drawn from multiple best practices organizations. Higher scores are given to projects that meet or exceed positive aspects of the decision criteria. Additionally, in this example, weights have been attached to criteria to reflect their relative importance in the decision process. To ensure consistency, each of the decision criteria should have operational definitions based on quantitative or qualitative measures.

BIBLIOGRAPHY

Aiken, L. R., and Lewis, A. (1996). Rating Scales and Checklists: Evaluating Behavior, Personality, and Attitudes. New York: John Wiley & Sons. [Covers theory, construction and evaluation of rating and attitude scales, checklists, and related questionnaires for research and practice in industrial, clinical, and educational contexts. A set of computer programs to assist in designing, administering, scoring, and analyzing various types of psychometric instruments is included with the book.]

Aiken, L. R., and Lewis, A. (1997). Questionnaires and Inventories: Surveying Opinions and Assessing Personality. New York: John Wiley & Sons. Covers the construction, administration, scoring, and interpretation of questionnaires, psychological inventories, and population surveys. A companion volume to Rating Scales and Checklists. Comes with a computer disk that assists in instrument construction.

Ammons, D. N. (1996). Municipal Benchmarks: Assessing Local Performance and Establishing Community Standards. Thousand Oaks, CA: Sage Publications. Presents relevant national standards developed by professional associations, with actual performance targets and performance results from a sample of governments.

Cohen, R. J., and Swerdlik, M. E. (1998). Psychological Testing and Assessment: An Introduction to Tests and Measurement. 4th ed. Mountain View, CA: Mayfield Publishing Company.

Davis, J. A., and Smith, T. W. (1994). General Social Surveys, 1972–1994: Cumulative Codebook. Chicago: National Opinion Research Center. Distributed by The Roper Center for Public Opinion Research, Storrs, Connecticut. The GSS codebook is available online at http://www.icpsr.umich.edu/gss/codebook.htm.

Fowler, F. J., Jr. (1995). Improving Survey Questions: Design and Evaluation. Thousand Oaks, CA: Sage Publications.

Gallup, G. (1997). The Gallup Poll. Wilmington, DE: Scholarly Resources, Inc. Volumes 1–3 covered 1935–1971 and were published by Random House (NY). Subsequent volumes have been published every 2 or 3 years. At this writing, the most recent was the volume covering 1995–1996, published in 1997.

Groth-Marnat, G. (1996). Handbook of Psychological Assessment. 3rd ed. New York: John Wiley & Sons. Reviews commonly used psychological assessment tests such as the Wechsler Intelligence Scales, Bender-Gestalt, Rorschach, Thematic Apperception Test (TAT), Minnesota Multiphasic Personality Inventory (MMPI/MMPI-2), projective drawings, and California Psychological Inventory. Discusses validity and reliability of each.

Halachmi, A. (1996). Organizational Performance and Measurement in the Public Sector:

Toward Service, Effort and Accomplishment Reporting. Greenwood Publishing Group.
Hambleton, R. (1991). Fundamentals of Item Response Theory. Thousand Oaks, CA: Sage Publications.
Hastings, P. K., and Southwick, J. C., eds. (1998). Index to International Public Opinion. Westport, CT: Greenwood Publishing Group. The first volume in this series, originally published by the Roper Public Opinion Research Center, appeared in 1974. At this writing, the most recent annual volume covered 1996–1997, published in 1998.
Hopkins, K. D. (1997). Educational and Psychological Measurement and Evaluation. Boston: Allyn and Bacon.
Impara, J. C., and Plake, B. S., eds. (1998). The Thirteenth Mental Measurements Yearbook. 13th ed. Lincoln, NB: Buros Inst., University of Nebraska Press. Published annually, this is the leading source for psychological scales. Has articles, bibliography, and critical reviews of psychological tests. Earlier volumes should be consulted also.
Keyser, D., and Sweetlands, R. C., eds. (1994). Test Critiques: Volume X. Kansas City, MO: Test Corporation of America. Published periodically, this covers over 700 tests in psychology, education, and business, giving a detailed description of each measure: applications and discussion of validity and reliability. Also a leading standard source.
Loewenthal, Kate M. (1996). Introduction to psychological tests and scales. London: UCL Press.
Miller, M. B. (1995). Coefficient alpha: A basic introduction from the perspectives of classical test theory and structural equation modeling. Structural Equation Modeling 2:255–273.
Miller, W. E., and Traugott, S. A. (1989). American National Election Studies Data Sourcebook, 1951–1986. Cambridge, MA: Harvard University Press.
Newmark, C. S., ed. (1996). Major Psychological Assessment Instruments. 2nd ed. Boston: Allyn and Bacon.
Osterlind, S. J. (1997). Constructing Test Items: Multiple-Choice, Constructed-Response, Performance, and Other Formats. Boston: Kluwer Academic Publishers.
Price, J. L., and Mueller, C. W. (1986). Handbook of Organizational Measurement. Marshfield, MA: Pitman.
Robinson, J. P., Athanasiou, R., and Head, K. B. (1969). Measures of Occupational Attitudes and Occupational Characteristics. Ann Arbor, MI: Institute for Social Research.
Robinson, J. P., and Shaver, P. R. (1991). Measures of Personality and Social Psychological Attitudes. New York: Academic Press.
Robinson, J. P., Shaver, P. R., and Wrightsman, L. S., eds. (1998). Measures of Political Attitudes. New York: Academic Press.
Smith, P., ed. (1996). Measuring Outcome in the Public Sector. London: Taylor & Francis.
Van Der Linden, Wim J., and Hambleton, R. K. (1997). Handbook of Modern Item Response Theory. New York: Springer Verlag.
Yeung, O. M., and Mathieson J. A. (1998). Global Benchmarks: Comprehensive Measures of Development. Washington, DC: Brookings Institution.

POLL. Note that Dialog Information Services and other vendors carry the POLL database, containing virtually all items asked in Gallup, Roper, Harris, and many other polls, with frequencies. Data are not available from POLL, but rather may be obtained from organizations such as the Inter-University Consortium for Political and Social Research (ICPSR) and the polling organizations themselves.

ERIC/AE Test Locator. This is an online service of the ERIC Clearinghouse on Assessment and Evaluation, the Library and Reference Services Division of the Educational Testing Service, the Buros Institute of Mental Measurements at the University of Nebraska in Lincoln, the Region III Comprehensive Center at GW University, and Pro-Ed test publishers. Located at http://www.ericae.net/testcol.htm, the site includes links to the ETS/ERIC Test File, the Test Review Locator, the Buros/ERIC Test Publisher Locator, and the CEEE/ERIC Test Database, as well as to the "Code of Fair Testing Practices" and "Test Selection Tips."

Psychological and intelligence tests online are linked at this website: http://www.vanguard.edu/psychology/webtesting.html

11

Research Designs

I. DEFINING THE METHODOLOGY

A ''Methodology'' section follows the ''Review of the Literature'' section in most empirical article, thesis, and dissertation outlines. The methodology section is the ''plan of investigation.'' It must not be ''tacked on.'' Rather, the researcher must demonstrate to the reader that the methodology is appropriate for investigating the relationships set forth in his or her model. Many researchers prefer a ''multitrait, multimethod'' (MTMM) approach, with each variable (trait) measured multiple ways (e.g., multiple survey items) and each relationship examined by multiple methods (survey research *and* case studies, for instance) so as to achieve a higher level of confirmation of results. Also, it is often a good idea to identify prominent alternative methodologies *not* used and explain why the methods actually selected are superior.

A. Research Designs

Research designs may be qualitative or quantitative, or a mixture of both. Qualitative research designs strive for indepth understanding of subjects through such techniques as participant observation or narrative analysis, or they may strive for indepth understanding of texts through such methods as exegesis or deconstruction. Some techniques that fall in the ''qualitative'' camp, such as content analysis, may be quantitative as well, involving extensive counting and statistical analysis of word patterns. Quantitative research designs, therefore, differ more in degree than kind from qualitative designs. Quantitative designs routinely involve larger sample sizes, more reliance on random sampling, greater use of statistical inference, and less use of case illustration of findings.

1. Qualitative Empirical Research

A qualitative approach to explanation may share one or more of the following orientations:

1. *A focus on intersubjective meaning*. Rather than assume there is one "true" meaning that must be established empirically, the researcher may take the view that there are as many true meanings as there are subjects. Moreover, the researcher him- or herself is apt to be a subject, affecting that which is observed. As in the classic Japanese movie *Rashomon*, each subject views reality (in the movie, a crime) from a different, but valid, perspective. There is no absolute truth, but by examining each subjective "truth" in turn, an intersubjective meaning is obtained.

2. *A focus on inducing meaning from observation*. Because of the importance of intersubjective meaning, the qualitative researcher may eschew formal hypotheses, believing they are antithetical to unbiased observation. Developing hypotheses to be tested may be seen as equivalent to imposing categories of perception on a complex phenomenon that is better understood by inducing insight and generalizing from observation.

3. *A holistic focus*. The qualitative researcher may believe that meaning is lost by disaggregating phenomena into small subtopics, each examined in narrow terms. This belief is sometimes associated with scorn for empirical research as missing the "big picture." The holistic researcher not only believes that the whole is greater than the sum of the parts investigated individually, but also that experimental and quasiexperimental research designs that seek to "control" variables actually separate them from their only valid context of meaning, which is the whole.

4. *Discovery in nature*. As a corollary of a holistic focus, the qualitative researcher is apt to believe that the subject of study must be viewed in its natural context, as it really exists. Just as the true nature of animal behavior cannot be studied in zoos, so the true nature of human behavior cannot be studied in experiments.

Qualitative approaches can be and usually are empirical approaches, but not in the experimental or quasiexperimental sense. Methods for doing qualitative analysis may involve participant observation; action research, in which the investigator is a change agent; open-ended, even free-associative interviewing; storytelling and narrative analysis; and other largely qualitative approaches. Coding of transcripts of interviews and other documents can be used to make qualitative analysis more empirical. With text management software, the researcher can assign code categories in the course as documents are received, then form natural aggregations of codes, observing relationships among code categories to induce generalizations in a process labeled "grounded theory."

Because of the subjective nature of much qualitative research, a greater burden is placed on the researcher to demonstrate that his or her coding methodology is replicable (that similar phenomena generate similar codes) and that there is high intercoder reliability. One method of establishing the validity of the researcher's coding schemes is to conduct a debriefing with participants in the process studied, soliciting reactions and trying to understand where and why participants react negatively to the terms of the researcher's schema.

Phenomenology is a qualitative approach to empirical study that emphasizes intersubjectivity and the other orientations of qualitative research listed above.

Ethnographic research builds on the same orientations of qualitative research as phenomenology but is differentiated from it. Ethnographic research can be inductive (inducing generalizations based on observations) or deductive (classifying observations based on an established framework). In both cases, however, observation is in a naturalistic setting and emphasizes the importance of cultural symbols in relation to subjective meanings assigned by various actors and populations in the study. Although often applied to the study of tribes and ethnic groupings, ethnographic research can focus on such contemporary subjects as mental hospitals or Internet chat rooms.

2. Case Studies

Case study research is a time-honored, traditional approach that illustrates issues of research design. Because only a few instances are studied, the case researcher will typically uncover more variables than he or she has data points, making statistical control (e.g., through multiple regression) an impossibility. Case study research may be used in its own right but is more often recommended as part of a multimethod approach (''triangulation'') in which the same dependent variable is investigated through the use of multiple procedures (such as case studies, survey research, archival data). In recent years there has been increased attention to implementation of case studies in a more systematic, standalone manner that increases the validity of associated findings.

Unlike random sample surveys, case studies are not representative of entire populations, nor do they claim to be. The case study researcher should take care not to generalize beyond cases similar to the one(s) studied. Provided the researcher refrains from overgeneralization, case study research is not methodologically invalid simply because selected cases cannot be presumed to be representative of entire populations. Put another way, in statistical analysis, one is generalizing to a population based on a sample that is representative of that population. In case studies, one is generalizing to a theory based on cases selected to represent dimensions of that theory.

Because of the type of generalization involved in case studies, case selection should be theory-driven. When theories are associated with causal typologies, the researcher should select at least one case that falls in each category. That cases are not quantitative does not relieve the case researcher from identifying what dependent variable(s) are to be explained and what independent variables may be relevant. Not only should observation of these variables be part of the case study, but ideally the researcher would study at least one case for every causal path in the model suggested by theory. Where this is not possible—often the case—the researcher should be explicit about which causal types of cases are omitted from analysis. Cases cited in the literature as counter-cases to the selected theory should not be omitted.

Cross-theoretic case selection. As multiple theories can conform to a given set of data, particularly sparse data as in case study research, the case research design is strengthened if the focus of the study concerns two or more clearly contrasting theories. This enables the researcher to derive and then test contrasting expectations about what would happen under each theory in the case setting(s) at hand.

Pattern matching is the attempt of the case researcher to establish that most cases are not inconsistent with each of the links in the theoretical model that drives the case study.

Process tracing is the more systematic approach to pattern matching in which the researcher attempts, for each case studied, to find evidence that each link in the theory-based causal model actually existed, was of the sign predicted by theory, and was of the effect magnitude predicted by theory. Process tracing cannot resolve indeterminancy (selecting among alternative models, all consistent with case information); however, it can establish in which types of cases the model does not apply. Controlled observation is the most common form of process tracing. Its name derives from the fact that the researcher attempts to control for effects by looking for model units of analysis (e.g., people in the case of hypotheses about people) that shift substantially in magnitude or even valence, on key variables in the model being investigated. In a study of prison culture, for instance, in the course of a case study an individual may shift from being free to being incarcerated; or in a study of organizational culture, an individual may shift from being a rank-and-file employee to being a supervisor. Such shifts can be examined to see if associated shifts in other variables (e.g., opinions) also change as predicted by the model. Controlled observation as a technique dictates that the case study (1) be long enough in time to chronicle such shifts, and (2) favor case selection of cases in which shifts are known to or are likely to occur.

Time series analysis is a special and more rigorous case of process tracing in which the researcher also attempts to establish that the existence, sign, and magnitude of each model link and the temporal sequence of events relating the variables in the model is as expected. This requires observations at multiple points in time, not just before-after observations, to establish that the magnitude of a given effect is outside the range of normal fluctuation of the time series.

Congruence testing is an even more systematic approach to pattern matching that requires the selection of pairs of cases identical in causal type, except for the difference of one independent variable. Differences in the dependent variable are attributed to incongruence on the independent. Where there are a large number of cases, it may be possible to replace congruence testing with statistical methods of correlation and control.

Explanation-building is an alternative or supplement to pattern matching. Under explanation-building, the researcher does not start out with a theory to be investigated. Rather, the researcher attempts to induce theory from case examples chosen to represent diversity on some dependent variable (such as cities with different outcomes on reducing welfare rolls). A list of possible causes of the dependent variable is constructed through literature review and brainstorming, and information is gathered on each cause for each selected case. The researcher then inventories causal attributes common to all cases, common only to cases high on the dependent variable, and common only to cases low on the dependent variable. The researcher comes to a provisional conclusion that the differentiating attributes are the significant causes, whereas those common to all cases are not. Explanation-building is particularly compelling when there are plausible rival explanations that can be rebutted by this method. Explanation-building can also be a supplement to pattern matching, as when it is used to generate a new, more plausible model after pattern matching disconfirms an initial model.

Grounded theory is a form of comparative case-oriented explanation-building popularized in sociology by Glaser and Strauss (1967), related to ethnography. The researcher examines cases that are similar on many variables but differ on a dependent variable, to discern unique causal factors. Similarly, the researcher may examine cases that are similar on the dependent variable, to discern common causal factors. In this way, advocates of grounded theory seek a continuous interplay between data collection and theoretical analysis. Whereas the conventional scientific method starts with a priori (preconceived) theories to be tested and then collects data, grounded theory starts with data collection and then induces theory. Although not strictly part of its methodology, ''grounded theory'' also implies a focus on generation of categories by the subjects themselves, not à priori creation of typologies by the researcher. In this it is similar to phenomenology.

In grounded theory, the researcher may even try to label variables in the terminology used by subjects in their perception of a phenomenon. In this way, grounded theory is context-based and process-oriented. Good grounded theory meets three criteria: (1) fit: it makes sense to those active in the phenomenon being studied; (2) generality: it can be generalized to a describable range of phenomena; and (3) control: it anticipates possible confounding variables that may be brought up by challengers to the theory. Also, the data for ''grounded theory'' may be broader than traditional case studies and may include participant observations, field notes, event chronologies, or other textual transcripts. As analysis of such transcripts is central, coding becomes an important issue, though it ranges from the informal to the quantitatively structured. As a rule, research based on grounded theory will have a tabular schedule of coded variables being tracked in the transcripts.

A brief example of grounded theory construction is provided by Strauss and Corbin (1990: 78):

> Pain relief is a major problem when you have arthritis. Sometimes, the pain is worse than other times, but when it gets really bad, whew! It hurts so bad, you don't want to get out of bed. You don't feel like doing anything. Any relief you get from drugs that you take is only temporary or partial.
>
> Grounded theory-building: One thing that is being discussed here is PAIN. One of the properties of pain is INTENSITY: it varies from a little to a lot. (When is it a lot and when is it little?) When it hurts a lot, there are consequences: don't want to get out of bed, don't feel like doing things (what are other things you don't do when in pain?) In order to solve this problem, you need PAIN RELIEF. One AGENT OF PAIN RELIEF is drugs (what are other members of this category?) Pain relief has a certain DURATION (could be temporary), and EFFECTIVENESS (could be partial).

Paradigms, in the jargon of grounded theory, consist of the following elements: the phenomenon (the dependent variable of interest), the causal conditions (the set of causes and their properties), the context (value ranges and conditions of the causal variables that affect the model), intervening conditions (intervening, endogenous variables in the model), action strategies (goal-oriented activities subjects take in response to conditions), and consequences (outcomes of action strategies).

Is case study research a substitute for scientific experimentation? It is interesting to note that case study research plays an important role in the natural sciences as well as social sciences. Many scientific fields, such as astronomy, geology, and human biology, do not lend themselves to scientific investigation through traditional controlled experiments. Darwin's theory of evolution was based, in essence, on case study research, not experimentation, for instance. It is true that a later researcher using case methods will of necessity be studying a different case, if only because he or she comes later, and therefore may come to different conclusions. Similarly, in experimental and quasiexperimental research the subjects will differ, meaning relationships may differ.

What makes research replicable in either case study or experimental research is not the units of analysis but whether the research has been theory-driven. If the case researcher has developed and tested a model of hypothesized relationships, then a future case researcher can replicate the initial case study simply by selecting cases on the basis of the same theories, then testing the theories through pattern matching. If pattern matching fails to uphold theories supported by the first case researcher, the second case researcher may engage in explanation building, as discussed above, to put forward a new model.

Aren't case studies unscientific because findings cannot be generalized? No. Generalizability of findings is a function of the range and diversity of settings in which a theory is tested, not of the testing methodology per se. It is true that randomization of subjects in experimental research and random sampling in quasiexperimental research, along with larger sample sizes, mean that research of this type can more easily lay claim to range and diversity than can case study research projects. Nonetheless, judicious case selection to identify cases illustrating the range of a theory (e.g., a theory about causes of divorce) may result in more generalizable research than, say, the attempt to test the same theory based on a random sample of students in one university. Moreover, if case research is replicated (discussed above), generalization of case-based findings can be enhanced further.

3. Quantitative Empirical Research

Quantitative empirical research designs fall into two broad classes: experimental and quasiexperimental. In both, the purpose of research design is to control for all factors that may influence the dependent variable(s) being studied. In experimental designs, control is achieved through randomization of subjects into treatment and control groups. Because the composition of each group is random, the researcher can assume that the effects of any unmeasured variables (e.g., political preferences, religious affiliations, medical conditions, etc.) ''wash out.'' That is, the researcher assumes that because of random assignment of subjects, all unmeasured factors are neutralized.

The same assumption cannot be made in real-life research settings, such as most studies of the effects of public policies, because it is impossible to randomize subjects into those receiving a ''treatment'' and those not. Instead, quasiexperimental research design attempts to achieve the same sort of control through statistical means as described below. Although much more problematic than true experimental research, quasiexperimental methods are well developed throughout the social sciences due to the necessity of dealing with real-life data.

4. Quasiexperimental Research Designs

Whereas in classic experimental research, the researcher assigns subjects at random to an experimental (treatment) group and to a control group, in quasiexperimental research the researcher has no such ability to randomize subjects. Instead the researcher must attempt to emulate an experimental situation by various multivariate statistical methods. In principle, experimental design is always better than quasiexperimental research design. In practice, often an experimental design is not feasible, ethical, or even lawful. Data may need to be analyzed on the basis of existing archival information, it may be impossible to randomize subjects, and pretest data may be absent. Even when randomized experiments are undertaken, they may become flawed because of such factors as attrition in the treatment group, in which case the wise researcher will have a ''fall-back'' quasi-experimental design for purposes of analysis. Often these ''fall-back'' methods involve results from random sample surveys of a population of interest.

(a) Sampling Designs. In research projects that involve data gathering, it is frequently not feasible to gather data on every possible subject. Instead, a sample is taken to represent the universe of all possible subjects. How the sample is taken will determine whether the researcher can make scientific statements about the significance of his or her findings (significance is discussed more extensively in Chapter 14). Such statements routinely take forms such as ''These results are significant within plus or minus three percentage points,'' or ''These results are significant at the .01 level.''

Only random sampling allows findings of significance. If one has an enumeration (data on all subjects) rather than a sample, then significance is irrelevant because there is *no* chance that the researcher's results are the result of the chance of sampling, which is what significance measures. If one has a nonrandom sample (e.g., a convenience sample of all students in a class, taken as representative of all students at a college), then one would like to make statements about significance but there is no valid, statistical way of doing so! For this reason, nonrandom samples are appropriate mainly for preliminary, exploratory phases of research.

In addition to wanting a random sample, the researcher needs to know how large a sample to gather. Various software packages exist to help the researcher determine the number of respondents needed in a sample. These, however, offer only guidelines. The truth is that the needed sample size depends on several factors, not all of which will be well defined by the researcher beforehand.

1. The smaller the effect the researcher is trying to prove, the larger the sample must be.
2. The more variables used by the researcher as controls on an effect, the larger the sample must be.
3. The more unequal to distribution of values of variables examined by the researcher, the larger the sample must be (e.g., a study of violence among homosexual couples will require a larger sample than a study of divorce rates among heterosexual couples, because homosexuality is rarer than heterosexuality and violence is rarer than divorce).
4. The statistical methods to be used may also influence the number of cases needed.

A study of large effects involving evenly distributed variables with no control relationships may require only 50 cases, whereas a study of small effects involving unequally distributed variables and two or three controls may require a thousand or more cases. The needed sample size does *not* depend on the size of the universe to be sampled. The same sample size will be needed for a sample of students at a college as for people in the United States, given the same variables and relationships to be studied. Even large-scale national surveys, such as those reported at election time, usually involve only 1,500 to 3,000 respondents. A useful tip is simply to notice the sample size used by other researchers engaged in research similar to that to undertaken by the writer.

(b) Nonequivalent Control Group Designs. Cook and Campbell (1979) outline 11 nonequivalent control group research designs. In each case, because of the nonequivalence of the comparison group, threats to validity are much more possible than in randomized experimental designs, and the researcher should consider all the types of validity threats (validity is discussed in a later chapter). Here are the 11 nonequivalent control group designs.

1. *One-Group Posttest-Only Design:* Lacking a pretest baseline or a comparison group, it is impossible to come to valid conclusions about treatment effect based solely on posttest information. Changes in the dependent variable may be the result of treatment or may be due to any number of causes of invalidity, such as history (other events coexisting with treatment), experimenter expectation (subjects seeking to provide responses known to be desired), as discussed in the section on validity. If this design is used, as in a single-shot case study, information must be gathered on pretest conditions, if only through respondent recollections.

2. *Posttest-Only Design with Nonequivalent Comparison Groups Design.* It is also impossible to come to valid conclusions about treatment effect based solely on posttest information on two nonequivalent groups, as effects may be caused by treatment or to nonequivalence between the groups.

3. *Posttest-Only Design with Predicted Higher Order Interactions.* Sometimes the expectation of the treatment effect interacts with a third variable. Instead of the expectation that treatment group subjects will be higher on the dependent, one has the expectation that the subjects will be higher if in the upper half of third variable Y, but lower (or not as high) if in the bottom half of Y. For instance, training may lead to greater productivity for high-education employees but not for low-education employees on the same tasks. The interaction creates two or more expectations compared with the simple one-expectation, one-group, posttest only design. Because there are more expectations, there is greater verification of the treatment effect. However, this design is still subject to possible challenges to validity because of such factors as history (subjects high in education had different experiences); it is just that the counterargument has to be more complex to account for the interaction and, therefore, may be somewhat less likely to be credible.

4. *One-Group Pretest-Posttest Design.* This is a common but flawed design in social science. It is subject to such threats to validity as history (events intervening between pretest and posttest), maturation (changes in the subjects), regression toward the mean (the tendency of extremes to revert toward averages), testing (the learning effect on the posttest of having taken the pretest), and most challenges discussed in the separate section on validity.

5. *Two-Group Pretest-Posttest Design Using an Untreated Control Group.* If a comparison group that does not receive treatment is added to what otherwise would be a one-group pretest-posttest design, threats to validity are reduced. Because the groups are not equivalent, there is still the possibility of selection bias (observed changes are the result of selection of subjects, such as working with more motivated volunteers in a treatment group—see two-stage least squares for a discussion of testing for selection bias). Much depends on the outcome. For instance, if the treatment group starts below the comparison group and ends up above after treatment, a stronger inference of a treatment effect exists than if both groups rise in performance, but the treatment group more so (this might well be caused by selection). A strongly recommended modification to this design is to have more than one pretest. Multiple pretests (at the same interval as between the last pretest and the posttest) help establish the performance trends in both the treatment group and the control group, and treatment should be revealed by a change in the trend line for the treatment group, but not the control group.

6. *Nonequivalent Dependent Variables Pretest-Posttest Design.* In this design, the researcher identifies dependent variables related to the treatment-related variable, but where treatment is predicted to have no effect. Then, if the variable thought to be affected by treatment does in fact change in the predicted direction, but there is no change in the other related dependent variables, again as predicted, then the inference is made that the change in question is the result of treatment, not some confounding cause such as test experience from the pretest.

7. *Removed-Treatment Pretest-Posttest Design.* In some situations, it is possible to both introduce a treatment and to remove it. If the dependent variable goes up after treatment and then goes down when treatment is removed, this is some evidence for the effect of treatment. Of course, if the variable goes up after treatment, it might come down on its own anyway because of a declining return or attrition effect. Cook and Campbell (1979) recommend at least two posttests after treatment and before removal of treatment to establish trend effects after treatment. The researcher also needs to beware of resentment effects caused by treatment removal, as these also might cause a decline in the variable measured, depending on the situation.

8. *Repeated-Treatment Design.* This design is similar to the preceding one but follows a pretest-treatment-posttest-removal of treatment-posttest-resto-

ration of treatment-posttest pattern. The expected treatment effect is for the dependent variable to increase after treatment, decline after removal of treatment, then increase again with restoration of treatment. Even if this outcome occurs, inference is not foolproof, as the decline phase may be caused by resentment at removal of treatment rather than direct adverse affects of removal of treatment, and the subsequent rise may not result from restoration of treatment but from removal of the source of resentment. Also, subjects may more easily become aware of experimenter expectations in this design and may seek to meet (or react against) expectations, thereby contaminating the study.

9. *Reversed-Treatment Pretest-Posttest Nonequivalent Comparison Groups Design*. This design is one in which the nonequivalent comparison group receives the opposite treatment (e.g., the treatment group receives participative leadership and the comparison group receives autocratic leadership). The expectation is that the posttest will show increase for the treatment group and decrease for the comparison group. Cook and Campbell (1979) suggest adding a no-treatment group and even a placebo group, where appropriate. Multiple pretests will improve this design by showing preexisting trends in the treatment and nonequivalent comparison group.

10. *Cohort Designs with Cyclical Turnover*. This design refers to the study of groups as they evolve over time, as in the study of a fourth grade class in year 1, the corresponding fifth grade class in year two, etc. The expectation is that the class average will increase in the posttest after treatment. This design is liable to the same challenges to validity as simple pretest-posttest designs, but it can be strengthened by partitioning the cohort into subgroups, according to their exposure to the treatment. In a study of the effects of television violence, for instance, the cohort may be divided into groups of high, medium, and low exposure to violent television shows. The expectation is that the partitions exposed more will show more change on the dependent variable. Where partitioning is not possible, having multiple pretests and posttests can establish trends to rebut "it would have happened anyway" arguments about the validity of conclusions under this design.

11. *Regression-Discontinuity Design*. One might hypothesize that if there is a treatment effect, then the slope of the regression line relating scores before and after treatment would be the same, but there would be a discontinuous jump in magnitude on the dependent variable immediately after treatment. This test requires verification that the relationship between pretest and posttest scores is linear, as two linear regressions (one before, one after treatment) on a curvilinear underlying relationship could spuriously appear to meet this test. Also, there may be a treatment effect taking the form of a steeper regression slope but no discontinuity at the point of treatment. Such a treatment effect is very difficult to differentiate from a simple curvilinear relationship.

(c) Interrupted Time Series Designs. Above, in the discussion of nonequivalent control group designs, it was suggested that pretest-posttest versions could be improved by having at least two sample pretests to establish linear tendencies apart from treatment. Cook and Campbell (1979) list six interrupted time series designs that extend this suggestion by having multiple pretests and posttests.

1. *Simple Interrupted Time Series Design.* This is the one-group pretest-posttest design augmented with multiple pretests and posttests. The trend found in multiple pretests can be compared with the trend found in multiple posttests to assess whether apparent posttreatment improvement may simply be an extrapolation of a maturation effect that was leading toward improvement anyway. There may be other confounding factors as well, such as failure to seasonally adjust data, confounding a seasonal effect with a treatment effect. In general, this design is liable to history-type challenges to validity: the possibility that other factors historically coterminous with the treatment actually led to the observed effect. Other threats to validity include selection bias, as results from nonrandom attrition of subjects in the posttest; instrumentation bias (the posttest is not equivalent to the pretest); and testing (there may be a learning effect from the pretest such that the observed effect is a test artifact rather than a treatment effect).

2. *Interrupted Time Series with a Nonequivalent No-Treatment Comparison Group.* This is the two-group pretest-posttest design that uses an untreated control group, but with multiple pretests and posttests. By having a comparison group, even if nonequivalent (not randomized), the same threats to validity can occur, but they occur in a more complex and hence more easily disproved way. For instance, if this design shows an improvement in the treatment but not comparison group, it may still be true that there is historical bias, but such bias must be unique to the treatment group for some reason, not including variables that also affect the comparison group. There could be seasonal bias, but only if the seasonal factors were thought to be uniquely associated with treatment, and so on.

3. *Interrupted Time Series with Nonequivalent Dependent Variables.* This is the nonequivalent dependent variables pretest-posttest design with multiple pretests and posttests. The object is to find dependent variables related to the one thought to be influenced by treatment, but where the related variables are not. Cook and Campbell (1979) give the example of influence of breathalyzer tests given by police when bars are open weekend nights, but not given at other times. The dependent variable of interest is accident rates on weekend nights. The related dependents are accident rates on weekday nights when bars are open, and accident rates at times when bars are not open. The expectation is that the treatment effect of breathalyzer testing will be significantly greater for weekend nights than at other times. Counterexplanations for lower accident rates (e.g., safer cars, stricter court treatment of offenders) must explain not only the lower accident rate on weekend nights, but also the lack of effect at other times. Of course,

confounding factors may well exist, but they must be unique to the dependent variable of interest.

4. *Interrupted Time Series with Removed Treatment.* This is the removed-treatment pretest-posttest design with multiple pretests and posttests, including ones in between the original treatment and its removal and, hence, is a more powerful test. For instance, the threat of history is reduced because any historical forces coincident with treatment would also have increased after treatment and decreased after removal, an unlikely circumstance. Ideally, removal of treatment does not occur until enough observations have been taken to rule out any seasonal or other cyclical effects.

5. *Interrupted Time Series with Multiple Replications.* This is simply the interrupted time series with removed treatment design, except that treatment and removal occur multiple times on a schedule. Circumstances rarely permit such a design, but it is stronger yet. By timing the replications randomly, the researcher is able to minimize contamination from cyclical factors. This design assumes one is dealing with a treatment effect that dissipates in a timely manner before the next replication, without carryover effects.

6. *Interrupted Time Series with Switching Replications.* This is a further refinement in which there are two groups, each serving as either the treatment or comparison group on an alternating basis, through multiple replications of treatment and removal. This requires an even higher level of researcher control over subjects, but it is a particularly strong design in ruling out threats to validity. It does not lend itself to studies in which the treatment intervention has been gradual or where treatment effect does not decay well.

5. Experimental Research Designs and Analysis of Variance

Experimental studies are characterized by the ability to randomize subjects into treatment and control groups. This randomization goes a long way toward controlling for variables not included explicitly in the study. Quasiexperimental studies, in contrast, have to control for confounding variables explicitly, because comparison groups are not true, randomized control groups. Case studies are a prototype of quasiexperimental design if pursued systematically, as discussed above. Analysis of variance (ANOVA) studies may be experimental or quasiexperimental but originated in the former.

(a) Types of Experimental Design. Cook and Campbell (1979) mention 10 types of experimental design, all using randomization of subjects into treatment and control groups. Note that the control group may receive no treatment, or it may be a group receiving a standard treatment (e.g., students receiving computer-supported classes versus those receiving conventional instruction; that is, the control group is not necessarily ‘‘no treatment,’’ as would be no classes in this example).

1. *Classic experimental designs.* Randomization of subjects into control and treatment groups is a classic experimental method, amenable to a variety of ANOVA designs, discussed separately.

2. *Lottery designs.* Used when lotteries are expected, as in some communities' manner of assignment of students to magnet schools, this eliminates a major impediment to randomization in social science situations, where it is frequently considered unethical or even illegal, or contrary to community standards, to offer benefits (a public policy treatment) to some citizens but not to others.

3. *Waiting list designs.* Used when demand outstrips supply, which also legitimates giving treatment to some citizens but not others, offering treatment to all is impossible because of limited supply (e.g., studies of clients vs a waiting-list group).

4. *Equivalent time series designs.* Used when treatment cannot be delivered simultaneously to all, also legitimizing giving treatment to some citizens but, temporarily, not to others, as when all employees are to receive training, but in rotations, such that different types of training can be delivered to different groups.

5. *Spatial separation designs.* Used when treatment groups are separated and have no experiment-relevant intercommunication, as when participative management is tried with a treatment group of new, randomly assigned employees in one location but not in another.

6. *Mandated change/unknown solution designs.* Used when change is required but there is no one clear solution, random assignment of subjects can gain acceptance, as in random assignment of students to classes with alternative textbooks.

7. *Tie-breaking designs.* Used in cases where receiving treatment is merit-based, as in some academic situations, those receiving tied scores on merit-based exams can be randomly assigned to a treatment and a control group.

8. *Indifference curve designs.* The attractiveness of the treatment can sometimes be adjusted to a point at which some people will be indifferent toward receiving or not receiving it, and thus may be randomly assigned to a treatment or a control group.

9. *New organizations designs.* Used when a new organization is established, such as one providing job training, opportunities may well arise that permit random assignment of clients to a control and a treatment organization.

10. *Mandated control designs.* Sometimes, as in the military, control levels are sufficiently high that random assignment to treatment and control conditions will be accepted as a matter of course.

(b) Analysis of Variance. Analysis of variance is used to uncover the main and interaction effects of categorical independent variables (called "factors") on an interval-dependent variable. The new general linear model (GLM) version of

ANOVA also supports categorical dependents. A "main effect" is the direct effect of an independent variable on the dependent variable. An "interaction effect" is the joint effect of two or more independent variables on the dependent variable. Regression models cannot handle interaction unless explicit cross-product interaction terms are added; however, ANOVA uncovers interaction effects on a built-in basis. There is also a variant for using interval-level control variables (analysis of covariance [ANCOVA], and for the case of multiple dependents, multiple analysis of variance [MANOVA], and there is a combination of MANOVA and ANCOVA called MANCOVA.

The key statistic in ANOVA is the F-test of difference of group means, testing if the means of the groups formed by values of the independent variable (or combinations of values for multiple independent variables) are different enough not to have occurred by chance. If the group means do not differ significantly, then it is inferred that the independent variable(s) did not have an effect on the dependent variable. If the F-test shows that overall, the independent variable(s) is related to the dependent variable, then multiple comparison tests of significance are used to explore just which value groups of the independent(s) have the most to do with the relationship.

The F-test is an overall test of the null hypothesis that group means on the dependent variable do not differ. It is used to test the significance of each main and interaction effect (the residual effect is not tested directly). For most ANOVA designs, F is between-groups mean square variance divided by within-groups mean square variance. (Between-groups variance is the variance of the set of group means from the overall mean of all observations. Within-groups variance is a function of the variances of the observations in each group weighted for group size.) If the computed F value is around 1.0, differences in group means are only random variations. If the computed F score is significantly greater than 1, then there is more variation between groups than within groups, from which we infer that the grouping variable does make a difference. Note that the significant difference may be very small for large samples.

If the data involve repeated measures of the same variable, as in before-after or matched pairs tests, the F-test is computed differently from the usual between-groups design, but the inference logic is the same. There is also a large variety of other ANOVA designs for special purposes, all with the same logic.

Unlike regression, ANOVA does not assume linear relationships and handles interaction effects automatically. Some of its key assumptions are that the groups formed by the independent variable(s) are relatively equal in size and have similar variances on the dependent variable ("homogeneity of variances"). Like regression, ANOVA is a parametric procedure that assumes multivariate normality (the dependent has a normal distribution for each value category of the independent[s]).

Analysis of variance focuses on F-tests of significance of differences in group means, discussed below. If one has an enumeration rather than a sample, then any difference of means is "real." However, when ANOVA is used for comparing two or more samples, the real means are unknown. The researcher wants to know if the difference in sample means is enough to conclude the real means do in fact differ among two or more groups (e.g., if support for civil liberties differs among Republicans, Democrats, and Independents). The answer depends on:

1. The size of the difference between group means, and
2. the sample sizes in each group. Larger sample sizes give more reliable information and even small differences in means may be significant if the sample sizes are large enough, and
3. the variances of the dependent variable (e.g., civil liberties scores) in each group. For the same absolute difference in means, the difference is more significant if, in each group, the civil liberties scores tightly cluster about their respective different means. Likewise, if the civil liberties scores are widely dispersed (have high variance) in each group, then the given difference of means is less significant.

The formulas for the t-test (a special case of one-way ANOVA) and for the F-test used in ANOVA thus reflect three things: the difference in means, group sample sizes, and the group variances. That is, the ANOVA F-test is a function of the variance of the set of group means, the overall mean of all observations, and the variances of the observations in each group weighted for group sample size.

One-way ANOVA tests differences in a single interval dependent variable among two, three, or more groups formed by the categories of a single categorical independent variable. Also known as univariate ANOVA, simple ANOVA, single classification ANOVA, or one-factor ANOVA, this design deals with one independent variable and one dependent variable. It tests whether the groups formed by the categories of the independent variable seem similar (specifically that they have the same pattern of dispersion as measured by comparing estimates of group variances). If the groups seem different, then it is concluded that the independent variable has an effect on the dependent (e.g., if different treatment groups have different health outcomes). One may note also that the significance level of a correlation coefficient for the correlation of an interval variable with a dichotomy will be the same as for a one-way ANOVA on the interval variable using the dichotomy as the only factor. This similarity does not extend to categorical variables with more than two values.

Two-way ANOVA analyzes one interval dependent in terms of the categories (groups) formed by two independents, one of which may be conceived as a control variable. Two-way ANOVA tests whether the groups formed by the categories of the independent variables have similar centroids. Two-way ANOVA is less sensitive than one-way ANOVA to moderate violations of the assumption of homogeneity of variances across the groups.

(c) ***Multivariate or n-way ANOVA.*** To generalize, n-way ANOVA deals with n independents. It should be noted that as the number of independents increases, the number of potential interactions proliferates. Two independents have a single first-order interaction (AB). Three independents have three first order interactions (AB,AC,BC) and one second-order interaction (ABC), or four in all. Four independents have six first-order (AB,AC,AD,BC,BC,CD), three second-order (ABC, ACD, BCD), and one third-order (ABCD) interaction, or 10 in all. As the number of interactions increase, it becomes increasingly difficult to interpret the model.

(d) ***Designs.*** Analysis of variance and ANCOVA have a number of different experimental designs. The alternative designs affect how the F ratio is computed in generating the ANOVA table. However, regardless of design, the ANOVA table is interpreted similarly—the significance of the F ratio indicates the significance of each main and interaction effect (and each covariate effect in ANCOVA).

Between-groups ANOVA design. When a dependent variable is measured for independent groups of sample members, where each group is exposed to a different condition, the set of conditions is called a between-subjects factor. The groups correspond to conditions, which are categories of a categorical independent variable. For the experimental mode, the conditions are assigned randomly to subjects by the researcher, or subjects are assigned randomly to exposure to the conditions, which is equivalent. For the nonexperimental mode, the conditions are simply measures of the independent variable for each group. For instance, four random groups might all be asked to take a performance test (the interval dependent variable), but each group might be exposed to different levels of noise distraction (the categorical independent variable).

This is the usual ANOVA design. There is one set of subjects: the "groups" refer to the subset of subjects associated with each category of the independent variable (in one-way ANOVA) or with each cell formed by multiple categorical independents (in multivariate ANOVA). After measurements are taken for each group, ANOVA is computed to see if the variance on the dependent variable between groups is different from the variance within groups. Just by chance, one would expect the variance between groups to be as large as the variance within groups. If the variance between groups is enough larger than the variance within groups, as measured by the F ratio (discussed below), then it is concluded that the grouping factor (the independent variable(s) does/do have a significant effect.

Completely randomized design. This is simply between-groups ANOVA design for the experimental mode (see above). Randomization is an effort to control for all unmeasured factors. When there is an à priori reason for thinking some additional independent variable is important, the additional variable may be controlled explicitly by a block design (see below) if categorical, or by ANCOVA if it is a continuous variable. In the nonexperimental mode, where there is no control by randomization, it is all the more important to control explicitly by these methods.

Randomized complete block design. Analysis of variance is an experimental design in which the subjects are matched on some control variable. The subjects are then divided into groups based on this control variable (sometimes called the "nuisance variable"). There must be exactly as many people in each block group as there are categories of the independent variable, to assure that each group has the same number of subjects measuring the same on the control (e.g., the same proportion of subjects by race). Then on a random basis, the members of each block are assigned to different categories of the independent variable (e.g., different dosages of a medication). When sample members are matched in this way, the F ratio is computed similarly to that in a repeated measures ANOVA (see below).

Latin square designs. These extend the logic of block designs to control for two categorical variables. Latin square designs also reduce the number of observations necessary to compute ANOVA. This design requires that the researcher assumes all interaction effects are zero. Normally, if one had three variables, each of which could assume four values, then one would need 43 = 64 observations just to have one observation for every possible combination. Under Latin square design, however, the number of necessary observations is reduced to 42 = 16. For a discussion of how to select the necessary observations under Latin square, see Iverson and Norpoth (1987, 80–84).

Graeco-Latin square designs. These extend block designs to control for three categorical variables.

Factorial ANOVA. Factorial ANOVA is for situations in which there is more than one factor (more than one independent, hence, for two-way ANOVA or higher), used to assess the relative importance of various combinations of independents. As such, it is not a true separate form of ANOVA design, but rather a way of combining designs. A design matrix table shows the intersection of the categories of the independent variables. A corresponding ANOVA table is constructed in which the columns are the various covariate (in ANCOVA), main, and interaction effects. See the discussion of two-way ANOVA below.

Factors are categorical independent variables. The categories of a factor are its groups or levels. When using factorial ANOVA terminology, 2 × 3 (two-by-three) factorial design means there are two factors, with the first having two categories and the second having three. A 2 × 2 × 2 factorial design has three factors, each with two categories. The order of the factors makes no difference. If you multiply through, you have the number of groups (often "treatment groups") formed by all the independents collectively. Thus a 2 × 3 design has six groups, and a 2 × 2 × 2 design has 8 groups. In experimental research, equal numbers of subjects are assigned to each group on a random basis.

GLM ANOVA. General linear model ANOVA is a replacement for factorial ANOVA starting in SPSS with version 8. The GLM approach is more generalized and supports use of categorical dependent variables. The GLM also provides additional output in the form of plots, post hoc tests, comparisons among estimated marginal means, nested designs, mixed models, and more.

Random effect models. Most ANOVA designs are fixed effect models (model I), meaning that data are collected on all categories of the independent variables. In random effect models (model II), in contrast, data are collected only for a sample of categories. For instance, a researcher may study the effect of item order in a questionnaire. Six items could be ordered 720 ways. However, the researcher may limit himself or herself to the study of a sample of six of these 720 ways. The random effect model in this case would test the null hypothesis that the effects of ordering are zero. For one-way ANOVA, computation of F is the same for fixed and random effects, but computation differs when there are two or more independents. The resulting ANOVA table still gives similar sums of squares and F ratios for the main and interaction effects, and is read similarly (see below) and Iverson and Norpoth (1987, 69–78). Random effect models assume normality, homogeneity of variances, and sphericity but are robust to violations of these assumptions (Jackson and Brashers, 1994: 34–35).

Random factors models are the same as random effect models. Do not confuse these terms with completely randomized design or randomized block design, which are fixed factor models. Random effects are factors that meet two criteria: (1) Replaceability: the levels (categories) of the factor (independent variable) are randomly or arbitrarily selected and could be replaced by other, equally acceptable levels; and (2) Generalization: the researcher wishes to generalize findings beyond the particular, randomly, or arbitrarily selected levels in the study.

Treatment by replication design is a common random effects model. The treatment is a fixed factor, such as exposure to different types of public advertising, whereas the replication factor is the particular respondents who are treated. Sometimes it is possible and advisable to simplify analysis from a hierarchical design to a simple treatment by replication design by shifting the unit of analysis, as by using class averages rather than student averages in a design in which students are a random factor nested within teachers as another random factor (the shift drops the student random factor from analysis). Note also that the greater the variance of the random effect variable, the more levels needed (e.g., more subjects in replication) to test the fixed (treatment) factor at a given alpha level of significance.

Mixed factorial design is any random effect model with one fixed factor and one random factor.

Effects shown in the ANOVA table for a random factor design are interpreted a bit differently from standard, within-groups designs. The main effect of the fixed treatment variable is the average effect of the treatment across the randomly sampled or arbitrarily selected categories of the random effect variable. The effect of the fixed by random (e.g., treatment by replication) interaction indicates the variance of the treatment effect across the categories of the random effect variable. The main effect of the random effect variable (e.g., the replication effect) is of no theoretical interest, as its levels are arbitrary particular cases from a large population of equally acceptable cases.

Treating a random factor as a fixed factor will inflate type I error. The F-test for the treatment effect may read as .05 on the computer output, but F will have been computed incorrectly. That is, the treatment effect will be .05 only for the particular levels of the random effect variable (e.g., the subjects in the replication factor). This test result is irrelevant to the researcher's real interest, which is controlling the alpha error rate (e.g., .05) for the population from which the levels of the random effect variable were taken.

Put another way, if a random factor is treated as a fixed factor, the researcher opens his or her research up to the charge that the findings pertain only to the particular arbitrary cases studied, and findings and inferences might well be different if alternative cases had been selected. The purpose of using a random effect model is to avoid these potential criticisms by taking into account the variability of the replications or random effects when computing the error term that forms the denominator of the F-test for random effect models.

Repeated measures or within-groups ANOVA design. When a dependent variable is measured repeatedly at different time points (e.g., before and after treatment) for all sample members across a set of conditions (the categories of an independent variable), this set of conditions is called a within-subjects factor and the design is called within-groups or repeated measures ANOVA. In the within-groups or repeated measures design, there is one group of subjects. The conditions are the categories of the independent variable, which is the repeated measures factor, and each subject is exposed to each condition and measured. For instance, four random groups might all be asked to take a performance test (the interval dependent variable) four times, once under each of four levels of noise distraction (the categorical independent variable).

The object of repeated measures design is to test the same group of subjects at each category (e.g., levels of distraction) of the independent variable. The levels are introduced to the subject in a counterbalanced manner to rule out effects of practice and fatigue. The levels must be independent (performance on one cannot affect performance on another). Each subject is his or her own "control": the different "groups" are really the same people tested at different levels of the independent variable. Because each subject is his/her own control, unlike between-groups ANOVA, in repeated measures designs, individual differences do not affect differences between treatment groups. This in turn means that within-group variance is no longer the appropriate error term (denominator) in the F ratio. This then requires different computation of error terms. SPSS makes these different calculations automatically when repeated measures design is specified. Repeated measures ANOVA is also much more affected by violations of the assumption of homogeneity of variances (and covariances in ANCOVA) compared with between-groups ANOVA.

Mixed designs is a term that refers to the fact that in repeated-measures ANOVA, there also may still be one or more between-subjects factors in which each group of the dependent variable is exposed to a separate and different category of an independent variable, as discussed above in the section on between-groups designs. Mixed designs are common. For instance, a performance test might be the interval dependent variable, noise distraction might be the within-subjects repeated factor (measure) administered to all subjects in a counterbalanced sequence, and the between-subjects factor might be mode of testing (e.g., having a pen-and-paper tested group and a computer-tested group). Repeated-measures ANOVA must be specified whenever there are one or more repeated factor measures, even if there are also some between-groups factors that are not repeated measures. Split-plot designs are a form of mixed design, originating in agricultural research, in which seeds were assigned to different plots of land, each receiving a different treatment. In split plot designs, subjects (e.g., seeds) are randomly assigned to each level (i.e., plots) of the between-groups factor (soil types) before receiving the within-subjects repeated factor treatments (i.e., applications of different types of fertilizer). In mixed designs, sphericity is almost always violated and, therefore, epsilon adjustments to degrees of freedom are routine before computing F-test significance levels.

Pretest-posttest designs are a special variant of mixed designs, that involve baseline testing of treatment and control groups, administration of a treatment, and posttest measurement. As Girden (1992, 57–58) notes, there are four ways of handling such designs:

1. One-way ANOVA on the posttest scores. This involves ignoring the pretest data and is not recommended.

2. Split-plot repeated measures ANOVA might seem to be appropriate because the same subjects are measured more than once. In this perspective, the between-subjects factor is the group (treatment or control) and the repeated measure is the test scores for two trials. The resulting ANOVA table will include a main treatment effect (reflecting being in the control or treatment group) and a group-by-trials interaction effect (reflecting treatment effect on posttest scores, taking pretest scores into account). This partitioning of the treatment effect is more confusing than analysis of difference scores, which gives equivalent results and is recommended.

3. One-way ANOVA on difference scores, where difference is the posttest score minus the pretest score. This is equivalent to a split-plot design if there is close to a perfect linear relation between the pretest and posttest scores in all

treatment and control groups. This linearity will be reflected in a pooled within-groups regression coefficient of 1.0. When this coefficient approaches 1.0, this method is more powerful than the ANCOVA method.

4. Analysis of covariance on the posttest scores, using the pretest scores as a covariate control. When pooled within-groups regression coefficient is less than 1.0, the error term is smaller in this method than in ANOVA on difference scores, and the ANCOVA method is more powerful.

In summary, ANOVA is sometimes thought of as being for just the experimental research designs discussed above. However, this generalization is incorrect. It is true that ANOVA emerges from the experimental tradition, but it is not limited to experimental design. In this context we may ask, "What designs are available in ANOVA for correlated independents?" Correlation of independents is common in nonexperimental applications of ANOVA. Such correlation violates one of the assumptions of usual ANOVA design. When correlation exists, the sum of squares reflecting the main effect of an independent no longer represents the unique effect of that variable. The general procedure for dealing with correlated independents in ANOVA involves taking one independent at a time, computing its sum of squares, then allocating the remaining sum to the other independents. One will get different solutions depending on the order in which the independents are considered. Order of entry is set by common logic (e.g., race or gender cannot be determined by such variables as opinion or income, and thus should be entered first). If there is no evident logic to the variables, a rule of thumb is to consider them in the order of magnitude of their sums of squares (Iverson and Norpoth 1987, 58–64).

B. Checklist

1. Can you explain what a research design is?
2. You *do* have a research design, don't you?
3. Can you explain convincingly how the variables in which you are interested will be illuminated by the design of your research?
4. If your dependent variable of interest involves change over time, does your research design provide for before-after or time series measurement? If not, have you defended alternative approaches to assessing change?
5. Is there a convincing discussion of how subjects were selected and assigned to groups, if groups were involved in your study?
6. Is there a relation between the theories on which your study is based and the selection of cases or subjects?
7. Have you addressed explicitly all of the assumptions of the research design you have selected (e.g., randomization in classic experiments; random sampling in survey research)?

8. If you have chosen a research design not involving randomization of subjects, have you developed a plan for controlling for variables that may affect your dependent variable?
9. Have you gone through the checklist of possible threats to the validity of your research design? (See Chapter 14 for this checklist).
10. Have you considered a multimethod approach in your research design? For instance, have you considered supplementing a quantitative approach with a qualitative one? Supplementing before-after survey research with a case study?
11. Have you discussed how your research design is tied to your choice of statistical procedures?
12. Are these procedures appropriate to your research focus?
13. Does your data meet the assumptions of the procedures you have selected?

C. Software

Designer Research is the research design module of *Methodologist's Toolchest*, which is expert system software for social research created by Ed Brent of Missouri State University. This Windows program helps researchers design efficient experimental or quasiexperimental designs for a wide range of problems. The program helps users identify plausible threats to validity for their problem and suggests strategies to address those threats. It advises the user when conflicting strategies are chosen and helps them select a coherent set of design strategies for the study. Features include extensive descriptions of design strategies, a detailed report, and extensive help. *Designer Research* is available from IdeaWorks, Inc. at the website http://www.ideaworks.com, and from Scolari Software (see below).

*NUD*IST* is software, standing for Non-numerical Unstructured Data Indexing, Searching, and Theorizing, which can be used in conjunction with grounded theory to create and analyze theories and provide a framework for understanding. It can handle coding categories and subcategories, supporting hierarchical indexing; browse and code documents and indexing databases; search for words and word patterns and combine them in indexes; "memo link" emerging codes and categories with their associated documents; and create new indexing categories out of existing ones. See Richards and Richards (1991). NUD*IST is available from Scolari Software at the website http://www.scolari.com.

BIBLIOGRAPHY

Anastas, J. W. (1999). Research Design for Social Work and the Human Services. New York: Columbia University Press. ISBN 0231118902.

Annells, M. P. (1997). Grounded theory method, part 1: Within the five moments of qualitative research. Nursing Inquiry 4:120–129; Grounded theory method, part II; options for users of the method. Nursing Inquiry, 176–180. A good two-part historical overview of the grounded theory method, relating it to theory, methodological issues, and practical procedures.

Bailey, M. T. (1992). Do physicians use case studies? Thoughts on public administration research. Public Administration Review (Jan/Feb): 47–55.

Booth, W. C., Colomb, G. G., and Williams, J. M. (1995). The Craft of Research. Chicago: University of Chicago Press. An overview of the research process.

Bordens, K. S., and Abbott, B. B. (1997). Research Design and Methods: A Process Approach. Fourth ed. Mountain View, CA: Mayfield Publishing Company.

Box, G. E. P., Hunter, J. S., and Hunter, W. G. (1978). Statistics for Experimenters: An Introduction to Design, Data Analysis, and Model Building. New York: John Wiley & Sons.

Brown, S. R., and Melamed, L. E. (1990). Experimental Design and Analysis. Quantitative Applications in the Social Sciences series no. 74. Thousand Oaks, CA: Sage Publications. Discusses alternative ANOVA designs and related coefficients.

Campbell, D. T., and Stanley, J. C. (1966). Experimental and quasi-experimental designs for research and teaching. In Gage, N. L., ed. Handbook of Research on Teaching. Chicago: Rand McNally.

Clark-Carter, D. (1997). Doing Quantitative Psychological Research : From Design to Report. Hove, East Sussex: Psychology Press.

Cook, D. T., and Campbell, D. (1979). Quasi Experimentation: Design and Analysis Issues for Field Settings. Chicago: Rand McNally.

Cox, D. (1992). Planning of Experiments. New York: John Wiley & Sons.

Creswell, J. W. (1994). Research Design : Qualitative and Quantitative Approaches. Thousand Oaks, CA: Sage Publications.

Creswell, J. W. (1997). Qualitative Inquiry and Research Design: Choosing among Five Traditions. Thousand Oaks, CA: Sage Publications.

Dean, A., and Voss, D. T. (1999). Design and Analysis of Experiments. New York: Springer Verlag.

Eisenhardt, K. M. (1989). Building theories from case study research. Academy of Management Review 14(4): 532–550.

Fraenkel, J. R., and Wallen, N. E. (1999). How to Design and Evaluate Research in Education. New York: McGraw-Hill.

Girden, E. R. (1992). Evaluating Research Articles from Start to Finish. Thousand Oaks, CA: Sage Publications.

Glaser, B. G., and Strauss, A. L. (1967). The Discovery of Grounded Theory: Strategies for Qualitative Research. Chicago: Aldine Publishing Co. The seminal work in grounded theory.

Goffman, E. (1963). Asylums. Garden City, NY: Anchor Books. A classic example of the ethnographic approach, in this case to study mental hospitals.

Hamel, J. (1993). Case Study Methods. Thousand Oaks, CA: Sage Publications. Covers history of the case study method.

Hinkelmann, K., and Oscar Kempthorne, eds. (1994). Design and Analysis of Experiments: Introduction to Experimental Design. Wiley Series in Probability and Mathematical Statistics. Applied Probability. New York: John Wiley & Sons.

Hoyle, R. H. (1999). Statistical Strategies for Small Sample Research. Thousand Oaks, CA: Sage Publications.

Iverson, G. R., and Norpoth, H. (1987). Analysis of Variance. Thousand Oaks, CA: Sage Publications. A readable introduction to one-way and two-way ANOVA, including Latin Square designs, nested designs, and discussion of ANOVA in relation to regression.

Kazdin, A. E. (1982). Single Case Research Designs. New York: Oxford University Press.

Kennedy, M. M. (1979). Generalizing from single case studies. Evaluation Quarterly, 3: 661–78.

Keppel, G. (1991). Design and Analysis: A Researcher's Handbook. 3rd ed. Englewood Cliffs, NJ: Prentice Hall.

Kirk, R. E. (1995). Experimental Design: Procedures for the Behavioral Sciences. Pacific Grove, CA: Brooks/Cole Publishing Co.

Lee, A. S. (1989). A scientific methodology for MIS case studies. MIS Quarterly March: 33–50. Using management information systems as a focus, Lee addresses problems of and remedies for case study research.

Leedy, P. D., Newby, T. J., and Ertmer, P. A. (1996). Practical Research: Planning and Design. Englewood Cliffs, NJ: Prentice-Hall.

Lehtonen, R., and Pahkinen, E. J. (1995). Practical Methods for Design and Analysis of Complex Surveys. New York: John Wiley & Sons.

Lucas, W. (1974). The Case Survey Method of Aggregating Case Experience. Santa Monica, CA: Rand.

Maxwell, J. A. (1996). Qualitative Research Design : An Iterative Approach. Thousand Oaks, CA: Sage Publications.

Mitchell, M., and Jolley, J. M. (1996). Research Design Explained. New York: Harcourt, Brace, Jovanovich.

Montgomery, D. C. (1996). Design and Analysis of Experiments. 4th ed. New York: John Wiley & Sons.

Naumes, W., and Naumes, M. J. (1999). The Art and Craft of Case Writing. Thousand Oaks, CA: Sage Publications. The authors have led case writing workshops for the Academy of Management and the Decision Sciences Institute, and they use their experiences to illustrate issues in case study research.

Richards, T. J. and Richards, L. (1991). The NUDIST qualitative data analysis system. Qualitative Sociology. 14:307–324.

Selwyn, M. R. (1996). Principles of Experimental Design for the Life Sciences. Boca Raton, FL: CRC Press.

Solso, R. L., Johnson, H. H., and Beal, M. K. (1997). Experimental Psychology : A Case Approach. Boston: Addison-Wesley Publishing Co.

Stake, R. E. (1995). The Art of Case Study Research. Thousand Oaks, CA: Sage Publications. Focuses on actual case (Harper School) to discuss case selection, generalization issues, and case interpretation.

Strauss, A. L., and Corbin, J. M. (1998). Basics of Qualitative Research : Techniques and Procedures for Developing Grounded Theory. Thousand Oaks, CA: Sage

Publications. Probably now the leading contemporary treatment of grounded theory.

Strauss, A., and Corbin, J. eds. (1997). Grounded theory in practice. London: Sage Publications.

U. S. General Accounting Office (1990). Case Study Evaluations. Washington, DC: USGPO. GAO/PEMD-91-10.1.9. Available online in .pdf format. Government manual for doing evaluation research using case studies.

Yin, R. K. (1994). Case Study Research. 2nd ed. Thousand Oaks, CA: Sage Publications.

12

Selecting Statistical Procedures

I. INTRODUCTION

A central element of research design for quantitative research is selection of appropriate statistical procedures. Much of this task is outside the scope of this book; however, in this chapter an attempt is made to outline some of the main considerations involved in this aspect of writing one's paper, thesis, or dissertation. The focus of procedure selection should be on the match of the statistical procedure to the nature of the dataset and to the analytic needs of the researcher. The focus is *not* on the level of sophistication of the procedure for its own sake. Part of the matching process is assuring that the data meet the statistical assumptions of the procedure chosen. The writer should be prepared not only to defend his or her selection of statistical technique but also to explain why other possibly appropriate procedures were rejected.

A. Selecting Statistical Procedures

1. Level of Data and Statistical Procedures

Selection of statistical procedures appropriate for your data starts with an understanding of the level of measurement of your variables. Ordinarily, you will have to select a statistical procedure that corresponds to the lowest level of measurement of one of any variable in your model. The levels of measurement, from lowest to highest, are listed below.

1. *Nominal data* has no order, and the assignment of numbers to categories is purely arbitrary (e.g., 1 = East, 2 = North, 3 = South, etc.). Because of

lack of order or equal intervals, one cannot perform arithmetic (+, −, /, *) or logical operations (>, <, =) on nominal data.

2. *Ordinal data* has order, but the intervals between scale points may be uneven. Rank data are usually (see below) ordinal, as in students' rank in class. The interval distance from the top student to the second-highest student may be great, but the interval from the second-ranked student to the third-ranked may be very close. Because of lack of equal distances, arithmetic operations are impossible with ordinal data, which are restricted to logical operations (more than, less than, equal to). For instance, given a person of rank 50 and a person of rank 25 in a school class of 100, where rank 100 is highest achievement, one cannot divide 25 into 50 to conclude that the first person has twice the achievement of the second. However, one can say the first person represents more achievement than the second person.

Because social scientists frequently use opinion survey data, which are often Likert scales (e.g., 1 = strongly agree, 2 = agree, etc.), and because social scientists often want to use interval-level techniques like multiple regression, there is a temptation to treat such ordinal scale data as if they were interval. In practice, it is very common to use such scales with interval procedures, provided the scale item has at least five and preferably seven categories. Most researchers would not use a 3-point Likert scale with a technique requiring interval data. The fewer the number of points, the more likely the departure from the assumption of normal distribution, required for many tests.

3. *Interval data* has order and equal intervals. Counts are interval, such as counts of income, years of education, or number of Democratic votes. Ratio data are interval data that also have a true zero point. Temperature is not ratio, because zero degrees is not "no temperature," but income is ratio because zero dollars is truly "no income." For most statistical procedures, the distinction between interval and ratio does not matter, and it is common to use the term "interval" to refer to ratio data as well. Occasionally, however, the distinction between interval and ratio becomes important. With interval data, one can perform logical operations, add, and subtract, but one cannot multiply or divide. For instance, if a liquid is 40° and we add 10°, it will be 50°. However, a liquid at 40° does not have twice the temperature of a liquid at 20° because 0° does not represent "no temperature"—to multiply or divide in this way, we would have to be using the Kelvin temperature scale, with a true zero point (0° Kelvin = -273.15 degrees Celsius). Fortunately, in social science the issue of "true zero" rarely arises, but researchers should be aware of the statistical issues involved.

A question that frequently comes up is, "Can one validly use ordinal data like typical Likert scale (1 to 5, strongly approve to strongly disapprove) survey items with statistical procedures that formally call for interval level data?" In a recent review of the literature on this topic, Jaccard and Wan (1996, 4) summarize, "for many statistical tests, rather severe departures (from intervalness) do not seem to affect Type I and Type II errors dramatically.'' Standard citations to literature showing the robustness of correlation and other parametric coefficients with respect to ordinal distortion are Labovitz (1967, 1970) and Kim (1975). Others are Binder (1984) and Zumbo and Zimmerman (1993). Use of ordinal variables such as 5-point Likert scales with interval techniques is the norm in contemporary social science. Here is a typical footnote inserted in research using interval techniques with Likert scales:

> In regard to our use of (insert name of procedure), which assumes interval data, with ordinal Likert scale items, in a recent review of the literature on this topic, Jaccard and Wan (1996: 4) summarize, ''for many statistical tests, rather severe departures (from intervalness) do not seem to affect Type I and Type II errors dramatically.'' Jaccard, James and Choi K. Wan (1996). *LISREL approaches to interaction effects in multiple regression*. Thousand Oaks, CA: Sage Publications.

Researchers should be aware that there is an opposing viewpoint. Thomas Wilson (1971) concludes, ''The ordinal level of measurement prohibits all but the weakest inferences concerning the fit between data and a theoretical model formulated in terms of interval variables.'' The researcher should attempt to discern if the values of the ordinal variable seem to display obvious marked departures from equal intervalness and qualify his or her inferences accordingly.

A second question is, ''Is it okay to use dichotomous variables in procedures like regression or path analysis that assume interval data?'' If one assumes the dichotomy collapses an underlying interval variable, there will be more distortion with dichotomization than with an ordinal simplification. Dichotomization of continuous variables attenuates the resulting correlations. Moreover, the degree of attenuation will be affected by the cutting points used in the dichotomization. If the underlying correlations are high (more than .7), the cutting points will have a nontrivial effect. Nonetheless, it is common to use dichotomies in interval-level techniques like correlation and regression.

In the ''old days'' of statistical inquiry, if you had nominal data, then you would have to content yourself with frequency distributions, crosstabulations, and related nominal-level measures of significance and association. If you had ordinal level data, then there were some additional, better measures of ordinal association and correlation. Only if you had interval data, or were willing to treat ordinal data as interval (see below), could you use more sophisticated quantitative procedures, such as regression and factor analysis. If you had interval data but your dependent was a dichotomy, you could use discriminant function analysis. You could get around some of the restrictions on categorical data by making the categories into separate dummy variables (making each value into a 0-or-1 dichotomous variable, leaving one of the values out) after which they could be used in multiple regression.

Today, the linear model of regression has been generalized (hence the general linear model, GLM, used in multinomial logistic regression) so that SPSS and other statistical packages can create dummy variables automatically for all categorical inputs and can generate computer coefficients (parameters) for variables regardless of level. Moreover, new estimation techniques, particularly maximum likelihood estimation (MLE), have largely replaced the older ordinary least squares (OLS) forms of estimation on which regression was based. The result is that level of data is less of a restriction today than it once was, *if* you are using new statistical procedures such as GLM multiple analysis of variance (MANOVA), multinomial logistic regression, or structural equation modeling. Also, SPSS CATEGORIES module supports a wide range of procedures for categorical data: PRINCALS, OVERALS, and CATREG are analogous to principal components, canonical correlation, and regression.

B. Statistical Procedures and Their Purposes

Selecting the statistical procedure appropriate to your research question is one of the most important decisions in an empirical paper, thesis, or dissertation. This is a difficult problem as multiple procedures might be used to address the same research problem. In general, the researcher is concerned with effect size, often expressed as a coefficient representing the magnitude of apparent effect of an independent variable on a dependent. However, with data that are a sample of a larger population, effect size is meaningful only when statistically significant (not because of chance of sampling). Many statistical procedures, discussed below, have associated coefficients for reporting both effect size and statistical significance and, indeed, researchers should report both effect size (association) and statistical significance. Statistical significance is discussed more fully in Chapter 14.

One broad distinction among statistical procedures is between "dependent procedures," which involve analysis of a dependent variable, and "nondependent procedures," which do not. Normally the research is investigating a dependent variable and wants a dependent procedure such as multiple regression, analysis of variance, or discriminant function analysis. As an extension of dependent procedures, sometimes the researcher is testing models involving variables that are dependent with respect to some variables and independent with respect to others. In such cases, the researcher may want to use model-testing procedures such as partial correlation, structural equation modeling, or hierarchical linear modeling. At other times, the researcher is simply trying to establish "the lay of the land" by determining which variables cluster with which other variables, in which case it may be appropriate to use a nondependent procedure such as factor analysis, cluster analysis, multidimensional scaling, or canonical correlation.

A range of statistical procedures is listed below, along with their corresponding type of research use.

Procedure	*Typical Use*
Chi-square	Assess significance of findings based on a random sample, including significance of tables and goodness-of-fit to particular (e.g., normal) distributions of data.
Measures of association	Assess bivariate effect size for categorical variables.
Correlation	Assess bivariate effect size for interval variables.
Partial correlation	Assess effect size of interval control variable(s) on correlation for small models.
Multiple regression	Assess overall and relative predictive power of a group of interval-independent variables on a single interval dependent variable.
Analysis of variance (ANOVA)	Assess significance of group differences on some categorical variable.
MANOVA	Assess significance of group differences on multiple categorical variables.
Analysis of covariance (ANCOVA)	Assess significance of group differences on a categorical variable, controlling for one or more interval covariate variables.
Multiple analysis of covariance (MANCOVA)	Assess significance of group differences on multiple categorical dependent variables, controlling for one or more interval covariates.
Canonical correlation	Assess effect size of a group of independent variables on a group of dependent variables.
Factor analysis	Assess the structure of a group of variables, including assessing if a group of indicators seems to measure the same dimension discriminant function analysis. Assess the effect of size and relative impact of a group of independent interval-level variables on a dichotomous dependent variable.
Cluster analysis	An umbrella term for a collection of procedures that seek to derive a set of criteria that classify cases into a parsimonious set of categories.
Correspondence analysis	A procedure widely used in marketing research to map alternatives (e.g., products) and their traits (e.g., colors, price ranges) onto coordinate systems, usually based on subjective survey data, to visualize the proximity of products to each other and to various traits.

Logistic regression	Assess the effect size and relative impact of a group of independent interval or categorical variables on a dichotomous or multinomial categorical dependent variables.
Path analysis	Assess the fit to sample data of one model of interval independent variables on mediating and dependent interval variables, as compared with an alternative or null model.
Structural equation modeling	Assess the fit to sample data of one model of latent independent variables on mediating and dependent latent variables, as compared with an alternative or null model, in which each latent variable is a function of multiple categorical or interval indicator variables.
Multilevel modeling	A variant on structural equation modeling that handles data aggregated at different levels (e.g., child, classroom, school, and school district levels).

Another way to look at the issue of selecting statistical procedures is to construct a decision tree, such as this one derived from criteria set forth by Tacq (1997), is shown in Figure 1.

Of course, there are many more statistical procedures than these, and of those listed, some can be refined to serve other than their typical purpose. Note, however, that statistical selection cannot be reduced to a mechanical choice. At the dissertation level, it is wise for the researcher to obtain the insight of a professional statistician before making a final selection of procedure.

C. Software for Statistical Selection

An excellent resource for statistical procedure selection has been placed online by Bill Troachim at http://trochim.human.cornell.edu/selstat/ssstart.htm.

Statistical Navigator is a Windows program that uses artificial intelligence reasoning and an extensive hypertext knowledge base to help researchers select appropriate statistical analyses for their research. *Statistical Navigator Professional* considers more than 200 different types of statistical analyses and includes hundreds of definitions of statistical terms. In the Browse mode, users can examine detailed descriptions of each type of analysis, including references and statistical packages that perform those analyses. Hypertext definitions of terms are available to help users understand these descriptions. In the Consult mode, users are asked questions about their research objectives and assumptions. Based on their answers, the program identifies the best analyses for their task. The program produces a detailed description of each recommended analysis along with references, statistical packages that perform the analyses, and a point-by-point summary of how the analysis does or does not fit their research problem.

WhichGraph is another module in the *Methodologist's Toolchest* that helps select appropriate business, statistical graphs, and maps from more than 100 possible graphical forms. It advises on stylistic issues for maximum presentation impact through the use of extensive hypertext descriptions and definitions.

Both *Statistical Navigator* and *WhichGraph*, as well as the larger *Methodologists' Toolchest* of which they are components (usable on a stand-alone basis,

1. Is the research problem dependent? ---- NO —> Go to non-dependent page

YES

Multiple regression
Partial correlation
Hierarchical regression
Path analysis
Discriminant function
Anova
Ancova
Manova
Mancova
Multivariate multiple regression
Multiple discriminant analysis
Loglinear analysis

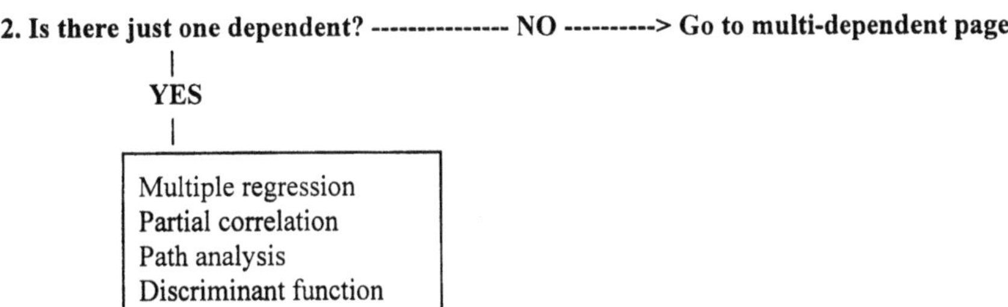

FIGURE 1 Decision tree.

Uni-Dependent Page

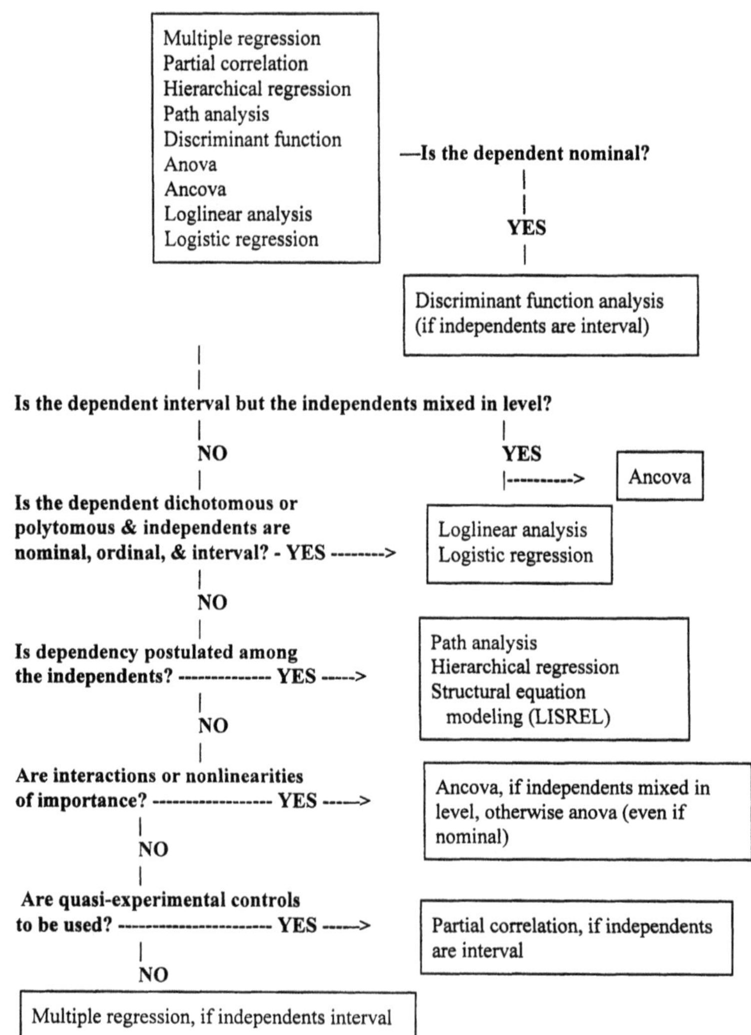

FIGURE 1 Continued.

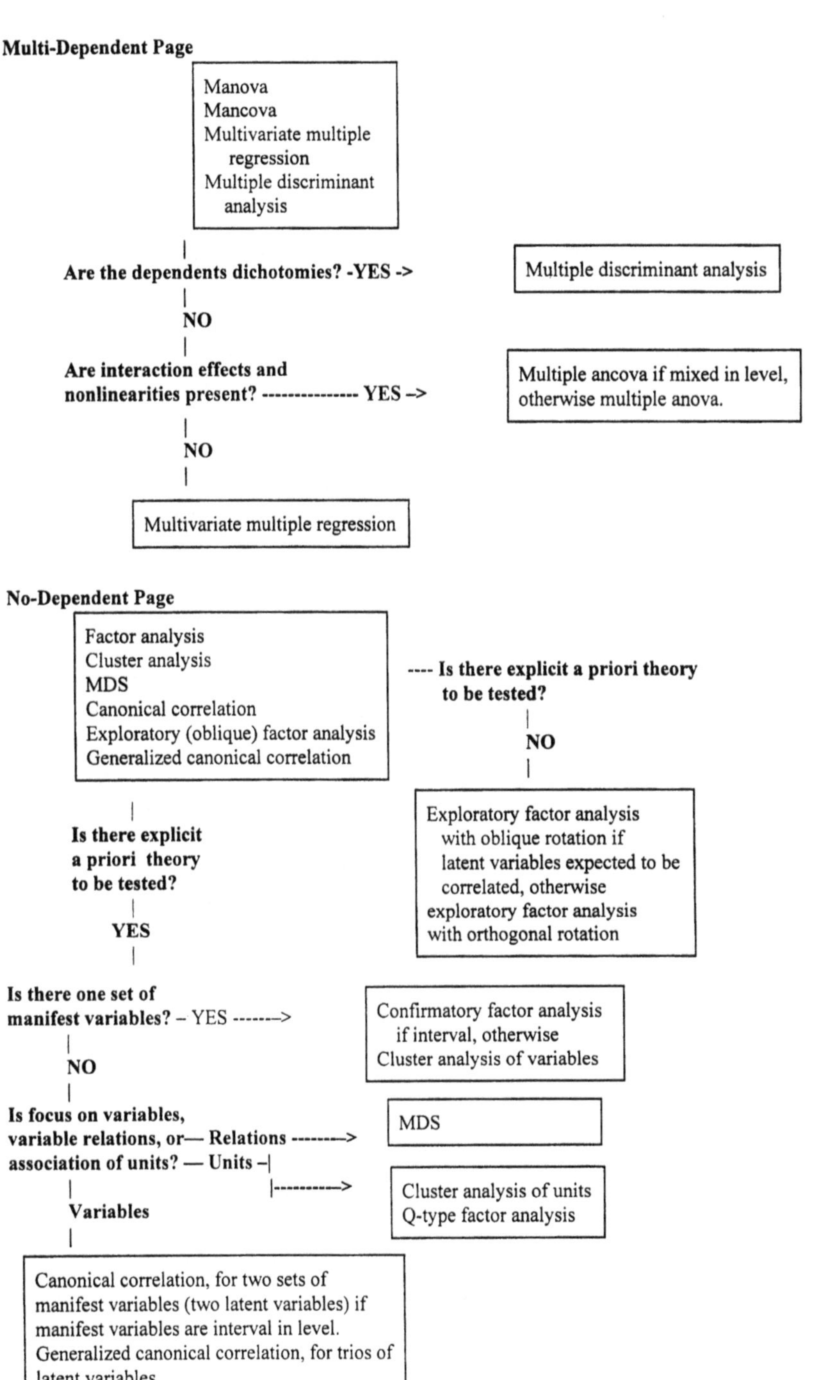
Multi-Dependent Page
Manova
Mancova
Multivariate multiple regression
Multiple discriminant analysis
Are the dependents dichotomies? -YES ->
Multiple discriminant analysis
NO
Are interaction effects and nonlinearities present? -------------- YES ->
Multiple ancova if mixed in level, otherwise multiple anova.
NO
Multivariate multiple regression
No-Dependent Page
Factor analysis
Cluster analysis
MDS
Canonical correlation
Exploratory (oblique) factor analysis
Generalized canonical correlation
---- Is there explicit a priori theory to be tested?
NO
Exploratory factor analysis with oblique rotation if latent variables expected to be correlated, otherwise exploratory factor analysis with orthogonal rotation
Is there explicit a priori theory to be tested?
YES
Is there one set of manifest variables? – YES ------->
Confirmatory factor analysis if interval, otherwise Cluster analysis of variables
NO
Is focus on variables, variable relations, or— Relations -------->
MDS
association of units? — Units –|
|---------->
Cluster analysis of units
Q-type factor analysis
Variables
Canonical correlation, for two sets of manifest variables (two latent variables) if manifest variables are interval in level. Generalized canonical correlation, for trios of latent variables.

Figure 1 Continued.

however) are available from Scolari Software, the software division of Sage Publications, Thousand Oaks, CA (http://www.scolari.com).

D. Checklist

1. Is the statistical procedure selected appropriate to the research question at hand?
2. Have you prepared a ''table of hypotheses, instruments, and statistical procedures?'' Such a table lists each of the hypotheses in your study, the survey scale, or other data collection instrument that will measure the variables of each hypothesis, and the statistical procedure that will test for the relationship contained in the hypothesis. This is a literal table and should appear in your list of tables after the table of contents.
3. Are clear operational definitions defined for each variable in the model?
4. Does the research instrument avoid all of the following?
    1. Vague items (e.g., Agree/Disagree ''Government is too big.'' Vague as to level of government: federal, state, local).
    2. Biased items (e.g., equal number of positive and negative wordings for same dimension to avoid yea-saying bias that respondents tend to agree with).
    3. Loaded items (e.g., respondents will tend not to want to ''prohibit'' things, but are more amenable to ''not allow'' the same things).
    4. Multidimensional items (e.g., Agree/Disagree ''The president is an effective leader of high integrity.'' Effectiveness and high integrity are two different dimensions).
    5. Nonmutually exclusive items (e.g., ''single'' may mean ''never married'' or ''divorced'').
    6. Nonexhaustive items (e.g., never married/married/divorced choices leave out widows/widowers and also committed gay relationships).
    7. Multiple items (e.g., ''Check any of the following that apply . . . ''). Each response on such items must be converted to a separate yes/no variable and the total of yes responses become an additional variable.
5. Do items code (separately) for no response and no answer?
6. Do items force choices (e.g., by omitting a ''neutral'' or ''no answer'' code) only where there is reason to think every respondent does, in fact, have a listed choice?
7. Is an appropriate method of data imputation undertaken for missing value? This requires an assessment of whether data are missing at

random. Treatment of data imputation is covered at the website http://www2.chass.ncsu.edu/garson/pa765/missing.htm.

8. If all missing values are not imputed, has the researcher chose listwise versus pairwise deletion of missing cases appropriately? Pairwise deletion deletes cases only for pairs with missing values, only when that pair figures in a computation. Listwise deletion deletes cases if a case has a missing value on any computation. Pairwise deletion preserves sample size. However, listwise deletion is required in some statistical procedures, such as structural equation modeling, so as not to violate statistical assumptions.
9. Is every table numbered and entered in the ''List of Tables'' that follows the table of contents? Note that (APA) American Psychological Association style, a common standard, calls for numbering using Arabic numerals throughout the work (*not* A, B, C; *not* I, II, III; *not* 1.1, 1.2, 1.3; *not* 1a, 1b, 1c, etc.).
10. Is every chart numbered and entered in the ''List of Charts'' that follows the table of contents?
11. Is every figure numbered and entered in the ''List of Figures'' that follows the table of contents?
12. Does every table, chart, and figure have a caption or title?
13. In each table, chart, and figure, are numbers rounded appropriately for easy reading?
14. For every table, chart, and figure, are variables listed by a meaningful name rather than by a cryptic computer code (e.g., ''% Hispanic with > 12 years school'' rather than ''PCTHGT12'')?
15. Does every table, chart, and figure have a source note? The APA style guide calls for notes to be indicated by the word ''Note,'' underlined, followed by a period (Note.).
16. For each table, chart, and figure, where appropriate, is there a note indicating the significance of the relationships depicted? It is a common practice when exact significance levels are not reported (e.g., $P = .032$) to list significance by the following symbols: $*P < .05$, $**P < .01$, $***P < .001$, where single, double, and triple asterisks in the body of the table, chart, or figure indicate the corresponding levels of significance. The researcher should also indicate in a note if one-tailed or two-tailed significance testing pertains to the table, chart, or figure.
17. For each table, chart, and figure, where appropriate, is there a note indicating the association, correlation, or effect size of the relationships depicted? Effect size needs to be reported, as for larger samples, relationships can be highly significant even when the effect is tiny.

18. For each table, chart, and figure, where needed, are there notes on information critical to intepretation, such as special definitions of terms, changes in data collection, or missing values?
19. Is each table, chart, or figure discussed or at least referenced by number in the body of the text?
20. When descriptive statistics are presented, as in tables of means, are standard deviations reported as well? Would this information be better presented through histograms of frequency distributions?
21. In each table, is the independent variable the column variable and are percentages calculated to add to 100% down each column? Interpretation will be difficult or impossible if this convention is not followed. If there is an overriding reason for placing the independent variable as the row variable, percentages must add to 100% across rows.
22. In each table, is the count presented as well as percentages? This implies reporting sample size as part of the row and column marginal totals.
23. In correlation, regression, discriminant analysis, path analysis, structural equation modeling, and other procedures that are part of the general linear model family, are standardized (beta) coefficients reported along with unstandardized weights? This allows easier comparison of the relative importance of the independent variables. Likewise, are significance tests listed for all coefficients? This aids in determining if effects are likely to be replicated in another sample.
24. If a linear procedure is used (e.g., OLS regression), has an explicit effort been made to demonstrate that the data relationships under investigation are, in fact, linear?
25. Depending on the statistical procedure selected, various data assumptions must be met. Common assumptions include normal distribution of variables, multivariate normality of variables, homogeneity of variances between groups, absence of high multicollinearity, and data selected randomly and independently. Have statistical tests (e.g., tests of homogeneity of variances) been applied to the data, demonstrating that the assumptions associated with the chosen statistical procedure have been met?

BIBLIOGRAPHY

Achen, C. and Shively W. P. (1995). Cross-Level Inference. Chicago: University of Chicago Press.

Binder, A. (1984). Restrictions on statistics imposed by method of measurement: Some reality, some myth. J Criminal Justice 12:467–481. Defends robustness of parametric techniques even when using ordinal data.

Jaccard, J. and Wan C. K. (1996). LISREL Approaches to Interaction Effects in Multiple Regression. Thousand Oaks, CA: Sage Publications.

Kim, J. O. (1975). Multivariate analysis of ordinal variables. Am J Sociol 81:261–298.

Labovitz, S. (1967). Some observations on measurement and statistics. Social Forces 46: 151–160.

Labovitz, S. (1970). The assignment of numbers to rank order categories. Am Sociol Rev 35:515–524.

Tacq, J. (1997). Multivariate Analysis Techniques in Social Science Research. Thousand Oaks, CA: Sage Publications.

Tarter, M. E. (1999). Statistical Curves and Parameters: Choosing an Appropriate Approach. Natick, MA: A. K. Peters, Ltd.

Wilson, T. (1971). Critique of ordinal variables. In: Blalock, H. M., ed. Causal Models in the Social Sciences. Chicago, Aldine.

Zumbo, B. D. and Zimmerman, D. W. (1993). Is the selection of statistical methods governed by level of measurement? Can Psychol 34:390–399. Defends robustness of parametric techniques even when using ordinal data.

13

Writing Fundamentals

I. TELLING A STORY

Every writing effort needs to tell a "story," whether that story is how a certain combination of chemicals can form a stronger bonding agent or how a certain sequence of social factors can cause a political revolution. The writer's story starts with an exposition of the intellectual problem. It has a beginning, middle, and end. The writer must make a convincing case that the problem is well identified, significant, and in need of research. The writer must avoid "topic shift," in which the focus set forth at the beginning differs from the focus of conclusions at the end. Usually the writer will want to relate the selected intellectual problem to social, economic, political, psychological, moral, or other problems that may be aided in their solution by the writer's research findings. Generalizations that summarize research findings are made concrete through judicious use of illustrative examples. The good writer never forgets that a central purpose of all writing is to motivate the interest of the reader.

II. SELECTED GRAMMAR FUNDAMENTALS

Even with the best style of writing, organization, and logical appearance of evidence, the researcher's presentation can be undermined by ignorance of the fundamentals of grammar, discussed briefly here before turning to more significant writing concerns.

The twelve most common grammatical mistakes of the elementary variety are:

1. Apostrophes denote possession. Wrong: womens' sports. Correct: women's sports.
2. Articles should be omitted when they are unnecessary. Wrong: ''The Norsemen discovered the Americas first.'' Correct: ''Norsemen discovered the Americas first.''
3. Capitalization is for proper names but not for things that are simply important. Wrong: ''the white house,'' ''the Federal Courts.'' Correct: ''the White House,'' ''the federal courts.''
4. Closing quotation marks always go after the punctuation mark. Wrong: ''Key terms include 'infrastructure', 'satisficing', and 'simulation'. Correct: ''Key terms include 'infrastructure,' 'satisficing,' and 'simulation.'''
5. Commas separate adjective lists where an ''and'' would be plausible, and otherwise they do not. Wrong: ''a little, old lady,'' ''an unprecedented long-awaited report.'' Correct: ''a little old lady,'' ''an unprecedented, long-awaited report.''
6. Hyphenation errors often occur when the user combines two familiar words into a non-word, but adding hyphens unnecessarily can be a problem also. Wrong: ''dataset,'' ''co-equal.'' Correct: ''data set,'' ''coequal.'' However, with widespread usage over time, what was formerly ungrammatical may become accepted: website, for instance, is now accepted in place of web site.
7. Plural nouns require plural verbs. Wrong: ''The data is compelling on this point.'' Correct: ''The data are compelling on this point.''
8. Run-on sentences need to be split into two or more sentences. Wrong: ''Norsemen discovered the Americas first they arrived by way of Iceland.'' Correct: ''Norsemen discovered the Americas first. They arrived by way of Iceland.''
9. Sentence fragments lack verbs. Wrong: ''Waiting for the necessary resources, including paper, pens, and ink cartridges, employees speedily warehousing incoming cartons in bulk containers.'' Correct: ''Waiting for the necessary resources, including paper, pens, and ink cartridges, employees speedily warehoused incoming cartons in bulk containers.''
10. Spelling errors can sabotage an otherwise compelling argument. Always use your spell-checker, but then proofread as well. A spell-checker will not catch all errors!
11. Unbalanced quotation marks and parentheses are a common grammatical problem: each must always be used in an opening and closing pair.
12. Verb tenses must be consistent. Wrong: ''Miller (1999) argued against the proposition, but Smith (1995) argues for it.'' Correct:

''Miller (1999) argued against the proposition, but Smith (1995) argued for it.''

The additional grammatical topics below are ones that seem to be stumbling blocks for college-educated writers who have mastered more elementary basics as avoiding double negatives, avoiding run-on sentences, using commas properly, and ensuring subject-verb agreement.

Parallel construction. One common grammatical error among college-level writers is failure to maintain parallel construction for coequal terms. Wrong: ''The French, the Germans, and Spanish all use the Eurodollar.'' Correct: ''The French, the Germans, and the Spanish all use the Eurodollar.'' Wrong: ''She gave an interesting report and very inspiring.'' Correct: ''She gave an interesting and inspiring report.'' Wrong: ''An election not of policy choices, but personality.'' Correct: ''An election not of policy choices but of personality.'' When nouns or adjectives are coequal, their use should be identical.

Clear antecedents for pronouns. The antecedent to which any pronoun is referring must be clear and unambiguous to the readers. Pronouns should refer to only one specific person or thing. Wrong: ''To help incoming students adjust to life with upperclassmen, mentors were assigned to them.'' (This is wrong because the pronoun ''them'' would ordinarily refer to the nearest subject, upperclassman, but here refers to the first subject, incoming students). Correct: ''Mentors were assigned to incoming students to help them adjust to life with upperclassmen.'' In general, it is usually wise to keep the distance from a pronoun to its antecedent small and to examine carefully clauses that begin with ''which,'' ''it,'' or ''that'' (e.g.: ''The students like the textbooks and the lab assignments, which were authored by G. Pennington Morse.'' Here ''which'' may refer to the textbooks, the lab assignments, or both). Likewise, to avoid vague referents, do not use terms like ''this,'' ''that,'' 'it,'' and ''which'' unless closely and clearly connected to the subjects to which they allude.

Comparing comparable things. The writer should be careful of comparison statements, making sure that comparisons are on the same footing. For instance, the sentence ''The level of interest in the current election is greater than the last election'' incorrectly compares ''level of interest'' with ''last election.'' A correct version would be, ''The level of interest in the current election is greater than the level of interest was during the last election.'' In addition to comparing apples with apples, comparison statements should make the basis of comparison explicit (not, for instance, ''Many people found his speech to be better,'' but rather, ''Many people found his speech to be better than his previous speeches.''

III. WRITING FUNDAMENTALS

The thesis statement. You must have a story to tell about your topic, not just an ''area'' to explore. For quantitative papers, there must be an empirical puzzle to solve. Your thesis statement must make a plausible, specific claim about your topic. Although plausible, this statement must nonetheless be arguable; informed people may dispute alternative explanations of what is being studied. The writer should clearly set forth the topic, the underlying problem or puzzle, the writer's explanation of the problem or puzzle (this explanation is the writer's thesis), and set forth alternative plausible explanations to be investigated (with the expectation that they will be found weaker than the author's explanation). These alternatives should not be of the "straw man" type or oversimplified dichotomies, but rather should fairly and honestly represent the complexity of all sides of an issue.

The "story line" is the logical presentation of examples and data that support the author's thesis more than alternatives (unless the author's thesis is to be rejected, which can be a valid scholarly conclusion also) and that provide an explanation of the puzzling topic selected for investigation. All components of the paper, thesis, or dissertation revolve explicitly around the story line, which the writer keeps in the forefront of the reader's attention throughout.

Critical paragraphs. In each section, the introductory and concluding paragraphs are critical. The former lays the foundation for information in the section, and the latter summarizes for readers where they have been taken. The introductory paragraph(s) will do the following:

1. Relate the section to the overall thesis of the paper, thesis, or dissertation.
2. Present basic who-what-where-when-why information as appropriate.
3. Set forth the scope of the section.

A second or more introductory paragraph may be needed to accomplish the following tasks:

1. Present any other essential background information, including examination of the assumptions made by the author and by those advocating competing explanations.
2. Define key terms.
3. Look ahead in general terms to key statistical or other findings of the section.

The concluding paragraph is also critical, providing the reader with a logical conclusion to the section, summarizing what has been demonstrated, and relating this to the overall story line of the paper, thesis, or dissertation. The concluding paragraph also provides a look ahead and a smooth transition into the next section.

Transitional sentences and paragraphs. Without good transitional sentences and paragraphs, the author's work will not read smoothly—it may even sink below choppiness to the point of seeming incoherent. The writer should never assume the reader understands the logic of the writer's story line in detail. The burden is on the writer to point out continually where the story has come from, where it is going, and what the overall point will have been when the story is finished. Transitional phrases should be used throughout the work (e.g., in addition, it follows that, furthermore, by comparison, by the same token, similarly, moreover, nonetheless, for instance, as an illustration, in conclusion, in summary, therefore, and so on). Of course, care must be taken to work transitional phrases into the text as natural expressions, not as mechanical devices inserted for their own sake. Repetition of key words and phrases may also aid in the construction of transitional sentences and paragraphs, through the use of concepts that have already been well developed for the reader as stepping-stones to lead into new concepts about to be discussed (e.g., in transitioning from a discussion of anomie to a discussion of alienation: "Just as we have demonstrated that anomie is a factor in suicide, so too it may be demonstrated that the related dimension of social alienation is also a factor.") Parallel construction, discussed below, can also reinforce transitional paragraphs.

Parallel construction. Parallel construction is a classic writing strategy, used effectively, for instance, by the writers of the Psalms. Redundancy can be effective in heightening audience interest, as President John F. Kennedy often demonstrated in his speeches, as in his famous "Ich bin ein Berliner" speech:

> "There are some who say that communism is the wave of the future. Let them come to Berlin. And there are some who say in Europe and elsewhere we can work with the Communists. Let them come to Berlin. And there are even a few who say that it is true that communism is an evil system, but it permits us to make economic progress. Lass' sie nach Berlin kommen. Let them come to Berlin." - JFK, remarks in the Rudolph Wilde Platz, West Berlin: June 26, 1963.

Similarly, a series of prepositional phrases can effectively describe something while grabbing reader attention (e.g., "He was a man of high principles, a man of strong convictions, of ruthless decisiveness in taking action toward his goals . . . "). Such parallel construction will seem redundant if overused, but some use of repetition can be very effective in hammering home central points in a way that heightens reader attention to the writer's story line.

Parsimonious writing. In spite of what has just been said of parallel construction, most of the time the writer should honor the principle of parsimony—that if the same information can be conveyed in fewer words, it should be. Examples of redundancy are too diverse and numerous to catalog but include such phrases as "a biography of his life," "consensus of opinion," "7:00 AM in the morning," "new innovations," "the usual custom," "the resulting consequence," "the outcome effect," and innumerable others. If one's word processor thesaurus will bring up one word in a phrase (e.g., "outcome" when another part of the phrase is highlighted (e.g., ''effect''), in most cases the writer needs to be more concise. Toyka (1995) lists many phrases that usually can be omitted altogether, such as ''For that matter,'' ''As a matter of fact,'' and ''For the most part.'' If the principle of parsimony applies to phrases, it applies even more to entire paragraphs that, of course, may also be redundant.

Body paragraphs. Paragraphs in the body of any section develop a single idea, each a logical building block in the intellectual edifice that the section, as a whole, represents. The logical order of body paragraphs is best dictated by the theory and hypotheses that form the core of empirical writing. However, at times the logical ordering of paragraphs may be historical order, process order, spatial order, or by order of importance of other phenomena to be compared or contrasted, depending on the purpose of the section. A typical paragraph will state its subtopic, relating it to the hypothesis under investigation in its section. It may also present statistical output or illustrative examples, providing evidence for the argument being made. When such evidence is presented, the reader should also be given information about the basis for selection of that evidence. Body paragraphs should not be so terse as to be abrupt and ''telegraphic,'' nor should they be rambling or verbose. Some redundancy is not inappropriate, however, particularly the practice of using the concluding sentence in a body paragraph to reiterate the key idea for that paragraph.

The jargon issue. One of the most difficult aspects of writing style to master is acquiring the ability to know just how much of the specialized terminology of one's discipline to use to appear ''professional'' without using jargon in a backfired attempt to impress. In general, the more specialized the audience, the freer the writer is to use specialized terms without defining them. The more general the audience, the less jargon may be used, and when used, the more it must be clearly defined. A common practice is to refer to a phenomenon (e.g., an organism in biology) by its scientific term the first time the reference is made, but to use the common term thereafter.

Active versus passive voice. English instructors who teach writing normally encourage the use of the active voice because it engages the reader more effectively than the passive voice. Even well-educated readers take longer to comprehend statements put in the passive rather than active voice. However, excessive use of the active voice in some disciplines can create an unprofessional writing tone (e.g., the passive voice is the dominant mode in legal writing and is common for bureaucratic reports). Also, when the agent of the verb is unknown, the passive voice is necessary (e.g., ''The door was closed to the public prior to the meeting.'') In general, the more creative the writing task, the more the conventional advice to use the active voice should be followed. Use of the active voice in the findings section of research papers and dissertations is appropriate as long as the word ''I'' remains limited. (Disparaged: ''I found social isolation increased suicide rates." "Suicide rates were increased by social isolation." Better: "Social isolation increased suicide rates.") Good writing style substitutes more active verbs for members of the "to be" family wherever appropriate. In most research writing, however, the passive voice is used in the methodology section to focus attention on procedures, not the researcher.

General-to-specific order of organization. As a rule of thumb, it is often best in the introductory portions of one's writing to progress from the general to the specific. This allows the reader to see the "big picture" first, so as to be in a better position to integrate and assimilate specific details. In contrast, in the ending discussion section, it is common to progress from the specific to the general, ending with the strongest generalizations warranted by the evidence one has marshaled. This allows the reader to see how the pieces fit together into a climactic conclusion.

A. Writing Fundamentals Checklist

1. Have you taken seriously the need to back-up your writing project? Avoid potential tragedy by making multiple back-ups and keeping some of them in different locations in case of major disasters such as fire. For electronic materials, use at least a three-phase back-up system. On day 1 back-up from disk A to disk B. On day 2, use disk B and back-up to disk C. On day 3, use disk C and back-up to A, etc. The simpler and more common method—to back-up from your hard disk to a back-up disk at regular intervals, runs a serious risk: you may have corrupted your files at the end of the day's work, then copied the corrupt files to your back-up, leaving you with nothing! It does happen, as do fires. Spending a little extra time for proper back-up is sound insurance.
2. Have you read some dissertations your faculty mentors think illustrate good writing, perhaps discussing with them what makes them fall in this category?
3. Have you established a suitable physical writing environment, such as a home office, a library carrel, a departmental office, or other space that affords quiet, privacy, and access to tools such as a computer and the Internet?
4. Have you established a clear writing schedule in your work week so that enough time is set aside on a scheduled basis for you reasonably to be expected to complete your research and writing on schedule? It works best for many people to schedule a regular writing time each day rather than to expect to do all one's work in a concentrated period such as Saturdays, even if the number of hours is the same.
5. If you are married, have you kept your spouse closely informed about your progress and timetable? Have you negotiated with your spouse some sort of exchange that recognizes the sacrifices involved in his or her support of your

thesis or dissertation efforts? Investing time and energy into that exchange does not detract from your writing; in the long run it is essential to it.

6. Have you established logical chapters and sections to your work, as described in the previous chapter on outlining? Is text broken into logical segments with an aesthetic amount of white space separating sections, and has each chapter started on a new page?

7. Have you avoided "paragraph sprawl"? That is, have you avoided digressions that are relatively unimportant to your story line? Such digressions may belong in endnotes, appendices, or the trash bin. Nothing is *completely* irrelevant to your topic, you must exercise sound judgment in protecting the centrality of your story line.

8. Are your paragraphs neither too long nor too short, instead sufficiently developing single subtopics in a logical progression from the beginning to the end of each section? However, although paragraphs are about 4 to 8 sentences long, a variety of paragraph lengths stimulates reader interest. Having many long paragraphs (more than 10 sentences) diminishes reader interest. Also avoid having any one-sentence paragraphs: a paragraph should contain a separate idea, *and* develop it, which requires a minimum of two sentences.

9. Unless it violates some formatting requirement of your department or publisher, it is best to start new paragraphs with an indent rather than a blank line. The former is more readable and allows use of blank lines to be reserved for separating sections, not paragraphs. Indenting is also better when it is necessary to print single-spaced at times and double-spaced at other times.

10. Likewise, are your sentences neither too short nor too long, and is sentence length varied within paragraphs? For instance, are longer explanatory sentences contrasted by short, to-the-point summary statements?

11. When you do use long and complex sentences, do the subject and verb come early and close together in the sentence construction, with complex clauses following rather than preceding the verb?

12. Have you added variety to your writing style by interjecting occasional exclamatory statements, or questions to the reader? Empirical writing generally assumes a dispassionate, professional tone; however, the reader will also want to sense that the writer cares about his or her subject and wishes to involve the reader in the writer's enthusiasm for his or her investigation.

13. Have you used quotations to good effect? Are all quotations relevant to your line of argument, and is that relevance explained clearly to the reader? Are citations given in full, standard format for all quotations? Have you avoided using so many quotations that your line of argument is interrupted and sinks into paragraph sprawl, piling on citations as a form of scholasticism? As a rule of thumb, use no more than one quote per paragraph.

14. Have you set longer quotations out using indented blocks? Note that for publication, longer quotes (as little as 25 words or more) and all figures,

tables, and charts probably require written permission of both the author and the publisher.

15. Have you used italics for book titles, foreign words, and specialized scientific terms? Have you used a limited amount of underlining to highlight terms or even points deserving emphasis? Have you limited sharply your use of all-capitals? Note that departments and publishers differ, so check (e.g., some publishers bar any italics, preferring only underlining in the manuscript, which gets converted to italics in print).

16. Have you followed convention and used ragged right margins, not full justification?

17. Where you have series of examples or points, have you made good use of numbered or bulleted lists, which are easier for readers to understand?

18. Have you avoided sentences which begin with "There are," "It is," and the like?

19. Have you been careful to stay in the same person and tense consistently? Do not switch unnecessarily from present to past tense (Green "finds" x, but Brown "found" y) or from first to third person ("I" or "we" find, but later "one" also finds).

20. Are you aware that it is customary to use the past tense in your abstract, methodology, and summary of conclusions sections? Check with your advisor on departmental practice regarding verb tense for scientific findings.

21. Are you aware that it is customary to use the present tense in your acknowledgments section?

22. Wherever possible and appropriate, have you worded your statements positively rather than negatively?

23. The first time any abbreviation or acronym is used, have you parenthetically or otherwise spelled out in full what it stands for? Note some departments and publishers require a glossary of abbreviations and acronyms in an appendix.

24. Have you avoided clichés (e.g., "rat race," "acid test," "in a nutshell"), slang ("cool," "bad," "rave"), euphemisms ("passed away" instead of died, "surgical strike" instead of bombing raid), and jargon (each discipline has their own)?

25. Have you avoided mixing metaphors (e.g., "This view once washed across the profession like a mighty wave, but now we have turned that page and gone on to different conclusions." [This mixes ocean and book metaphors.])?

26. Have you used "who" with verbs and "whom" with prepositions? Wrong: "I don't know whom that was." "That is who it was for." Correct: "I don't know who that was." "That was whom it was for."

27. Are all tables, figures, and charts placed near the text that refers to them? Note that for each table, figure, or chart, there should be a reference to it in the text, by number (e.g., "As Figure 12 shows. . . ."), and it should have a

caption. Most publishers prefer all tables, figures, and charts to appear at the end of the manuscript, numbered, each on a separate page, with its caption, and there is a call-out to it in an appropriate location in the text (e.g., "Figure 12 about here"). Some publishers want the caption repeated in the call-out.Do not place text inside a table, chart, or graph. Instead, any such text belongs in the caption or the body of the section itself.

28. In mathematical writing, are all equations numbered?

29. Have you spelled out all numbers in the text of ten or fewer, using Arabic numerals for larger numbers or for any number in a paragraph that contains larger, Arabic numerals?

30. Did you proofread? Twice? Many feel proofreading in hard copy rather than one's computer monitor is more reliable.

31. Throughout, did you present your findings in an assertive and unapologetic manner, avoiding such unnecessary phrases as "I believe that . . . " or "The findings suggest the possibility that. . . ." Readers know your findings are your opinion and are based on your estimates of the probabilities of factors involved. It is better to present your findings in a straightforward, self-confident manner.

IV. RESOURCES ON WRITING FUNDAMENTALS

Online Writing Centers. Numerous colleges and publishers provide online writing centers that cover the fundamentals of college writing. Some good ones include:

Broome Community College Writing Center—http://www.sunybroome.edu/~writecenter
NCSU Online Writing Lab—http://www2.ncsu.edu/ncsu/grammar/
Researchpaper.com's Writing Center—http://www.researchpaper.com/writing.html
Troy State Writing Center—http://trojan.troyst.edu/studserv/html/writingcenter/handouts.html

BIBLIOGRAPHY

General

Atchity, K. (1986). A Writer's Time: A Guide to the Creative Process, from Vision through Revision. New York: L/A House Books/W. W. Norton & Co. A good discussion of the general process of writing a book-length manuscript.

NSF Guide to Proposal Writing (updated annually). Written for undergraduate research grants, but has general applications to writing proposals. http://www.nsf.gov.

Troyka, L. Q. (1995). Quick Access: Reference for Writers. New York: Simon & Schuster. Covers writing fundamentals, including lists of phrases to be avoided.

Zinsser, W. (1988). Writing to Learn. New York: Harper and Row. Emphasis on writing as a learning process, not just a telling process.

Selected Fields: Economics

Field, W. J., Wachter, D. R. and Catanese, A. V. (1985). Alternative ways to teach and learn economics: Writing, quantitative reasoning, and oral communication. J Econ Educ 16:213–217.

Henry, L. H. (1986). Clustering: Writing (and learning) about economics. College Teaching 34:89–93.

Jacobsen, J. P. (1994). Incorporating data collection and written reports in microeconomics. J Econ Educ 25:31–43.

Manzer, J. P. (1991). Writing strategies for basic business and economics. Business Education Forum 45.5:43–45.

Selected Fields: Political Science

Cornacchia, E. J. (1989). Write on! Strategies for the overburdened instructor. Political Science Teacher 2(3):15–16.

Goodman, M. R., and Lanser, S. (1987). The teaching of writing in political science: Defining a stronger disciplinary role. Teaching Political Science 14(2):60–66.

Selcher, W. A., and McClellan, F. E. (1990). Sequential writing assignments in international relations and American government survey courses. Political Science Teacher 3(3):14–16.

Selected Fields: Psychology

Dunn, D. S. (1994). Lessons learned from an interdisciplinary writing course: Implications for student writing in psychology. Teaching of Psychology 21(4):223–227.

Madigan, R., and Brosamer, J. (1990). Improving the writing skills of students in introductory psychology. Teaching of Psychology 17(1):27–30.

McGovern, T. V., and Hogshead, D. L. (1990). Learning about writing, thinking about teaching. Teaching of Psychology 17(1):5–10.

Nodine, B. F., ed. (1989). Psychologists teach writing. [Symposium]. Teaching of Psychology 17(4): 4–61.

Radmacher, S. A., and Latosi-Sawin, E. (1995). Summary writing: A tool to improve student comprehension and writing in psychology. Teaching of Psychology 22: 113–115.

Sternberg, R. J. (1993). For the article writer . . . how to win acceptances by psychology journals: 21 tips for better writing. Am J Mental Retard 97(6):709–712.

Wade, C. (1995). Using writing to develop and assess critical thinking. Teaching of Psychology 22:24–28.

Selected Fields: Sociology

Adams, D. S. (1986). Writing with sociological imagination: A time-line assignment. Teaching Sociology 14(3):200–203.

Anderson, L., and Holt, M. (1990). Teaching writing in sociology: A social constructionist approach. Teaching Sociology 18(2):179–184.

Cadwallader, M. L. and Scarboro, C. A. (1982). Teaching writing in a sociology course: A case study in writing across the curriculum. Teaching Sociology 9(4):359–382.

Green, C. S., and Klug, H. G. (1990). Teaching critical thinking and writing through debates. Teaching Sociology 18(4):462–471.

Kamali, A. (1991). Writing a sociological student term paper: Steps and scheduling. Teaching Sociology 19(4): 506–509.

Karcher, B. C. (1988). Sociology and writing across the curriculum: An adaptation of the sociological journal. Teaching Sociology 16(2):168–172.

Roberts, K. A. (1993). Toward a sociology of writing. Teaching Sociology 21(4):317–324.

14

Fallacies, Reliability, Validity, Significance, and Association

I. THE LOGIC OF THE STORY

Telling a story in an empirical paper, thesis, or dissertation invariably involves at least a minimum exposure to the logic of statistical fundamentals, a topic treated in this chapter. Statistical fallacies need to be avoided. The measures of variables in your model need to be reliable. The research design must be valid. Findings must be significant and must demonstrate appropriate level of association. Without these fundamentals, even the application of sophisticated statistical procedures to good data will not be enough.

A. Fallacies

The most common fallacy in social science is the "ecological fallacy." A term coined by Robinson (1950), the ecological fallacy assumes that individual-level correlations are the same as aggregate-level correlations. Robinson showed that individual-level correlations may be larger, smaller, or even reverse in sign compared with aggregate level correlations. For instance, at the state level there is a strong correlation of race and illiteracy, but this largely disappears at the individual level. The reason is that many African-Americans live in the South, which has high illiteracy for whites as well as minorities. More generally, what is true at one level of aggregation (e.g., states) need not be true at another level (e.g., individuals or nations).

There is no good ''solution'' to the problems posed by the ecological fallacy. The monograph by Langbein and Lichtman (1978) addressed this long ago. They debunked a number of purported procedures, such as ''homogenous grouping'' (restricting analysis to aggregate units that do not vary on variables of interest, as by looking at counties very high in Catholicism and counties very high in Protestantism to assess the individual-level voting behaviors of Catholics and Protestants), which they note has ''disabling defects'' (p. 39).

Langbein and Lichtman found the best of bad alternatives to be ''ecological regression'' (pp. 50–60), a technique that involves using regression to model the effects of grouping. Ecological regression, however, has been criticized as vulnerable to statistical bias. Ecological regression fails whenever factors affecting the dependent variable covary with the independent variable(s). Epstein and O'Halloran (1997) give a good critique of ecological regression, noting, ''For instance,'' (in a study in which the dependent is votes for the minority candidate) ''say that voter registration rates are not constant across districts, but rather minority registration rates increase as the percent of African-American voters in a district rises. In such a case, ecological regression would attribute the rise in the number of votes for the minority candidate to polarized voting, when in fact it is partly due to increased minority registration'' (p. 4). Epstein and O'Halloran propose logit and probit techniques instead of ecological regression. For current reading, see Achen and Shively (1995) and King (1997).

There is a strong temptation to make individual level statements (e.g., ''Being poor increases the chance one will shoplift'') when in fact one has only aggregate-level data (e.g., state data show more shoplifting in states with lower median income). However, such statements are fallacious. There is only one good solution: design research to collect data at the level on which one wishes to make generalizations. In particular, generalizations about individuals require data on individuals.

B. Reliability

In telling your research story, one of the first things you want to communicate is evidence that your measures, on which your entire empirical study is based, are reliable. Reliability is a measure of the extent to which an item, scale, or instrument will yield the same score when administered in different times, locations, or populations, when the two administrations do not differ in relevant variables. Reliability coefficients are forms of correlation coefficients.

In this context, ''scores'' are the subjects' responses to items on an instrument (e.g., a mail questionnaire). Observed scores may be broken down into two components: the true score plus the error score. The error score, in turn, can be broken down into systematic error (nonrandom error reflects some systematic bias, as due, for instance, to the methodology used—hence also called method error) and random error (resulting from random traits of the subjects—hence also called trait error). The greater the error component in relation to the true score component, the lower the reliability, which is the ratio of the true score to the total (true + error) score.

The forms of reliability below measure different dimensions of reliability; thus, any or all might be used in a particular research project.

Split-halves reliability, which measures equivalence, is also called parallel forms reliability or internal consistency reliability. It is administering two equivalent batteries of items that measure the same thing in the same instrument to the same people. The closer the correlation is to 1.0, the more the reliability (the more one may be sure the forms are equivalent).

Test-retest reliability, which measures stability over time, is administering the same test to the same subjects at two points in time. The appropriate length of the interval depends on the stability of the variables that causally determine that which is measured. A year might be too long for an opinion item but appropriate for a physiological measure.

Interrater reliability, which measures homogeneity, is administering the same form to the same people by two or more raters/interviewers so as to establish the extent of consensus on use of the instrument by those who administer it. For categorical data, consensus is measured as number of agreements divided by total number of observations. For continuous data, consensus is measured as the Pearsonian correlation between the ratings for pairs of raters. Since Pearson's r makes no assumptions about rater means, a t-test of the significance of r reveals if interrater means differ. For small samples (< 15), Pearson's r overestimates test-retest correlation and, in this situation, intraclass correlation may be used instead of Pearson's r. Note that raters should be as blind as possible to expected outcomes of the study and should be randomly assigned.

"Cronbach's alpha" is the most common form of reliability coefficient. By convention, alpha should be .70 or higher to retain an item in a scale. Cronbach's alpha is discussed further in the section on standard measures and scales, along with other coefficients such as Cohen's kappa.

"Triangulation" is the attempt to increase reliability by reducing systematic (method) error through a strategy in which the researcher uses multiple methods of measurement (e.g., survey, observation, archival data). If the alternative methods do not share the same source of systematic error, examination of data from the alternative methods gives insight into how individual scores may be adjusted to come closer to reflecting true scores, thereby increasing reliability.

"Calibration" is the attempt to increase reliability by increasing homogeneity of ratings through feedback to the raters, when multiple raters are used. Raters meet in calibration meetings to discuss items on which they have disagreed, typically during pretesting of the instrument. The raters seek to reach consensus on rules for rating items (e.g., defining the meaning of a "3" for an item dealing with job satisfaction). Calibration meetings should not involve discussion of expected outcomes of the study, as this would introduce bias and undermine validity.

C. Validity

A measure may be reliable but not valid, but it cannot be valid without being reliable. That is, reliability is a necessary but not sufficient condition for validity. A study is valid if its measures actually measure what they claim to and if there are no logical errors in drawing conclusions from the data. There are a great many labels for different types of validity, but they all have to do with threats and biases that would undermine the meaningfulness of research. Be less concerned about defining and differentiating the types of validity (researchers disagree on the definitions and types, and yes, they do overlap) and be more concerned about all the types of questions one should ask about the validity of research (researchers agree on the importance of the questions).

1. Internal Validity

Internal validity has to do with defending against sources of bias that would affect the cause-effect process being studied by introducing covert variables. When there is lack of internal validity, variables other than the independent(s) being studied may be responsible for part or all of the observed effect on the dependent variable(s). If no causal phenomenon is under study, internal validity is not at issue.

The Hawthorne effect (experimenter expectation) is a type of internal validity issue. Do the expectations or actions of the investigator contaminate the outcomes? (Named after famous studies at Western Electric's Hawthorne plant, where work productivity improvements were found to reflect researcher attention, not interventions like better lighting).

Mortality bias is a second internal validity issue. Is there an attrition bias, such that subjects later in the research process are no longer representative of the larger initial group? *Selection bias* is a third internal validity issue. How closely do the subjects approach constituting a random sample, in which every person in the population of interest has an equal chance of being selected? When multiple groups are being studied, there can be differential selection of the groups that can be associated with differential biases with regard to history, maturation, testing, mortality, regression, and instrumentation (that is, selection may combine differentially with other threats to validity mentioned on this page). See section on two-stage least squares regression for a discussion of testing for selection bias.

Evaluation apprehension is a fourth internal validity issue. Does the sponsorship, letter of entry, phrasing of the questions, or other steps taken by the researcher suffice to mitigate the natural apprehension people have about evaluations of their beliefs and activities, and to give answers that are designed to make themselves "look good?"

There are also special internal validity problems involving control groups (social interaction threats to validity):

Control awareness. Is the control group aware it is a control group and not receiving the experimental treatment? If so, the control group may exhibit compensatory rivalry, resentful demoralization, or other attitudes and actions that may contaminate study results. Treatment imitation or diffusion is also a type of control awareness invalidity that arises from the control group imitating the treatment or benefiting from information given to the treatment group and diffused to the control group.

Compensatory equalization of treatments. Were those administering the setting pressured, or did they decide on their own, to compensate the control group's lack of the benefits of treatment by providing some other benefit for the control group? Parents may pressure school administrators, for instance, to provide alternative learning experiences to compensate for their children in the control group not receiving the special test curriculum being studied in the experimental group.

Unintended treatments. The Hawthorne effect (see above) is an example in which the experimental group was also receiving the unmeasured "treatment" of researcher attention. However, either the experimental or control group may receive different experiences that constitute unmeasured variables.

Finally, there are special internal validity problems of before-after studies and time series:

Instrumentation change. Variables are not measured in the same way in the before and after studies. A common way for this to occur is when the observer/raters, through experience, become more adept at measurement.

History (intervening events). Events not part of the study intervene between the before and after studies and have an effect. Did some historical event occur that would affect results? For instance, outbreak of a war often solidifies public opinion behind the commander-in-chief and could be expected to affect a study of causes of changes in presidential support in public opinion polls, even if the items had nothing to do with foreign policy.

Maturation. Invalid inferences may be made when the maturation of the subjects between the before and after studies has an effect (e.g., the effect of experience), but maturation has not been included as an explicit variable in the study.

Regression toward the mean. If subjects are chosen because they are above or below the mean, one would expect they will be closer to the mean on remeasurement, regardless of the intervention. For instance, if subjects are sorted by skill and then given a skill test, the high- and low-skill groups will probably be closer to the mean than expected.

Test experience. The before study affects the after study in its own right, or multiple measurement of a concept leads to familiarity with the items and hence a history or fatigue effect.

2. Statistical Validity

Statistical validity has to do with basing conclusions on proper use of statistics. Violation of statistical assumptions is treated elsewhere in the discussion of each specific statistical procedure. In addition, the following general questions may be asked of any study:

Reliability, discussed above. Has the research established the statistical reliability of his/her measures? (A measure is reliable if measurement of the same phenomena at different times and places yields the same measurement.)

Type I errors and statistical significance. A type I error is when the researcher thinks there is a relationship, but there really isn't. If the researcher rejects the null hypothesis, ask these questions:

1. If data are from a random sample, is significance established to be of an appropriate level (usually .05 in social science)?
2. Are significance tests applied to à priori hypotheses, or is a shotgun approach used in which large numbers of relationships are examined, looking a posteriori for significant ones. If the latter, note that one table or relationship in 20 will be found to be statistically significant just by chance alone, by definition of .05 significance.

Type II errors and statistical power. A type II error is when the researcher thinks there is no relationship, but there really is. If the researcher has accepted the null hypothesis, ask these questions:

1. Has the researcher used statistical procedures of adequate power?
2. Does failure to reject the null hypothesis merely reflect small sample size?
3. Interaction and nonlinearity. Has the researcher taken possible interaction effects and nonlinear effects into account? Is there interaction among multiple treatments?
4. Causal ambiguity. Has the researcher misinterpreted the causal direction of relationships, particularly in correlative studies?

3. Construct Validity

Construct validity has to do with the logic of items that comprise measures of social concepts. A good construct has a clear operational definition that allows specific indicators to be selected for it. A poor construct is associated with indicators that may be construed as measuring something other than the construct. Construct validity is also involved in assertion of relationships, as when evidence cited by one researcher to show A is related to B is interpreted by another researcher as evidence that A is related to X, Y is related to B, or even that X is related to Y. Multimethod, multitrait methodologies, discussed below, are considered to have higher construct validity.

4. Convergent Validity

Convergent validity, which is a type of construct validity, refers to the principle that the indicators for a given construct should be at least moderately correlated among themselves. Poor convergent validity among the indicators for a factor may mean the model needs to have more factors.

4. Discriminant Validity

Discriminant validity, also a type of construct validity, refers to the principles that the indicators for different constructs should not be so highly correlated as to lead one to conclude that they measure the same thing. Some researchers use $r = .85$ as a rule-of-thumb cutoff for this assessment. Some researchers use the criterion that the correlations testing convergent validity should be higher than those testing discriminant validity, on the rationale that items measuring the same thing should correlate more highly with themselves than with other things.

5. Face Validity

Face validity has to do with items seeming to measure what they claim to (studies can be internally valid and statistically valid, yet use measures lacking face validity). Are the measures that operationalize concepts ones that seem by common sense to have to do with the concept? Or could there be a naming fallacy? Indicators may display construct validity, yet the label attached to the concept may be inappropriate. Are the labels attached to constructs overly general? For instance, in a small group study of corruption, "monetary incentives" may be used to induce participants to covertly break the rules of a game. The researcher may find "monetary incentives" do not lead to corruption, but what may be involved would be better labeled "small monetary incentives," whereas "large monetary incentives" may have a very different effect.

6. Concurrent Validity

Concurrent validity has to do with the correlation between instrument measurement items and known and accepted standard measures as, for instance, the correlation of coordinates using recreational GPS (global positioning systems) units bought at Radio Shack with coordinates found using commercial mapping-quality GPS units. Likewise, do new measures for a given concept exhibit generally the same direction and magnitude of correlation with other variables as do measures of that concept already accepted within the social science community? For instance, does a new measure of ''alienation'' exhibit the same general correlative behavior as established scales of social anomie? Cross-validation is a type of concurrent validity, asking if the researcher has made efforts to cross-validate subjective items with objective measures where possible.

7. External Validity

External validity has to do with possible bias in the process of generalizing conclusions from a sample to a population, to other subject populations, to other settings, or to other time periods. The question raised is, ''To what population does the researcher wish to generalize his/her conclusions, and is there something unique about the study sample's subjects, the place where they lived/worked, the setting in which they were involved, or the times of the study, that would prevent valid generalization?'' Naturally, when a sample of observations is nonrandom in unknown ways, the likelihood of external validity is low, as in the case of convenience samples.

8. Multi method, multitrait (MMMT) strategies for increasing validity

Monomethod and monotrait biases. Use of a single data-gathering method or a single indicator for a concept may result in bias. Various data-gathering methods have their associated biases (e.g., the yea-saying bias in survey research, where people tell pollsters what they think they want to hear). In the same vein, has the researcher used randomization of items to eliminate order effects of the instrument or established the unimportance of order effects? Likewise, basing a construct like ''work satisfaction'' on a single item dealing with, say, socializing with peers at work, biases the construct toward a particularistic meaning.

In an MMMT validation strategy, the researcher not only uses multiple indicators per concept, but also gathers data for each indicator by multiple methods or from multiple sources. For instance, in assessing the concept of ''tolerance,'' the researcher may have indicators for racial tolerance, religious tolerance, and sexual orientation tolerance, and each may be gathered from the subject, the subject's spouse (assessing tolerance indicators for subject, not spouse), and the subject's parent (assessing tolerance indicators for subject, not parent).

A correlation matrix is created in which both rows and columns reflect the set of three tolerance indicators, grouped in three sets—once for subject data, once for spousal data, and once for parental data.

Convergent validity is assessed by correlations between the same tolerance indicator between two methods (e.g., racial tolerance with subject data and with spousal data). One expects these correlations to be at least moderate to demonstrate convergent validity.

Discriminant validity is assessed by correlations between different indicators across different methods. One expects these correlations to be low to demonstrate discriminant validity.

Common method variance is assessed by correlations between different indicators using the same method. One expects these correlations to be as low as those assessing discriminant validity to demonstrate methodological invariance.

D. Significance

Significance is the percent chance that a relationship found in the data is just the result of an unlucky sample, such that if we took another sample we might find nothing. That is, significance is the chance of a type I error: the chance of concluding we have a relationship when we do not. Social scientists often use the .05 level as a cutoff: if there is 5% or less chance that a relationship is just due to chance, we conclude the relationship is real (technically, we fail to accept the null hypothesis that the strength of the relationship is not different from zero). Significance testing is not appropriate for enumerations or nonrandom samples because it only deals with the chance of type I error based on a random sample. Any relationship, not matter how small, is a true relationship (barring measurement error) for an enumeration. We would like to make inferences for nonrandom samples, but that is impossible.

Confidence limits set upper and lower bounds on an estimate for a given level of significance (e.g., the .05 level). The confidence interval is the range within these bounds. For instance, for normally distributed data, the confidence limits for an estimated mean are the sample mean plus or minus 1.96 times the standard error, as discussed in the section on normal-curve z-tests. As another example, confidence limits are often reported in the media in relation to opinion polls, as when the percentage of Americans who support the president's policies is said to be, say, 60%, plus or minus 3 percentage points. Some researchers recommend reporting confidence limits wherever point (e.g., mean) estimates and their significance are reported. This is because confidence limits provide additional information on the relative meaningfulness of the estimates. Thus, significance has a different meaning when, for example, the confidence interval is the entire range of the data, as compared to the situation in which the confidence interval is only 10% of the range.

Where significance deals with type I errors, power deals with type II errors. A type II error is accepting a false null hypothesis (thinking you do not have a relationship when, in fact, you do). Power is $1 - q$, where q is the chance of making a type II error. Social scientists often use the .80 level as a cutoff: there should be at least an 80% chance of not making a type II error. This is more lenient than the .05 level used in significance testing. Leniency is justified on the ground that greater care should be taken in asserting that a relationship exists (as shown by significance < .05) than in failing to conclude that a relationship exists. Obviously, the .80 level of power is arbitrary, and the researcher must set the level appropriate for his or her research needs. In general, there is a trade-off between significance and power. Selecting a stringent significance level such as .001 will increase the chance of type II errors and thus will reduce the power of the test. However, if two types of significance tests show the same level of significance for given data, the test with the greater power is used. It should be noted that in practice, many researchers do not consider or report the power of the significance tests they use, although they should.

Parametric tests make distributional assumptions, particularly that samples are normally distributed. When these assumptions are met, parametric tests are more powerful than their nonparametric counterparts and are preferable. Common parametric tests are the binomial one-sample test of significance of dichotomous distributions, t-tests of the difference of means, normal-curve z-tests of differences of means and proportions, and F-tests in analysis of variance.

Nonparametric tests do not assume the normal distribution. Common examples are chi-square tests of the significance of crosstabs and goodness-of-fit, Fisher's exact test for 2-by-2 tables with a cell < 5, the one-sample runs test of randomness, the Kolmogorov-Smirnov goodness-of-fit test , various tests for two independent samples (Mann-Whitney U, Wald-Wolfowitz runs, Kolmogorov-Smirnov Z, and Moses extreme reactions tests); tests for more than two independent samples (Kruskal-Wallis, median, and Jonckheere-Terpstra tests); tests for two dependent samples (McNemar, marginal homogeneity, Wilcoxon, and sign tests); tests for more than two dependent samples (Friedman, Kendall's W, and Cochran Q tests); and resampling methods for nonparametric significance estimates (bootstrapping, jackknifing).

Significance testing involves several assumptions about the researcher's data.

1. Random sampling is assumed for inferential statistics (significance testing). "Inferential" refers to the fact that conclusions are drawn about relationships in the data based on inference from knowledge of the sampling distribution characteristics of known common forms of data distribution, notably the bell-shaped normal curve. When significance is reported for enumeration or nonrandom data, such uses should be accompanied by a footnote such as: "Because the present study does not use randomly sampled data, significance tests are not appropriate for inferential analysis. However, significance is reported here as an arbitrary criterion in deference to its widespread use in social science for exploratory analysis of nonrandom data."

2. Sample size is assumed not to be small. Since significance tests reflect both strength of association and sample size, making inference based on small samples may lead to excessive type I errors, even for moderate or strong relationships.

3. Substantive significance should not be assumed merely because statistical significance is demonstrated. For large samples, even very weak relationships may be statistically significant.

4. A priori testing is assumed. That is, the significance tests undertaken should be ones selected a priori based on theory. If a posteriori tests are done, say, on all possible crosstabulations in a dataset to determine which are significant, then for the .05 significance level, one would expect one test in 20 to be a type I error. Put another way, a posteriori testing a nominal alpha significance level of .05 really is testing at an effective level that is much more lenient.

5. Correspondence of significance levels with research purpose is assumed. Specifically, it is inappropriate to set a stringent significance level in exploratory research (a .10 level is acceptable in exploratory research). Likewise, it is inappropriate to set a lenient significance level in confirmatory research (a .10 level is not acceptable in most confirmatory research settings).

6. Intervening and common anteceding variables are absent for purposes of causal inference. The observed significant relationship between A and B may be spurious if they share a common anteceding cause (e.g., ice cream sales and fires appear related, but that is only because they share a mutual anteceding cause—heat of the day). If there is an intervening variable (A causes C, which causes B), the relationship of A to B is indirect.

E. Association

Association refers to a wide variety of coefficients that measure strength of relationship, defined various ways. In common usage, "association" refers to measures of strength of relationship in which at least one of the variables is a dichotomy, nominal, or ordinal. Correlation, which is a type of association used when both variables are interval, is discussed separately. Reliability, which is a type of association used to correlate a variable with itself, usually in assessing interrater similarity on a variable, is also discussed separately.

A relationship can be strongly significant, even when the association of variables is very weak (this may happen in large samples, where even weak associations may be found significant). Also, two variables may be strongly but not significantly associated (this may happen in small samples). That is, significance coefficients reflect not only the strength of association but also sample size. This is why researchers should report measures of both significance and of association.

Where measures of significance test the null hypothesis that the strength of an observed relationship is not different from what would be expected due to the chance of random sampling. Significance coefficients reflect the strength of relationship, sample size, and sometimes other parameters. Therefore, it is possible to have a relationship that displays strong association but is not significant (e.g., all males are Republicans and all females are Democrats, but the sample size is only 8) or a relationship that displays an extremely weak association but is very significant (e.g., 50.1% of males are Republicans compared with 50.0% of females, but sample size is 15,000 and the significance level is .001). Because significance and association are not at all equivalent, researchers ordinarily must report both significance and association when discussing their findings. Note also that significance is relevant only when one has a random sample, whereas association is always relevant to research inferences.

Most *coefficients of association* vary from 0 (indicating no relationship) to 1 (indicating perfect relationship) or -1 (indicating perfect negative relationship). As discussed below, there are various types of "perfect relationship" and various types of "no relationship," however. Which definitions the researcher selects may strongly affect the conclusions to which he or she comes. When particular coefficients are discussed later in this section, their definitions of perfect and null relationships are cited, and this is one important criterion used by researchers in selecting among possible measures of association. If you wish to skip the rather long discussion below, just keep in mind that most, but not all coefficients of association define "perfect relationship" as strict monotonicity and define a "null relationship" as statistical independence.

Specific measures of association. With the exception of eta, when data are mixed by data level, the researcher uses a measure of association for the lower data level. Thus, for nominal-by-ordinal association, one would use a measure for nominal-level association.

Measures of dichotomous association (2-by-2 tables) include percent difference, Yule's Q, Yule's Y, and the risk coefficient. Measures for nominal association include phi, contingency coefficient, Tschuprow's T, Cramer's V, lambda, and the uncertainty coefficient. Eta is a measure for nominal-by-interval nonlinear association. Measures of ordinal association include gamma, Kendall's tau-b and tau-c, and Somers' d. Kappa is an association measure for interrater agreement (rows and columns are the same variable).

For interval variables, one refers to correlation rather than association, but both are measures of strength. Correlation is a bivariate measure of association (strength) of the relationship between two variables. It varies from 0 (random relationship) to 1 (perfect linear relationship) or -1 (perfect negative linear relationship). It is usually reported in terms of its square (r2), interpreted as percent of variance explained. For instance, if r2 is .25, then the independent variable is said to explain 25% of the variance in the dependent variable.

There are several common pitfalls in using correlation. Correlation is symmetrical, not providing evidence of which way causation flows. If other variables also cause the dependent variable, then any covariance they share with the given independent variable in a correlation will be falsely attributed to that independent. Also, to the extent that there is a nonlinear relationship between the two variables being correlated, correlation will understate the relationship. Correlation will also be attenuated to the extent there is measurement error, including use of subinterval data or artificial truncation of the range of the data. Correlation can also be a misleading average if the relationship varies, depending on the value of the independent variable (''lack of homoscedasticity''). Many of these problems apply to measures of association also.

In SPSS, most measures of association are found in the SPSS CROSSTABS module. From the menu, select Statistics, Summarize, Crosstabs. In the ''Crosstabs'' dialog box, click the ''Statistics'' button, then in the ''Crosstabs: Statistics'' dialog box, check the measures you want. However, SPSS does not offer Yule's Q, Yule's Y, or Tschuprow's T. Another SPSS Inc. product, SYSTAT, offers Yule's Q and Yule's Y.

1. Significance in Theory and Practice

Robert Matthews (1999) is among those who have pointed out that findings of significance based on Bayesian inference are not always as reliable as they seem. He cites, for instance, several laboratory studies of medicines for heart attack victims in the 1990s. Clinical trials suggested a clot-busting drug called anistreplase could, for instance, double survival chances. The same level of effect was claimed for magnesium injections, again based on clinical trial data. In 1995, however, studies of actual heart attack victims in hospital wards found no effect for magnesium injection and only a small effect for anistreplase. Another study, comparing actual death rates from 1989 to 1992, after ''wonder'' therapies like thrombolytic therapy, with death rates in 1982 to 1984, before such therapies, found no effect at all of the therapies. The reason for the discrepancy between highly significant results in the laboratory and little or no effect in hospital wards is that the randomization of subjects in laboratory studies does not appear to control for all variables, as theory suggests it should. Instead, in actual hospital situations, other variables appear to mitigate the theoretically ''significant'' effects of certain drugs and therapies. These other variables may include differences between the pool of laboratory patients and the much larger pool of actual heart attack patients in hospitals—a Hawthorne effect of experimentation—high levels of specialization, and eminence of laboratory doctors compared with hospital doctors—a journal preselection-of-articles bias favoring positive results—or other unknown factors.

Matthews notes that significance of findings is not tantamount to validation. The ability to replicate findings in realistic conditions is in many ways a much more important ''test of significance'' than the mathematical coefficients of statistical significance found in any one laboratory or other study. The inferential statistics on which significance testing rests—Bayes' theorem, printed 2 centuries ago in his ''Essay Towards Solving a Problem in the Doctrine of Chances,'' has been equated among some researchers as the scientific method for proving what is "truth." However, the fact is that different researchers using different data can use statistical tests of significance to "prove" different and contradictory findings.

F. Checklist

The "Ethical Guidelines for Statistical Practice" of the American Statistical Association (1999) provide one good checklist for all types of empirical writing. Among their guidelines, some paraphrased here, are those listed below. The ASA considers it professionally unethical not to observe all the points on this checklist!

1. Are statistical protocols clearly defined for the stage of analysis (exploratory, intermediate, or final) *before* looking at the data for that stage?
2. Likewise, are technical criteria to justify the practical relevance of the study determined *before* the research looks at the data?
3. Is sample size determined beforehand, with no adding to the sample after partial analysis of the data?
4. Has the researcher guarded against the possibility that his or her predisposition might predetermine the result?
5. Are data selection or sampling methods used that are designed to assure valid analyses, given the statistical approach selected (often this means random sampling)? Are any problems in following the sampling protocol in practice reported fully?
6. Is the statistical methodology used regarded as standard for the data situation, not yesterday's preferred method, now derogated in favor of newer, better techniques?
7. Does the researcher have adequate statistical and subject-matter expertise? The researcher may need to supplement his or her efforts by adding consultants to the research team.
8. Does the statistical methodology used address the multiple potentially confounding factors in observational studies and use due caution in drawing causal inferences?
9. If a frequentist statistical test is employed, such as bootstrapped estimates of significance, does the researcher recognize that any frequentist statistical test has a random chance of indicating significance when it is not really present?
10. Does the researcher understand that running multiple tests on the same data set at the same stage of an analysis increases the chance of obtaining at least one invalid result?
11. Does the researcher understand that selecting the one "significant" result from a multiplicity of parallel tests poses a grave risk of an incorrect conclusion?

12. Has the researcher disclosed fully all tests of significance, including ones that are inconclusive or contrary to the researcher's findings?
13. Has the researcher disclosed any conflicts of interest? Has the researcher disclosed all financial backers of the research project?
14. Would the researcher's findings stand up to peer review?
15. Where appropriate, have valid alternative statistical approaches been considered in terms of scope, cost, and precision and a justification given for the approach selected?
16. Has the researcher reported statistical and substantive assumptions made in the study, including assessments of the extent to which the study meets assumptions, and consequences for findings of not meeting assumptions?
17. Are the sources of the data reported and their adequacy assessed?
18. Does the researcher report all data cleaning and screening procedures used, including any imputation of missing data?
19. Does the researcher clearly and fully report the steps taken to guard validity?
20. Does the researcher footnote or identify the computer routines used to implement the analytic methods?
21. Are potential confounding variables not included in the study discussed?
22. Where volunteered or other nonrepresentative data are analyzed, are appropriate disclaimers given?
23. Are data shared with the scholarly community so results can be verified through replication?
24. Is the analysis appropriate to the audience? For the general public, convey the scope, relevance, and conclusions of a study without technical distractions. For the professional literature, strive to answer the questions likely to occur to your peers.
25. Is the researcher aware of and observant of rules for the protection of human and animal subjects?
26. Has the researcher estimated needed sample size in advance so as to avoid the use of excessive or inadequate numbers of research subjects?
27. In collecting data, has the researcher avoided or minimized the use of deception?

BIBLIOGRAPHY

Achen, C., and Shively, W. P. (1995). Cross-Level Inference. Chicago: University of Chicago Press.

American Statistical Association (1999). Ethical Guidelines for Statistical Practice. Washington, DC: American Statistical Association, Committee on Professional Ethics. Approved by the Board of Directors, August 7, 1999. Available at http://www.cbs.nl/isi/fundamental.htm.

Campbell, D. T., and Stanley, J. C. Experimental and quasi-experimental designs for research on teaching. In: Gage, N. L., ed. Handbook of Research on Teaching. Chicago: Rand McNally. The seminal article on types of validity.

Cook, T. D., and Campbell, D. T., Quasi-experimentation: Design and Analysis Issues for Field Settings. Boston: Houghton-Mifflin, 1979. Chapter 2 is a classic statement of types of validity.

Ebel, R. L. (1951). Estimation of the reliability of ratings. Psychometrika 16:407–424.

Epstein, D., and O'Halloran, S. (1997). Who needs ecological regression? Measuring the constitutionality of majority-minority districts.'' Midwest Political Science Conference, 1997. Available at http://wizard.ucr.edu/polmeth/working_papers97/epste97.html.

Garson, G. D. (1976). Political Science Methods. Boston: Holbrook Press. Chapter 11 covers most measures of association. See also any standard introductory textbook on statistics associated with survey research.

Haggard, E. A. (1958). Intraclass Correlation and the Analysis of Variance. New York: Dryden.

Henkel, R. E. (1976). Tests of Significance. Thousand Oaks, CA: Sage Publications.

Huttner, H. J., and van den Eeden, P. (1995). The Multilevel Design: A Guide with an Annotated Bibliography. Westport, CT: Greenwood Press. An overview of statistical approaches to problems involving data at multiple levels, such as studies in education with student, classroom, school, and district level data.

King, G. (1997). A Solution to the Ecological Inference Problem. Princeton: Princeton University Press.

Langbein, L. I., and Lichtman, A. J. (1978). Ecological Inference. Series: Quantitative Applications in the Social Sciences, No. 10. Thousand Oaks, CA: Sage Publications. Explores ways of using aggregate data for individual-level models. There are no good answers, but the authors outline ''ecological regression'' as the best of bad alternatives.

Liebetrau, A. M. (1983). Measures of Association. Quantitative Applications in the Social Sciences Series No. 32. Newbury Park, CA: Sage Publications.

Litwin, M. S. (1995). How to Measure Survey Reliability and Validity. Survey Kit Series, Vol. 7. Thousand Oaks, CA: Sage Publications.

Matthews, R. (1999). Factions: The use and abuse of subjectivity in scientific research. Paper, European Science and Environment Forum, 4 Church Lane, Barton, Cambridge CB3 7BE, UK.

McNemar, Q. (1969). Psychological Statistics. 4th ed. New York: Wiley, p. 322. Covers F tests for intraclass correlation.

Robinson, W. S. (1950). Ecological correlations and the behavior of individuals. Am Sociol Rev 15:351–357. Coined the term ''ecological fallacy'' and helped overturn the then-common practice of using aggregate data for individual-level models.

15

Datagraphics

I. INTRODUCTION

Although paper, thesis, and dissertation writing is far from pictorial journalism, graphics have an important role to play in "telling the story," even in serious research. Moreover, graphics can be used effectively at many points in the outline—from presentation of one's thesis and hypotheses, to representation of one's research design, to visualization of findings based on one's data. Selecting the proper form of data visualization can be critical to the effective communication of the author's thesis. In fact, data visualization has become a major field of study in its own right.[1]

II. DATA VISUALIZATION

Data visualization has developed greatly in the last two decades, particularly with the advent of personal computers and their capacity for interactive 3-D representation and animation. This poses a problem for writers of papers, theses, and dissertations because data may now be represented better on computers than on paper. It is becoming common for journal and other scholarly websites to maintain superior graphics on the Internet with references to them from the print version of articles.

Data visualization includes datagraphics of the conventional types—charts, plots, diagrams, and figures—but it also includes rotatable three-dimensional representations of data and the possibility of using animation to represent a fourth dimension, such as time. However sophisticated the data representation, the cardinal rule of data visualization is that the distances depicted in the representation should correspond proportionately to the variable magnitudes being represented. Most instances of ''lying with graphs'' involve violation of this rule. Tufte (1983: 57) refers to the ''lie factor'' in graphs, which is the ratio of the size of an effect in the graphical representation to the size of the effect in the actual data. For instance, he gives an example of a *New York Times* graph that showed the mandated fuel economy increase in cars going from 18 miles per gallon to 27.5 (a 53% increase). In contrast, the line representing 27.5 in the graph is 783% larger than the line representing the 18. Thus, for this graph the lie factor is (783/53) = 14.8. Had the line representing the 27.5 been only 53% larger than the line representing the 18, then the lie factor would have been (53/53) = 1.0, where 1.0 is scientifically accurate graphical representation. Tufte (1997) further observes that graphic abusers may emulate the operating principles of a stage magician: never explain what is to be done; never do the same trick twice; and obscure small important movements with large unimportant ones.

Data visualization can involve opportunities for graphic abuse, especially with regard to use of axes, data selectivity, and measurement adjustment. Common abuses of axes inviting misinterpretation include (1) not starting the origin at 0, as the viewer normally assumes, but rather presenting only an attenuated range of the data so as to exaggerate effect sizes; or (2) starting the origin at 0, not using equal intervals as tick marks, but rather allowing different scales at different ranges of the axis, so as to exaggerate effect sizes for selected ranges. A third type of graphic abuse is to switch the X and Y axes. The informed viewer is accustomed to the horizontal X axis representing the causal variable and the vertical Y axis representing the effect variable. Reversing these, for example to obtain a steeper and more dramatic line, can promote misinterpretation rather than helpful data visualization.

Graphic abuse is also possible based on selectivity of the points represented. A famous and tragic example of this concerned analysis of the O-rings used in the fuel system of the ill-fated 1986 Challenger spacecraft. Later analysis showed O-ring failure at low temperatures to have been the likely source of the Challenger disaster. In prelaunch analysis of O-ring failure and ambient temperature, NASA had discarded data points involving no O-ring failure, all of them involving mild ambient temperatures. O-ring failures occurred at a range of temperatures, but the correlation of failure with low temperature was difficult to spot (and was not spotted) in the absence of all the data. Had all data points been retained, data visualization would have shown much more clearly the association of O-ring failure with low ambient temperature. All forms of data visualization are subject to abuse if only selected data ranges, years, areas, etc., are included in the dataset, because the viewer lacks the proper basis for comparison.

Measurement adjustment, or lack of it, can be a third area of graphic abuse. Perhaps the most common example is the failure to represent money value in inflation-adjusted terms. Unadjusted graphs of monetary value routinely show increasing effect sizes but the effect may disappear once inflation is taken into account. Government agencies not infrequently change their methods and basis of measurement; ignoring that can easily lead to profound misrepresentations of data. For instance, depicting changes in population density of the United States in the 19th century, ignoring the geographic expansion of the country, would be a form of graphic abuse. When multiple variables are being represented, measured in different magnitudes (e.g., education 0–26 years, income 0–billions), visualization of relationships can be difficult. Standardized data, in which all data points result from subtracting the mean and dividing by the standard deviation, make comparison across variables easier to interpret validly.

Graphics themselves can be their own form of graphic abuse. Three-dimensional representations are commonly used because of their media-worthiness, but empirical tests on human subjects routinely show that two-dimensional data representations are interpreted more validly than three-dimensional representations of the same data. Likewise, a typical form of graphic exaggeration is the use of mirrored images, where bars, icons, or other images used to represent an amount are mirrored immediately beneath in some way (e.g., as a shadow or to contain the label), conveying a subjective impression of doubling effect sizes.

A. Data Visualization in Conceptualization

1. Conceptual Spaces

Conceptual spaces graphically depict the intersection of important variables in the research study at hand (Figure 1). This intersection forms categories, which may be types of people, relationships, or other phenomena being explained in the study.

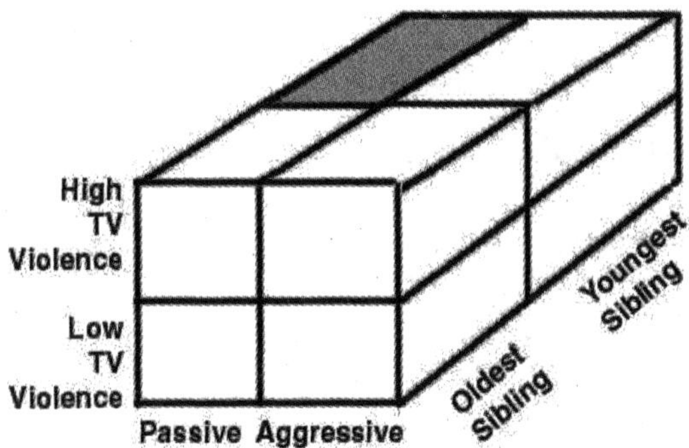

FIGURE 1 Example of conceptual space.

Of course, unlike the three-dimensional figure above, conceptual spaces may have a different dimensionality. In fact, two-by-two conceptual spaces are perhaps the most common form of "theoretical framework" in research.

B. Datagraphics in Research Design

1. Method Flow Charts

Method flow charts are used to depict the chronological logic of procedures discussed in the methodology section of one's work (Figure 2). Like other flow charts, outcomes are represented as rectangles, processes as diamonds, and sequences as lines or arrows.

Use of a method flow chart may seem redundant inasmuch as the research method processes and outcomes will be discussed in text, but most readers, faculty included, will find it easier to follow the methodological discussion if it is also visualized in flow chart format.

C. Datagraphics in Visualization of Findings

1. Histograms

Histograms represent a single variable. However, an array of histograms can be used to represent a second variable. *Pie chart* presentation is an alternative univariate graphical representation.

A profile or polygon plot is a histogram in which the bars have been replaced by a line connecting the midpoints where the top of the bars would be,

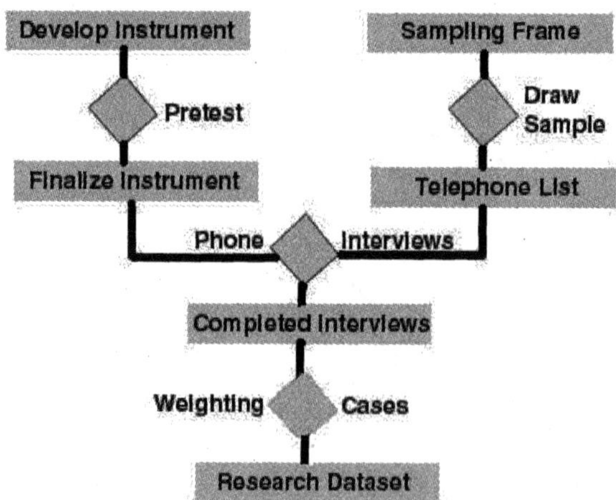

FIGURE 2 Method flow chart.

thus forming a polygon. This is appropriate when the categorical variable represented by the bars is actually a categorized continuous variable (such as income ranges).

A star plot is a variant of the profile plot for bivariate visualization. For k values of a categorical variable (e.g., regions), draw k equally spaced rays emanating from a point, such that the length of the line reflects the value of a second variable (e.g., median family income). Connecting the endpoints of the rays creates the ''star'' polygon, which gives this type of plot its name.

2. Cross-tabulations

Tables are one of the simplest forms of data display. Note that it is customary that the rows are the dependent variable and the columns are the independent. Moreover, percentages should add to 100% in the direction of the independent (column) variable. To do otherwise is to confuse the reader.

3. Stem and Leaf Displays

Stem and leaf displays attempt to go beyond the insights provided by simple bar charts and histograms by using data to literally build frequency bars, thereby providing more information. For instance, in a study of age of first marriage, we may find people married at a range of ages from, say, 14 to 75, though with a distinct skew toward younger ages. If we take the first digit of age (e.g., ''2'' for people in their 20s) as the ''stem'' and the remaining digit as the ''leaf'' we can construct a display such as the following:

Age at First Marriage

Stem	Leaf
1	4566777888899999
2	0000000111112222222222222233333334444455555566666777788889999
3	00000111112222223334444455566777889
4	000011233445789
5	12238
6	34
7	1

The length of the leaf bar displays the same information as a frequency distribution: in this case, that most people sampled marry in their 20s, as indicated by the ''2'' stem value for the longest leaf bar. Unlike the usual histogram, however, the actual values of the data can be read by combining the stem and leaf values. In this illustration, the two people who first married in their 60s were ages 63 and 64, for instance.

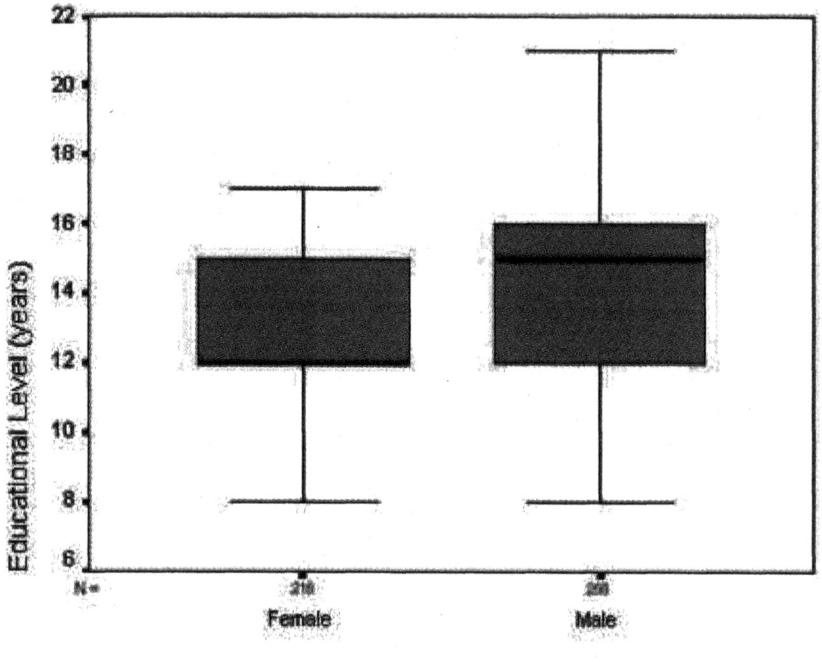

FIGURE 3 Box plots.

4. Box Plots

Box plots (as shown in Figure 3) are a way of displaying the distribution of a single variable. There are many variants. In one version, the box plot is a bracket followed by a line, a box, a dot within the box, another line, and an end bracket. The brackets and the line represent the low and high values (the range) of the variable. The box shows the one standard deviation limits. The dot in the box shows the mean. In the SPSS version, each box shows the brackets are still the extreme values, but the box is the interquartile range and the line (not dot) within the box is the median. For normal distributions, which are not strongly skewed, the box should be more or less in the center of the box plot.

5. Points in Property Space

Two-dimensional data may be represented as points on a two-dimensional plot, with or without grid lines, either with the origin (0 on both dimensions) in the lower left or in the middle (to show all four quadrants), suitable when negative values are present. It is customary for the dependent variable to be the vertical y-axis, and for the first independent variable to be the horizontal x-axis. In addition to position, color, size, shape, orientation, and texture may be used to represent up to five additional polytomous dimensions, although the more dimensions, the less effective the graph for visualization purposes.

Where the points in space form a series, they may be connected to form a *line graph*, showing the trend on one variable by another (Figure 4).

A *difference line chart*, as shown in Figure 4, depicts two variables with respect to a third. In this example, current salary and beginning salary are depicted in relation to educational level.

6. Scatterplots with Regression or Smoothed Average Lines

The addition of regression lines or Loess smoothed average lines can aid the viewer in understanding trends in the point data, although such lines may invite unwarranted extrapolation outside the range of the data or unwarranted interpolation between discrete data points. Axes can be the logs of variables to represent curvilinear relationships. Note that scatterplots are two-dimensional representations and can mislead the reader when understanding the impact of a third variable is critical. That is, a scatterplot of X-Y pairs of observations ignores any pattern

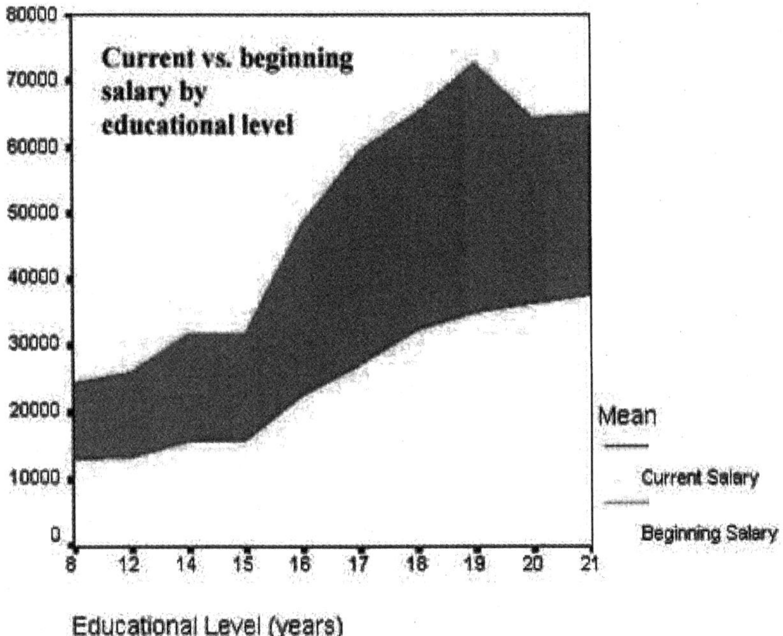

FIGURE 4 Difference line chart.

arising from the association of third variable Z with X or Y. Imagine a three-dimensional space with X, Y, and Z axes, revealing a pattern extending along Z. Then imagine rotating the space to view the X and Y axes and flatten the space to two dimensions, causing the pattern associated with Z to disappear. A number of approaches are used to take account of multidimensional data (Figure 5):

(a) Scatterplots with Plotting Symbols Instead of dots, a scatterplot can use symbols to represent a third dimension (e.g., the letters e, w, n, s to represent the variable "region").

(b) Three-Dimensional Scatterplots. It is possible to draw a three-dimensional representation of a scatterplot on a two-dimensional surface. This is done by taking a perspective drawing of a set of X, Y, Z coordinates and viewing the resulting cube from an angle above and to the side (Figure 6). It is hard to judge depth in such representations, a problem often addressed by making the dots larger in the foreground, nearer the origin. One can also use drop lines to the X, Y surface to show the X, Y location of the X, Y, Z points.

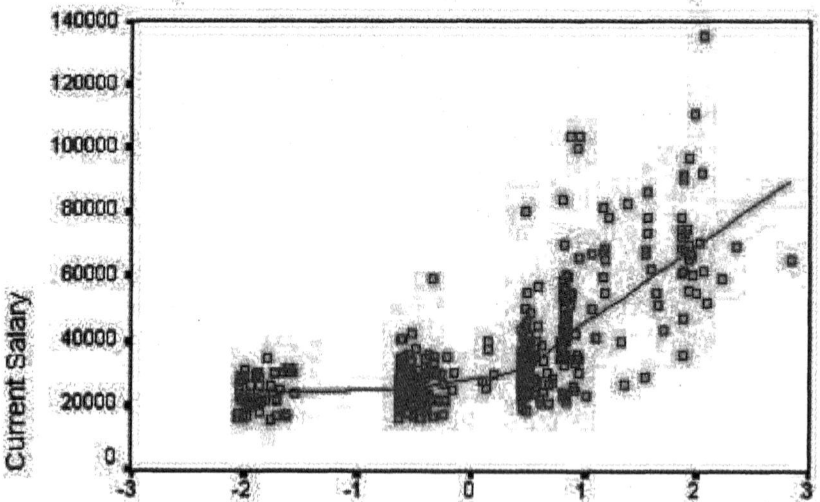

FIGURE 5 Scatterplot with Loess smoothing line.

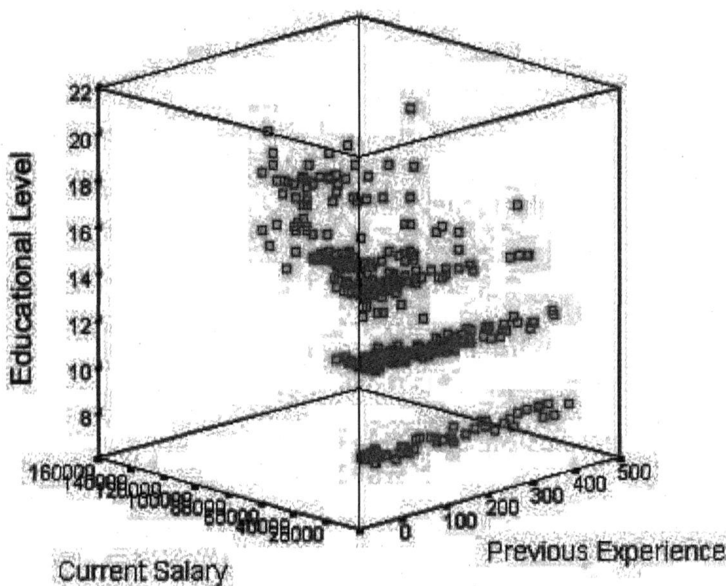

FIGURE 6 Three-dimensional scatterplot with full frame.

*(c) **Bubble Plots.*** Bubble plots are an alternative way of representing a third dimension in a scatterplot. Instead of dots, open circles (bubbles) are used to represent a third dimension, with the size of the bubble representing the magnitude of a third variable Z (Figure 7). If X causes Y and Z has no effect, large and small bubbles will be on both sides of the X, Y regression line. If Z has an effect on Y and X does too, the larger bubbles will be above the X, Y regression line. If Z has an effect and X does not, there will be a cloud of bubbles rather than a line, with the larger bubbles higher on Y.

*(d) **Glyph Plots.*** Five variables can be represented by this extension of scatterplots with plotting symbols. If an open circle is used in place of a dot, the size of the circle can represent a third variable. The length of a line segment emanating from the middle of the circle can represent a fourth variable. The direction of the line segment, with the 12:00 position representing 0, can represent a fifth variable. Glyph plots are sometimes called "van plots." They are effective only when the number of cases is small enough not to lead to excessive overplotting of symbols.

*(e) **Scatterplot Matrices.*** A scatterplot matrix is an array of X-Y scatterplots used to represent any number of variables (Figure 8). Variable names appear in the diagonal cells of a table, each row or column of which is a different variable.

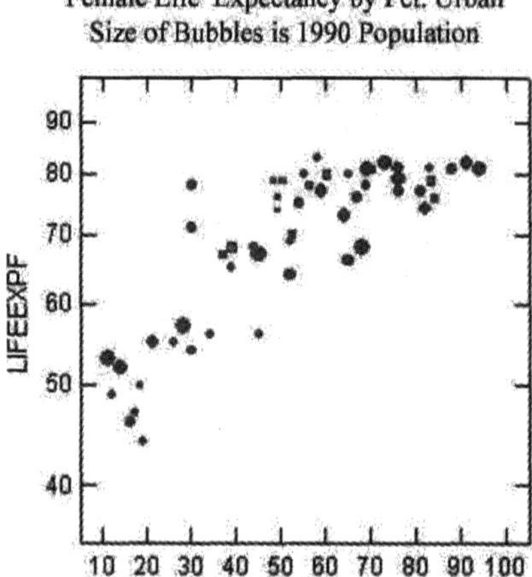

Figure 7 Systat bubble plot.

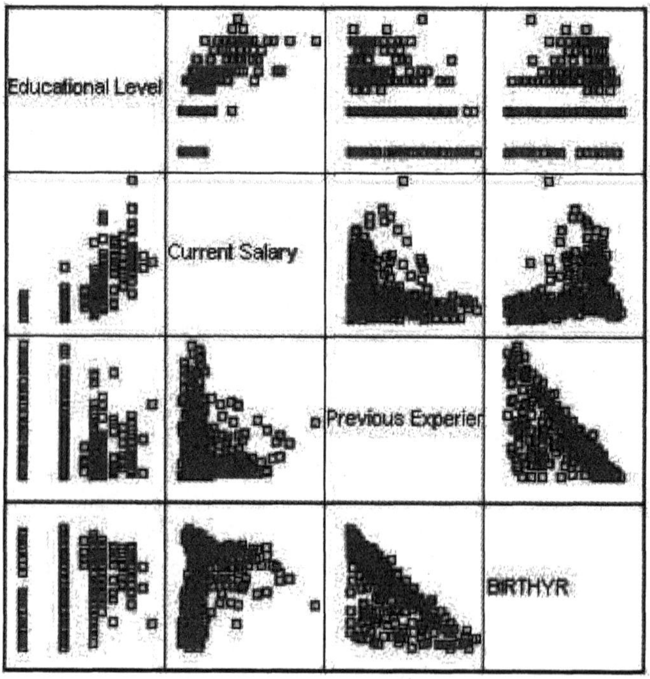

Figure 8 Scatterplot matrix.

The variable names serve as the axis labels for the corresponding scatterplots that appear in all the off-diagonal cells. Often output drops tick marks and scale values, showing only the dot scatterplots themselves. Using scatterplot matrices, it is easy to see which pairs of variables are correlated, but it is still hard to discern interaction effects involving multiple variables. The triangle above the diagonal contains the same information as the triangle below the diagonal, except with axes reversed, so some researchers just display the lower triangle plus the diagonal labels, and this is called a ''half-matrix.'' However, researchers such as Jacoby (1997: 42) argue that seeing the full matrix promotes understanding among one's readers.

(f) Conditioning Plots. In the case of a categorical control variable Z, a conditioning plot shows the X, Y scatterplot for each value (condition) of Z, arraying the scatterplots in a panel (row), also called a ''casement display.'' In the case of a continuous control variable, Z must be sliced into intervals. This is tricky, as too broad or too narrow slices will fail to reveal the effect of the Z variable. One approach is to use overlapping slices to make sure a full range of slicing possibilities is represented.

(g) Coplots. Coplots are conditioning plots for continuous variables, except that a ''given panel'' appears above the scatterplot panels. The given panel shows the portion of the range for each slice of the conditioning (control) variable for the corresponding scatterplot. The ranges are depicted as line segments, with the width of the given panel representing the entire range of Z. The left-most line segment is the range of the slice for the left-most scatterplot in the ''dependence panel'' containing the actual scatterplots, and so on. If there are too many slices for one dependence panel, the panels will be stacked, and the given panel will be divided into an equal number of corresponding panels.

A *two-way coplot* handles two conditioning variables by creating a matrix of corresponding plots instead of a single panel.

(h) Trellis Displays. A trellis display is a type of conditioning plot, similar to coplots, but there is no ''given panel.'' Instead there is a strip label on top of each dependence panel, with a darkened bar representing the slice depicted by the scatterplot. That is, the top left-right borders of each X-Y plot in the panel is taken as the range of Z, and within this range a bar indicates the range of the slice of Z depicted by that scatterplot.

(i) Biplots or Vector Plots. In a biplot, all variables are standardized. The mean of all variables is taken as the origin for a set of vectors (rays) representing the variables under analysis. The angle of any two vectors corresponds to their degree of correlation, with a right angle indicating zero correlation, acute angles representing positive correlation (bringing the vectors closer), and obtuse angles

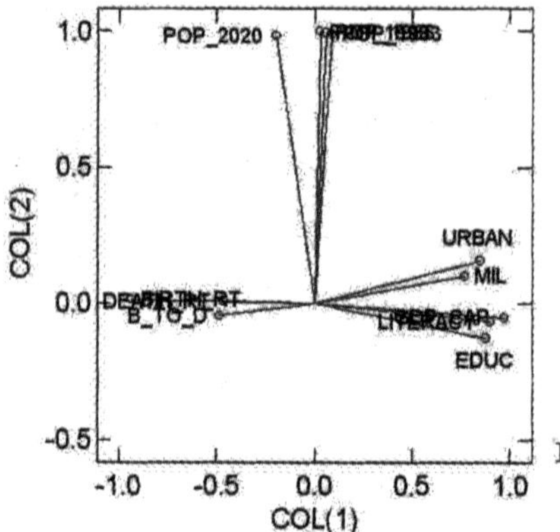

Figure 9 Systat vector plot.

representing negative correlation (Figure 9). The length of the vectors corresponds to the percent of variance accounted for in that variable by all the other variables in the plot. The points are cases as in other scatterplots, but they are located further from the biplot origin when they have higher values on the vectors, and closer to vectors with which they are most associated.

(j) Line Graphs. Line graphs are similar to points in property space, but the points are connected, indicating the interpolation is permitted to estimate dimension values at points not actually measured.

(k) Isometric Surfaces. Isometric (fishnet) surfaces are commonly used to represent three dimensions. The three-dimensional aspect can mean that high front values obscure viewing of values further to the back of the representation. However, this problem disappears with modern surface mapping software, which supports user-determined viewing angles and rotations, enabling viewing of the entire surface.

D. Software for Data Visualization

All major statistical programs, such as SPSS, Systat, SAS, S-Plus, Stata, and IBM Visualization Data Explorer, have extensive data visualization features, as do most spreadsheets. For instance, SPSS does basic histograms, box plots, scatterplots with regression lines or Loess smoothing lines, plots with multiple symbols for categorical variables, three-dimensional scatterplots, and scatterplot matrices. SAS also does biplots. Systat has some of the most extensive graphics capabilities, doing glyphs and bubble plots. S-Plus does coplots. No one package does everything, although with each new software version, each package is more complete. Hundreds of other packages illustrate one or another type of data visualization. The output of almost all packages can be cleaned and improved by first moving the datagraphic into an actual graphics package, of which Adobe Photoshop is the industry leader and choice of professionals. A few selected packages are summarized below.

1. SPSS Diamond

SPSS Diamond is a visualization tool that goes beyond three-dimensional graphs by using color, shapes of data points, and angles to express information at higher dimensions. It supports, for example, fractal foam plots in which the center circle represents the main dependent (e.g., IBM stock price) and the location of other shapes represent related variables (e.g., other stocks), whereas the shape, size, distance, and tilt of surrounding shapes indicate other characteristics (e.g., variation in stock prices and the shape of its distribution). Diamond was developed by the Exploratory Data Visualization Group at IBM Research Division's T.J. Watson Research Center in Yorktown Heights, New York, but is distributed by SPSS. SPSS Diamond can read SPSS data files as well as SYSTAT, BMDP, SAS, Excel, Lotus, dBase, and ASCII formats.

2. SAS Graphics Modules

SAS/Graph is SAS's base graphics module, featuring extensive graphics (e.g., dot charts with error bars, bubble charts). At this writing, a new version called *SAS/Graph Multidimensional Charts* was in the experimental release stage. Multidimensional Data Visualization Version 7 SAS/AF Objects is an SAS module for interactive multidimensional bar charts, histograms, pie charts, and more. SAS/SpectraView is also an interactive multidimensional data visualization tool. One can create geometric data models using three-dimensional volumes with cutaway capabilities, isometric surfaces, two- and three-dimensional charts, stacked contours, cutting planes, and more, with all models subject to user scaling and rotation. One can concurrently view several models using four display windows and rotate and zoom each view, either independently or collectively, to change viewing perspective and to aid in data analysis.

3. Slicer-Dicer

Slicer-Dicer is data visualization software for data in three or more dimensions. It creates arbitrary orthogonal and oblique slices, rectilinear blocks and cutouts, isosurfaces, and projected volume depictions of the researcher's data. One can also generate animation sequences featuring continuous rotation, moving slices, blocks, parametric variation such as time animation, oblique slice rotation, and varying transparency. Scaling and rotation are controllable by the user. The accompanying CD-ROM includes hundreds of megabytes of sample data, including portions of the National Library of Medicine Visible Man data set. For information, go to http://www.slicerdicer.com/. For illustrations of Slicer-Dicer output, go to http://www.slicerdicer.com/gallery.html to find examples of astrophysical jet animation, global winds simulation, seismic data, the visible man (including animated versions), ocean temperature, and more.

4. VR Charts

VRCharts is a three-dimensional ''virtual reality'' data visualization product. The viewer can ''fly'' over, under, around, and through charts in real time, interactively. Two companion products, VR Presenter and VRPlayer, allow VRCharts visualizations to be integrated into Microsoft PowerPoint presentations, the leading slide-show presentation package. The VRPlayer module allows virtual reality slide shows created by the other components to be played back in conjunction with PowerPoint. For information, go to http://www.vrcharts.com/.

E. Checklist

1. Have you considered that data visualization will make your statistical arguments more compelling and will even aid your own understanding of your data?

2. Have you selected separate, appropriate forms of data representation for the univariate, bivariate, and multivariate portions of your statistical presentation rather than, say, relying on univariate histograms to make your multivariate argument?

3. Have you considered whether to standardize your data before plotting? Standardization (subtracting the mean, dividing by the standard deviation, so scores have a mean of 0 and a standard deviation of 1.0) is desirable when you want to control for differences in means and variances between variables. For instance, using standardized policy data would keep education on a par with sanitation expenditures, whereas in unstandardized terms, education expenditures would dominate the histogram. With unstandardized data, one would be viewing the absolute expenditures on different local policy arenas. With standardized date, one would be viewing which localities were relatively high or low on a policy area, controlling for differences in mean expenditure (controlling for the fact that large cities spend more on everything compared to small cities).

ENDNOTES

1. Leading forums for research on data visualization include the Association for Computer Machinery's Siggraph conferences and journals and conferences, the IEEE Visualization conference and related publications, and Eurographics.

BIBLIOGRAPHY

Arnheim, R. (1960). Visual Thinking. Berkeley: University of California Press.

Cleveland, W. S. (1993). Visualizing Data. New Jersey: Hobart Press.

Friedhoff, R. M., and Benzon, W. (1989). Visualization: The Second Computer Revolution. New York: Harry N. Abrams, Inc.

Globus, A., and Raible, E. (1994). 14 Ways to say nothing with scientific visualization. IEEE Computer 27(7):86–88.

Haber, R. N., ed. (1969). Information-Processing Approaches to Visual Perception. New York: Holt, Rinehart and Winston, Inc.

Jacoby, W. G. (1997). Statistical Graphics for Visualizing Univariate and Bivariate Data. Thousand Oaks, CA: Sage Publications. This summary was written with social scientists in mind but is broadly relevant.

Kulikowski, J. J., Walsh, V., and Murray, I. J. (1991). Limits of Vision. Boston: CRC Press Inc.

Nielson, G. M., Hagen, H., and Muller, H. (1997). Scientific Visualization: Overviews, Methodologies, Techniques. Washington, DC: IEEE Computer Society.

Thalmann, D., ed. (1990). Scientific Visualization and Graphics Simulation. New York: John Wiley and Sons.

Tufte, E. R. (1983). The Visual Display of Quantitative Information. Cheshire, CT: Graphics Press. Tufte is by far the leading authority on data visualization in social science, and this is the work that established his reputation.

Tufte, E. R. (1990). Envisioning Information. Cheshire, CT: Graphics Press. This volume covers maps, layering, interaction effects, and graphics for the display of categorical data.

Tufte, E. R. (1997). Visual Explanations. Cheshire, CT: Graphics Press. This third volume covers depiction of cause-effect relationships and narratives, including coverage of the use and abuse of scale in animations and simulations, such as the NASA Venus fly-over simulation, which exaggerated the vertical dimension by a factor of two.

16

Research Ethics

I. RESEARCH ETHICS

Research ethics have traditionally been taken for granted. In recent years, however, the academic community recognized this as a mistake. Today, ethical training is a component of professional education required by the accrediting commissions of most disciplines. Courses on ethics proliferate, as do regulations issued by funding agencies. It is likely that the beginning researcher who gives no systematic forethought to ethics will neglect one or more of the guidelines discussed in this chapter. In contrast, scrupulous attention to ethical guidelines enhances the credibility of the researcher and lends further credence to his or her findings. Thus having explicit, high ethical standards is in the researcher's self-interest, as well as being in the interest of the scholarly community as a whole.

A. Conflicts of Interest

A conflict of interest is a clash between the researcher's concern for the public interest and his or her private interests or allegiances.[1] For instance, it would be a conflict of interest if the researcher used his or her research to further personal interests, which might conflict with the public interest. The researcher must be very careful regarding outside affiliations or relationships that could affect the objectivity of his or her research judgments. Gifts or favors from those being researched could affect the objectivity or integrity of the researcher's contribution and are not to be accepted.

The subject of conflicts of interest contains many gray areas. Many scientists receive grant funding from corporations or agencies that have vested interests in outcomes or have a clear point of view regarding conclusions. This has been a common problem with medical research and pharmaceutical company funding, for instance. Negative findings may lead to lack of funding for future projects, creating a conflict of interest that entices researchers to put findings in "the best possible light" or even suppress findings contrary to the interests of the funder. In recent years, some funding sources have even required approval of any publications emanating from research they fund, raising very serious ethical questions. Variations on such problems are widespread. Another arena has to do with classified military research, in which scientific studies are not held to the same standard of peer review as in civilian research. Even social scientists surveying government agencies, nonprofit groups, and private sector firms may find themselves under pressure to put things in the best possible light, not for funding reasons but simply so that they will not find access closed to them in future surveys. Another conflict of interest in this gray area is when graduate students find themselves putting things in the best light to conform more closely to the orientations of their thesis advisor or members of their doctoral committee. In general, if the researcher finds himself or herself putting things in the best light, there is probably a conflict of interest ethics problem.

Ethical behavior includes the obligation to present the appearance of being ethical. Thus, for instance, nepotism is unethical, as in hiring one's spouse in a research project, even if the spouse is fully qualified for the job. Likewise, the researcher is expected to recuse himself or herself from peer review of manuscripts arising from his or her own academic institution, even if he or she would, in fact, give a thorough and honest opinion. On the other hand, restricting the choice of research assistants in a grant project to one's own institution is considered acceptable, as is refusing to distribute research data to other scholars before exercising the right to first publication.

B. Misconduct

The National Science Foundation (NSF) defines misconduct as (1) fabrication, falsification, plagiarism, or other serious deviation from accepted practices in proposing, carrying out, or reporting results from activities funded by NSF; or (2) retaliation of any kind against a person who reported or provided information about suspected or alleged misconduct and who has not acted in bad faith (NSF 1991:22287). The Public Health Service defines misconduct as "fabrication, falsification, plagiarism, or other practices that seriously deviate from those that are commonly accepted within the scientific community for proposing, conducting, or reporting research. It does not include honest error or honest differences in interpretations or judgments of data" (PHS 1989: 32449).

In 1989, the Committee on Science, Engineering, and Public Policy (COSEPUP) of the National Academy of Sciences (NAS), the National Academy of

Engineering, and the Institute of Medicine (IOM) initiated a major study on scientific responsibility and the conduct of research. This committee defined "misconduct in science" as fabrication, falsification, or plagiarism, in proposing, performing, or reporting research. Misconduct was not defined to include errors of judgment; errors in the recording, selection, or analysis of data; differences in opinions involving the interpretation of data; or misconduct unrelated to the research process. Fabrication was defined as making up data or results. Falsification is changing data or results. Plagiarism, of course, is using the ideas or words of another person without giving appropriate credit.

There is no disagreement that fabrication, falsification, and plagiarism are forms of research misconduct. However, there *is* disagreement about such phrases as "other serious deviation from accepted practices," as this could be construed to bar creative, nonconventional approaches to science. Some definitions of misconduct have included "deception," but researchers may object that some forms of deception are appropriate in and necessary to certain types of experiments in psychology and other disciplines. Furthermore, scientists should not be penalized for posing hypotheses that prove to be wrong, or even for making arguments that are considered fallacious by other scientists or prove to be empirically false. Nonetheless, the researcher should be aware that many practices besides fabrication, falsification, and plagiarism can be considered misconduct.

C. Protection of Human Subjects

In 1991, some 16 federal agencies formally adopted a set of regulations on the protection of human subjects, included in the Code of Federal Regulations, Title 45, Part 46 (45 CFR 46). These regulations require review of all research protocols involving human subjects to minimize risks, ensure risks are reasonable in relation to anticipated benefits, and ensure informed consent to maintain the rights and welfare of subjects. The review is normally conducted by a formally constituted Institutional Review Board (IRB) at one's academic institution. A privacy statement, to be given to all human subjects, is usually part of the IRB application. The privacy statement assures subjects of confidentiality and apprises them candidly of any risks of participating in the study at hand.

Taking the National Science Foundation guidelines as typical, the relevant rules are these (see http://www.nsf.gov/search97cgi/vtopic):

> 207 Protection of Human Research Subjects Under NSF-Supported Projects
> 207.2 Policy
> a. The protection of the rights and welfare of human subjects involved in research, development, and related activities supported by NSF funds is the responsibility of the performing institution regardless of the funding mechanism.

207.3 Exemptions

The following categories of research activities involving human subjects are exempt from the Common Rule regulations:

a. Research is exempt if conducted in established or commonly accepted educational settings, involving normal educational practices, such as research on regular and special education instructional strategies, or research on the effectiveness of or the comparison among instructional techniques, curricula, or classroom management methods.

b. Research involving the use of educational tests (cognitive, diagnostic, aptitude, achievement) is exempt if information taken from these sources is recorded in such a manner that subjects cannot be identified, directly or through identifiers linked to the subjects.

c. Research involving survey or interview procedures is exempt. However, research involving survey or interview procedures is not exempt from Institutional Review Board (IRB) review where all of the following conditions exist:

responses are recorded in such a manner that the human subjects can be identified, directly or through identifiers linked to the subjects;

the subject's responses, if they became known outside the research, could reasonably place the subject at risk of criminal or civil liability or be damaging to the subject's financial standing or employability;

and the research deals with sensitive aspects of the subject's own behavior, such as illegal conduct, drug use, sexual behavior, or use of alcohol.

Nevertheless, all research involving survey or interview procedures is exempt, without exception, when the respondents are elected or appointed public officials or candidates for public office.

d. Research involving the observation (including observation by participants) of public behavior is exempt. However, this category of research is not exempt where all of the following conditions exist:

observations are recorded in such a manner that the human subjects can be identified, directly or through identifiers linked to the subjects;

the observations recorded about the individual, if they became known outside the research, could reasonably place the subject at risk of criminal or civil liability or be damaging to the subject's financial standing or employability;

and the research deals with sensitive aspects of the subject's own behavior such as illegal conduct, drug use, sexual behavior, or use of alcohol.

e. Research involving the collection or study of existing data, documents, records, pathological specimens or diagnostic specimens is exempt. This exemption is applicable if these sources are publicly available or if the information is recorded by the investigator in such a manner that subjects cannot be identified, directly or through identifiers linked to the subjects.

207.4 Responsibilities

a. Performing institutions. Except for research that is exempted (see 207.3, above), no human subjects may be involved in any NSF-supported project until the project has been reviewed and approved by the appropriate IRB as provided in the Common Rule. In the event research funded by NSF is undertaken without the intention of involving human subjects, but it is later proposed to use human subjects in the research, the research shall first be reviewed and approved by an IRB.

b. Research by unaffiliated individuals. No individual may receive NSF funding for research involving human subjects unless the Program Officer affirms that the research is exempt or the PI obtains an appropriate review as specified below.

c. NSF Program Officer. The responsibility for affirming that the research satisfies the "Common Rule" rests with the Program Officer. If the Program Officer certifies that the research is exempt (see 207.3), no further review is necessary.

In most cases, the applicant institution will have an IRB set up in conformance with the "Common Rule." This typically means that the institution will have a currently approved Multiple Project Assurance (MPA) on file with NIH's Office of Protection from Research Risks (OPRR). The IRB will certify that the research is exempt or else will approve it via an expedited (chair's only) or full committee review.

Rarely, an institution or unaffiliated PI will have no assurance and no hopes of getting one from OPRR or any other federal agency participating in the "Common Rule." In that case, the best alternative is for the PI to contact a nearby institution with a valid MPA, normally a nearby state University or research facility, and to arrange for that institution's IRB to review the proposal and certify it as conforming to the Human Subjects regulations.

Guidelines from the National Institutes of Health summarize regulations for ethics and human subjects: "The fundamental principle of human subjects protection is that people should not (in most cases) be involved in research without their informed consent, and that subjects should not incur increased risk of harm from their research involvement, beyond the normal risks inherent in everyday life.'' (See http://www.nih.gov:80/grants/oprr/humansubjects/guidance/belmont.htm).

D. Ethics and Grant Proposals

Most funding agencies as well as academic departments now require an ethics statement as part of a thesis, dissertation, or grant proposal. A 1998 National Science Foundation Workshop summarized the concerns to be addressed by the ethics statement, broadly applicable to most types of research (NSF, 1998: 23), and this is reproduced below.

> Research proposals should show an awareness of ethical issues that may be involved with the project. The researcher should show how decisions may be made throughout the research project, from planning and implementation to analysis. The proposal, or related human subjects certification, should discuss how such issues related to privacy and confidentiality will be addressed, that is, what safeguards will be put into place to make sure that the work and reports that come out do not damage the individuals who have participated. The integrity and anonymity of subject-teachers, administrators, children, and parents must be respected. Clear statements need to be made regarding who will own the data and who will report on them.
>
> Researchers are well aware of the need to safeguard the privacy of human subjects and to make sure that their participation in a research project does not place them in any personal jeopardy because of what they do or say. Indeed, many projects would be impossible to conduct if participants felt that their opinions, perceptions, or behaviors were to be attributed to them in any specific way. In large-scale studies, it has been fairly easy to provide confidentiality by reporting data only at the group level and by placing limitations on the size of the group for which data will be presented in any disaggregated form. (Usually, the requirement is at least 10 subjects in a group.)
>
> Where small samples are used, assurance of confidentiality may pose a significant challenge. Proposals should address the issue of confidentiality and explicitly address how the rights of subjects will be protected, even if that protection may limit some aspects of the research itself. Even if only a small number of people will be able to recognize the identity of a respondent, that recognition may be sufficient to cause personal embarrassment and harm. Sowder (1998) points out that some research has led to, and perhaps even rested on, a relationship of trust between the researcher and the subject. Thus, the researcher is duty

bound to address the manner in which the data will be presented since presentation can have serious personal consequences.

Researchers who collect large data sets that might be used by others should explain in the proposed statement of work that they have plans for making the data available to others for secondary analysis. It is recommended that all data sets be released to other researchers, with complete documentation, by one year after the publication of results.

E. Checklist

1. Have you filed your research with your college's IRB for ethics clearance if it involves human or animal subjects?
2. Have you also filed a conflict-of-interest form, usually required separately by the research office of your academic institution, research staff, and contract employees?
3. Have you scrupulously avoided fabrication, falsification, and plagiarism?
4. Have you avoided using inappropriate statistical or other methods of measurement to enhance the significance of research findings?
5. Have you avoided misrepresenting speculations as fact?
6. In your write-ups of your results, have you been forthright about problems and shortcomings in your data collection and sampling?
7. Have you reported relevant negative as well as positive findings?
8. Have you avoided releasing preliminary research without sufficient data to allow peers to judge the validity of your results?
9. Have you made provision to retain your data and research records for a reasonably long time, so as to be able to allow others to verify what you have reported?
10. Have you given peers reasonable access to data that support findings in papers you have published?
11. Have you avoided making use of any information in breach of any duty of confidentiality to your subjects, associates, or peers?
12. Have you avoided all forms of misuse of funds?
13. Have you avoided all forms of sexual harassment?
14. Have you avoided exploiting graduate research assistants?

II. RESOURCES

Numerous examples of resources on research ethics are to be found by exploring the website of the ''Ethics Center'' at the following address: http://ethics.cwru.edu. Dr. Caroline Whitbeck has developed this center with an NSF grant from the Ethics and Value Studies Program. The WWW Ethics Center, created with support from the NSF in 1995, focuses especially on ethics in engineering and science. Now hosted at Case Western Reserve University, the Center also spans sociology, ecology, history, computer ethics, and psychology. An ''Ethics in a Corporate Setting'' section focuses on ethical problems associated with high-technology corporations. The Center's website has a keyword index, glossary, a 12,000 item bibliography, case studies, and a list of ethics-related organizations with their acronyms and links to their sites.

The Online Ethics Center for Engineering and Science, located at http://onlineethics.org/, is a related website that provides engineers and scientists with resources useful for understanding ethically significant problems that arise in their work. The website is associated with the International Conference on Ethics in Engineering and Computer Science. Caroline Whitbeck's essay, ''Trustworthy Research, Editorial Introduction,'' provides an historical background to current ethics issues in engineering and science (http://onlineethics.org/essays/connect.html).

The National Institutes of Health Office of Protection from Research Risks is charged with overseeing human subjects issues in the biomedical sciences supported by the National Institutes of Health. Since it is the largest federal government office dealing with human subjects issues, it takes a de facto lead in the area. See http://www.nih.gov:80/grants/oprr/oprr.htm.

Social science professional associations maintain information on ethics:

American Anthropological Association:http://www.ameranthassn.org/ethics.htm
American Political Science Association: http://www.apsanet.org/ ethics.html
American Psychological Association: http://www.apa.org/ethics/ ethics.html
American Sociological Association: http://www.asanet.org/ecoderev.htm
Archaeological Institute of America: http://www.archaeological.org/ ethics.html
Society of Professional Archeologists: http://www.smu.edu/~anthrop/sopa.html#CODE_OF_ETHICS
Society for Applied Anthropology: http://www.telepath.com/sfaa/sfaaethic.html

The Centre for Applied Ethics is located at the University of British Columbia. Its website covers Health Care Ethics, Business Ethics, Computer and Info-Tech Ethics, Environmental Ethics, Moral/Ethical Decision Making, Media Ethics, Animal Welfare and the Ethics of Animal Use, Professional Ethics, Science and Technology Ethics, and Miscellaneous Ethics Resources at http://www.ethics.ubc.ca/.

The Center for Bioethics at the University of Pennsylvania maintains a virtual library of bioethics articles at http://www.med.upenn.edu/~bioethic/library/resources/bioethics.html.

"Ethics Links," maintained by Saint Joseph's College faculty member Timothy McFarland, covers Ethics Links; Bioethics Links; Business Ethics Links; Computer Ethics Links; Environmental Ethics Links; Catholic Sources; Ethics in Science and Technology; Theological Resources; and Supreme Court Cases at http://www.saintjoe.edu/~timm/core10lks.html.

The "Ethics in Science" site, maintained by Virginia Polytechnic Institute faculty member Brian Tissue, covers science ethics resources and selected essays on ethics in science, with an emphasis on chemistry, at http://www.chem.vt.edu/ethics/ethics.html.

The Eubios Ethics Institute is a New Zealand/Japanese center focusing on bioethics. Its site has numerous links to online journals, other ethics centers, and more, at http://www.csu.edu.au/learning/eubios/Info.htm.

"Scientific Misconduct" is a website that maintains an annotated bibliography on such issues as fraud and plagiarism, at http://www.lemoyne.edu/OTRP/otrpresources/otrp_sci-misc.html.

ENDNOTES

1. This section is based on National Science Foundation (1997).

BIBLIOGRAPHY

American Psychological Association. (1982). Ethical Principles in the Conduct of Research with Human Participants. Washington, DC: American Psychological Association.

Barnbaum, D. R., and Byron M. (2000). Research Ethics Text and Readings. Englewood Cliffs, NJ: Prentice-Hall.

Brody, B. A. (1998). The Ethics of Biomedical Research: An International Perspective. New York: Oxford University Press.

Chastain, G., and Landrum R. E. (1999). Protecting Human Subjects: Departmental Subject Pools and Institutional Review Boards. Washington, DC: American Psychological Association.

Elliott, D., and Stern J. E., eds. (1997). Research Ethics: A Reader. Hanover, NH: University Press of New England.

Gallup, G., and Beckstead J. (1988). Attitudes toward Animal Research. Am Psychol 43(6):474–476.

Kimmel, A. J. (1996). Ethical Issues in Behavioral Research: A Survey. Cambridge, MA: Blackwell.

King, N. M. P., and Stein J. eds. (1999). Beyond Regulations: Ethics in Human Subjects Research (Studies in Social Medicine). Chapel Hill, NC: University of North Carolina Press.

Koocher, G. P. (1998). Protection of Participants in Sensitive Social Research: A Special Issue of "Ethics and Behavior." Hillsdale, NJ: Lawrence Erlbaum Associates.

Koocher, G. P., and Keith-Spiegel P. (1998). Ethics in Psychology: Professional Standards and Cases. Oxford Textbooks in Clinical Psychology, vol 3. New York: Oxford University Press.

Levine, R. J. (1988). Ethics and Regulation of Clinical Research. New Haven: Yale University Press.

Mayland, H. F., and Sojka R. E., eds. (1992). Research Ethics, Manuscript Review, and Journal Quality: Proceedings of a Symposium on the Peer Review-Editing Process. Washington, DC: American Society of Agronomy.

National Academy of Sciences, Committee on Science, Engineering, and Public Policy (COSEPUP). (1992). Responsible Science: Ensuring the Integrity of the Research Process, vol. 1. Washington, DC: National Academy Press.

National Academy Press. (1995). On Being a Scientist, Responsible Conduct in Research. Washington, DC: National Academy Press, 2nd ed. Recommended reading as listed in National Science Foundation program announcements.

National Academy Press. (1997). Adviser, Teacher, Role Model, Friend. On Being a Mentor to Students in Science and Engineering. Washington, DC: National Academy Press. Recommended reading as listed in National Science Foundation program announcements.

National Science Foundation. (1991). Misconduct in science and engineering. Federal Register 56 (May 14): 22286–22290.

National Science Foundation. (1997). Conflicts of Interest and Standards of Ethical Conduct. NSF Manual No. 15. Arlington, VA: NSF.

National Science Foundation. (1998). Research Methods in Mathematics and Science Education Research: Report of a Workshop. Arlington, VA: NSF. Workshop on Education Research Methods, Division of Research, Evaluation and Communication, National Science Foundation, November 19–20, 1998, The Hilton Hotel, Balston, Virginia. Obtained from http://www.ehr.nsf.gov/ehr/rec/pubs/report10.doc Nov. 18, 1999.

Newman, D. L., and Brown R. D. (1996). Applied Ethics for Program Evaluation. Thousand Oaks, CA: Sage Publications.

Penslar, R. L. (1995). Research Ethics: Cases and Materials. Bloomington, IN: Indiana University Press.

Pincus, H. A., Lieberman J. A., and Ferris S., eds. (1999). Ethics in Psychiatric Research: A Resource Manual for Human Subjects Protection. Washington, DC: American Psychiatric Association.

Professional Ethics. (1995). Special issue on research ethics. Professional Ethics 4:3–4. Recommended reading as listed in NSF program announcements.

Public Health Service (PHS). (1989). Responsibilities of awardee and applicant institutions for dealing with and reporting possible misconduct in science. Federal Register 54 (August 8):32446–32451.

Resnick, D. B. (1998). The Ethics of Science: An Introduction. New York: Routledge. (Philosophical Issues in Science).

Sales, B. D., and Folkman S., eds. (2000). Ethics in research with human participants. Washington, DC: American Psychological Association.

Shrader-Frechette, Kristin (1994). Ethics of Scientific Research. New York: Rowman and Littlefield. (Issues in Academic Ethics).

Sieber, J. E. (1992). Planning Ethically Responsible Research: A Guide for Students and Internal Review Boards. Newbury Park, CA: Sage Publications.

Sowder, J. T. (1998). Ethics in mathematics education research. In: Sierpinska A., and Kilpatrick J., eds. Mathematics Education as a Research Domain: A Search for Identity, Book 2. Norwell, MA: Kluwer Academic, pp 427–442.

Stanley, B. H., Sieber J. E., Nelton G. B., and Melton G. B. eds. (1996). Research Ethics: A Psychological Approach. Onaha, NE: University of Nebraska Press.

Steneck, N. H. (1994). Research universities and scientific misconduct: History, policies, and the future. J Higher Ed 65 (3):54–69.

Sugarman, J., Mastroianni A. C., and Kahn J. P., eds. (1998). Ethics of Research with Human Subjects: Selected Policies & Resources. New York: University Publishing Group.

U.S. Department of Health and Human Services, Public Health Service, National Institutes of Health. Office for Protection from Research Risks. (1993). Protecting Human Research Subjects: Institutional Review Board Guidebook. Washington, DC: U. S. Government Printing Office.

U.S. Department of Health and Human Services, Division of Policy and Education, The Office of Research Integrity. (1995). Integrity and Misconduct in Research. Washington, DC: U. S. Government Printing Office.

Whitbeck, C. (1998). Ethics in Engineering Practice and Research. New York: Cambridge University Press.

17

Data-Gathering Strategies

DATA-GATHERING STRATEGIES

There are many different strategies for collecting data: experiments, simulations, participant observation, case studies, focus groups, survey research, analysis of archival data, and content analysis are leading examples. A combination of strategies is sometimes advisable because multitrait, multimethod analysis can be more valid than monistic approaches. That is, having multiple measures of each concept, measured multiple ways, may lead to valid results more than single measurements taken through one strategy. For example, using focus groups to back up survey questionnaire data or case studies to back up statistical analysis of archival data are common combinations of data gathering strategies.

Data collection strategies are divided into qualitative and quantitative, but both require a systematic approach. Participant observation, case studies, and focus groups are primarily qualitative approaches, although quantitative data may also be gathered. Survey research, statistical analysis of archival data, and content analysis are primarily quantitative approaches, although some open-ended qualitative information may also be gathered. Qualitative-based examples flesh out and give validation to quantitative conclusions, whereas quantitative-based conclusions validate generalizations made on the basis of cases and qualitative observations. Again, a multimethod strategy is preferable to any single strategy.

Response taking, document analysis, and observation underlie all data gathering strategies. Participant observers interview people, analyze organizational documents, and observe behavior. Case study analysts interview role players and analyze case documents. Focus group researchers gather responses from group discussion and observe group behaviors. Survey researchers focus on questionnaire responses but also use interviewer observations and cross-check responses against documented data. Analysts of archival data and content analysts focus on document analysis but also may interview those responsible for archiving to understand data validity and reliability. Experimenters rely almost exclusively on observation.

A. Types of Data-Gathering Strategies

There is a very large number of data gathering strategies, ranging from laboratory instrumentation measuring movements and temperatures to psychoanalytic inkblot projection tests measuring subjective perceptions. Other methods include experiments with controls, modeling and simulation, observation of small group behavior, reflective discussion, and secondary analysis of archival data, to name a few. Below we are able to present only a few data gathering strategies, but they illustrate many of the issues surrounding data collection in general.

1. Participant Observation

Participant observation provides first-hand information, yields high face validity, and involves reliance on relatively simple and inexpensive methods. The downside of participant observation as a data gathering technique is increased threat to the objectivity of the researcher, unsystematic gathering of data, reliance on subjective measurement, and possible observer effects (observation may distort the observed behavior).

The objectivity issue. Participation is a form of investment of time, energy, and self, and as such, it raises obvious questions of possible bias. However, defenders of participant observation find greater bias in allegedly neutral instruments such as survey questionnaires. These, they say, involve the imposition of an externally conceived "scientific" measuring device (the questionnaire) on individuals who do not perceive reality according to that external conception (Bruyn, 1966).

The phenomenological approach to participant observation emphasizes intersubjective understanding and empathy. Bruyn (1966) outlined four elements in this approach:

1. Awareness of time: Record the temporal phases of research according to the sequence of experience of the observer in relation to the milieu (e.g., newcomer, provisional member, categorical member, personalized rapport, and imminent migrant—that is, as the researcher is about to leave the community).
2. Awareness of the physical environment: Record the relations of people

to their physical environment as they perceive it, not as the researcher conceptualizes or even experiences it.

3. Awareness of contrasting experiences: Record the experiences of people under contrasting social circumstances; meanings cannot be assessed under one set of circumstances because they are relative to the setting.
4. Awareness of social openings and barriers: Record the changes in meaning as the participant observer is admitted into narrower social regions, transitioning from stranger to member to insider. Determining vocabulary concepts is a major focus of participant observation, seeking to illuminate the intersubjective meanings of critical terms.

In general, in the phenomenological approach, the participant observer seeks out the meaning of the experiences of the group being studied from each of the many different perspectives within it.

The empirical approach to participant observation emphasizes participation as an opportunity for in-depth systematic study of a particular group or activity. Zelditch (1962) outlined three elements of this approach:

1. Enumeration of frequencies of various categories of observed behavior, as in interaction analysis. Often there is an explicit schedule of observation geared to hypotheses framed in advance of participation. As Reiss (1971) observes, participation may lead to alteration of hypotheses and observation schedules; the attempt to observe systematically is ongoing.
2. Informant interviewing to establish social rules and statuses. There may be systematic sampling of informants to be interviewed, content analysis of documents encountered, and even recording of observations in structured question-and-answer format.
3. Participation to observe and detail illustrative incidents. Where the phenomenological approach emphasizes the participant observer experiencing meanings through empathy, the empirical approach emphasizes systematic observation and recording of the milieu. This distinction is, of course, more a matter of emphasis than a dichotomy.

2. Case Studies

Case study research is a time-honored, traditional approach to the study of topics in social science and management, but it also finds application in such scientific fields as botany or meteorology. Case study research may be used in its own right but is more often recommended as part of a multimethod approach (triangulation) in which the same dependent variable is investigated using multiple procedures (such as case studies, survey research, archival data). Case study methodology was discussed in an earlier chapter.

3. Focus Groups

Focus group research is based on facilitating an organized discussion with a group of individuals selected because they were believed to be representative of some class (e.g., the class of consumers of a product, the class of voters). Discussion is used to bring out insights and understandings in ways that simple questionnaire items may not be able to tap. Focus group research has long been prominent in marketing studies (Morgan, 1988), in part because market researchers seek to tap emotional and unconscious motivations not amenable to the structured questions of conventional survey research. The interaction among focus group participants brings out differing perspectives through the language that is used by the discussants. People get caught up in the spirit of group discussion and may reveal more than they would in the more formal interview setting.

As discussants ask questions of each other, new avenues of exploration are opened. In discussions, multiple meanings are revealed as different discussants interpret topics of discussions in different ways. Interaction is the key to successful focus groups. In an interactive setting, discussants draw each other out, sparking new ideas. The reactions of each person spark ideas in others, and one person may fill in a gap left by others. One may even find a form of collaborative mental work, as discussants build on each other to come to a consensus that no one individual would have articulated on their own.

Drawbacks of the focus group method include the potentially strong influence, one way or the other, of the discussion moderator; the difficulty of separating individual viewpoints from the collective group viewpoint; and the difficulty of obtaining a representative sample within a small focus group. In a group context, individuals may be less willing to reveal sensitive information because assurance of confidentiality is lost, in spite of the practice of urging participants not to reveal discussions of the group. The focus group method may also have positive or negative effects on the subjects, particularly when members of the group are associated in work or other social contexts.

Focus groups are generally a poor choice when quantitative information is desired (such as when one wants to know the percentage of people who will buy product X or vote for candidate X). The small size of focus groups makes any estimates of quantitative proportions unreliable, even if the members of the focus group are representative of the target population. By the same token, focus group research is a poor choice for multivariate research, in which one again needs the stability of large random samples to be able to disaggregate the effects of explanatory variables through statistical techniques. Finally, focus group research is a poor choice for predicting future action in settings yet to emerge because focus group discussants will articulate their views in terms of their own present experiences.

Note that focus group research differs from group interviewing, in which a standard survey instrument is administered to respondents simultaneously. In focus studies, in contrast, there is no standard instrument, only a topic to be explored through the exchange of group discussion. For instance, a start-up topic question might be, ''What are the present satisfactions and dissatisfactions with X and those of Y?'' The discussants have a strong influence on the subtopics that are examined and the insights yielded. Where survey research, even group survey research, requires a priori theory or at least a list of subtopics as a guide for selection of items to be included in the survey instrument, there is no à priori theory in focus group research. Focus groups are a method of choice when the dynamics that determine outcomes are not well known and surprises are expected, as in marketing research in which focus groups are brought together to react to product or candidate ads.

The role of the focus group moderator is to facilitate, not dominate discussion. The moderator encourages the participation of everyone and seeks to limit the domination of discussion by a few discussants. The moderator may also give prompting questions (probes) to elicit expansion on interesting subtopics, such as ''Give us an example of . . . ,'' ''Tell us more about that,'' ''Keep talking,'' or ''Can someone summarize what we've been saying.'' The moderator will not ask closed-ended, yes-no questions, such as ''Do you prefer X?'' instead always using nondirective prompts like ''What is your reaction to X?'' The moderator may also seek to return conversation to the topic at hand. Finally, the moderator may take notes or record the conversation of the group, although often that role is left to an assistant moderator. The moderator must record overt statements and be sensitive to omissions, choice of words, nonverbal communications, expressions of emotion, energy levels, and the roles played by the discussant. Because of the strong role of the moderator, usually the same one is used if there are multiple groups, in an attempt to control for the influence of the moderator.

In terms of implementation, some recommend a focus group size of 6 to 10, although both smaller and larger examples can be found. Focus group facilitators, however, usually regard even 10 as becoming unwieldy and counterproductive. Most studies bring the focus group together for one session, but a sequence of meetings is also possible, usually for one or two hours each. Taped excerpts from one meeting may be played back to a subsequent group to obtain reactions. The broader and more ambitious the purposes of doing focus group research, the more groups are necessary. A study of ''women's attitudes toward health services'' will require many more groups than one on ''Boston consumers' preferences for detergent,'' for instance. Use of follow-up groups, bringing back past participants, can be very fruitful.

Often ''ice-breaking exercises'' are used to start a focus group discussion. One example is the ''eyes closed exercise,'' in which the moderator asks members of the focus group to close their eyes, imagine the last time they were involved with the subject of the study, and to articulate their remembrance of this. This sharing of experiences while eyes are closed is intended to break down formalities and get conversation rolling as discussants feel closer as a result of the sharing experience. Another example of an ice-breaking exercise is to have the discussants draw a cartoon or picture of the best of worst aspects of X, then share their work with the group. A third example is word association, asking discussants quickly and without thinking to finish prompts like ''The worst thing about X is. . . .'' or ''People who like X tend to be. . . .'' Participants write their answers on a sheet of paper, then share them with the group. Many other projective exercises are possible.

The number of topics explored per meeting is usually at most three (often just one), with subtopics under each. Meetings are usually held in neutral locations such as hotel meeting rooms (not, for instance, in the workplace in a study involving employees). Participants may be selected at random or through information, using a snowball reference technique in which the first informant recommends others, who in turn recommend yet others. Participants should be informed of the purposes of the focus group study. Often they are encouraged to participate on a first-name basis, which encourages informality and openness while suggesting greater anonymity. The ethics guidelines regarding use of human subjects, discussed in a previous chapter, apply to focus groups.

Focus groups are not a panacea for tapping ''true'' feelings. People often do not themselves understand their own motivations and preferences and thus cannot articulate them well. People have complex, even conflicting motivations that may come together in unpredictable ways given only slightly varying ways of presenting a stimulus. People may give acceptable or politically correct responses in front of peers, and they may act differently in real situations compared with hypothetical ones. They may be aware of the study's sponsorship and tell the researcher what they believe he or she wants to hear. People tend to express views that enhance their own image of themselves, and they also may formulate opinions ''on the spot,'' lacking any real commitment to what they say. And people lie.

4. Survey Research

Survey research is the method of gathering data from respondents thought to be representative of some population, using an instrument composed of closed structure or open-ended items (questions). This is perhaps the dominant form of data collection in the social sciences, providing for efficient collection of data over broad populations, amenable to administration in person, by telephone, and over the Internet. Some forms of survey research by telephone or the Internet may be completely automated. Critics of survey research methodology hold it to be a method that artificially forces respondents to formulate opinions, masking the complexity of conflicting views and unconscious biases within each respondent, and critics note that in many arenas (e.g., race relations) survey items poorly predict actual behavior.

In some areas, such as voting, there appears to be a close correspondence between how respondents say they will vote and how they actually do vote subsequently. In other areas, such as race-related attitudes, the discrepancy between what people say and what they do appears to be substantial. Tartar (1969) found 65% of respondents changed their behavior away from surveyed attitudes when confronted with actual situations requiring behavioral response. An early survey by Ehrlich (1969: 34) concluded, "Studies on the relation of attitudes and behavior have almost consistently resulted in the conclusion that attitudes are a poor predictor of behavior." Ehrlich gave seven reasons for this gap:

1. There may be no clear way for an attitude to become expressed in a behavior.
2. Attitudes may reflect fantasy or sublimation more than realistic responses.
3. Individuals may not be willing to disclose honest expression of certain opinions.
4. Individuals may translate opinions into action in unpredictable ways, such as suppression and inaction, displacement into other arenas, and rationalization.
5. Individuals may lack the informational resources to act.
6. Individuals may lack the opportunity to act.
7. Individuals may lack the sense of efficacy to act.

The survey "instrument" is the schedule of questions or response items to be posed to respondents. "Items" are the individual survey questions or statements for which a response is solicited from the respondent. Ordinarily, "interviews" refers to the face-to-face administration of a survey instrument, whereas "questionnaires" is a term that refers to mail or other indirect methods of administration. "Response structure" refers to the format of items, which may be open-ended or structured. Structured items may be multiple choice, multiple response, dichotomies, rank lists, or a variety of other formats.

A social science model can be depicted graphically as a set of variables (represented by circles) connected by a set of causal effects (represented by single-headed arrows) and correlations (represented by double-headed arrows). The survey should, at a minimum, include items pertaining to each circle and arrow in the model. Multiple items to measure each variable and relationship are preferred.

Typically, after an introduction that discloses sponsorship, a survey begins with nonthreatening items that arouse interest. The first question should be clearly related to the announced purposes of the survey (not a background item, for instance). Some recommend the second question be open-ended, to allow the respondent to "get into" the subject. Nonthreatening background information questions (e.g., demographic information) should be posed early so these controls will be available if the respondent fatigues and does not answer all the later items. The survey then proceeds to attitude questions, often sequencing from general and less-threatening items toward more specific and more sensitive items. Sensitive background items, particularly the income item, are usually put at the end. However, the more toward the end of the survey an item is, the lower its response rate is apt to be. For this reason, balancing the foregoing considerations, it is desirable to administer the survey with different forms with different orders so as to lessen the order/response bias.

Filter items allow the elimination of unqualified respondents during post-processing (e.g., respondents who lack minimum information to respond intelligently). Cross-check items are internal check items that test consistency with other responses. Asking age at one point and date of birth at another would be a pair of cross-checked items. An extension of this is the split-form interview, which might be administered to both partners in a marriage with a view toward cross-checking for consistency. Random probe items of an open-ended nature are randomly interspersed by item and by survey form such that any one respondent is only probed on a few items. Probe items are "Could you tell me a little more about what you mean?" or "Could you give me an example of what you mean?" Probe responses are used to better understand the meaning of frequency distributions of responses to the corresponding structured items.

Bias may creep into survey items in a variety of ways. The types of bias are enumerated below, as they constitute things to watch out for in many types of data collection, not just survey research:

1. *Ambiguity*. Questions should be specific, avoiding generalities, for example, "On a scale from 1 to 10, how popular is the president at this time?" This example begs the question, "popular with whom?" Some respondents will answer the item in terms of popularity with themselves, others will answer in terms of popularity with their peers, and some will respond in terms of their recollection of past opinion polls. Items often need to be anchored in one or more of the familiar journalistic dimensions: who, what, when, where, why, and how? If it is possible for respondents to interpret questions in dissimilar terms, they will. "Have you participated in a political rally?" is also ambiguous, for instance, because participation is undefined and some will answer affirmatively, having passed within earshot of a political speaker, whereas others will answer negatively because, even though they attended rallies, they were not the organizers. As a third example, "Do you favor government policy toward crime control?" leaves ambiguous the level of government (local, federal, state), as well as just what dimension of law enforcement is at issue. As a fourth example, when value

preferences are requested by ranking "above average," "average," "below average," etc., ambiguity is introduced unless the question is answered, average in comparison with what? In general, all pronouns, nouns, and noun-phrases should have a clear referent.

2. *Mutual exclusivity*. When multiple response items are allowed, bias is introduced if the items are not mutually exclusive, yet only a single item may be selected.

3. *Nonexhaustive response set*. Bias is introduced when the response alternatives available to the respondent leave out valid choices they would otherwise make. The most common example is leaving out such responses as "neutral" or "don't know" when, in fact, respondents may well be neutral or actually may not know, rather than hiding their "true" responses, which the researcher is trying to force out by omitting these categories. Ambiguous terms, such as "parents," can also lead to nonexhaustive response sets, as by omitting the distinction between birth parents and adoptive parents. Likewise, "single" may omit the distinction between "never married," "widowed," and "divorced."

4. *Ranking* can be a challenging task. Many survey researchers recommend that respondents not be asked to rank more than four or five items. Beyond that, respondents may give arbitrary rankings just to get past the item.

5. *Loaded terms*. Example: "Do you lean more toward the pro-life or the pro-abortion position on issue of termination of late-term pregnancies where the health of the mother is threatened?" This example is biased because one position is labeled with its most favorable label (pro-life, rather than anti-abortion), whereas the other position is labeled with its less favorable label (pro-abortion, rather than pro-choice). As another example, more people will "not allow" something than will "forbid" the same thing.

6. *Leading questions*. Example: "Do you favor an increase in the federal minimum wage to $8.00?" This example is not as leading as an item of the type, "You favor X, don't you?" but it is still leading because it does not legitimize both affirmative and negative responses. A negative response may appear stingy or mean-spirited toward the poor, and this may bias the survey toward too many affirmative responses. A better method is to phrase such policy options in the form, "Some people favor X, whereas other people are opposed to X. What is your opinion?"

7. *Recall items*. People's ability to recall the past is limited. The more current and specific the question reference, the better. If recall is necessary, the time frame should be as recent as possible and not longer than 6 months, unless the reference is to major events (e.g., marriage, changing jobs, buying a car).

8. *Unfamiliar terms and jargon*. Example: "Do you consider environmental regulation of wetlands to be an invasion of the sovereignty of the states?" Terms such as "sovereignty" are apt not to be well understood by typical survey populations. When a term not in popular usage must be used in an item, such as

an item asking opinions about the Civil Rights Act of 1964, the interviewer must precede the item with a brief explanation. Wherever possible, familiar terms should be substituted for unfamiliar terms.

9. *Requiring inaccessible information.* An item may use familiar terms but require information most respondents would not know. For instance, a question about Stalin's treatment of the Cossacks might have been acceptable long ago, but today's population of respondents is apt to know little about this subject and perhaps not even recognize "Stalin." As a second example, the item, "Is your family income above, about equal to, or below the official poverty rate for a family of four?" is flawed, among other reasons, because people are not apt to know what dollar amount is the referent today, making the item unacceptable for a determination of fact (although possibly acceptable for a determination of self-perception).

10. *Multidimensionality.* A form of ambiguity arises when items are multidimensional. Example: "On a scale of 1 to 10, please rank the performance of the president." The respondent may be torn between multiple dimensions: personal versus official performance, or domestic versus foreign policy performance, for instance. Example two: "Do you believe President Clinton lied under oath in the Monica Lewinsky scandal, impairing his effectiveness as president?" This item calls for two opinions: one on lying under oath and one on subsequent effectiveness. It should be broken into two separate items.

11. *Compound items.* Items with compound clauses may not be multidimensional but may involve undue complexity (see below). For instance, the item, "Do you have or have you ever had a physical, mental, or other health condition that lasted more than 6 months and that has limited the kind of work you could do on your job?" is better broken into two items: "Do you have or have you ever had a physical, mental, or other health condition that lasted more than 6 months?" and the follow-up item, "If you answered yes to the previous question, did this condition limit the kind of work you could do on your job?"

12. *Complexity and memory overload.* It is possible to overtax the respondent by requiring an excessive memory burden. The more complex the item, the easier it is to overload memory. The explanation should not demand that the respondent learn complex new material. Simply using double negatives in an item may introduce undue complexity. If there are more than five alternatives, a show card should be used to allow the respondent to view the alternatives, not simply hear them orally in an interview situation.

13. *Poor grammatical format.* Weak grammatical format can introduce bias. For instance, the item, "Would you say that you approve very strongly, strongly, . . ." presents "dangling alternatives," which the respondent must memorize before even knowing what the question is. This format is frustrating and may bias responses toward the first-presented response, or toward negativity. Putting the subject first is the preferred order.

14. *Hypothetical items.* Hypothetical items (e.g., "What would you do if . . .") creates a difficult challenge for respondents. Seriously considering such items requires time for imagination and consideration. People tend to base responses to such items on their most-related actual experiences, and it may be better to ask about such experiences directly.

15. *Inappropriate assumptions.* Items should not contain false or arguable premises. The respondent should not be required to make a false or arguable assumption to respond to an item on its face. For instance, "How much improvement in your life would passage of the Equal Rights Amendment make? A great deal, some, very little, or none?" is an item that assumes that the effect of ERA passage could not be negative on a respondent, forcing respondents who believe the effect would be negative to either skip the item or give a response that does not represent their views.

16. *Mismatched item and response set.* The response categories should be appropriate to the dimension probed by the item. For instance, "How unusual do you think it is for a person to donate $100 or more to a presidential candidate? A great deal, some, very little, or none?" is a mismatch because "a great deal unusual," "some unusual," etc., are not grammatically acceptable responses and will confuse respondents.

Pretesting is considered an all-but-essential step in survey research. No matter how experienced the survey researcher, pretests almost invariably bring to light item ambiguities and other sources of bias and error. In fact, Converse and Presser (1986: 65) argue cogently that a minimum of two pretests are necessary, with pretest sizes of 25 to 75 administered to respondents similar to those who will be in the final sample. The first pretest may have up to twice the number of items as the final, as one purpose is to identify weaker items and drop them from the survey. Items may also be dropped if the first pretest shows they exhibit too little variance to be modeled. The first pretest will also have many more probe items than the final, and respondents may even be told they are being given a pretest and their help solicited in refining the instrument. Other purposes of the first pretest are to see if respondent interest is aroused, if respondent attention can be maintained, if interviewers and respondents feel the survey has a natural flow, and if interviewers experience problems such as need to repeat questions, need to correct misinterpretations of questions, need to handle volunteered information, sections where the respondents wanted to say more, or questions that seemed sensitive. The first pretest results, hopefully, in a much-changed, finished instrument. The second pretest is used simply for polishing, trimming, rearranging, and other refinements, but not for adding new dimensions or making major substantive changes in the survey. If such changes prove necessary, a third pretest will also be needed.

After pretesting, if there is any remaining doubt about the reliability of one or more items, the researcher should consider split sample comparisons, in which two versions of the same item appear on two different survey forms administered randomly. If the mean responses of the comparison subsamples differ significantly, the inference is made that the two versions represent two different items, not two versions of the same item. Of course, survey error also includes such factors as faults in sampling, coding, tabulating, data processing, interviewer bias, researcher bias, and data misinterpretation.

In survey research, items may be open-ended or structured. Open-ended items are frequently used as complements rather than alternatives to structured items. As a follow-up to a structured item, an open-ended item can bring to light unanticipated interpretations and variations in the meaning of responses. For instance, in a ranking item about job satisfaction, a structured response may show "income" to be the most important satisfaction factor, but a follow-up open-ended item may show some respondents mean "high income," whereas other respondents mean "steady income." Open-ended items are not necessarily more accurate, however. An open-ended question may elicit one range of preferences, yet when other choices are presented in a structured question, respondents may well alter their open-ended preferences to rerank in the light of previously unconsidered alternatives in the structured item. Ideally, one would use both, with an open-ended probe question after every structured item. However, the time and fatigue costs of the interview would be prohibitive, which is why random probe questions are used, as discussed above.

Survey research items may also force a choice, or they may provide for a "no opinion" option. It is very tempting to leave out "no opinion," "not sure," and "don't care" options in structured questions. Forcing a choice not only yields the direction of preference, but also requires the respondent to give a more considered response. However, forcing a choice does distort the responses of individuals who genuinely have no opinion, are genuinely unsure, or genuinely do not care. When the researcher can assume everyone really has an opinion, then forced choice is justified. If not, the researcher should retain the no preference options, or should consider filter and intensity questions. Filter questions precede an item and are of the type, "Here is a statement about X. Not everyone has an opinion on this. Here is the statement: . . . Do you have an opinion on that?" If the respondent answers "Yes" to the filter question, then a forced-choice item is presented. Intensity items follow forced choice items and ask "How strongly do you feel about that: extremely strongly, very strongly . . . ?" A separate intensity item is needed because extremity on the forced choice item is not equivalent to intensity: one may hold an extreme position nonintensely and may intensely hold a middle position. In using forced choice rather than offering a "no opinion" option, the researcher is assuming that those who would have given "no opinion" responses will be low intensity on the intensity item, but not necessarily in the middle on the forced choice item itself.

There are specialized techniques for getting a more valid response to highly sensitive questions. This issue is treated in depth by Fox and Tracy (1986). The randomized response strategy takes subjects ''off the spot'' by mixing randomized responses with real ones. The basic randomized response method: consider the question, ''Have you ever used marijuana?'' Respondents can be told to flip a coin or use some other randomizing device, then if heads appear (not seen by the interviewer), respondents are told to answer the question honestly but to answer ''Yes'' regardless if tails appear. If the result for a survey is 60% ''Yes,'' we can reason that the true response rate is 20% (half of true ''Yes'' responses will also be part of the 50% expected tails-determined ''Yes'' responses and half not, so the true percentage is twice the excess of the observed response [60%], less the random response [50%]). Fox and Tracy extend this to polytomous and quantitative responses and discuss various refinements as well as alternative approaches that have proved problematic.

Finally, in survey research you must decide how to handle the fact that not all respondents answer all items in your questionnaire. The most common methods are:

1. Archival comparison. Means and proportions from survey data are compared with known archival data, as by comparing percent female in one's sample with percent female in the census district one was polling.
2. Wave extrapolation. Data are coded according to whether the survey was received in the first instance or in the second or third wave of call-backs to subjects who had not yet responded. If there is, say, a smaller percent female in each successive wave, it is inferred that the figure would be lower still among nonrespondents.
3. Nonresponse surveys. It is also possible to undertake a very intensive effort to get responses from a random sample of nonrespondents, perhaps offering added inducements to participate.

Andrew Gelman, Gary King, and Chuanhai Liu (1998) presented an alternative method of analyzing a series of independent cross-sectional surveys in which some questions are not answered in some surveys and some respondents do not answer some of the questions posed. The method is also applicable to a single survey in which different questions are asked, or different sampling methods are used, in different strata or clusters. The method involves multiply imputing the missing items and questions by adding to existing methods of imputation designed for single surveys a hierarchical regression model that allows covariates at the individual and survey levels. Information from survey weights is exploited by including in the analysis the variables on which the weights were based and then reweighting individual responses (observed and imputed) to estimate population quantities. Diagnostics for checking the fit of the imputation model are also developed based on comparing imputed to nonimputed data. The authors illustrate with the example that motivated this project: a study of pre-election public opinion polls, in which not all the questions of interest are asked in all the surveys, so that it is not feasible to impute each survey separately.

A great deal of software exists for survey research. SPSS, for instance, in addition to its comprehensive statistical modules, also offers *Software with Confidence*, an expert system for guiding the researcher through instrument construction; *SPSS Data Entry*, for entering survey or other data; and *SPSS* Tables, for specialized tabular output of results. Saris (1991) reviews survey software, as do Vasu and Vasu (1998) and Couper (1998).

SDA is a set of programs for the documentation and Web-based analysis of survey data. There are also procedures for creating customized subsets of datasets. This set of programs is developed and maintained by the Computer-assisted Survey Methods Program (CSM) at the University of California, Berkeley. The website gives access to the demonstration SDA archive, related documentation, and several datasets. See http://socrates.berkeley.edu:7502/.

Westat, located at http://www.westat.com/method.html, is a leader in the development of instruments for survey research, focus groups, and other methodologies. For instance, Westat evaluates and refines data collection methods for the Current Population Survey of the Bureau of Labor Statistics, medical surveys for the Social Security Administration, and the Bureau of the Census with the 2000 Census.

Eform is software for placing survey forms on the web, collecting information to online databases, and generating appropriate reports. Most web-based surveys require special programs (CGI scripts) on one's server, but *Eform* processes responses on their web server and e-mails results to the researcher. Web reports are automatically generated each time a response is received. Contact Beach Tech, 4131 Vincent Avenue South, Minneapolis, MN 55410; (612) 924-9193; (800) 323-0434. A free demo version of *EForm* can be downloaded from their website.

Other vendors of online survey or data collection systems include Epic Data Inc., http://www.epicdata.com/; *FieldWorker*, for mobile data collection, including spatial information from a global positioning system (GPS), at http://www.fieldworker.com/; and *VoCarta* speech recognition software for mobile field data collection, at http://www.datria.com/.

B. Checklist

1. Have you clarified what your units of analysis are (people, cities, companies, nations, etc.)?

2. Have you considered the need for/possibility of multilevel analysis (individual level, organizational level, etc.)?
3. Have you carefully defined the sampling frame(s) needed in your study? That is, have you clarified what, specifically, is the universe of cases from which your units will be taken? This is directly related to the level of generalization you wish to entertain for conclusions of your study and is relevant whether you are doing qualitative case studies or empirical survey research.
4. Have you set forth in detail the procedures and rationale for how you will select cases from your sampling frame (simple random sample, cluster sample, expert-identified sample, etc.)?
5. Have you considered what control variables might confound findings relating your independent and dependent variables? Are these control variables adequately represented in your survey or other data-collection protocol?
6. Have you looked for other sources of bias in your data collection methodology?
7. If you are relying on others for data (e.g., your committee chairperson, the agency at which you work), have you come to an unambiguous and firm agreement about when you will have access to the data, what format it will be in, and what rights you will have regarding publication and other use of the data?
8. If you are relying on others for data, are you satisfied that the variables measured by that data adequately operationalize the variables in the hypotheses that comprise your model? If not, is the shortcoming sufficiently small that you have been able to obtain the approval of all members of your committee anyway?
9. If you are relying on assistants to collect data, have you implemented a formal and adequate training process for them?
10. If you are relying on assistants to collect data, does your research design include a provision for testing interrater reliability?

BIBLIOGRAPHY

Adler, P. A., and Adler, P. (1994). Observational techniques. In: Denzin N. and Lincoln Y. S., eds. Handbook of Qualitative Research. Newbury Park: Sage, 1994, 377–392.

Arksey, H., and Knight, P. T. (1999). Interviewing for Social Scientists: An Introductory Resource with Examples. Thousand Oaks, CA: Sage Publications. Covers design, triangulation, human subjects protection, report writing, and other basic topics.

Bogdan, R. (1972). Participant Observation in Organizational Settings. Syracuse, NY: Syracuse University Press.

Bourque, L. B., and Clark, V. A. (1992). Processing Data: The Survey Example. Thousand Oaks, CA: Sage Publications. Quantitative Applications in the Social Sciences Series No. 85. A nontechnical work that covers designing forms, pretesting, training data collectors, data entry, and data preparation, including handling nonresponse, missing data, and outliers.

Chandler, J., Davidson, A. I., and Harootunian, H. eds. (1994). Questions of Evidence: Proof, Practice, and Persuasion across the Disciplines. Chicago: University of Chicago Press. A dozen essays from Critical Inquiry that explore what is considered legitimate evidence and the history and the uses of inquiry.

Converse, J. M., and Presser, S. (1986). Survey Questions: Handcrafting the Standardized Questionnaire. Thousand Oaks, CA: Sage Publications. Quantitative Applications in the Social Sciences Series No. 63.

Couper, M. (1998). Computer Assisted Survey Information Collection. New York: John Wiley & Sons.

Ehrlich, H. (1969). Attitudes, behavior, and the intervening variables. Am Sociol 4(1): 29–34. Cited in relation to the gap between attitudes and behavior.

Eisenhardt, K. M. (1989). Building theories from case study research. Acad Management Rev, 14:516–531.

Flores, J. G., and Alonso, C. G. (1995). Using focus groups in educational research. Eval Rev 19(1):84–101.

Fox, J. A., and Tracy, P. E. (1986). Randomized Response: A Method for Sensitive Surveys. Thousand Oaks, CA: Sage Publications. Quantitative Applications in the Social Sciences Series No. 58. Covers randomized response methods to encourage response to sensitive items.

Gelman, A., King, G., and Liu, C. (1998). Not asked and not answered: Multiple imputation for multiple surveys. J Am Stat Assoc March, 1998.

Glaser, B. G., and Strauss, A. (1967). The Discovery of Grounded Theory: Strategies for Qualitative Research. Chicago: Aldine Publishing Co. The seminal work in grounded theory.

Hamel, J. (1993). Case Study Methods. Thousand Oaks, CA: Sage Publications. Covers history of the case study method.

Kreuger, R. A. (1988). Focus Groups: A Practical Guide for Applied Research. London: Sage.

Krueger, R. A., and Casey, M. A. (2000). Focus Groups: A Practical Guide for Applied Research. Thousand Oaks, CA: Sage Publications.

LaPiere, R. T. (1934). Attitudes vs. actions. Social Forces (13):230–237. This is the classic article challenging survey research and empirically showing its limitations.

Merton, R. K., and Kendall, P. L. (1946). The focused interview. Am J Sociol 51:541–557.

Morgan, D. L. (1997). Focus Groups as Qualitative Research. 2nd ed. London: Sage Publications. First edition, 1988.

Roberts, C. W., ed. (1997). Text Analysis for the Social Sciences: Methods for Drawing Statistical Inferences from Texts and Transcripts. Hillsdale, NJ: Lawrence Erlbaum.

Saris, W. E. (1991). Computer-Assisted Interviewing. Quantitative Applications in the Social Sciences Series No. 80, Thousand Oaks, CA: Sage Publications.

Spradley, J. P. (1997). Participant Observation. Austin, TX: Holt Rinehart & Winston; ISBN: 0030445019.

Strauss, A., and Corbin, J. (1990). Basics of Qualitative Research: Grounded Theory Procedures and Techniques. Newbury Park, CA: Sage Publications. Probably now the leading contemporary treatment of grounded theory.

Stewart D. W., and Shamdasani, P. N. (1992). Focus Groups: Theory and Practice. London: Sage Publications.

Strauss, A., and Corbin, J., eds. (1997). Grounded Theory in Practice. London: Sage Publications.

Tartar, D. (1969). Toward prediction of attitude-action discrepancy. Social Forces 47(4): 398–404. Cited in relation to the gap between attitudes and behavior.

Vasu, M. S., and Vasu, E. S. (1998). Computers, survey research, and focus groups in public administration research and practice. In: Garson, D., ed. Information Technology and Computer Applications in Public Administration. Hershey, PA: Idea Group Publishing, 1998, pp 196–219.

Yin, R. K. (1994). Case study research. 2nd ed. Thousand Oaks, CA: Sage Publications.

18

Data-Gathering Resources

I. DATA-GATHERING RESOURCES

Before one can search for data, the researcher must have a clear concept of his or her question or problem. Refining one's search for data may involve identifying the intended use of the data. It may be helpful to sketch out the data tables one hopes to incorporate in a dissertation or other research project. From such mock-up tables, or from circle-and-arrow diagrams of the causal relationships being modeled, the researcher may be able to ''work backward'' to define the variables that in turn define the datasets that are needed.

Datasets have data dictionaries, codebooks, or other documentation. These define the variables to be found in a given dataset and their values, as well as such crucial information as how missing data are coded, if there have been changes over time in the way certain variables have been measured, and if variables have been measured differently for different subjects (e.g., differently in different states). In some cases, the documentation may also list published articles and books known to have used the dataset in question.

There are many types of research resources for purposes of finding data. Listing them would fill many volumes and such a list would be obsolete before it was completed. However, this section calls attention to a sample of leading current examples.

A. Data Libraries and Gateways

National digital library strategies are supported by the National Science Foundation (NSF) and other organizations such as the Council on Library and Information Resources (CLIR), whose web page on digital libraries is http://www.clir.org/programs/diglib/diglib.html. Further, CLIR is administrative home to the Digital Library Federation (DLF), which includes university research libraries, the Library of Congress, the National Archives, and the New York Public Library. The goal of DLF is to establish the conditions necessary for the creation, maintenance, expansion, and preservation of a distributed collection of digital materials accessible to scholars and the wider public.

Data libraries archive datasets used widely in social science. The Inter-University Consortium for Political and Social Research (ICPSR), for instance, functions as the depository for many datasets, analyses of which appear in social science journals (http://www.icpsr.umich.edu/). Major categories of ICPSR data holdings include Census Enumerations, Community, Urban Studies, Conflict, Aggression, Violence, Economic Behavior, Attitudes, Education, Elites and Leadership, Geography and Environment, Government Structures, Policies, Health Care, Facilities, Instructional Packages, International Systems, Legal Systems, Legislative, Deliberative Bodies, Mass Political Behavior, Attitudes, Organizational Behavior, Social Indicators, and Social Institutions.

The Harvard-MIT Data Center (HMDC) is a central contact point for many other archives and data suppliers. It maintains a large library of electronic data and an extensive codebook library. The HMDC web site has been awarded the title ''Best Political Science Research Web Site, 1999'' by the American Political Science Association (CMS). Many features of this site are unique, such as more than 500 online subsettable datasets, sophisticated browsing and searching options, automatic ordering of new datasets from other repositories, and interactive data exploration. Its largest project currently is the creation of a data center (VDC)—a free, open, portable, self-installing data server, using the protocols for communication and searching from their ongoing Digital Libraries Project and their recently completed Record of American Democracy project (the largest collection of combined census and electoral data set ever created). The website is at http://data.fas.harvard.edu/.

Michigan's Guide to Statistical Computing Resources on the Internet (http://asa.ugl.lib.umich.edu/chdocs/statistics/stat_guide_home.html) is one of the foremost general purpose data gateways.

The Networked Social Science Tools and Resources resource (NESSTAR), is a search engine that provides data discovery, location, browsing, and the dissemination of information through the Internet. Users may also analyze and download data and documentation. Information is available across organizational and national boundaries. Based on a standard proposed by an international committee of data librarians and statisticians, the NESSTAR software development builds on state-of-the-art technology like Java, XML and CORBA. An overview of the program is available on line at www.nesstar.org/.

Princeton University Data and Statistical Services (DSS) provides reference and consulting support to users of electronic data. Its data library is a collection of more than 24,000 machine-readable files. Electronic data are gathered primarily for the social sciences but also for the sciences and humanities. Data are available for the United States and foreign countries. The Data Library includes extensive holdings for Economic Time Series and U.S. Census Data and a range of other subject areas spanning historical and contemporary events, factual and pinion-oriented studies, and single and multiple country coverage. Some data are restricted to the Princeton community but much are available to outside researchers. The website is at http://www.princeton.edu/~data/.

Other data libraries and gateways on the Internet are:

http://www.co.calstate.edu/as/HTML/homepage.html, Analytic Studies Data Library;

http://www.lib.virginia.edu/socsci/arl/, Association of Research Libraries (ARL) Statistics;

http://www.brown.edu/Facilities/University_Library/general/guides/SSDS/SSDSHelp.html, Brown University Social Science Data Services (SSDS);

http://WWW.ciesin.org/, CIESIN: The Consortium for International Earth Science Information Network;

http://www.ciser.cornell.edu, Cornell Institute for Social and Economic Research (CISER), Data Archive;

http://www.nsd.uib.no/cessda/, Council of European Social Science Data Archives (CESSDA);

http://dawww.essex.ac.uk/, Data Archive, UK;

http://odwin.ucsd.edu/jj/idata/, Data on the Net, San Diego State University;

http://www.macroint.com/dhs/dhsarch.html, Demographic and Health Surveys Data Archive;

http://www.data-archive.ac.uk, Essex, Data Archive at the University of (The Economic and Social Research Council, UK);

http://www.berinsteinresearch.com/stats.htm, Finding Statistics Online;

http://www.un.org/Depts/unsd/global.htm, Global Statistics;

http://data.fas.harvard.edu/, Harvard MIT Data Center (social science);

http://www.radcliffe.edu/murray/data/index.htm, Henry A. Murray Research Center Data Archive (women's studies, Radcliffe College);

http://datalib.library.ualberta.ca/iassist/index.html, IASSIST (social science data librarians);

http://www.issp.org/data.htm, International Social Survey Programme;

http://www.icpsr.umich.edu/, ICPSR Home Page;

http://www.icpsr.umich.edu/contents.html, ICPSR site search;
http://www.sscnet.ucla.edu/issr/da/, ISSR social science data archive;
http://www.un.org/Depts/unsd/refs3.htm, National Publications and Statistical Yearbooks, Current Statistics and Internet Sites;
http://www.lib.umich.edu/libhome/data/, Numeric Data Services at the University of Michigan Library;
http://acit.cgu.edu/acit/Datasets/datalist.html, OnLine Datasets, Claremont Graduate University;
http://www-rcade.dur.ac.uk/, Resource Centre for Access to Data on Europe;
http://www.un.org/Depts/unsd/social/main.htm, Social Indicators, UN;
http://www.psc.lsa.umich.edu/SSDAN/, Social Science Data Analysis Network;
http://artemis.calstatela.edu/, Social Science Data Base;
http://www3.huji.ac.il/www_magar/il-home.htm, Social Sciences Data Archive (Hebrew University of Jerusalem, Israel);
http://ndad.ulcc.ac.uk/, UK National Digital Archive of Datasets (NDAD);
http://statlab.stat.yale.edu/SSDA/ssda.html, Yale University, Social Science Data Archive;
http://www.uib.no/nsd/diverse/utenland.htm, World Map of Social Science Data Archives.

B. Government Agencies

Government agencies increasingly make data available directly. The National Technical Information Service (NTIS), for instance, functions as the archivist for all federally funded research. The U.S. Census Bureau, the Department of Justice, and the Bureau of Labor Statistics are among the many federal agencies making large datasets available for research purposes.

Census data online:

Aging. Grandparents Day 1998 provides statistical information at http://www.census.gov/ Press-Release/cb98-ff.10.html.

The 1997 American Community Survey Online has census data for more than 65,000 areas accessible on the Internet at http://www.census.gov/cms/www. The 1997 data appear in both summary and area-profile formats.

The black population in the United States: March 1997 (Update), P20–508. Detailed statistical tabulations on the civilian, noninstitutional, black population of the United States; based on the March 1997 Current Population Survey. The Internet address is http://www.census.gov/population/socdemo/www/race/black.html.

Changes in median household income: 1969 to 1996. Reports trends in income changes between 1969 and 1996, at http://www.census.gov/hhes/www/income.html.

American FactFinder, located at http://www.census.gov/dads/www. The Bureau of the Census' effort to disseminate federal data to the American public.

Geographic mobility: March 1997 (Update), P20–510. Detailed characteristics of movers such as age, sex, race and Hispanic origin, educational attainment, occupation, income and homeowner/renter status for Northeast, South, Midwest and West; special table for "Sunbelt." The Internet address is http://www.census.gov/cgi-bin/main/newsite.

Government expenditures. U.S. and State government revenue and expenditures, http://www.census.gov/govs/www/index.html.

Hispanics. Census Bureau Facts for Features. Hispanic Heritage Month, provides statistical information at http://www.census.gov/Press-Release/cb98-ff.11.html. For another report on Hispanic immigration, showing California to be most effected, go to http://www.census.gov/population/www/ estimates/statepop.html for state data and to http://www.census.gov/population/www/estimates/countypop.html for county data.

Estimates of the Population of States by Age Groups and Sex: 1990 and 1997, PPL-109. State population estimates by detailed age and sex as of July 1997. The report is available on the Internet and in paper listings, with a few exceptions. The Internet address is http://www.census.gov/cgi-bin/main/newsite.

Marital Status and Living Arrangements: March 1997 (Update), P20–506. Report consists of 1 state-level, 3 summary, 9 detailed, and 12 historical tables, with marital-status characteristics of total population and living arrangements of children and adults. The Internet address is http://www.census.gov/population/www/socdemo/ms-la.html.

Hot Sites is a new feature of the U. S. Census. Go to http://www.census.gov, then click on News, then on Hot Sites. This will bring you to custom census information on such topics as those for African-Americans, Hispanics, or American Indians as a group.

The State and Metropolitan Area Data Book Fifth Edition (1997–98) is available in PostScript document format (.pdf) at http://www.census.gov/statab/www/smadb.html. The 268-page document contains data tables that give state and metropolitan breakdowns on a wide range of social, economic, and demographic variables. The site also contains information on ordering the CD-ROM version.

Selected government data resource and research sites:

http://www.census.gov/, Bureau of the Census;

http://lcweb2.loc.gov/frd/cs/cshome.html, Army Area Handbooks;
http://www.ojp.usdoj.gov/bjs/, Bureau of Justice Statistics;
http://stats.bls.gov:80/datahome.htm, Bureau of Labor Statistics data page;
http://www.gsa.gov/fdac/, catalog of federal domestic assistance;
http://www.census.gov/mp/www/index2.html, CENSTAT-electronic subscription service;
http://www.unchs.org/indicat/indihome.htm, Centre for Human Settlements Indicators Programme;
http://www.communityhealth.hrsa.gov/, Community Health Status Indicators Project;
http://members.aol.com/copafs/, Council of Professional Associations of Federal Statistics;
http://www.uncjin.org/stats/ccrimes.html, crime by country, UN;
http://www.albany.edu/sourcebook/, criminal justice statistics sourcebook;
http://www.ojp.usdoj.gov/bjs/dcf/contents.htm, drugs and crime facts;
http://europa.eu.int/en/comm/eurostat/eurostat.html, The Statistical Office of the European Communities, EUROSTAT;
http://www.access.gpo.gov/omb/omb003.html, Federal budget;
http://fjsrc.urban.org/index.shtml, Federal Justice Statistics Resource Center;
http://www.fedstats.gov, FEDSTATS;
http://govinfo.kerr.orst.edu/, Government Information Sharing Project;
http://www.nttc.edu/gov_res.html, government information sources;
http://www.access.gpo.gov, GPO access (Government Printing Office);
http://aspe.hhs.gov/98gb/intro.htm, Green Book of Entitlement Programs, HHS;
http://www.nara.gov/nara/electronic/tlintro.html, National Archives and Records Administration data files;
http://www.usda.gov/nass/, National Agricultural Statistics Service;
http://www.icpsr.umich.edu/NACJD/, National Archive of Criminal Justice Data;
http://www.ed.gov/NCES/, National Center for Education Statistics (NCES);
http://www.health.org/, The National Clearinghouse for Alcohol and Drug Information;
http://www.ncjrs.org/database.htm, National Criminal Justice Research Service database;
http://www.ntis.gov/, National Technical Information Service (NTIS);
http://www.nvc.org/, National Victim Center;
ftp://ftp.ssa.gov/pub/statistics/, Social Security Administration public information server;

http://www.whitehouse.gov/fsbr/ssbr.html, Social Statistics Briefing Room;
http://www.statistics.gov.uk/statbase/mainmenu.asp, StatBase (UK);
www.unl.edu/SPPQ/sppq.html, State Politics and Policy Quarterly data archive;
http://www.stat-usa.gov, STAT-USA;
http://www.census.gov:80/stat_abstract/, Statistical Abstract of the United States;
http://www.census.gov/prod/www/statistical-abstract-us.html, Statistical Abstract of the United States;
http://www.itl.nist.gov/div898/strd/, statistical reference datasets;
http://www.education.unesco.org/educprog/stat/spreadsheets/index.html, statistical tables on education;
http://www.unicef.org/statis/, UNICEF statistics;
http://www.fbi.gov/ucr.htm, Uniform Crime Reports, FBI;
http://www.un.org/Depts/unsd/, United Nations Monthly Bulletin of Statistics;
http://www.disastercenter.com/crime/, United States crime statistics;
http://travel.state.gov/links.html, U. S. Embassies;
http://usda.mannlib.cornell.edu/usda/, USDA Economics and Statistics System;
http://computing.oac.ucla.edu/census/census1.htm, User's Guide to Online Census Data on the Web;
http://www.who.org/whosis/whosis.htm, World Health Organization Statistical Information System.

C. Survey Organizations

Survey organizations also make data available directly, as well as provide training in survey methods. POLL, available online through commercial services such as Dialog Information Systems, enables researchers to identify previously asked survey items. Among the Internet-accessible survey sites are:

http://europa.eu.int/en/comm/dg10/infcom/epo/eo.html, EUROPINION Continuous Tracking Survey (CTS);
http://www.gallup.com/The_Poll/thepoll.asp, Gallup Poll;
http://www.icpsr.umich.edu/GSS/, General Social Survey;
http://www.louisharris.com/home_content.html, Harris Poll;
http://www.icpsr.umich.edu/, The Inter-University Consortium for Political and Social Research (ICPSR);
http://www.ncpp.org/, National Council on Public Opinion Polls;
http://www.norc.uchicago.edu/, National Opinion Research Center;
http://newfederalism.urban.org/nsaf/, National Survey of America's Families;

http://www.people-press.org/, Pew Research Center;
http://www.pollingreport.com/, Polling Report;
http://www.portraitofamerica.com/, Portrait of America;
http://www.publicagenda.org/, Public Agenda;
http://www.irss.unc.edu/data_archive/pollsearch.html, Public Opinion Poll question database (IRSS);
http://www.jstor.org/journals/0033362X.html, Public Opinion Quarterly;
http://www.aapor.org/poq/, Public Opinion Quarterly Index;
http://www.epinet.org/pulse/pulse.html, Pulse;
http://www.lib.uconn.edu/RoperCenter/, The Roper Center;
http://www.lib.virginia.edu/socsci/pums.html, U.S. Census Public Use Microdata Samples (PUMS).

D. Other Online Data Resources

The Internet is increasingly a gateway to a large number of online research resources. The Educational Resources Information Center (ERIC) database is available free online, as is the Library of Congress catalog, and access is available to archives associated with many newspapers, policy institutes, university research centers, and interest groups. Use the buttons to the left to explore further.

1. Sites about Online Searching

http://www.windweaver.com/searchguide.htm, tips on using web search engines;
http://www2.chass.ncsu.edu/garson/PA540/dialog.htm, DIALOG: Introduction to Bibliographic Searching Online;
http://www.inform.umd.edu:8080/EdRes/Topic/Guides/, Internet subject guides;
http://www.learnthenet.com/english/, Internet tutorial;
http://www.learnthenet.com/english/html/15wsrch.htm, introduction to searching the Web.

2. Sites for Books and Bibliography

http://www.amazon.com/, Amazon.com;
http://www.barnesandnoble.com, Barnes and Noble.com;
http://www.columbia.edu/acis/bartleby/bartlett/, Bartlett's quotations;
http://wwwcrl.uchicago.edu/, Center for Research Libraries;
http://crlcatalog.uchicago.edu/, Center for Research Libraries catalog;
http://library.dialog.com/bluesheets/, Dialog Bluesheets Online;
telnet://dialog.com, Telnet to DIALOG (largest online vendor of bibliographic database access; account number and password required);

http://library.dialog.com/search_aids.html, DIALOG help (search);
http://www.jisc.ac.uk/subject/socsci/, Economic and Social Research Council (UK);
http://www.elibrary.com/, Electric Library;
http://ericir.syr.edu/Eric/, ERIC bibliographic database;
http://ericir.syr.edu/Eric/plweb_faq.html, ERIC FAQ sheet;
http://ipl.sils.umich.edu/ref/, Internet public library (University of Michigan);
http://lcweb.loc.gov/catalog/, Library of Congress search system;
http://lcweb2.loc.gov/, Library of Congress ''American Memory'' digital collection search;
http://www.cs.cmu.edu/books.html, online books;
http://www.yorku.ca/nathanson/search.htm, organized crime and corruption bibliographic database;
http://srsweb.nsf.gov/it_site/index.htm, social and economic implications of information technologies bibliographic database;
http://sosig.ac.uk/, SOSIG (UK, social science).

3. Sites for Legislation and Law Data

http://www.lexis.com/, Lexis-Nexis Home Page;
http://thomas.loc.gov:80/, U. S. Congress ''Thomas'' Site;
http://www.law.cornell.edu/uscode/, U. S. Code;

4. Sites for Data on Cities, States, and Nations

http://www.BestPlaces.net/, Best Places Net;
http://pathfinder.com/money/bestplaces/, Best Places to Live;
http://www.mayors.org/uscm/meet_mayors/cities_online.html, Cities Online;
http://www.city.net, City.Net;
http://lcweb2.loc.gov/frd/cs/cshome.html, Country Studies (Library of Congress);
http://www.prb.org/prb/info/stateweb.htm, Data web sites for the 50 states;
http://www.unc.edu/depts/nnsp/abtnnsp.htm, National Network of State Polls (NNSP);
http://www.prb.org/, Population Reference Bureau;
http://www.census.gov/statab/www/smadb.html, State and Metropolitan Area Data Book;
http://io.aspensys.com/SOCDS/SOCDS_Home.htm, State of the Cities;
http://www.census.gov/sdc/www/, State Data Centers;
http://www.econ.ag.gov/pubs/usfact/, State Fact Sheets;

http://io.aspensys.com/SOCDS/SOCDS_Home.htm, State of Cities Data System (HUD);
http://www.states.org/contents/index.html, States Inventory Project;
http://govinfo.kerr.orst.edu/usaco-stateis.html, USA Counties;
www.ibe.unesco.org/Inf_Doc/Nat_reps/wdepfome.htm, World Data on Education website.

5. Political Data

http://politicsusa.com/PoliticsUSA/resources/almanac/, The Almanac of American Politics;
http://www.freedomchannel.com/almanac/almanac_of_amer_pol.cfm, Almanac of American Politics;
http://www.umich.edu:80/~nes/, The American National Election Studies;
http://www.umich.edu:80/~nes/search.htm, American National Election Studies Search;
http://www.klipsan.com/usp32-96.htm, Atlas of United States Presidential Elections;
http://www.vote-smart.org/congress/index.html, Campaign Finance Contributions to members of U.S. Congress;
http://www.publicampaign.org/ColorOfMoney/, Color of Money (campaign contributions);
http://130.241.116.20/, Comparative Election Administration Study Data Archive (CEAS/DA);
http://venus.census.gov/cdrom/lookup/, Congressional District Data, U. S. Census;
http://www.tray.com/fecinfo/, FEC Info;
http://dodgson.ucsd.edu/lij/, Lijphart Election Archives;
http://www.usmayors.org/uscm/elections/99elections.asp, Mayoral Elections Database;
http://www.sos.state.mi.us/cfr/cfonl.html, Michigan Campaign Finance Reporting System;
http://data.fas.harvard.edu/ROAD/, ROAD (Record of American Democracy electoral and socioeconomic data down to U. S. precinct level);
http://clerkweb.house.gov/evs/index.htm, Roll Call votes, U.S. House (The Office of the Clerk, U.S. House of Representatives);
http://www.vanishingvoter.org/, Vanishing Voter.

6. Sites for News and Media Data

http://www.enews.com/, E-News.com electronic newsstand;
http://www.yahoo.com/news_and_media/, Electronic Newspapers and Media;
http://www.euromktg.com/globstats/, Global Internet Statistics;

http://www.internetindicators.com/, Internet Economy Indicators;
http://aa.mlive.com/ap/0417webrace.html, Internet use;
http://www.trac.org/, Telecommunications Research and Action Center.

7. Economic Data Sites

http://www.bea.doc.gov/beahome.html, Bureau of Economic Analysis;
http://stats.bls.gov/homtoc.htm, Bureau of Labor Statistics Handbook;
http://www.tcb-indicators.org/, Business Cycle Indicators;
http://www.commerce.net/research/, Commerce Net Research Center;
http://www.compustat.com/, COMPUSTAT;
http://www.tcb-indicators.org/, Conference Board;
http://stats.bls.gov/cpihome.htm, Consumer Price Index;
http://www.census.gov/epcd/cbp/view/cbpview.html, County Business Patterns;
http://www.gpo.ucop.edu/catalog/econind.html, Current Economic Indicators;
http://www.census.gov/ftp/pub/cir/www/, Current Industrial Reports;
http://stats.bls.gov/cpshome.htm, Current Population Survey;
http://www.epinet.org/datazone/, DataZone;
ftp://econ.lsa.umich.edu/pub/Dow-Jones/, Dow Jones Historical Data;
http://www.ny.frb.org/rmaghome/, Economic Research;
http://bos.business.uab.edu/data/data.htm, Economic Time Series, Ted Bos;
http://economagic.com/, Economagic: Economic Time Series Page;
http://www.bls.gov/eag.table.html, Economy at a Glance;
http://www.ecommerce.gov/, Electronic Commerce Policy, U. S. Dept. of Commerce;
http://stats.bls.gov/ecthome.htm, Employment Cost Trends;
http://europa.eu.int/en/comm/dg10/infcom/epo/eb.html, Eurobarometers;
http://www.frbsf.org/system/fedinprint/, Fed in Print;
http://www.stls.frb.org/fred, Federal Reserve Economic Data (FRED);
http://www.bog.frb.fed.us/, Federal Reserve System;
http://www.stls.frb.org/fred/, Federal Reserve Economic Databases;
http://www.ny.frb.org/, Federal Reserve Bank of New York;
http://www.stls.frb.org/fred/dataindx.html, Federal Reserve Board, St. Louis;
http://www.globalfindata.com/guide.htm, Global Financial Database, Guide to;
http://dsbb.imf.org/gddsweb/siteinfo.htm, International Monetary Fund, General Data Dissemination Site;
http://www.ita.doc.gov/, International Trade Administration;
http://www.tcb-indicators.org/leihistory/leihistory.htm, Leading Economic Indicators;

http://www.nber.org/data_index.html, National Bureau of Economic Research;

http://www.lib.virginia.edu/socsci/nipa, National Income & Product Accounts Data Visualization System;

http://www.umich.edu/~psid/, The Panel Study of Income Dynamics;

http://stats.bls.gov/ppihome.htm, Producer Price Index;

http://www.sba.gov/, Small Business Administration;

http://www.tradeport.org/ts/countries/, Tradeport Country Library;

http://www.streeteye.com/, Wall Street Journal, StreetEYE;

http://www1.whitehouse.gov/fsbr/esbr.html, White House Economic Statistics Briefing Room.

8. Research Methodology Sites

http://www.biostat.washington.edu/Vlib/, BioStatistics Virtual Library;

http://trochim.human.cornell.edu/index.html, Center for Social Research Methods, Bill Trochim;

http://netec.wustl.edu/CodEc.html, CodEc–Programs for Economics and Econometrics;

http://elsa.berkeley.edu/, Econometrics Laboratory Software Archive;

http://gurukul.ucc.american.edu/econ/gaussres/GAUSSIDX.HTM, GAUSS Archive at American University;

http://eclab.econ.pdx.edu/gpe/, Gauss Programming for Econometricians;

http://www.econotron.com/, GAUSSX (Econotron);

http://www.wolverinesoftware.com/, GPSS;

http://math.montana.edu/~umsfjban/STAT438/Stat438.html, Graphical Data Analysis;

http://www.stat.ucla.edu/textbook/, The Internet Statistical Textbook;

http://raven.cc.ukans.edu/~keds, Kansas Event Data System (KEDS);

http://www.mathsource.com/, Mathematica Library;

http://www.ams.org/mathscinet/, MathSciNet;

http://www.mathsoft.com/, Mathsoft homepage;

http://polmeth.calpoly.edu/, Political Methodology website;

http://www.estima.com/tour/ratstour.htm, RATS tour;

http://www.stat.math.ethz.ch/~roosen/S-faq.html, S+ FAQ's by Charles Roosen;

http://www.isor.vuw.ac.nz/~office/Smanual/Smanual.html, S+ Introduction;

http://www.stat.cmu.edu/s-news/, S-News Archive at Statlib;

http://www.sas.com/, SAS Institute;

http://www.yorku.ca/dept/psych/lab/sas/, SAS Help, Michael Friendly;

http://www.spss.com, SPSS homepage;

http://data.fas.harvard.edu/hdc/spsshelp.shtml, SPSS Help, Harvard-MIT Data Center;
http://www.stata.com, STATA homepage;
http://www.stat.cmu.edu/stata/stata/, STATA Archive at Statlib;
http://data.fas.harvard.edu/hdc/statahelp.shtml, STATA Help, Harvard-MIT Data Center;
http:/www.stat.cmu.edu/, StatLib Index of Statistical Software;
http://GKing.Harvard.Edu/stats.html, Statistical Software, Gary King;
http://www.stat.ufl.edu/vlib/statistics.html, Statistics Virtual Library;
http://www2.chass.ncsu.edu/garson/PA765/statnote.htm, StatNotes;
http://www.tspintl.com/, TSP (for economic time series analysis).

9. Geographic and Spatial Information Sites

http://www.esri.com/data/online/, ArcData Online;
http://www.ciesin.org/, Consortium for International Earth Science Information Network (CIESIN);
http://plue.sedac.ciesin.org/plue/ddviewer/, CIESIN Mapping Service;
http://130.166.124.2/USpage1.html, Digital Atlas of the United States;
http://www.maproom.psu.edu/dcw/, Digital Chart of the World;
http://edcwww.cr.usgs.gov/landdaac/, Earth Resources Observation Systems Data Center;
http://www.esri.com/, Environmental Systems Research Institute (publishers of *ArcView* and *ArcInfo*, and vendors of data);
http://www.fgdc.gov/clearinghouse/, Federal Geographic Data Committee;
http://mcphee.wustl.edu/gissoft.htm, Geographical Information Services;
http://www.census.gov/pub/geo/www/, Geographic Services and Information, U. S. Census;
http://www-nmd.usgs.gov/www/gnis/, Geographic Names Information System;
http://www.frw.ruu.nl:80/nicegeo.html, Geography Sites;
http://www.blm.gov/gis/, Geospatial Home Page (BLM);
http://www.lib.berkeley.edu/UCBGIS/gisnet.html, GIS Resources on the Internet;
http://www.geo.ed.ac.uk/home/giswww.html, GIS WWW Resources List;
http://www.grid.unep.ch/, Global Resources Information Database;
http://www.cast.uark.edu/local/hunt/index.html, Guide to on-line and free U.S. spatial data;
http://www.lagesi.caltech.edu., Laboratory for Global Environmental Science Information;
http://magic.lib.uconn.edu/, Map and Geographic Information Center;
http://www.mapquest.com/, MapQuest;

http://www.cgrer.uiowa.edu/servers/servers_references.html, Maps and references;

http://ptolemy.gis.virginia.edu/gicdoc/dlg/dlg.html, National Digital Map Library;

http://nsdi.usgs.gov/, National Geospatial Data Clearinghouse (USGS);

http://nsdi.epa.gov/nsdi/, National Geospatial Data Clearinghouse (EPA);

http://water.usgs.gov/lookup/getgislist, Spatial Data Sets for Water;

http://www.iko.unit.no/gis/gisen.html, Starting points for GIS/ cartography;

http://www.census.gov/themapit/www/, Thematic Mapping Service, U.S. Census;

http://tiger.census.gov/, Tiger Mapping Service;

http://www.bts.gov/gis/ntatlas/background.html, U.S. Dept. of Transportation–GeoSpatial Data;

http://www.census.gov/cgi-bin/gazetteer, U.S. Gazetteer;

http://water.usgs.gov/public/watuse/, Water Use in the United States.

10. Sites for General Information

http://factfinder.census.gov/, American Factfinder;

http://www.library.cornell.edu/okuref/research/tutorial.html, Cornell Guide to Research Writing;

http://www.eb.com, Encyclopedia Britannica online;

http://www.itools.com/research-it/research-it.html, Research-It;

http://pathfinder.com, Time-Warner Pathfinder.

11. Other Data Sites

http://www.demographics.com/Publications/AD/index.htm, American Demographics;

http://www.arda.tm/, American Religion Data Archive;

http://intarch.york.ac.uk/ahds/index.html, Archaeology Data Service;

http://nces.ed.gov/, Center for Education Statistics;

http://wwwgateway.ciesin.org, CIESIN Gateway (demographics);

http://www.studorg.nwu.edu/seed/EnviroInfo.html, Internet Environmental Information;

http://csf.Colorado.EDU/isa/data-arc.htm, International Studies Association Data Archive;

http://www.icpsr.umich.edu/NACDA/index.html, National Archive of Computerized Data on Aging;

http://nccs.urban.org/, National Center for Charitable Statistics;

http://www.statistics.gov.uk/, United Kingdom Statistics Site;

http://www3.itu.int/unions/search.cgi, United Nations International Organizations Network Search (UNIONS).

12. Search Engines

http://www.alltheweb.com, All the Web;
http://altavista.digital.com, AltaVista;
http://www.excite.com, Excite;
http://www.google.com, Google;
http://www.hotbot.com, HotBot;
http://www.lycos.com, Lycos;
http://www.metacrawler.com, MetaCrawler;
http://webcrawler.com, WebCrawler;
http://www.yahoo.com, Yahoo.

19

Drawing Inferences and Making Generalizations

I. THE CONCLUSION

The conclusion is perhaps the most important segment of the dissertation or research paper. This is true partly because the conclusion presents the "bottom line" of the researcher's findings, with implications for theory and practice. But equally important is the fact that evaluators of the researcher's efforts are likely to ask whether the conclusion is consistent with the introduction (did the researcher do what he or she set out to do?) and whether the conclusion is supported by the evidence the researcher has marshaled (did the researcher generalize to the appropriate universe, and did the research avoid asserting conclusions that do not rest on the data actually collected in the present study?).

Stephen Toulmin (1979) set forth the six elements of reasoning, all of which must be present in the conclusion. The "claim" is the debatable assertion found in hypotheses. The "grounds" are the evidence supporting the claim. The "warrant" explains how the grounds support the claim. The "rebuttal" lists the conditions under which the warrant and grounds support the claim. The "modality" indicates the level of confidence or certainty the researcher has in the claim. Finally, the "backing" sets forth the "givens"—the assumptions on which the whole argument rests.

A full conclusion will have all six elements, although they are rarely labeled as such. For instance, in a study of the causes of drug use, a conclusion might state, "Given the prevailing American culture of individualism and freedom of choice (the backing), the more television role models make light of marijuana use, the more subsequent actual marijuana use (the claim). This is because such models increase dissonance among competing forces of socialization and legitimate individual free choice as a prime value (the warrant) as evidenced by the survey data in Table I (the grounds), at least for the urban population of teenagers studied (the modality).''

The better the previous sections of your dissertation or research paper, the easier it is to write the conclusions. Keep in mind that a good conclusion is relatively short, hitting the main points of your research. The reader should not have to wade through endless detail to understand what you have found. However, the conclusion is not the same as an abstract. In some scientific and technical fields, conclusions may be very succinct but in general, the typical organization of the concluding chapter contains the following elements, although not necessarily labeled as such:

1. A summary of the most important findings of the study, both supporting and not supporting the author's hypotheses.
2. A discussion of each important finding in relation to significant literature in the field (does it confirm, disconfirm, revise prevailing views?)
3. A reiteration of the limitations of the study in terms of generalization to broader populations or other settings and conditions.
4. A discussion of the implications of the study for future development of the field. This is the focus of the next chapter.
5. A final conclusion discussing implications of the study for current theory in the field.

The third step, generalization of one's findings, is particularly crucial, and this topic is covered below.

II. DRAWING INFERENCES AND MAKING GENERALIZATIONS

One of the most common downfalls in the writing of empirical papers, theses, and dissertations is the improper drawing of inferences and making of conclusions. Having invested so much time and energy in the investigative process, the researcher may well feel a desire to make strong assertions and conclusions of which he or she is convinced, suppressing the fact that the actual data gathered by the researcher are limited in nature and call for much narrower pronouncements of more limited scope. Even in published articles and books, one will find this common error of reasoning, which easily can become compounded by later, uncritical researchers citing as gospel truth the sweeping conclusions of an earlier author. In this way, the true development of the discipline is impaired even when the researcher-author is not called to task specifically. Often, of course, errors of generalization and inference *are* noticed, leading to sometimes insurmountable problems at the time of thesis defense or publication.

A. Conclusions and the Scientific Method

Conclusions may be based on classification, observation, induction, or deduction. Aristotle noted classification as a means to knowledge based on formulating exclusive definitions, then assigning cases to the classes thus created. Aristotle also discussed observation, defined as the process of gathering evidence through the senses, such as seeing, hearing, and tasting. Induction was the mode espoused by Francis Bacon (1561–1626), the English philosopher who argued that the methodology of science must be universally based on the process of making generalizations induced from observations of multiple cases (not just observation of single cases).

Almost the opposite was argued by Karl Popper, a 20th century philosopher who held that the methodology of science must be based on deducing specific conclusions from general theories and their corollaries: generalized questions are analyzed to formulate predictions of outcomes by deductive reasoning, after which is it useful to apply tests, as tests can only disprove theories. That is, many theories will be consistent with any given set of facts, so one cannot validly start with a set of facts and induce a single ''correct'' theory. Rather, one must start with a theory and test it against facts.

Drawing inferences and making generalizations properly is directly linked to appropriate use of the scientific method. At one level, the scientific method follows the hypothetico-deductive model: hypotheses are derived from theories and then tested empirically using experiments, random samples, and exact observation. The scientific method can be described in terms of solving puzzles. Selecting a topic begins with noticing a puzzling phenomenon, a mystery—something that calls for explanation. The researcher posits various possible explanations for the puzzling phenomenon. These are hypotheses. If the hypothesis is true, the researcher asks, then what should be the consequences? What will be the evidence that it is true? What would falsify the hypothesis? The answers to these questions become the tests for the hypotheses.

Of course, in reality the process of discovery may be much less systematic than this model suggests. Unexpected observations, even outside the framework of an experiment, may yield interesting findings that advance science. Sometimes new conclusions are not based on new evidence at all but rather on better analysis and logic applied to existing evidence. Moreover, much research is exploratory, without benefit of systematic theories and hypotheses. The hypothetico-deductive version of the scientific method does not fully describe how science actually works, as evidence may arise outside the context of hypothesis testing. However, it is nonetheless true that in the conclusion section of one's dissertation or research report, there must be evidence that supports each concluding statement.

In formulating conclusions, a distinction must be made between conclusions about a theory and conclusions about hypotheses derived from that theory. There are three possible explanations when unexpected results appear or when an experiment or quasiexperiment comes up with negative results, leading the researcher to fail to reject the null hypothesis that there is no difference between the results found and chance. The three explanations are:

1. The theory is wrong, and hence hypotheses derived from the theory are often wrong, including the present one with null results.
2. The theory is correct, but the hypothesis has not been derived correctly from the theory, so testing that hypothesis is not a good test of the theory.
3. The hypothesis is correctly derived, but the procedure for testing it is flawed, either in concept or in the steps involved in carrying out the procedure, so whether right or wrong, the underlying theory is not tested validly.

Rejection of underlying theory is only one of three possible explanations for negative results, and the researcher should be very cautious before conclusions are drawn that reject a theory. The more widely the theory is accepted, the more thorough and numerous the tests will be before it is rejected. The less well understood and accepted the procedures used for testing a theory, the more multiple methods of testing will be appropriate.

B. Making Inferences

Inference has to do with "external validity." External validity, in turn, has to do with possible bias in the process of making conclusions about a population based on data from a sample. The inferences may be to a population, to other subject populations, to other settings, or to other time periods. The question raised is, "To what population does the researcher wish to generalize his/her conclusions, and is there something unique about the study sample's subjects, the place where they lived/worked, the setting in which they were involved, or the times of the study that would prevent valid generalization?"

When the data in one's sample came about through convenience, availability, self-selection, or some other nonrandom process, generalization may be impossible. Nonrandom methods of obtaining one's units of analysis, be they people, agencies, or nations, introduce potential biases of unknown proportions. If the researcher has randomly sampled data, however, then statistical assumptions can be made validly in ways that allow generalization of findings from the sample data to the population at large.

C. Types of Generalizability

Researchers often distinguish three types of generalizability of conclusions, going beyond applying the conclusion to the original subjects. These are not mutually exclusive forms, and meeting the criteria of all three is a worthy goal.

1. *Sampling generalizability*. Inferences about a population based on a sample of that population require that the sample be randomly selected and large enough for the level of confidence desired. This is the issue of statistical inference and statistical significance. It deals with generalization from a sample to *one* population.
2. *Treatment generalizability*. The treatment or independent variable effect must be the same for *various* populations. Example: a tutorial software program is shown to improve test scores by similar percentages for both high school students and adult learners, or for both African Americans and whites. This form of generalizability is sometimes called *transferability*. In the field of educational and psychological tests and measurements, ''generalizability theory'' has to do with using analysis of variance techniques to develop a ''generalizability coefficient,'' which summarizes the treatment generalizability of a test under varying conditions (see Shavelson, 1991).
3. *Measurement generalizability*. For the same population measured using different methods, the treatment or independent variable effect is found to be the same. This is, of course, the multimethod strategy, as when survey research results are corroborated by the results of focus group methodology or archival research of records.

To have statistical generalizability, the researcher must use a random sample (or have enumeration data on all cases, in which case sampling generalizability is irrelevant). To have treatment generalizability, the researcher must test the treatment or apply the causal model to diverse populations and see if similar results are obtained. To have measurement generalizability, the researcher must use multiple methods of measurement.

D. The Trade-Off between Model Precision and Generalizability

There is a tradeoff between model precision and generalizability. Precision means the degree to which the quantitative model is allowed to predict the observed data by virtue of making the model more and more complex. For instance, in structural equation modeling, inductive expert systems, neural network analysis, and a variety of other statistical modeling techniques, full parameterization (allowing the model to be as complex as possible) will ''predict'' the observed data totally. To take another example, brute-force curve-fitting software exists that will test the data against every conceivable modeling equation, returning the one that explains the data best, often a very complex formula with many high-level power terms and interaction terms for which the researcher can find no corresponding theoretical or intuitive explanation.

What has happened in such cases is that what has been modeled is the noise in the dataset as well as the general relationships in which the researcher is really interested. The researcher would prefer to model only the underlying relationships, for then the results have the hope of being generalizable. This is why goodness of data fit coefficients in many statistical techniques reward parsimony (models that are less parameterized but still predict much of the data). It is also why better statistics texts caution against automated, brute-force methods of arriving at models but instead recommend that all parameters have a theoretical justification.

This is not to say that the simplest, most parsimonious model is best. Model misspecification refers to omitting significant variables or including extraneous ones and to correctly indicating the direction of arrows connecting the variables in the model. When a misspecification error is corrected by changing the model, all parameter estimates in the model are subject to change, not only in magnitude, but sometimes even in direction. There is no statistical test for misspecification, but as a rule of thumb, the lower the overall effect (e.g., R^2 in multiple regression, goodness of fit in logistic regression), the more likely it is that important variables have been omitted from the model and that existing interpretations of the model will change when the model is correctly specified. If a model has been misspecified, generalizations from statistical results are prone to great error as all coefficients may change after proper specification.

There is no precise solution to the problem of the tradeoff between model precision and generalizability. Nonetheless, the researcher should be very aware that tradeoffs exist and should seek to construct parsimonious models. The more complex and fully parameterized the model, the less likely it is to be generalizable and the more the researcher will need to demonstrate generalizability through explicit proofs.

E. Building Confidence in Conclusions

Many ''conclusion'' sections in dissertations, journal articles, and other empirical writing are actually nonconclusions. That is, the authors say such things as, ''The variables we have studied are important, and the relationships are complex and warrant further research.'' Some merit may be found in researchers not ''sticking their necks out'' too far in their conclusions, but it is nonetheless important that conclusions be strong enough that the assertions could be falsified by further research and more data. If on reading one's concluding section, the reader cannot really get a ''handle'' on something testable and empirically falsifiable, then the researcher has ''waffled'' the conclusions and spun a web of abstractions designed more to mystify and finesse the audience than to promote scientific inquiry. Conclusions should be no stronger than warranted by the evidence, but however sweeping or limited the conclusions may be, they should be expressed with enough clarity that they may be tested empirically by other researchers. This is how disciplines advance.

In modern times, methodologists have increasingly drawn a distinction between testing hypotheses and testing models. This distinction goes to the heart of the scientific method because it is based on the understanding that the hypothetico-deductive model cannot prove any set of hypotheses to be ''correct,'' as many models and sets of related hypotheses will fit any set of data. This was recognized decades ago and the customary advice then was to anticipate counterhypotheses that might be put forward by critics of one's findings, and to evaluate and rebut them explicitly one by one. This is still good advice and much better than not anticipating alternative hypotheses for a given set of facts.

However, the distinction between testing hypotheses and testing models goes beyond anticipating counterhypotheses. The process of testing hypotheses proceeds one hypothesis at a time, looking at the significance of the relationships it engenders (if a random sample) and at the effect sizes of these relationships, to see if they are of the direction and magnitude predicted. If there are many hypotheses, the actual significance level will be lower than the nominal (usually .05) one used in one-at-a-time testing, but this can be addressed by using a more stringent test (e.g., .001). In contrast, the process of testing models de-emphasizes significance testing of hypotheses and instead focuses on using measures of fit to indicate whether one model conforms to observations better than another. An entire web of relationships, often depicted in a circle-and-arrow diagram of the relationships of variables in a model, is evaluated simultaneously. Instead of testing an hypothesis and anticipation counterhypotheses, the researcher is urged to test models and countermodels. Of course, to have conclusions about models rather than individual hypotheses requires the researcher to have anticipated this in his or her methodology section and to have selected appropriate tools, such as structural equation modeling.

Confidence in conclusions goes beyond simply demonstrating that a particular set of experimental or survey data is consistent with an hypothesis being investigated. The researcher may seek to increase confidence in conclusions in any or all of four ways:

1. There should be a systematic discussion of possible threats to validity, discussed in a previous chapter.

2. Enough information should be presented that other researchers in your discipline could replicate your study and arrive at the same conclusion.

3. There should be a systematic discussion of the relation of current find-

ings to other findings in the literature, reconciling differences for the reader. Reconciliation may be by elucidation of differences in effects caused by differences in variables, perhaps unmeasured in prior studies; differences caused by measurement methods, perhaps better in the current study; or differences resulting from logical inference, perhaps more rigorous in the current study.

4. Wherever possible, each variable should be measured by multiple traits (e.g., multiple items in a survey instrument) and by multiple methods (e.g., by focus groups or experiments as well as survey research). A multi trait, multi method approach will build confidence in both the constructs used in the model tested by the researcher and the procedures used for the tests themselves.

With regard to the last of these three points, the dissertation writer whose research focuses on human subjects would do well to include case studies, narrative analysis, content analysis, focus groups, or other textually rich data-gathering strategies in addition to strategies that are statistically based, such as survey research and archival analysis of data. The purpose, of course, is to be in a position to use text-rich methods to reinforce—vividly and concretely for specific subjects—the generalizations based on broad statistical evidence.

F. Checklist

1. If there is such a heading at all, and even though some summarization is involved, have you headed your major findings as ''Conclusions'' or ''Findings'' rather than ''Summary?''
2. Have you related your generalizations and inferences clearly back to your dissertation or research paper thesis?
3. Is there close integration between your conclusion section and the literature review you did at the beginning?
4. Have you completed data analysis in earlier chapters, so the conclusion section can focus on findings?
5. Have you focused on important findings in your concluding chapter, leaving minor and trivial findings to the earlier chapters or sections of your work?
6. Have you used data visualization effectively in presenting your conclusions?
7. Have you avoided generalizing on data about one population to another? For instance, feminists often criticize generalizations made based on studies of male subjects when these generalizations are then applied to women.
8. Have you evaluated all available data, including evidence that only partially supports or is contrary to your hypotheses?
9. Is your sample large enough that you are confident you are not viewing chance variations?

10. Have you distinguished between long-term trends and short-term changes? That is, is your time period of observation long enough to allow you to distinguish fluctuations from true relationships?
11. Have you used control variables in your analysis where suggested by the literature or common sense? For instance, many relationships disappear when economic factors are controlled.
12. Do you have a sound basis for asserting what is a cause and what is an effect in each relationship in your model? Time sequence information helps in this regard but does not prove a prior event causes a subsequent event. One can rule out that the subsequent event causes the prior event, however.
13. Have your generalizations about causation avoided the usual logical fallacies?
    Post hoc fallacy: That one phenomenon follows another in time sequence does not prove causation.
    Prior cause fallacy: One thing may correlate with another only because both share a common prior cause.
    Mediating cause fallacy: One thing may correlate with another, but only by transmission of that effect through a third mediating variable.
    Insignificant effect fallacy: Some causes may indeed be causes, but they are insignificant in light of much more important causes.
    Confused cause-effect fallacy: Cause and effect are reverse of what is asserted, or reciprocal.
14. Where averages are used to reach conclusions, have you considered threats to the meaningfulness of measures of central tendency, such as outliers and bimodal distributions?
15. Have you avoided obvious logical inconsistencies or hyperbole, which will lead readers to dismiss your argument as a whole?
16. If you have cited other statistical studies in support of one or more of your arguments, are you confident that these articles have not been rebutted or superceded in the existing literature? Are you confident that the studies cannot be challenged on grounds of bias of the researcher, small sample size, lack of random sampling, low response rate, nonsignificant results, or significant results with trivial effect sizes?
17. Where statistical significance is involved, have you avoided discussing ''nearly significant'' results (e.g., those at the .056 level)? It is generally considered improper not to use your significance cut-off (.05) as a firm criterion for deciding which findings should be treated as being different from chance.
18. In your summaries of findings, have you avoided referring to things like ''Hypothesis 8a,'' ''Group C,'' and ''the C182 variable,'' instead

using descriptive English labels to aid the reader in following your explanation?

19. If you have cited authorities as added evidence in support of one or more of your arguments, are you confident of the expert's credentials and reputation? Citing persons with known biases will undermine rather than reinforce your conclusions.
20. Likewise, if you have cited testimony as added evidence in support of your arguments, are you confident that the testimony is without important inconsistencies and told from an unbiased viewpoint?
21. If you do not have enumeration data, have you demonstrated sampling generalizability through statistical tests of significance?
22. Have you attempted to demonstrate treatment generalizability by obtaining data based on different populations? If not, does your discussion section discuss possible treatment limits to generalizability?
23. Have you used multiple methods of measurement to demonstrate measurement generalizability? If not, does your discussion section discuss possible methodological biases limiting generalizability?
24. Have you evaluated the limitations of your study objectively, avoiding an apologetic tone?
25. In discussion limitations, have you distinguished limitations and delimitations? Delimitations are restrictions that the researcher has imposed deliberately on his or her study (e.g., in a study of the effects of testosterone on aggressiveness, restricting the study to males). Limitations are constraints on the generalizability of the study outside the control or intent of the researcher (e.g., low response rate, failure to obtain a random sample, or other violations of inferential assumptions, undermining valid generalization).
26. Is your conclusion consistent with your abstract?
27. Is your major conclusion and the major dependent variable reflected in keywords in your title?

BIBLIOGRAPHY

Dewey, J., ed. (1917). Creative Intelligence: Essays in the Pragmatic Attitude. New York: Henry Holt and Co.

Douglas, R., Harte, L., O'Hara, J. (1998). Drawing Conclusions. Belfast, Ireland: Blackstaff Press. Oriented toward historical examples, elementary level.

Englebretsen, G. (1998). Line Diagrams for Logic: Drawing Conclusions. Lewiston, NY: Edwin Mellen Press. Problems in Contemporary Philosophy, Vol. 40.

Firestone, W. A. (1993). Alternative arguments for generalizing from data as applied to qualitative research. Educational Researcher 22(4):16–23.

Fyans, L. J., ed. (1983). Generalizability theory: Inferences and practical applications. In: New Directions for Testing and Measurement. Vol. 18. San Francisco: Jossey-Bass.

Ginzberg, C. (1989). Clues: Roots of an evidential paradigm. In: Clues, Myths, and the Historical Paradigm. Baltimore, MD: The Johns Hopkins University Press, 1989, pp 96–125.

King, G., Keohane, R. O., and Verba, S. (1994). Designing Social Inquiry: Scientific Inference in Qualitative Research. Princeton, NJ: Princeton University Press. Presents a unified approach to valid descriptive and causal inference in qualitative research.

Kuhn, T. S. (1962). The Structure of Scientific Revolutions. Chicago: University of Chicago Press. This work described how science works in terms of "paradigm shifts," which are changes in general theories that in turn force alternative explanations of existing and new facts.

Kuhn, T. S. (1977). The Essential Tension. Chicago: The University of Chicago Press.

Mead, G. H. (1917). Scientific method and individual thinker. In: Dewey, J., ed. Creative Intelligence: Essays in the Pragmatic Attitude. New York: Henry Holt and Co., 1917, pp 176–227.

Popper, K. R. (1959). The Logic of Scientific Discovery. New York: Basic Books. A classic articulation of the positivist view of the nature of scientific reasoning.

Roberts, C. W., ed. (1997). Text Analysis for the Social Sciences: Methods for Drawing Statistical Inferences from Texts and Transcripts. Hillsdale, NJ: Lawrence Erlbaum.

Shavelson, R. J. (1991). Generalizability Theory: A Primer. Series: Measurement and Methods in the Social Sciences. Vol. 1. Thousand Oaks, CA: Sage Publications. Generalizability theory is an extension of reliability theory, assessing how psychological and other test instruments vary across conditions. Generalizability coefficients are interpreted similarly to the reliability coefficient and reflect a ratio based on a variance components ANOVA model, looking at generalization facets (usually testing conditions, such as locations) and differentiation facets (what is being discriminated by the measurement instrument, usually persons).

Toulmin, S. E. (1958). The Uses of Argument. New York: Cambridge University Press.

Toulmin, S. E., Rieke, R., and Janik, A. (1979). An Introduction to Reasoning. New York: Macmillan Publishing Co.

20

Pointing Ahead

I. INTRODUCTION

The conclusion is an all-important section in any research writing. Given human nature, the conclusion is not infrequently the first-read section of your writing! It is certainly considered the ''bottom line'' when the value of your work is assessed. As such, it deserves the utmost attention and care. Some consider it akin to the lawyer's summation address to a jury before a verdict. Doctoral students are likewise apt to feel it is their last chance for favorable consideration before judgment by their committee. The summary section of the conclusion reiterates the research problem and recalls the justification of its importance, relating that to key prior research literature; then describes the major findings of the researcher regarding the research problem; then draws implications. A conclusion thus has four ''Rs:'' reiteration of important results, reply to anticipated objections, reflection on the theory and the broader context of the current research project, and recommendations for future research and policy. The ''pointing ahead'' section discussed in this chapter focuses on the last two, reflection and recommendation.

II. POINTING AHEAD

It is very common in the conclusion to have a section in which one points ahead to further research that might build on the work you have just completed. This grows naturally out of that part of the conclusion in which the researcher explains how his or her research relates to topics of theory and policy that were outlined in the literature review and embedded in the researcher's hypotheses. The pointing-ahead segment of the conclusion serves three essential purposes:

1. It reiterates the limitations on the researcher's study, indicating further work yet to be done.
2. It indicates a research agenda that the researcher may wish to follow in his or her own future research.
3. It places the researcher's study in the context of the growth of the discipline, particularly the advancement of theory.

For the doctoral student, the pointing ahead segment serves a fourth function, as during the dissertation defense, the researcher is very likely to be asked precisely how the research project relates to theory and policy in the discipline.

The stronger the researcher's conclusions, the more easily they will be related to future steps in the development of theory or the pursuit of a research agenda. Conversely, the more the researcher's conclusions are of a general nature, side-stepping the paramount issues of the field, the more difficult the pointing ahead segment of the conclusion will be. A clearly articulated conclusion usually will engender relatively clear implications that call for further research. When the writing in question is a doctoral dissertation, evaluators will also often ask, "How difficult was the original question and how well answered was it?" Wishy-washy conclusions may forestall the criticism that comes from sticking one's neck out, but they are also likely to elicit the judgment that the researcher has set himself or herself a very low hurdle.

A. From Research Project to Research Agenda

It is not always necessary that the researcher formulate a research agenda based solely on his or her study. Three common sources of existing research agendas may be appropriate as pointing ahead contexts for future research: agendas of funding agencies, agendas of research conferences, and agendas of professional associations.

1. Agendas of Funding Agencies

Funding agencies, such as the National Science Foundation and other public and private funding organizations, routinely have formal research agendas. These, obviously, may provide context for that section of the writer's conclusions that deals with related future research and research agendas. An illustration is that from the National Institute for Occupational Safety and Health (NIOSH) (below and Table 1):

> NIOSH and its public and private sector partners have developed the National Occupational Research Agenda (NORA) to provide a framework to guide occupational safety and health research in the next de-

TABLE 1 Priorities in the NIOSH Research Agenda

Category	Priority Research Areas
Disease and injury	Allergic and irritant dermatitis
	Asthma and Chronic Obstructive Pulmonary Disease
	Fertility and pregnancy abnormalities
	Hearing loss
	Infectious diseases
	Low back disorders
	Musculoskeletal disorders of the upper extremities
	Traumatic injuries
Work environment and workforce	Emerging technologies
	Indoor environment
	Mixed exposures
	Organization of work
	Special populations at risk
Research tools and approaches	Cancer research methods
	Control technology and personal protective equipment
	Exposure assessment methods
	Health services research
	Intervention effectiveness research
	Risk assessment methods
	Social and economic consequences of workplace illness and injury
	Surveillance research methods

cade—not only for NIOSH but also for the entire occupational safety and health community. Approximately 500 organizations and individuals outside NIOSH provided input into the development of the Agenda. This attempt to guide and coordinate research nationally is responsive to a broadly perceived need to address systematically those topics that are most pressing and most likely to yield gains to the worker and the nation. Fiscal constraints on occupational safety and health research are increasing, making even more compelling the need for a coordinated and focused research agenda.

Source: http://www.cdc.gov/niosh/nora.html.

2. Conference Research Agendas

It is not uncommon to find professional conferences, or at least tracks, panels, or papers associated with conferences, that set forth a research agenda in one's field. An example is this research agenda on aging and development, from the

"Research on Aging, Vienna Conference, 1999," organized by the United Nations:

> This project represents a major initiative of great significance in the area of ageing and development. It will involve the most prominent researchers and policy planners. It will influence the development of national public policy on ageing and shape the world of scientific gerontology in the decades to come. The objective is to develop a worldwide research agenda on aging for the twenty-first century to serve as a back-ground for policy response to population and individual ageing, particularly in developing countries.
> *Source*: http://www.unagenda.org/

3. Research Agendas of Professional Associations

Many professional associations have research committees or similar groups that have formulated formal research agendas for the field. An example is the research agenda drafted by the Research Committee of the World Society of Victimology (WSV):

> The World Society of Victimology has set up a research committee to direct the task of defining and updating the society's research agenda. The new research committee does not set out to dictate the subject matter of research carried out by the society's members. Rather, the committee aims to provide members with an overview of key and emergent themes in victimological research. These themes are intended to inform the society's members while providing them with a stimulus for academic debate and policy development. The committee intends to pick up on current research themes that reflect broad interest from the society's members. Alongside emergent popular themes, the committee will endeavour to highlight 'gaps' in the victimological research base; that is, areas which are at the embryonic stage of research development or areas where the committee feels more research is needed. 'New' areas of victimological research will draw from the expertise and traditions of other research areas which are often at the margins of victimology's self-imposed remit. In opening up the victimological gaze to other disciplines, the committee is attempting to portray the society's wide-ranging and progressive research front to non-members who might be encouraged to delve further into the victimological arena.
>
> Major themes for research:
>
> 1. Defining 'Victims' and Defining Victimology
> 2. The United Nation's Declaration and the Law
> 3. The Impact of Politics, Policy and Populism on Victims
> 4. Power Inequalities

5. Helping Victims
6. Restorative Justice, Victims and Victimology
7. Repeat Victimization
8. Transnational Victims
9. Developing Methodologies for Victimological Research

Source: http://www.victimology.nl/ivwdb/resagenda.html

The WSV document goes on to spell out in considerable detail the research agenda under each of these headings.

B. Additional Resources

One of the specific online resources that may be of use to the researcher trying to place his or her work in the context of looking ahead to future work is the National Technical Information Service (NTIS), which is File 6 on Dialog Information Services (www.dialog.com), the leading vendor of online bibliographic information. The NTIS database contains information on most government-funded research projects, including ones that are current. As such it is one way of revealing what state-of-the-art research is focusing on. The researcher, of course, should also consult leading research funding organizations in his or her specific field. By being aware of state of the art research, the dissertation writer is in a better position to understand where research is going in his or her field, and to place his or her own study in this broader context, using this information in the pointing ahead section to discuss not only what the researcher would like to do next individually, but also what the field is apt to do next in areas that relate to the project at hand.

The NTIS provides summaries of research funded by U. S. government agencies. It also provides analyses prepared by federal agencies and their contractors or grant recipients. The NTIS is the vehicle for making available to the public unclassified distribution reports for sale from agencies such as NASA, Department of Defense (DOD), Department of Education (DOE), Housing and Urban Development (HUD), Department of Transportation (DOT), Department of Commerce, and some 240 others. Additionally, some state and local government agencies offer summaries of their reports to the database. The NTIS also provides access to the results of government-sponsored research and development from countries outside the United States. Organizations that currently contribute to the NTIS database include: the Japan Ministry of International Trade and Industry (MITI); laboratories administered by the United Kingdom Department of Industry; the German Federal Ministry of Research and Technology (BMFT); the French National Center for Scientific Research (CNRS); and many more. (Source: Dialog Blue Sheets at http://library.dialog.com/bluesheets/html/bl0006.html).

Several online databases are also available for searching for conferences and conference papers that may contain recent formulations of research agendas related to the researcher's project, as discussed above. One of these is the Inside Conferences (IC) database produced by the British Library. It covers all papers given at every congress, symposium, conference, exposition, workshop, and meeting received at the British Library Document Supply Centre (BLDSC) since October 1993. Some 16,000 proceedings are indexed, covering a wide range of subjects, and more than 500,000 bibliographic citations for individual conference papers are added each year. Most records are in English, with many languages represented in the source documents. This is File 65 on Dialog Information Services (Source: Dialog Blue Sheets, http://library.dialog.com/bluesheets/html/bl0065.html).

Likewise, the Conference Papers Index (CPI, which is File 77 on Dialog Information Services) covers more than 100,000 scientific and technical papers presented at more than 1,000 major regional, national, and international meetings annually. The CPI provides titles of the papers as well as the names and addresses (when available) of the authors of these papers. Also included are announcements of any publications issued from the meetings, in addition to available preprints, reprints, abstract booklets, and proceedings volumes, including dates of availability, costs, and ordering information. Primary subject areas covered include the life sciences, chemistry, physical sciences, geosciences, and engineering. (Source: Dialog Blue Sheets, http://library.dialog.com/bluesheets/html/bl0077.html). There is also MediConf: Medical Conferences and Events (Dialog File 431), which provides comprehensive listings of conferences and exhibitions in the fields of medicine, biotechnology, and pharmacology.

C. Example

One of the best resources for the pointing ahead section of the conclusion is the research agenda of the funding agency or agencies that is most concerned with one's research topic. To illustrate, below are excerpts from the research agenda of the NSF's initiative on research on human capital (National Science Foundation, 1999). Reading such funding agendas provides insight, whether at the early brainstorming phase of paper, thesis, and dissertation writing or at the end, when one is considering further research steps.
Example: An NSF Agenda for Future Research on Human Capital

> This report identifies six areas of substantial research importance, where further work in the social and behavioral sciences promises significant returns . . .
>
> 1. Employing a Productive Workforce

If America is to remain competitive in the world economy, American workers must have the skills required to compete effectively. It is also essential that the strategic decisions of firms and the organization of the workplace be conducive to full utilization of workers' skills. Future research in this area can improve our understanding of how human behavior, group behavior, and organizational structure relate to employment and productivity. Such work can have a substantial effect on the private sector as it works to design and staff workplaces for the future that are productive and that support a reasonable quality of life for workers and their families . . .

2. Educating for the Future

Not all of America's youth are being adequately educated for the future, as indicated by the poor performance by U.S. students on standardized tests, high school drop out rates and extensive criticism of the public schools. Schools face increasingly difficult challenges in preparing a wide range of students to be productive and involved citizens. For instance, violence is a major concern inside many schools; growing population diversity means schools must cope with issues of multiculturalism, bilingualism, and racism; changes in family structure suggest that children are receiving less help and support at home for their school work

3. Fostering Successful Families

Families play a pivotal role in the creation of human capital. Families must be able to provide children and adolescents with the resources to become competent adults and productive citizens and (eventually) to be effective parents themselves. American families are undergoing radical changes, however, and there is concern that today's children are not being nurtured as effectively as in the past. More limited economic opportunities are putting new stresses on lower-income families, while the growing number of single-parent families at all income levels is creating a new set of challenges and potential problems for parents and children . . .

4. Building Strong Neighborhoods

Neighborhoods and the capital they contain (both social, physical, and human capital) strongly shape social networks and the daily activities of local residents. A neighborhood environment can facilitate or inhibit the life chances of its residents. As our society becomes increasingly urban and segregated by race, class, and income, the neighborhoods may be increasingly important in shaping the opportunities of their residents. Research on neighborhoods includes looking at the importance of social networks among geographically proximate adults and children, the role of neighborhood organizations and institutions on the lives of residents, the negative effects of crime, decaying housing, or gangs within a neighborhood, and the causes of local economic development . . .

5. Reducing Disadvantage in a Diverse Society

America is and always has been a society of diverse peoples. Growing immigration has led to increases in diversity in recent years. Diversity has been linked to disadvantage as certain groups, identified by race or ethnicity, have long faced different economic opportunities and outcomes, limiting their contribution. To develop the human skills of all citizens of this country, we need to find ways to meet the social challenges that diversity represents . . .

6. Overcoming Poverty and Deprivation

Problems of poverty and deprivation have been remarkably stubborn in the United States. In 1992, 37 million Americans (14.5 percent of the population) lived in families whose income was below the U.S. poverty line. Other problems of deprivation, beyond income poverty, may be even more disturbing: growing homelessness, rising incarceration rates due to violence and drugs, or high illiteracy rates. Scientific research on poverty and deprivation has helped to better define and describe the causes of poverty and has been instrumental in both designing policies to combat poverty and in accurately evaluating their effectiveness . . .

7. Data Needs

Our research on human capital issues is limited by the data available. There are several key areas where additional attention to data set design and collection could provide substantial scientific rewards.

The extension of longitudinal data sets. Over time, persons invest in skills, form families, and make employment decisions. While point-in-time data on individual behavior is useful, many of the human capital questions discussed in this report demand longitudinal data. Existing longitudinal data sets have vastly increased our knowledge of dynamic behavior. Their ongoing collection and extension is crucial. For instance, we are just beginning to have enough data within the Panel Survey of Income Dynamics to relate childhood family characteristics to the labor market outcomes of young adults 10 to 15 years later.

Collecting data from multiple sources with multiple perspectives. Research on human behavior is complex because human beings are affected by so many external forces. Much of our data focuses on limited aspects of human behavior. For example, economists tend to collect data on income and employment; sociologists focus on family and neighborhood environments; psychologists ask about mental and cognitive functioning. More data sets need to link information from multiple disciplinary perspectives. This may mean including economic and psychological measures on individual surveys, and linking this with external data on neighborhood and school characteristics, as well as the workplace where individuals are employed. Only with this sort of multiple-source and multiple-perspective information, can we effectively investigate the linkages between individuals and families, families and neighborhoods, and families and public or private institutions.

Embedded studies, that merge alternative forms of empirical analysis. Some of the most promising new empirical work in recent years has used multiple empirical techniques, administering large-scale individual surveys of employment and family behavior while also directing more intensive interview techniques to a subset of the survey population. . . .

8. Methodological Needs

Methodological limitations also constrain research on human capital issues. Across the social and behavioral sciences, there is a need for greater development of our theoretical and analytical tool-kit to analyze key questions.

Analytical techniques for dynamic questions. Questions about dynamic behavior require complex modeling and empirical techniques, that estimate the effect of multiple events in a persons' past history on current behavior. While our understanding of time-dependent analysis has greatly increased over the past few years, there are still serious limits to what we can do. Expanded methodologies for dynamic modeling would provide much clearer answers to questions about sequential employment and promotion patterns, movements in and out of schooling and training among younger workers, or changes in family composition over time.

Models that link individual behavior to family and environmental characteristics. Providing better policy prescriptions from research on human capital issues requires better modeling of the simultaneous nature of the interactions between individuals and their families. It also requires the development of better models that link micro-level development and decision-making processes among individuals with the macro-level institutions and environments with which individuals interact.

Improved techniques for policy evaluation. There has been steady progress within the social and behavioral sciences improving the methodologies that are available to evaluate the effectiveness of political interventions. Further development in this area is necessary, however, as new work continually uncovers methodological difficulties with past evaluation strategies. The use of experimental random-assignment techniques to evaluate social programs has flourished in recent years, and further expansion of this methodology to new settings may produce substantial new knowledge. . . .

D. Checklist

1. Have you searched for existing relevant research agendas from funding agencies, research conferences, and professional associations, seeking to relate your project to these research agendas?
2. Have you concentrated on your one, two, or three research suggestions that are most directly related to your findings? Avoid the "laundry list" approach and focus on a few compelling priorities.
3. Have you concentrated on direct next steps, not a wish list of long-range research goals pertaining to the same topic?

BIBLIOGRAPHY

Easterly, W., King, R., Levine, R., and Rebelo, S. (1992). How Do National Policies Affect Long-Run Growth?: A Research Agenda. Washington, DC: World Bank. An economics example of research agendas.

Kerckhoff, A. C., ed. (1996). Generating Social Stratification: Toward a New Research Agenda. Series on Social Inequality. Boulder, Co: Westview Press. Illustrates how to situate studies in the context of previous research and pointing toward a future research agenda.

Levine, F. J., and Rosich, K. J. (1996). Social Causes of Violence: Crafting a Science Agenda. Washington, DC: American Sociological Association. Highlights recent research and identifies priorities for further study based on a workshop of leading social scientists.

National Research Council, Committee on Biological Diversity in Marine Systems. (1995). Understanding Marine Biodiversity: A Research Agenda for the Nation. Washington, D.C.: National Academy Press. A natural science example.

National Science Foundation. (1999). A Strategic Plan for the Human Capital Initiative. Washington, DC: NSF. Obtained online 11/23/99 at http://www.nsf.gov/sbe/ses/sociol/works1.htm#rtftoc6. Illustrates research agendas set forth by funding agencies in connection with grant programs.

Rumelt, R. P., Schendel, D. E., Teece, D. J., eds. (1996). Fundamental Issues in Strategy: A Research Agenda. Cambridge, Ma: Harvard Business School Press. Focuses on interdisciplinary research agenda for strategic management.

21

The Thesis or Dissertation Committee

I. THE DISSERTATION PROCESS

Never overlook the fact that the writing process is one of socialization into the discipline. Formally the student is told that the purpose of the paper, thesis, or dissertation is to demonstrate the ability to analyze challenging subjects in the discipline and, in the case of dissertations, to advance the discipline itself. However, the writing process is more. It is also a ritual in the sense that its various incarnations—paper, thesis, dissertation—are stages of passage into acceptance and respect as a full-fledged colleague among fellow researchers in the discipline. One enters the dissertation process as a student and emerges as a younger colleague.

As a ritual, the writing process has three major aspects over and above empirical research itself. These are the aspects of contact, networking, and collegiality.

1. The writing process involves establishing contact with and soliciting advice from faculty and other members of the relevant profession. Do not be afraid, even as an undergraduate paper writer, to ask for advice and help, particularly after you have equipped yourself with the background to ask intelligent questions. Today, online discussion lists in particular subfields also may provide an appropriate forum for posing such questions.

2. The writing process involves establishing yourself in a network of scholars, at least for writers of dissertations. By sharing your work and questions, showing appreciation for work that has gone before you, and reaching out to others, you are becoming part of a network of scholarship. The "Lone Ranger"

approach to research is not the goal of dissertation writing even though, of course, your work is expected to be your own. Nonetheless, the writing process is seen as a launching pad for your entry into relevant scholarly networks. Completing a dissertation entirely in isolation from others often will be held against you.

3. The writing process as an academic ritual involves both networking and presentation of one's work to the community of scholars, whether as a seminar paper presentation, presentation of a conference paper, or a formal defense of one's dissertation. Presentation and defense demonstrates your ability to relate your subject to the broader context of the discipline, showing that you have studied and can relate articulately to a tradition of research, showing that you are striving to make a contribution to your field—in short, that you have been well socialized as a professional in your discipline and represent yourself as such to others.

II. THE THESIS OR DISSERTATION COMMITTEE

A. Committee Selection

In most academic settings, the thesis or dissertation writer is free to select the members of his or her committee. This involves two distinct types of choices: selection of one's principal advisor and selection of the rest of the committee. The more straightforward of the two is selection of a principal advisor, as in most cases this is dictated by the subject matter of one's research. Even when one's department is large enough to have two or three faculty members in the field of one's dissertation, there will normally be one faculty member whose specialization is closest to the dissertation topic. Sometimes, of course, the actual process works very differently; the masters or doctoral student takes courses with a professor or serves as a research assistant, becomes involved with the faculty member's work, and is offered an opportunity to develop a dissertation that builds on the faculty member's data and line of research, with the faculty member becoming both a mentor and principal advisor. Selecting a faculty member outside the area of specialization of the thesis or dissertation generally is inadvisable, as the student will fail to get the much-needed benefit that an experienced advisor can provide. It is better for the student to be flexible and consider shifting his or her topic to one within the scope of research of a departmental faculty member. However, if specialization is not determinant, the masters or doctoral student must either select a faculty member who can be of generic assistance (a methodologist, for example) or who simply seems friendly and willing to spend the time necessary.

In selecting advisors, word of mouth invariably plays a large role However, most departments issue a booklet or have a web page containing full or abbreviated faculty vitae that may be consulted to understand their specializations and current research more fully. Not infrequently, this will provide considerably more information than word of mouth alone. Reading the works cited in faculty vitae gives the student a basis for visiting and initiating discussions with a faculty member, with a view toward identifying potential principal advisors and members of one's dissertation committee. Reading other students' dissertations recently completed under the direction of particular faculty members can serve the same purpose.The student will normally take elective courses with prospective advisors and committee members, so thinking about committee selection is appropriate from the outset of the student's graduate career.

The principal advisor has a number of responsibilities vis-a-vis the doctoral student. The principal advisor first and foremost plays a mentoring role, helping the student to define his or her dissertation topic and plan his or her research strategy and timeline. The advisor may also suggest other members of the dissertation committee. Throughout the dissertation proposal process, the advisor will assist in obtaining the support of all members of the committee, providing valuable feedback to the candidate. The advisor will also read each chapter of the dissertation as it is written, evaluating work to date before dissertation chapters are circulated to the rest of the committee or to larger audiences. Finally, the principal advisor ordinarily will assist the doctoral student in placement of his or her scholarly work in conferences and publications and will later assist in career placement.

In most institutions, a masters committee will have three or four members and a doctoral dissertation committee will have three to five. If the student has a choice, a larger number usually is better, as larger committees are more apt to be run openly, in a manner not dependent on personality, and because larger committees provide more protection against faculty attrition (faculty leaves, deaths, retirements, and other departures, which can delay the student's dissertation). For each level of degree, the university may require that the committee include at least one member outside the student's major department. Outside members may be one of two types: some outside members from other disciplines, but who nonetheless specialize in the area of the dissertations; others may be graduate school representatives whose interest is largely restricted to monitoring the due process of the dissertation defense.

There are essentially three major strategies for selecting the rest of one's committee, each with pros and cons.

The low road. The first strategy is to pick as members of one's committee those faculty who, through the graduate student grapevine, are known to be "easy." That is, certain faculty may have the reputation of spending little time considering or even reading the graduate student's work. They provide little feedback and they do not ask unfriendly questions at the thesis defense itself. As a downside, such faculty provide little mentoring and little entree into later collegial relationships. More dangerous, "easy" faculty may leave the student writer unprotected from fundamental criticism of his or her work—criticism that will eventually surface if research design and execution are not up to standard. That is, the ''low road'' seems easier and faster in the short run but may leave one shortchanged in the long run.

The high road. The second strategy is to pick as members of one's committee the most able experts in one's substantive area and in research methodology. In this strategy, one seeks to be challenged through a high level of early feedback. By securing a ''buy-in'' from the faculty experts available for committee service, there is a much higher probability that few obstacles will arise in the defense itself. Moreover, such faculty are in a better position to put the graduate student researcher in contact with other experts across the country and internationally, introducing him or her to the true network of research in the subject area. Also, expert faculty are more likely to have access to grants and data that may be of immeasurable assistance to the thesis or dissertation effort. The danger, of course, is possible cooptation into the research agenda of the faculty member, sacrificing the student's true interests for those of the faculty expert.

The middle road. A third strategy, somewhat Machiavellian in nature, is to pick as committee chair a ''high road'' expert, but then to fill the rest of the committee with faculty with reputations for never being obstructionist. While giving the student writer less feedback, such a committee composition may sometimes speed the thesis or dissertation process by minimizing internal committee disagreements. However, the student is rarely free to fill the rest of his or her committee simply on this basis. The principal advisor may have strong preferences. It is expected that at least one member of the committee be a subject-matter expert in the area of the dissertation. Some institutions will insist one member be a methodologist. All these rules and traditions may severely constrain the actual choice of the dissertation committee.

Regardless of the road taken, the student candidate should always select the committee chair first, then consult closely with him or her as to the other members of the committee. Academic departments are not free from politics and personalities, and selection of feuding faculty members on the same committee is a recipe for an unnecessarily protracted thesis or dissertation process. Likewise, a faculty member may have a peer reputation as ''dead wood'' in a department due to low productivity or may be seen as an eccentric not accepting prevailing theories. In these cases, the masters or doctoral student will be well advised to look elsewhere for a principal advisor. An overall objective should be committee balance. If the student perceives an area of weakness in his or her study, that may be reason to make sure that a well-respected faculty expert in that area is included on the committee.

Methodology is a second consideration, as most masters or doctoral students remain in need of methodological guidance during the writing of the dissertation; thus, selection of a committee member who can play this guiding role is important. The methodology member of the committee will be the student's ally in defending his or her statistical procedures during the dissertation defense, assuming the methodologist's advice has been sought and heeded. Also, in some fields, ''methodology'' comprehends technology and equipment, and an advisor who operates at the state of the art may provide both knowledge of and access to needed tools. Particularly if the student proposes to use an unconventional methodology, it is important that the committee include a member who is an authority on that methodology and can validate the student's use of it.

It must be noted that there is the possibility of abuse in the advisor-student relationship. Most universities have explicit ethics statements proscribing abusive behavior of faculty thesis advisors. The most common forms of abuse are these:

1. Faculty conflicts of interest over ownership of data and authorship of works based on that data. Note that it is *not* customary for the dissertation advisor's name to appear on the dissertation when published in book form or in articles based on the dissertation.
2. Dictating a topic that is peripheral to or outside of the student's desired area of specialization.
3. Dictating a topic that is too narrow to establish the student's significant contribution to knowledge in the discipline and too narrow to provide the student with expertise in a new skill.
4. Unreasonable delay in the student's thesis or dissertation agenda caused by unrelated faculty priorities.
5. Sexual harrassment.

In principle, ethics board actions by a masters or doctoral student against his or her faculty advisor are possible, but the real use of departmental ethics statements is not after-the-fact; rather, they are to help anticipate problems before they arise. For instance, the student is reminded to come to clear understandings beforehand about ownership and use of datasets and authorship of articles based on the data. However, once a situation of abuse has emerged, the most common student action is to switch advisors. Bringing a formal charge before an ethics board is a very serious matter that might ruin careers. With such high stakes involved, one may expect formal charges to meet resistance and to carry efforts to bring the credibility of the student into question. For these reasons, bringing formal ethics charges is not advisable if the student does not have very clear and compelling evidence.

Candidate/advisor ethical issues are sometimes a problem when the masters or doctoral student is doing research and writing based on data collected by the faculty advisor. However, other situations raising ethical issues also occur, as when advisors encourage a succession of masters or doctoral students to write dissertations on a series of specialized topics too narrow to establish the reputation of the doctoral student. However, by using the combined work of several doctoral students, the faculty member is able to present research on a broader topic of more impact. Classified research, which restricts peer review and publication, can also lead to ethical problems and should make the masters or doctoral student alert to issues that may be involved.

In spite of best intentions on all sides, personal conflicts between a candidate and his or her advisor or committee members may arise. Discussing issues openly and honestly is usually the best policy. Going into such discussions with a non accusing attitude, expecting that the faculty member will want to help ameliorate the situation is appropriate. In fact, faculty members have strong incentives to avoid unnecessary dissension with doctoral candidates and masters students and usually do in fact want to solve interpersonal problems. If direct efforts to resolve differences fail, it is not inappropriate to change advisors. Discuss this with your department chairperson, who may make helpful recommendations. Use the utmost diplomacy and do not burn bridges when switching advisors, as doing otherwise will detract from your status as an emerging professional and colleague.

In some masters or doctoral programs, once a committee is established, an immediate decision is the choice between a conventional thesis or dissertation or another option , such as one or more extended research papers. Such options are instituted by some universities, presumably to speed the path to publication in professional journals. This, of course, can be in the interest of the student as well as the institution. On the other hand, the traditional dissertation provides invaluable experience in pursuing a major research challenge, preliminary to writing a full-length book. Where data are readily available, however, the research article path is undeniably a shorter route to the degree.

B. The Proposal Meeting

At first, your advisor may have more ideas about your dissertation than you do. Eventually, however, the balance shifts as you get deeper and deeper into your work. Inevitably, you will become more knowledgeable about the specialized topic and will develop theories and hypotheses of your own. A good advisor will support you in following your own instincts and directions, while at the same time warning you about directions already tried and failed by others. When you are ready to present your proposal to your entire committee, you should be thoroughly grounded by having your theories, hypotheses, literature review, data collection strategy, and proposed statistical methodology well worked out.

The purpose of the proposal meeting is to get advice on whether and how to proceed. This may prove to be an iterative process involving feedback and more than one proposal meeting. The masters or doctoral student should consider it a good proposal meeting if good advice is generated, even if another meeting is required to secure the desired approval. It is even possible you will change your focus and your committee will change. Note, however, that some departments have rules requiring that approval be secured by, say, the second such meeting. This sort of rule is apt to be the case when the proposal is part of the oral examination process. In such cases, however, there ordinarily are less formal proposal meetings before the proposal defense at the oral examination.

Questions asked by the committee at the proposal stage may seem critical, but their purpose actually is to help the student to strengthen his or her dissertation design. Questions typically include a focus on the definition of the problem and the operationalization of key variables, questions of validity and research design, whether possible confounding variables have been controlled, and if the methodology is suited to the purposes at hand. The student may also be asked if standardized measurement instruments, if available, have been used and if not, why not? Also, has the student a firm grasp on literature related to the proposed topic, even going so far as to be aware of who the principal other scholars are active in this area? Overall, the purpose of questioning is not at all the same as in an examination. If a proposal is not accepted, it is only because the committee feels that it is not feasible, not conceptually sound, or is of insufficient originality and importance—all things the student does well do discover early, before the brunt of dissertation labor.

At a good proposal meeting, you can expect several types of feedback:

1. Brainstorming of additional ideas
2. Advice on broadening or, more likely, narrowing the scope of your proposal
3. In some cases, constructive advice to shift to another more feasible or promising topic, or at least to set reasonable expectations
4. Suggestions about other researchers to contact and with whom to network

Proposal meetings are not examinations, but this is not to say that some preparation is not necessary. You may anticipate being asked what you have you read, what courses you have taken, and to whom you have talked in preparing your proposal. The proposal document itself follows the outline for a dissertation, discussed in an earlier chapter, but it emphasizes three critical sections: presenting your theories and hypotheses, your preliminary literature review, and your proposed data collection and analytic methodologies.

The proposal meeting typically runs about 2 hours. The student is usually given 30 to 45 minutes to review his or her proposal, but frequent interruptions for questions can make the presentation part last an hour and a half. It is acceptable during questioning to admit you have not yet looked into certain things, or even to thank the committee members for suggesting things you had not yet anticipated. The more your approach is unconventional, the more you must make the case for your reasoning and methodology. Making one's case is key to a successful proposal meeting. In particular, you should not tediously present every aspect of your proposal. You should use overheads and other visual aids, supplementing these with handouts.

The proposal meeting is not a one-time-and-it's-over thing. In most departments the masters or doctoral student will meet with his or her committee to report progress about biannually, with periodic e-mail contact with committee members between reporting sessions. Some revisions in scope and method may emerge from these review meetings. The masters or doctoral student should take care to listen to any warnings that arise in these meetings, particularly warnings about necessary changes in direction contingent on findings or problems in data collection or methodology. Such warnings may be expressed in very polite terms, or even casually; nonetheless, your committee is trying to tell you something, ignoring which could put you on the path to a long dissertation process. At the same time, if you yourself see the need to reorient the dissertation in a new direction, it is essential to understand that this requires sign-off by your committee at one of the review meetings for your dissertation.

C. Checklist

1. Did you understand that the advisor to whom you were assigned on entry to your program was probably an arbitrary selection, and did you take a proactive attitude in seeking to define your own area of specialization and to have a subject-appropriate advisor assigned to you relatively early in your graduate career so as to maximize the time to develop a collegial relationship of trust and mutual respect?
2. Have you selected as your principal advisor a faculty member who is in the same area of specialization as the topic on which you will be writing your thesis or dissertation, and have your selection criteria given weight to choosing a faculty member who is interested in taking the time and effort to be your teacher and mentor? (And do you understand this is different from selecting a faculty member who is warm and affable, but may not be a good mentor and teacher?)
3. Have you selected as your principal advisor a faculty member who is willing to provide you with a good level of feedback on your writing, marking up your manuscripts and providing editorial as well as substantive guidance?
4. Once you have tentatively selected a principal advisor, have you talked to other masters or doctoral students ahead of you who have had this individual as their thesis or dissertation advisor, to get an understanding of their experiences? Did they feel fairly treated? Did they feel they were neither neglected nor micromanaged? Did they find the advisor aided them in timely completion of their theses or dissertations? Did they receive assistance in career placement referrals and recommendations after completing their theses or dissertations?

5. Have you included on your committee at least one faculty member expert in the qualitative or quantitative methodology you will use at the core of your research design? If none of your subject experts qualify as methodology experts for the procedures you will be using, you should seriously consider adding a methodologist to your committee list.

6. Have you developed a schedule for your drafts that allows committee members to anticipate when you will make time demands on them for reading and feedback, and that allows for an adequate number of days for them to respond to your requests?

7. Have you negotiated your writing schedule with your advisor to determine if you are to present one chapter at a time, getting intermediate feedback, or if some other arrangement is preferred?

8. Have you made a point of visiting and obtaining the views of all committee members? You don't want to be blind-sided by an uncommunicative committee member who says almost nothing for the entire period of writing, then comes in at the paper, thesis, or dissertation defense with fundamental criticisms, often of a methodological nature. You need to get *all* committee members to buy into your research design and methodology early in the writing process, just as you need to keep all committee members informed of changes.

9. Have you defined a stopping criterion for your research, clarifying for your committee what you consider "finished" and securing their agreement to this criterion before you undertake the bulk of your work?

10. Have you secured an explicit understanding from your committee regarding the status of your dissertation should you arrive at negative results? Some advisors, committees, or departments will accept a methodologically sound dissertation effort that results in null findings. Others will make acceptance of a dissertation contingent on getting acceptable results.

11. Can you formulate for your committee a clear one-sentence statement of what your dissertation will demonstrate?

12. Have you defined your topic such that it has a reasonable chance of meeting the general criterion for masters or doctoral dissertations, that they constitute a "substantial, original contribution to knowledge?"

13. Where your topic cuts across areas, have you solicited for committee membership an expert in each of these areas? For instance, in a study on recidivism among black prison inmates, do you have experts on African-American culture as well as on criminology?

14. Have you anticipated and rehearsed for common types of questions that may be posed at your initial proposal meetings? How did you come to this topic? How does it relate to theory in your field? What will be the nature of your data? What statistical procedures will you apply? Can you give concrete illustrations of your generalizations? Can you define your key concept? Can you

explain your core idea in some depth? Are you familiar with who the key scholars are in your specialization, and are you familiar with their work? Similarly, are you familiar with the classics in your specialization, and how your work confirms, modifies, or rebuts such works?

15. Do you have a confident mental attitude about your research, conveying your enthusiasm for it in a professional way? Consider practicing your proposal presentation by standing at a blackboard, using chalk to present your key points visually, making your key points with a view toward effective and interesting presentation as well as merely getting out the facts about your dissertation.

16. Have you effectively used data visualization in your proposal meeting to show how your results might appear when your work is complete—to show what it is you are hoping to present at the end?

17. Consider asking for permission to tape-record your proposal meeting. Your later review may help you tune in to the full ramifications of suggestions.

18. At your proposal meeting, directly ask what you should seek to accomplish before the next, follow-up meeting. Have follow-up meetings, or at least follow-up contacts, en route to your dissertation defense.

19. In your written proposal presentation, have you attended to the basics, such as grammar, spelling, and editing? Have you properly handled tables, figures, references, footnotes, formulas, headers, footers, pagination, spacing, margins, your table of contents, and other formatting specifications using the manual of style prescribed by your department? Although clerical in one sense, a thoroughly professional format will help your proposal presentation to be taken as professional in substance as well.

20. Have you been thorough and generous in acknowledging attributions and credit?

BIBLIOGRAPHY

Association of Graduate Schools in the Association of American Universities (1990). Institutional Policies to Improve Doctoral Education. Washington, DC: Association of American Universities.

Bowen, W. G., and Rudenstine, N. L. (1992). In Pursuit of the Ph.D. Princeton, NJ: Princeton University Press.

Council of Graduate Schools (1991). The Role and Nature of the Doctoral Dissertation. Washington, DC: Council of Graduate Schools.

Fine, M. A. and Kudek, L. A. (1993). Reflections on determining authorship credit and authorship order on faculty-student collaborations. American Psychologist 48: 1141–1147.

Hawley, P. (1993). Being Bright is Not Enough: The Unwritten Rules of Doctoral Study. Springfield, IL: Charles C. Thomas.

LaPidus, J. B. (1990). Research Student and Supervisor. Washington, DC: Council of Graduate Schools.

Locke, L. F., Spirduso, W. W., and Silverman, S. J. (1999). Proposals That Work: A Guide for Planning Dissertations and Grant Proposals. Thousand Oaks, CA: Sage Publications. A widely-used guide to the proposal process.

Mauch, J. E., and Birch, J. W. (1998). Guide to the Successful Thesis and Dissertation: A Handbook for Students and Faculty. 4th ed. New York: Marcel Dekker. Chapter 5 deals with the dissertation committee.

Westmeyer, P. M. (1994). A Guide for Use in Planning, Conducting, and Reporting Research Projects. 2nd ed. Springfield, IL: Charles C. Thomas.

22

The Thesis or Dissertation Defense

I. INTRODUCTION

There is a typical timeline for defending one's dissertation. During the 2 years of coursework prior to taking comprehensive examinations, the doctoral candidate is thinking of possible dissertation topics, exploring them with faculty, and writing course seminar papers related to possible topics. Normally, the student will pass a comprehensive examination in the spring of his or her fourth semester. That summer, he or she will select a topic, re-read related seminar papers, search for key literature and read it, draft a dissertation proposal, and perhaps write an initial chapter of the dissertation as a practice exercise. This is also the time the dissertation student should work with his or her advisor on dissertation grants in support of the proposed research (see Chapter 25). In the fall after the comprehensive examinations, the doctoral student will revise his or her dissertation proposal and submit two or so chapters to his or her advisor (usually the problem chapter and the literature review chapter, and perhaps the methods chapter). The proposal should be defended before the full committee by later that fall. Data collection commences simultaneously, with a view toward completing it by the end of the following spring.

That spring, one year after the comprehensives, the doctoral student will have written drafts of about four critical chapters of the dissertation, including the problem, literature review, and methodology chapters. Some type of formal meeting or informal contact is made with other committee members early in this process to assure their approval of the overall approach. During the subsequent summer, the doctoral student will have collected all his or her data and will complete two or three additional chapters. That fall is devoted to writing the concluding chapter and revising all chapters. The doctoral student works with his or her principal advisor on preparations for both the dissertation defense and for the subsequent job search. The doctoral student will revise his or her vita, consult with the departmental and university career placement personnel, and will prepare a portfolio of his or her work. Presenting preliminary dissertation results at a professional conference and participating in the job interviewing components of that conference are common tasks for the spring of the second year after the comprehensive examinations. The passage of the actual doctoral defense that spring is the culmination of four years of doctoral work.

The dissertation defense is typically only two hours, but it comes at the pinnacle of an educational pyramid that has taken the student two decades to construct. Ideally the student's research purposes, methods, and findings are already well-known to the thesis or dissertation advisor, and an approving consensus has been forged through recurring contacts of the student and advisor with all committee members. In this happy circumstance, the dissertation defense is simply a collegial discussion of the state of the art in the student's area of specialization, followed by a pro forma vote and a round of well-deserved congratulations. However, this scenario is far from guaranteed and the student is well advised to prepare for the defense as one would for any other critical meeting in the world of business, government, or academia.

II. THE THESIS OR DISSERTATION DEFENSE

One of the paramount concerns of the thesis or dissertation writer should be to maximize interchange with committee members early in the writing process. Most criticism that arises at the thesis or dissertation defense stage has to do with such fundamentals as the match of measured indicators to theoretical concepts, the match of research purposes to qualitative and quantitative methods, and the nature of the research design. By securing buy-in from the committee early in the process, the dissertation defense is far more likely to have a happy outcome.

A. What the Dissertation Defense Is

The dissertation defense is different from an examination, even though it has exam-like elements. It is also different from the proposal presentation at the outset of the research process. Certainly it is true that the dissertation defense is where the validity of the researcher's research design, execution, and inferences are tested against the knowledge of the field held by the faculty members most related to the topic of the dissertation. However, the defense is more than that. It is a ceremonial ritual of admission to the status of research colleague, leaving behind the status of student. The dissertation defense is about proving one is a colleague who will be a credit to one's department as one goes out into the professional world. It is not just about avoiding mistakes in writing up one's findings.

American graduate students can be glad that the ceremonial aspects of the dissertation defense are not of the traditional European sort, held in a large auditorium and attended by scholars in full regalia. Being forced to answer difficult questions posed by scholars one may not have known was a fearsome rite of passage, although not an unfair one as in publishing the new researcher must expose himself or herself to similar criticism from other professionals one does not know. American doctoral dissertation defenses are far less threatening, but the student should not forget their aspect as a rite of passage into a new status.

In one view, the dissertation defense is a performance. Like an actor, the wise candidate pays attention to scripting, rehearsal, costume, props, supporting actors, and other aspects of the dramaturgy of the event. Scripting may involve developing an opening presentation that highlights the student's original contribution while defending it behind clear delimitations of scope. Rehearsal may call for prior simulation of the defense, complete with fellow students playing roles of members of the examining committee. Costume ordinarily involves dressing as one would if one were indeed a colleague. Props involve visual aids, handouts, and related equipment. Supporting actors may involve pre-arranged questions posed by the principal advisor. In terms of dramaturgy, there should be a beginning, a middle, and an ending, preferably climactic, built on the original findings of the study.

There are three possible outcomes to a dissertation defense: pass, conditional pass, and failure to be approved. Some departments also provide for a fourth outcome, deferred decision, which indicates failure on the immediate proposal, need for major revision, but also indicates the committee has faith in the candidate to undertake the revisions and pass a subsequent dissertation defense. In cases of failure, the department may or may not allow one or more additional attempts.

Unconditional pass/approval is, of course, the Holy Grail of the dissertation defense, occurring when all committee members agree the dissertation is acceptable without revision. Conditional pass/approval may reflect relatively minor issues of editing, inserting missing information, or rephrasing specific sections. This is done by the student in cooperation with the principal advisor, who must certify the conditions are met, after which the dissertation is sent for information purposes (not revote) to other committee members, to the library, and to other recipients as specified by university procedures. However, the requirements of conditional approval may be much more serious, involving significant revisions of substance and necessitating another meeting of the committee and another vote on whether the dissertation is now ready to accept. Regardless of the committee vote, even in cases of no-pass, the student may expect concrete and constructive instructions from the principal advisor on how to proceed.

B. Strategies for the Dissertation Defense

Writing a dissertation or even a thesis or paper can be a process that requires emotional support. The process leading up to a thesis or dissertation defense is a long one. Although often overlooked, emotional support may be the single most important factor in determining whether the writing project will be completed successfully. Support factors include a sympathetic committee chair; at least one committee member who can provide informal reassurance and mentoring; a family setting that recognizes the importance of the writing effort; and a work setting whose demands do not overwhelm the research endeavor. Taking occasional breaks may actually accelerate research in the long run. A particularly effective support mechanism is regular meetings with other students engaged in the same type of research process. A good support system can help overcome common fears, such as the fear that only you have insecurities, that no one cares, or that you have taken on the impossible. Support systems can also provide tangible aid in the form of suggestions, insights, and emotional comfort. A student with a good support system will come into the thesis or dissertation defense with a momentum that gives an advantage.

The best strategy for being prepared for the defense of your paper, thesis, or dissertation is to make sure you are thoroughly familiar with your own work. The kinds of questions you will be asked are relatively predictable for the most part, so it is not a bad idea to anticipate them and prepare answers for each. Questions should include the following:

1. What is the purpose of your study and is it presented as an empirically verifiable problem that is clearly delimited in scope?
2. What are the assumptions of your study and are they accepted in your field?
3. How does your thesis or dissertation question relate to the literature in your field?
4. What makes it a contribution to the literature?
5. What is/are your dependent variable(s)?
6. What scales operationalize your variables, and how do you know if they are valid?
7. What are your hypotheses?
8. Why did you pick the qualitative or quantitative procedures that you did to test each hypothesis, rather than another procedure?
9. What are your findings in terms of significance, if a random sample is involved?
10. What are your findings in terms of effect size?
11. What are the implications of your findings for theory in the field, and have you avoided overgeneralizing the implications of your findings?

12. What next research steps would be appropriate as follow-on to your study?

There are, of course, additional questions that may be asked. Does your title accurately reflect the nature of your proposal? Does your research follow ethical guidelines, as regarding the use of human or animal subjects? Have you fully detailed all your data gathering and analytical procedures, including reproducing all instruments used? You may even want to use these and other questions to rehearse a mock defense with your peers, much as law students may use mock trials as a learning experience.

In almost any paper, thesis, or dissertation defense, you will be allotted a substantial portion of time to make your case in your own way. You will not be able to control the entire meeting, but you should enter the meeting with a clear plan of how you want your defense to go. You will want a good 20-minute outline, overheads or other visuals, handouts, and background documents as appropriate. Keep in mind that 20 minutes of reading time is much more than 20 minutes of presentation time, so limit your outline. You want to be proactive but not defensive. It is better to admit to not knowing the answer to a few questions than to jeopardize your credibility by guessing or trying to "fudge" an answer. In most cases, however, you should get off to a good start because of the tradition of your principal advisor asking the first question at the dissertation defense, a question normally shared with you beforehand.

Eventually the questioning will be over and the principal advisor will ask the candidate to leave the room while the committee deliberates. Normally, there is relatively quick consensus on passing, as that agreement should have been well-anticipated by the principal advisor who otherwise should not have convened the dissertation defense. However, various reservations will come out during deliberations, of which the principal advisor will take note. The usual ruling is conditional acceptance of the dissertation, where the condition is revising the dissertation manuscript for final acceptance. Normally these revisions are sufficiently minor that they are left to the principal advisor and no additional meeting of the dissertation committee occurs. The deliberations will usually take about 10 minutes and be followed by the candidate re-entering the room as a new colleague in the profession, greeted with smiles, handshakes, and congratulations.

C. Checklist

1. Have you prepared for the defense by pursuing a high level of interaction with your committee members early in the writing process, seeking a "buy-in" on your research question, measurement instruments, statistical procedures, and overall research design?

2. Have you clarified with your faculty committee members which of their criticisms are seen as important and which are seen as minor?

3. Where faculty disagree on advice to you in early feedback, have you come to some sort of negotiated understanding, perhaps with the help of your committee chairperson?

4. Have you asked members of your committee beforehand what questions or types of questions they will be asking at the defense? As the defense is not an examination, this is not an inappropriate thing to ask and the student may find cooperative attitudes that greatly allay anxiety and assist preparation for the defense. However, such forewarning is a blessing when it is given, not a student right.

5. Have you formed a support group with other students pursuing your degree, and do you meet regularly for emotional and intellectual support?

6. Have you determined through your principal advisor if the thesis defense will be assessed through any evaluation forms or other written criteria? If so, have you studied these criteria with a view toward making sure that you provide evidence of satisfactory performance for each specified criterion?

7. Have you made the effort to hold a simulation of your dissertation defense, using fellow students in the role of committee members? Part of the simulation should be getting those who participated to comment on your body language and nonverbal cues as well as the substance of your presentation.

8. Have you tape recorded your presentation and listened to yourself?

9. Have you planned the physical setting of your presentation, including such things as the lectern, an overhead projector, a flip chart pad and easel, markers and chalk, a projector for PowerPoint slide shows, and other materials you will need?

10. If you have a choice, go with a formal lectern rather than simply sitting at the seminar table. You want your presentation to seem akin to a formal address to a conference of colleagues, not informal class discussion.

11. Use visual aids, such as charts, tables, photographs, diagrams, models, film, and other aids as appropriate. At the very least, distribute to committee members' seats beforehand a printed copy of your overhead slide show so there is no strain in reading tables or flipping back to information presented earlier. Never use a visual aid that is hard to see and read.

12. Make sure there is a clock in the room for defense of your thesis or dissertation so you can time your presentation appropriately.

13. Have you planned an opening script that highlights the original contribution of your work, delimits its scope, and defines its relation to the literature of your discipline?

14. Have you planned a middle section of your talk that is concise, enlivened by visual aids, and yet comprehensive in tabulations and coefficients provided in handouts?

15. Have you planned the ending of your talk to convey your own sense of interest in your topic and findings, and to pose questions that invite committee discussion on terms you wish to the focus of your defense?

16. When you are asked questions during your presentation, do not be afraid to ask questions for clarification so that you fully understand what you are supposed to respond to.

17. Have you avoided boring your committee with information they already know, instead concentrating on what they need to know? Keep in mind the ''less is more'' principle for presentations.

18. Remember to thank your advisor and members of the committee at the end of your presentation.

19. After your successful defense, have you checked that the proper paperwork is done to assure that your dissertation is copyrighted, microfilmed, and indexed with Dissertation Abstracts and University Microfilms, Inc., as is the case at nearly all research universities? This will make your dissertation available to electronic literature searches by others and put you on the path toward becoming a cited scholar.

BIBLIOGRAPHY

Davis, G. B. and Parker, C. A. (1997). Writing the Doctoral Dissertation. New York: Barron's Educational Series. Also covers the defense of the dissertation.

Mitchell, L. (1996). The Ultimate Grad School Survival Guide. Princeton, NJ: Peterson's.

Peters, R. L. (1997). Getting What You Came For: The Smart Student's Guide to Earning a Master's or Ph.D. New York: Noonday Press.

Ritter, B., and Trudeau, P. (1997). The Women's Guide to Surviving Graduate School. Thousand Oaks, CA: Sage Publications.

23

Quantitative Research Writing in the Humanities

I. CONCEPTUALIZING IN THE HUMANITIES

The humanities, which comprehend philosophy, history, literature, and language, commonly involve a different type of writing than occurs in empirical papers in the natural and social sciences. Frequently there is a focus on epistemology (studying the nature of knowledge and knowing) and axiology (studying the implications of ethics, morality, and values), and creative writing or artistic performance has a place as well. However, the line between the humanities and the sciences is not as evident as might first appear. Concepts in the humanities may touch on the sociology of knowledge, for instance, which is a well-established social science field, as is cultural anthropology, whose focus is on culture, including values. These examples illustrate the interest of the social sciences as well as the humanities in epistemology and axiology, respectively.

At the same time, there are innumerable humanistic studies that are empirical in nature, whether dealing with artificial intelligence and cognition in philosophy, semantic analysis in languages, social history using archival data, or content analysis in literature. Although writing in the humanities does not usually follow the standard scientific model emulated in much of the social sciences and practiced throughout the natural sciences, there are still some similarities. Prime among these is recognizing the importance of creating a framework for analysis.

A framework is the basis on which you will argue your thesis. It serves as an organizing structure for your arguments and functions as a reference point for your readers. Readers will look for a clear description of your framework at the end of your introductory thesis statement. Moreover, you should reference your framework explicitly in each of your major sections, using it to provide a transition from one section to the next. Finally, you will want to come back to your framework in your conclusion, showing how your research has extended, modified, clarified, or otherwise improved the intellectual foundation you established at the beginning.

A framework is a set of concepts that highlight patterns in the data and information you will be presenting in your paper, thesis, or dissertation. Ideally, frameworks are already part of the body of theory well known in your discipline and directly applicable to your topic. More often, however, frameworks are something you construct based on such prototypes as the following:

1. Typology of contrasting categories: the researcher asserts that all phenomena of interest fall into one of the categories. For instance, the researcher may assert that individuals may be classified as introvert or extrovert; that marriages may be classified as male dominant, egalitarian, or matriarchal; or that personalities may be classified as passive, aggressive, or passive/aggressive.

2. Two-dimensional spaces, often represented in two-by-two attribute tables: the researcher assets that all phenomena of interest fall into one of the categories formed by the intersection of two or more dimensions. An example would be the assertion that cultures may be classified into one of four categories in a space in which the x axis goes from self-oriented to other-oriented and the y axis goes from particularistic to universalistic; or the assertion that the symbolism in a novel may be classified according to an x axis that goes from images of darkness to images of light and a y axis that goes from male symbols to female symbols.

3. Developmental stages: the researcher asserts that all phenomena of interest will be found at one of a specified series of points of development, which occur in a set order. An example would be the assertion that Maslow's "need hierarchy" explains levels of motivation in an army unit; or the assertion that Kohlberg's stages of moral development explain differences in the behavior of officials in different nations.

4. Functionalism, in the sense of finding the positive functions of phenomena ordinarily seen as negative: an example would be the assertion that corruption mitigates problems of totalitarian social orders by providing the flexibility to achieve goals otherwise frustrated by a rule-bound system.

5. Contrarianism, in the sense of turning accepted wisdom on its head: the framework engages the interest of the reader and provides a structure onto which to lay the writer's thesis. An example would be the assertion that political apathy is more important to the stability of social order than is democratic participation.

6. Hermeneutics is a major approach to the study of texts, around which most of the humanities disciplines revolve. Hermeneutics grows out of a long tradition in biblical exegesis and scholarship, although as a technique it can be used by humanities and social science scholars alike to throw light on all sorts of textual materials not limited to the religious sphere. The hermeneutic scholar attempts to establish a dialogue with the text, looking at it from a number of viewpoints, including that of the researcher, and trying to understand the meaning of the text for the writer. Erik Erikson's *Young Man Luther* is a famous example, representing a form of psycho-history.

The humanities thesis is often introduced with a statement which shows there is a controversy to be investigated, such as "Although most writers on _____ have argued _____, it is the contention of the present thesis that _____." As a general rule, the writer wants to convince the reader early on that what will be discussed is something the reader does not already know. Settling controversies, or at least addressing them, is central to this purpose. Therefore, the thesis needs to be followed by, and contrasted with, alternative plausible theses about the same subject. Ideally, the writer wants to show that these alternative theses are believed in by various authorities or by public opinion, in order to show that he or she is not merely batting down "straw man" arguments.

A. Reviewing the Literature in the Humanities

Like other domains, the humanities have a variety of bibliographic reference works available as invaluable research aids. Most are available in print, on CD-ROM, and online. Your university's research library may be able to connect you to these bibliographic services. Alternatively, most are available through commercial services such as DIALOG, the nation's largest vendor of online reference databases (http://www.dialog.com). Below, some of the leading humanities reference resources are listed and described, all available online unless otherwise noted.

1. *Academic Search FullTEXT Elite*. This resource, not limited to the humanities, indexes and abstracts over 3,200 journals. For 1,200 of them, the full text is available. Started in 1984 (full text since 1990), it is updated daily.

2. *America: History and Life*. File 38 on Dialog, this service provides historical coverage of bibliography pertaining to the United States and Canada from prehistory to the present. Coverage is since 1954, with selected coverage to 1946. As of 1999 there were about 400,000 bibliographic listings, including coverage of some 2,000 American and selected foreign historical journals. In addition to adding about 10,000 regular listings each year, about 6,000 book and media reviews are indexed annually. About 90% of the listings are English-language and all the abstracts are in English.

3. *Archives USA*. This resource provides information on primary source materials from more than 4,800 American manuscript repositories, as well as records of more than 109,000 manuscript and other special collections. The service includes the Directory of Archives and Manuscript Repositories in the United States (DAMRUS), the National Union Catalog of Manuscript Collections (NUCMC), and indexing from the National Inventory of Documentary Sources in the United States (NIDS). It is updated quarterly.

4. *Art Abstracts*. File 435 on Dialog, Art Abstracts draws from 300 worldwide periodicals, yearbooks, and museum bulletins. Coverage from 1984, with abstracting since 1994, it has 400,000 records, updated monthly.

5. *ARTbibliographies Modern*. File 56 on Dialog, this database covers current literature, articles, books, dissertations, and exhibition catalogs on art and design, with full coverage of 19th- and 20th-century studies. Started in 1974, it more than over 225,000 records, updated semiannually by about 12,000 records per year.

6. *Art Index*. This resource indexes articles and book reviews taken from about 225 periodicals, yearbooks, and museum bulletins. It covers archaeology, architecture, art history, city planning, crafts, landscape architecture, film, fine arts, folk art, graphic arts, industrial design, interior design, and photography. Started in September 1984, the *Art Index* is updated quarterly.

7. *Art Literature International*. Files 176 and 191 on Dialog, this service abstracts and indexes current publications in the history of art. It is published by RILA, the International Repertory of the Literature of Art, and corresponds to the printed publication, *RILA*. Coverage from 1973, with more than 150,000 records, updated semiannually.

8. *Arts and Humanities Citation Index* (*Arts and Humanities Search*). File 439 on Dialog, this resource covers multiple humanities disciplines, indexing more than 1,300 journals worldwide. Citations make available the article bibliographies. Started in 1975, the online version covers from 1980, with more than 2 million records, updated weekly.

9. *ATLA Religion Database*. This database indexes journal articles, essays, and book reviews in all fields of religion, covering the most recent 10-year period. It is updated semiannually.

10. *Avery Index to Architectural Periodicals*. This database indexes more than 1,000 archaeology, city planning, interior design, historic preservation, and architecture journals. Started in 1977, it is updated daily.

11. *Bibliography of Asian Studies Online (BAS)*. Emphasizing the humanities and social sciences, this resource contains more than 410,000 citations on East, Southeast, and South Asia published worldwide since 1971. Emphasis is placed on 100 "most important" Asian Studies journals. It is updated quarterly. There is also a print version, *Bibliography of Asian Studies (BAS)*.

12. *Bibliography of the History of Art (BHA).* File 190 on Dialog, this database abstracts and indexes history of art publications. Earlier, this series appeared as RILA (International Repertory of the Literature of Art, File 191 on Dialog) and RAA (Repertoire d'Art et d'Archeologie). Coverage since 1991, with 150,000 records, updated quarterly.

13. *Biography Master Index (BMI).* File 287 on Dialog, this provides biographical information on some 4 million people in all fields of endeavor. It incorporates listings from more than 700 biographical dictionaries such as *Who's Who in America.* The print version is Gale Research's eight-volume publication, *Biography and Genealogy Master Index* (2nd edition, 1980), and its annual updates and a similar microfiche product, *Bio-Base.* Updated annually.

14. *Books in Print.* File 470 in Dialog, this venerable reference covers some 1.9 million books currently in print, declared out of print, or soon to be published titles in all subjects. The print versions of this resource are *Books in Print, Subject Guide to Books in Print, Forthcoming Books, Books in Print Supplement,* and the *Out of Print-Out of Stock Index.* Online since 1994, it is updated bimonthly.

15. *Book Review Index.* File 137 on Dialog, this database has more than 3 million reviews of more than 1 million books and periodical titles. Coverage since 1969 based on nearly 500 periodicals and newspapers. Updated about three times a year.

16. *Britannica Online.* The leading encyclopedia is now available in a fully searchable and browsable version that also includes *Merriam Webster's Collegiate Dictionary,* the *Britannica Book of the Year,* and links to sites selected by Britannica editors. Updated regularly.

17. *The Civil War: A Newspaper Perspective.* This provides the searchable full text for some 12,000 "major articles" from Union and Confederate newspapers such as the New York Herald, the Charleston Mercury, and the Richmond Enquirer, published between November 1, 1860 and April 30, 1865.

18. *CommSearch.* CommSearch provides searchable citation information, abstracting, table of contents listings, and some full text for literature pertaining to scholarly communication.

19. *Contemporary Women's Issues.* This database gives worldwide full-text access to journals, newsletters, and research reports pertaining to topics such as development, human rights, the workplace, violence and exploitation of women, education, politics, family life, pay equity, legal status of women, lesbian concerns, women's health, gender equity, and reproductive rights. Started in 1992, it is updated weekly.

20. *DISCovering Authors.* This resource provides biographies and critical essays on some 300 novelists, poets, dramatists, and others from a variety of cultures, nations, and time periods. Contents include biographic profiles, full-

text critical essays, and a bibliography and summary of media adaptations of the author's works. Updated every 3 years.

21. *Dissertation Abstracts.* File 35 on Dialog, this "must use" resource, *Dissertation Abstracts*, indexes and abstracts doctoral dissertations from most American, Canadian, and selected foreign institutions of higher learning. Since 1988, it has also provided coverage of masters' theses. Coverage from 1861, with 1.6 million records, it is updated monthly.

22. *Education Abstracts.* Covers more than 400 periodicals, yearbooks, and books on education. The focus includes preschool, elementary, secondary, and higher education; special and vocational education; comparative and multicultural education; adult and continuing education; computer technology; teacher education, evaluation, and methods; school administration and parent-teacher relations; and issues such as government funding and prayer in the schools. Started in 1983, abstracting began in 1994. It is updated monthly.

23. *English Poetry Online.* Covers more than 1,350 English-language poets from the Anglo-Saxon period to the end of the nineteenth century, providing full text.

24. *Ethnic Newswatch.* This full-text database has more than 450,000 articles from 200+ ethnic, minority, and native press newspapers, magazines, and journals. Covers since 1992.

25. *Historical Abstracts.* File 39 on Dialog, this major reference provides coverage of world history from 1450 to the present. Note that the United States and Canada are excluded as they are covered in America: History and Life. There are some half-million references, obtained from more than 200 historical, humanities, and social science journals worldwide. Some 20,000 citations are added annually. Coverage from 1954, with more than half a million records, updated six times a year.

26. *Historical Statistics of the United States.* This online and print publication of the Census Bureau contains time series data on a wide variety of topics, including demographic, economic, educational, and political information. Covers from historical times through 1970.

27. *History of Science and Technology.* This resource contains citations from more than 1,000 journals, covering the history of science and technology and allied historical fields.

28. *International Index to Music Periodicals (IIMP).* The IIMP indexes and abstracts music-related articles from 350 music periodicals from more than 20 countries. Music features from *The New York Times* and *The Washington Post* are included. Started in and covering from 1996.

29. *Linguistics & Language Behavior Abstracts (LLBA).* File 36 on Dialog, this reference acovers all aspects of the study of language, including phonetics, phonology, morphology, syntax, and semantics. Complete coverage is also given to various fields of linguistics, including descriptive, historical, compara-

tive, theoretical, and geographical linguistics. It is published by Sociological Abstracts and covers since 1973, with more than 200,000 records, updated quarterly.

30. *Magill's Survey of Cinema*. File 299 on Dialog, this database provides full-text articles on more than 1,800 notable films. Compiled by writers and cinema specialists based on information from the Academy of Motion Picture Arts and Sciences, the American Film Institute, the film archives at the University of California at Los Angeles, and the University of Southern California. The print version is published annually by Salem Press in multiple volumes. Coverage from 1902, with more than 34,000 records, updated throughout the year.

31. *MLA Bibliography*. The leading bibliographic reference for literature, this reference indexes more than 3,000 journals, monographs, series, working papers, and proceedings on literature, language, linguistics, and folklore. Started in 1963, it is updated quarterly.

32. *NoveList*. This online service lets one find new authors and titles based on keyword searching and browsing of more than 1,000 theme-oriented booklists, award-lists, and fiction-related websites.

33. *Periodical Abstracts*. Indexes more than 1,600 popular and general magazines and journals. Includes the full text of the articles from 490 journals. Started in 1971, with full text since 1991. Updated daily.

34. *Philosopher's Index*. The leading bibliographic reference for philosophy. It contains author-written abstracts on 15 fields of philosophy, published in journals and books since 1940. About 80% of the citations are articles, with the rest taken from books and contributions to anthologies. More than 480 journals are covered from 38 countries. It has some 210,000 records, adding about 10,000 annually. It covers since 1940.

35. *Primary Search*. Indexes and abstracts 116 children's magazines. Full text included for many. Covers since 1984.

36. *Wilson Humanities Abstracts Full Text*. File 436 on Dialog, this database covers more than 400 periodicals across the humanities, with full text for about 100 of these. Coverage from 1984, with almost a half-million records, updated monthly.

37. *WorldCat*. This is a union catalog of materials held in libraries worldwide.

B. Checklist

1. Have you clearly indicated which aspects of your paper, thesis, or dissertation constitute your own original contribution to your discipline?
2. Where you have set forth your research plan, have you justified each of your major methodological choices? Have you explained why you rejected major alternatives?

3. Have you carefully defined all the key terms in your study?
   In each major section, have you led with your most important points?
4. Within each major section, have you grouped points logically by descending levels of importance as indicated by descending levels of outline headings?
5. Have you read your work aloud at least once, listening for and then correcting the ''story line'' for better flow and emphasis?
6. Have you written the ''story'' in the active rather than passive voice? The active voice is preferred in most settings, especially in the humanities.
7. Have you considered the possibility of gaining help from a professional editor, particularly if English is not your native language?

BIBLIOGRAPHY

A. General

Mahoney, M. J. (1990). Human Change Processes. New York: Basic Books. Mahoney interprets change in terms of axiology, seeing an axial shift in 20th century history.

B. Fine Arts

Ameigh, T. M. (1993) Learn the language of music through journals. Music Educators Journal 79(5):30–32.

Beaty, D., and Schoenewolf, C. R. (1973). A marriage of English and music. Music Educators Journal 59(7):64–65.

Ernst, K. (1995). Art in your curriculum: Seeing meaning: Connecting writing and art. Teaching Prek-8(3):33–34.

Padgett, R. (1985). Camel serenade: New computer writing and art. Teachers and Writers Magazine 16(3):9–10.

Scali, N. (1991). The work of Beatrix Potter: A model for integrating fine art, writing, and science using technology. Writing Notebook 8(4):24–25.

Scali, N. (1991). Writing and art: Tools for self-expression and understanding. Writing Notebook 9(2):19–20.

Scali, N. (1992). Using art to enrich writing and reading. Writing Notebook 9(4):42–43.

Scali, N. (1993). The gift of writing. Writing Notebook. 10(4):39.

C. English

Beason, L. (1993). Feedback and revision in writing across the curriculum classes. Research in the Teaching of English 27:395–422.

Heap, S. (1997). Computer-assisted writing. On-Call 11(2):46–51.

Mansfield, M. A. (1993). Real world writing and the English curriculum. College Composition and Communication 44(1):69–83.

Shumaker, R. C., Dennis, L., and Green, L. (1990). Advanced exposition: A survey of patterns and problems. Journal of Advanced Composition 10(1):136–144.

D. History

Galt, M. F. (1992). The story in history: Writing your way into the American experience. Teachers and Writers 24(1):1–7.
Holsinger, D. C. (1991). A classroom laboratory for writing history. Social Studies Review 31(1):59–64.
Stockton, S. (1995). Writing in history: Narrating the subject of time. Written Communication 12(1):47–73.

E. Foreign Languages

Tabor, K. (1984). Gaining successful writing in the foreign language classroom. Foreign Language Annals 17(2):123–124.
White, A. S., and Caminero, R. (1995). Using process writing as a learning tool in the foreign language class. Canadian Modern Language Review 51(2):323–329.

F. Philosophy

Carella, M. J. (1983). Philosophy as literacy: Teaching college students to read critically and write cogently. College Composition and Communication 34(1):57–61.
Fishman, S. M. (1997). Student writing in philosophy: A sketch of five techniques. New Directions for Teaching and Learning 69:53–66.
Glesne, C., and Peshkin, A. (1992). Becoming Qualitative Researchers: An Introduction. New York: Longman.
Jason, G. J. (1985). Using philosophical dilemmas to teach composition. Teaching English in the Two-Year College 12(3):185–190.
North, S. M. (1986). Writing in a philosophy class: Three case studies. Research in the Teaching of English 20(3):225–262.
Seidman, I. E. (1991). Interviewing as Qualitative Research. New York: Teachers College Press.

24

Quantitative Research Writing in the Natural Sciences

I. CONCEPTUALIZING IN THE NATURAL SCIENCES

The natural science model is the leading framework for empirical study, not only in the natural sciences but also in the social sciences as well (see Behling, 1980). Research advances in the natural sciences can come about in several ways, as noted by Tice and Slavens (1983: 418). Logical positivists believed scientific advance occurred through discrete verifications of phenomena. Karl Popper preferred instead to emphasize the centrality to science of discrete falsifications of phenomena, believing nothing could be affirmatively verified, only ruled inconsistent with observed data. Thomas Kuhn, in contrast, emphasized the role of new paradigms in creating scientific revolution, transcending discrete empirical studies. Polanyi, arguing with Kuhn, saw the progress of science lying in growing consensus rather than revolution.

Conceptualization in science is closely associated with the scientific method, which involves collecting observations on a phenomenon, then analyzing these observations in terms of a model, theory, or set of hypotheses. A valid theory explains a large range of observations while being parsimonious in the number of assumptions it makes. A valid theory is also useful as a predictive tool, enabling us to anticipate the implications of new information. Also, measurements must be replicable so other scholars can verify the researcher's findings. All these aspects of scientific conceptualization are not unique to natural science, nor are experimental methods using control groups unique. What differentiates research in the natural sciences is only a matter of degree: experimentation is more feasible, diminishing the need to rely on quasi-experimental methods; quantitative measurement is more possible, reducing the relevance of qualitative research methods; and real-time measurement of phenomena is also more appropriate, lessening reliance on archival information. Also, in practical terms, funding levels are higher, enabling more thorough forms of instrumentation and investigation.

A. Researching the Scientific Literature

The natural sciences, in part because of their impact on the economy, have perhaps the richest array of bibliographic reference works available as invaluable research aids. Most are available in print, on CD-ROM, and online. Your university's research library may be able to connect you to any or all of these bibliographic services. Alternatively, most are available through commercial services such as DIALOG, the nation's largest vendor of online reference databases (http://www.dialog.com). Below, some of the leading natural sciences reference resources are listed and described, all available online unless otherwise noted.

1. *ACM Digital Library*. Contains citations and full-text of articles from ACM journals and magazines most dating back to 1991, available at http://www.acm.org/dl/. There is also a print version *ACM Guide to Computing Literature*.

2. *Aerospace Database*. File 108 in Dialog, the Aerospace Database abstracts scientific and technical documents, books, reports, conference papers, and articles on aerospace research in more than 40 countries. Coverage includes aeronautics, astronautics, and space sciences, as well as aspects of chemistry, geosciences, physics, communications, and electronics. The print equivalent is the *International Aerospace Abstracts (IAA)*. Covers from 1962, with more than 2 million records, updated monthly.

3. *Agricola*. File 10 on Dialog, this is the leading reference for agriculture and related literature, as indexed by the National Agricultural Library (NAL). The print versions are the *Bibliography of Agriculture* and the *National Agricultural Library Catalog*. Coverage extends to journal articles, books, theses, patents, software, audio visual materials, technical reports and agricultural experiment station reports. *Agricola* started in 1970, has more than 3.4 million records, and is updated monthly.

4. *Agricultural and Environmental Biotechnology Abstracts*. Covers biotechnology, molecular biology, plant genome studies, biopesticides, carbohydrates, oil and chemical spills, enzymes, genetic engineering, organic acids, patents, proteins, soil microorganisms, waste disposal, vaccines, and much more. Covers from 1993 to the present, updated bimonthly. Contains about 20,000 records, with about 2,500 records added annually.

5. *AGRIS.* File 203 on Dialog, this international information system for agricultural sciences and technology corresponds in part to the printed publication, *Agrindex,* published monthly by the Food and Agriculture Organization (FAO) of the United Nations.

6. *Algology, Mycology & Protozoology Abstracts.* Covers algae, fungi, protozoa, or lichens, and their reproduction, growth, life cycles, biochemistry, genetics, and infection and immunity in man, other animals, and plants. Topical coverage extends to environmental impact, genetic engineering, vaccine development, and many other areas. Contains more than 175,000 records, with about 10,000 added annually. Started in 1982, updated monthly.

7. *Analytical Abstracts.* File 305 on Dialog, this service covers analytical chemistry, including inorganic chemistry, organic chemistry, pharmaceutical chemistry, environmental science, agriculture, instrumentation, and more. Based on some 1,300 journals, as well as conference papers, books, standards, and technical reports, it covers since 1980 and has more than 250,000 records.

8. *Animal Behavior Abstracts.* Covers neurophysiology, behavioral ecology, genetics, applied ethology, and numerous related topics, based on coverage of all important journals dealing with the biology of one or more taxonomic groups. Started in 1982, it contains more than 90,000 records, with about 6,000 added annually. Updated monthly.

9. *APILit.* Files 354 and 954 of Dialog, this is the database of the American Petroleum Institute's Literature Abstracts on the petroleum, petrochemical, natural gas, and energy related industries.

10. *Applied Science & Technology Index.* This resource indexes journal articles, meeting reports, industry news, book reviews, interviews, and new product reviews from about 300 English-language sources. The major focus is on the fields of aeronautics and space science; artificial intelligence; fire and fire prevention; civil, electrical, and mechanical engineering; textiles and fabrics; mathematics; robotics; and metallurgy. Started in 1983, it is updated monthly.

11. *Aquatic Sciences and Fisheries Abstracts.* File 44 on Dialog, this leading aquatic science reference, ASFA covers more than 5,000 serial publications, books, reports, conference proceedings, translations, and limited distribution literature. ASFA is associated with the Aquatic Sciences and Fisheries Information System (ASFIS), formed by four United Nations agency sponsors and two international partners. Topical areas include aquaculture, water pollution, conservation, environmental quality, fisheries, marine environments, meteorology, oceanography, policy and legislation, and wildlife management. Started in 1978, it contains about 700,000 records, with more than 40,000 added annually. Updated monthly.

12. *Automated Patent Service (APS).* This is a full-text database on U.S. Patents, developed by the U.S. Patent and Trademark Office. Does not include patent drawings. Updated weekly on Monday evenings.

13. *Bacteriology Abstracts (Microbiology Abstracts: Section B: Bacteriology).* This is a medically oriented reference for microbiology and bacteriology, also of interest to environmentalists, medical and veterinary laboratory science, agricultural research, cell biology, genetics, toxicology, and more. Started in 1982, it contains 230,000 records, with 15,000 added annually. Updated monthly.

14. *Beilstein Information.* This database corresponds to the *Beilsteins Handbuch der Organische Chemie* and provides coverage of chemical structures. It is updated regularly.

15. *Bioengineering Abstracts.* Deals with bioengineering topics like instrumentation, imaging, biomechanics, biochemistry, microbial technology, food science, genetic engineering, medical applications, and more. Started in 1993, it covers 60,000 records. About 12,000 records are added annually. Updated monthly.

16. *Biological Abstracts.* The leading, comprehensive reference for worldwide journal literature in biology and the life sciences. It covers about 6,500 journals in agriculture, biochemistry, biotechnology, ecology, immunology, microbiology, neuroscience, pharmacology, public health, and toxicology. Started in 1980, with full abstracting in 1985. Updated quarterly. See listing below for *BIOSIS Previews.*

17. *Biological Abstracts/RRM.* This extends coverage to reports, reviews, meeting papers, books and chapters, review articles, and U.S. patents. Started in 1995, it is updated quarterly.

18. *Biological and Agricultural Index.* This resource indexes some 250 international English-language journals in agricultural science and biology, including animal science, biochemistry, botany, cytology, ecology, entomology, environment, forestry, genetics, horticulture, marine sciences, microbiology, nutrition, soils, veterinary medicine, and zoology. Started in 1983.

19. *Biology Digest.* This resource indexes and abstracts biology and life science literature worldwide, with an emphasis on the high school or undergraduate college level. The audience is students and instructors, not researchers. Started in 1989, it has about 24,000 records. Updated nine times a year.

20. *BIOSIS Basics.* This is the journals-only subset of the BIOSIS biological abstracts database.

21. *BIOSIS Previews.* Files 5 and 55 on Dialog, this is an online version from *Biological Abstracts* (*BA*), and *Biological Abstracts/Reports, Reviews, and Meetings* (*BA/RRM*) (formerly *BioResearch Index*). See listing for *Biological Abstracts.*

22. *Biotechnology and Bioengineering Abstracts.* This resource covers biotechnology, bioengineering, aquatic science, agricultural science, biomedical engineering, environmental science, genetic engineering, marine science, and more. Started in 1982, it has more than half a million records. Updated monthly.

23. *Books in Print.* This venerable reference covers some 1.9 million books currently in print, declared out of print, or soon to be published titles in all subjects. The print versions of this resource are *Books in Print, Subject Guide to Books in Print, Forthcoming Books, Books in Print Supplement,* and the *Out of Print-Out of Stock Index.* Online since 1994, it is updated bimonthly.

24. *CAB Abstracts.* This resource covers agriculture, forestry, and allied disciplines like crop husbandry, veterinary science, nutrition science, rural development, and more. It is sponsored by the Centre for Agriculture and Biosciences International. Started in 1972. Updated quarterly.

25. *Calcium and Calcified Tissue Abstracts.* Covers biological and medical implication of calcium. Started in 1982, it has 60,000 records. Updated quarterly with more than 4,000 records added annually.

26. *Cambridge Scientific Abstracts (CSA).* This reference incorporates some 60 databases in life and environmental sciences, and engineering. Databases include Aquatic Sciences and Fisheries Abstracts, Computer and Information Systems Abstracts, Conference Papers Index, Ecology Abstracts, Entomology Abstracts, Genetics Abstracts, Health and Safety Sciences Abstracts, Materials Business File, Microbiology Abstracts, Pollution Abstracts and TOXLINE.

27. *CASSIS* and *ASIST.* These databases cover patent literature. CASSIS covers current classification information for U.S. patents since 1790 and patent titles since 1969. Patent abstracts are available for the most recent 2-year period. ASIST includes the Manual of Classification and the Index to Patent Classification.

28. *Chemical Abstracts (CASearch).* Files 308–314 and 399 on Dialog, CASearch is a giant chemistry database of 13 million citations to worldwide chemistry literature since 1967. Chemical substances are represented by CAS Registry-unique numbers assigned to each specific chemical compound, such that corresponding substance information may be searched in Dialog chemical substance files such as CHEMSEARCH™ (Dialog file 398). All records from the 8th Collective Index Period forward are contained in Dialog file 399. Updated weekly.

29. *Chemical Engineering and Biotechnology Abstracts (CEABA).* File 315 of Dialog, this is the online version of the print publications *Chemical Engineering* and *Biotechnology Abstracts,* produced by The Royal Society of Chemistry and DECHEMA, the German Society for Chemical Equipment, Chemical Technology and Biotechnology. Covers since 1970, with more than 450,000 records, updated monthly.

30. *CHEMNAME and CHEMSEARCH.* CHEMNAME is file 301 on Dialog and CHEMSEARCH is file 398. These nonbibliographic databases record all chemical substances registered through the Chemical Abstracts Service, with one record per chemical entity. They cover all CAS Registry Numbers, molecular

formula, CA Substance Index Names, synonyms, complete ring data, and other chemical substance information. CHEMNAME covers chemical substances in the CAS Registry System cited in Chemical Abstracts two or more times from 1967 through the most recent monthly update. Records for substances in CHEMNAME are also contained in CHEMSEARCH. CHEMSEARCH covers all chemical substances registered since 1957, including substances that have been cited in the CAS literature since 1967. The files are used to support Dialog searching for specific substances on various Dialog chemical files. CHEMNAME covers since 1967 with 3.3 million records, updated monthly. CHEMSEARCH covers from 1957, has 18 million records, and is updated monthly.

31. *Chemoreception Abstracts*. This covers chemoreception, with implications for neurobiology, chemistry, biochemistry, molecular biology, and the physiology of taste, smell, internal chemoreception, and chemotaxis. Started in 1982, it has 30,000 records. Updated quarterly.

32. *CHEMTOX Online*. File 337 on Dialog, this database covers environmental, health, and safety data for chemical substances associated with EPA or other legislation or regulation, including carcinogens listed by the U. S. National Toxicology Program and others, or substances that have properties that might lead to later legislation or regulation. More than 11,000 records, updated quarterly.

33. *CINAHL*. This database indexes some 900 allied health journals in 13 disciplines, including nursing. Started in 1982.

34. *Clinical Reference System*. This patient-oriented service provides thousands of essays covering adult health, behavioral health, cardiology, drug and medication information, pediatric health, senior health, women's health, and sports medicine.

35. *Cochrane Library*. This service includes multiple databases, including the Cochrane Database of Systematic Reviews, the Cochrane Controlled Trials Register, the Database of Abstracts of Reviews of Effectiveness (DARE), and the Cochrane Review Methodology Database. This service is the leading resource for effects of specific health-related interventions and practices, as well as research methodology.

36. *Compendex*. This provides indexes and abstracts in engineering and technology. The print version is the *Engineering Index*. Started in 1986, it is updated monthly.

37. *Computer and Control Abstracts*—see *INSPEC*.

38. *Computer and Information Systems Abstracts*. This is the leading reference for computer science, information systems research, and related fields. Covers such topics as artificial intelligence, computer programming and hardware, imaging systems, bioengineering, control systems, instrumentation, and many more. Started in 1981, it has 300,000 records. Updated monthly.

39. *Computer Database*. Available on InfoTrac Web, this database provides a combination of indexing, abstracts and full text for leading business and

technical publications in the computer, telecommunications and electronic industries. See http://www.galegroup.com/tlist/sb5087.html.

40. *Conference Papers Index.* File 77 on Dialog, this database has citations to papers and poster sessions from major scientific and technical meetings worldwide. Specialization in the life sciences, environmental sciences, and the aquatic sciences. Records include complete ordering information. Coverage since 1973, updated bimonthly, with about 2 million records.

41. *Current Biotechnology Abstracts.* File on Dialog, this is the online version of the print *Current Biotechnology* published by The Royal Society of Chemistry. Covers since 1983, with more than 100,000 records, updated monthly.

42. *Derwent Biotechnology Abstracts.* File on 357 Dialog, this database covers biotechnology, genetic engineering, biochemical engineering, fermentation, cell culture and waste disposal, pharmaceuticals, downstream processing, and more. Coverage since 1982, with 250,000 records, updated biweekly.

43. *Dissertation Abstracts.* File 35 on Dialog, this "must use" resource indexes and abstracts doctoral dissertations from most American, Canadian, and selected foreign institutions of higher learning. Since 1988, it has also provided coverage of masters' theses. Coverage from 1861, with 1.6 million records, it is updated monthly.

44. *EIS: Digests of Environmental Impact Statements.* Provides concise summaries of federal environmental impact statements. Started in 1985, it has about 7,000 records. Updated monthly, adding about 1,800 records per year.

45. *Electrical and Electronics Abstracts*–see *INSPEC.*

46. *Electronics and Communications Systems Abstracts.* Provides abstracts for electrical engineering, control engineering, circuit design, and related fields in electronics, telecommunications, and multimedia. Started in 1981, it has more than 180,000 records. Updated monthly, with about 10,000 records added annually.

47. *Elsevier BioBase.* File 71 on Dialog, this new new life sciences database is a superset of the print *Current Awareness in Biological Sciences* (CABS). Coverage from 1994, with 1 million records, updated weekly.

48. *Energyline.* File 69 on Dialog, this closed database is the online version of the print *Energy Information Abstracts.* Coverage includes books, journals, Congressional committee prints, conference proceedings, speeches, and statistics. Covers 1971–1993, with 87,000 records, no further updates.

49. *Energy Science & Technology.* Files 103 and 803 on Dialog, this database is the former *DOE ENERGY* database. It provides multidisciplinary coverage of scientific and technical research literature. The print versions are *Energy Research Abstracts* and *INIS Atomindex.* Coverage from 1976, with nearly 4 million records, updated biweekly.

50. *Engineering Index (Ei Compendex).* Files 8 and 208 on Dialog, the *Ei Compendex* database is the online version of the print *Engineering Index.* It

abstracts 4,500 worldwide journals on civil, energy, environmental, geological, and biological engineering; electrical, electronics, and control engineering; chemical, mining, metals, and fuel engineering; mechanical, automotive, nuclear, and aerospace engineering; and computers, robotics, and industrial robots. Coverage from 1970, with about 4 million records, it is updated weekly.

51. *Entomology Abstracts.* Covers entomology, phylogeny, morphology, physiology, anatomy, biochemistry, and other scientific aspects of insects, arachnids, myriapods, onychophorans, and terrestrial isopods. Started in 1982, it has 170,000 records. Updated monthly.

52. *Environmental Abstracts (Enviroline). Enviroline* is the online version. It abstracts more than 1,000 worldwide primary and secondary publications on environmental management, technology, planning, law, political science, economics, geology, biology, and chemistry. Coverage from 1975, with about 200,000 records, updated monthly.

53. *Environmental Bibliography.* File 68 on Dialog, this database surveys more than 400 journals to cover water, air, soil, and noise pollution; solid waste management; health hazards; urban planning; global warming; and other environmental topics. The print equivalent is *Environmental Periodicals Bibliography.* Coverage from 1973 with abstracts since 1997, with more than 600,000 records, updated monthly.

54. *Environmental Health Information Service (EHIS).* Full text access to publications from the National Institute of Environmental Health Sciences, including Environmental Health Perspectives.

55. *Environmental Sciences,* a database from Cambridge Scientific Abstracts covering environmental issues including pollution, air quality, toxicology, and related bibliography.

56. *Environmental Sciences & Pollution Management.* This major resource abstracts about 4,000 scientific journals and other publications from a wide variety of disciplines, including agricultural science, aquatic science, bacteriology, ecoology, environmental engineering, toxicology, and others. Started in 1981, it has about 1.2 million records. Updated monthly, with 80,000 records added annually.

57. *Federal Research in Progress.* File 266 on Dialog, this database covers federally funded research in the physical sciences, engineering, and life sciences. Current coverage only, with about 175,000 records, reloaded monthly.

58. *Fish and Fisheries Worldwide.* This resource indexes and abstracts to worldwide fish and fish-related literature. The print version is the U.S. Fish and Wildlife Service's *Fisheries Review*, augmented by other fisheries databases. Started in 1971.

59. *Food Science and Technology Abstracts (FSTA).* Covers food science applications of biotechnology, biochemistry, chemistry, physics, microbiology,

engineering, and toxicology, as well as economics and legislation, based on some 1,600 scientific journals, Started in 1969, it is updated quarterly.

60. *General Science Abstracts* . File 98 on Dialog, this popular reference indexes (and has selective full text for) more than 150 United States and United Kingdom journals on anthropology, astronomy, biology, computers, earth sciences, medicine and health, and other disciplines. Started in 1984 with abstracts from 1994 and full text since 1995, with half a million records, it is updated monthly.

61. *Genetics Abstracts*. This resource covers genetics, recombinant DNA technology, molecular genetics, immunology, ecology, and numerous genetics specialties. It started in 1982 and has more than 200,000 records. Updated monthly.

62. *GeoArchive.* File 58 on Dialog, this database covers geoscience, hydroscience, and environmental science, based on about 5,000 serials, books from 2,000 publishers, as well as geological maps and doctoral dissertations. The print equivalents are *Geotitles*, *Hydrotitles*, *Geoscience Documentation*, and the *Bibliography of Economic Geology*. Coverage from 1974, with 700,000 records, updated monthly.

63. *GEOBASE.* File 292 on Dialog, this database covers world research articles in physical and human geography, earth and environmental sciences, ecology, and related disciplines. It covers more than 2,000 journals fully and another 3,000 selectively, as well as books, monographs, conference proceedings, and reports.

64. *GeoRef.* File 89 on Dialog, this reference contains 1.6 million records on geology, geography, geophysics, and related disciplines. The print versions are the *Bibliography and Index of Geology*, *Bibliography of North American Geology*, *Bibliography and Index of Geology Exclusive of North America*, *Bibliography of Theses in Geology,* and the *Geophysical Abstracts.* Coverage for North America is since 1785, and since 1933 for the rest of the world, with more than 2 million records, updated biweekly.

65. *Health and Safety Science Abstracts.* This reference covers public health, safety, and industrial hygiene.Topics include aviation and aerospace safety; environmental safety; nuclear safety; medical safety; occupational safety; and ergonomics; health- and safety-related aspects of pollution, waste disposal, radiation, pesticides, epidemics, and many others. Started in 1981, it has about 120,000 records. Updated monthly, with more than 5,000 records added annually.

66. *History of Science and Technology*. This resource contains citations from more than 1,000 journals, covering the history of science and technology and allied historical fields. See http://libweb.princeton.edu:2003/databases/about/tips/html/hst.html.

67. *Human Genome Abstracts.* Covers development from the Human Genome Project and many others, with a focus on topics like gene therapy, cloning,

immunogenetics, genetic screening, and more. Started in 1981, it has 25,000 records.

68. *IEEE/IEE Electronic Library.* This is a leading reference for electrical engineering, including coverage of related aspects of computer science and more. Focuses on standards. Started in 1988.

69. *Immunology Abstracts.* This is a database for immunology as a subfield of biomedical science. Started in 1982, it has more than 225,000 records. Updated monthly, with about 1,800 records added annually.

70. *Industrial and Applied Microbiology.* This referenc covers microbiology applications in agricultural, food and beverage, chemical, and pharmaceutical industries. Started in 1982, it has more than 140,000 records. Updated monthly, with about 10,000 records added annually.

71. *Information Science Abstracts.* File 202 on Dialog, this database indexes and abstracts about 300 periodicals in information science and library science worldwide. Coverage from 1966, with 200,000 records, updated nine times a year.

72. *INSPEC.* Files 2, 3, and 4 on Dialog, this resource indexes and abstracts articles in physics, electronics, electrical engineering, control technology, information technology, and computing. The print versions are *Physics Abstracts, Electrical and Electronics Abstracts*, and *Computer and Control Abstracts.* Started in 1989, with 12 million records, it is updated quarterly.

73. *Life Sciences Collection.* File 76 on Dialog, this database abstracts from more than 5,000 serials in biology, medicine, biochemistry, biotechnology, ecology, and microbiology, and some aspects of agriculture and veterinary science. It corresponds to print versions of about 20 abstracting periodicals. Coverage from 1982, with 1.8 million records, updated monthly.

74. *MathSci.* File 239 on Dialog, this database covers worldwide literature on mathematics, statistics, and computer science and related fields of operations research, econometrics, engineering, physics, biology, and others. It is composed of eight subfiles: *Mathematical Reviews* (from 1940), *Current Mathematical Publications* (current only), *Current Index to Statistics* (1975–1994), *Index to Statistics and Probability* (1910–1968), *ACM Guide to Computer Literature* (1981–1989), *Computing Reviews* (from 1984), *Technical Reports in Computer Science* (from 1954), and *STRENS Recreational Mathematics.* Overall, covers mathematics from 1959, statistics from 1910, and computer science from 1954, with 2 million records, updated monthly.

75. *MathSciNet.* This service corresponds to the print *Mathematical Reviews* and *Current Mathematical Publications.* The former is covered from 1940 and most else since 1980. The former is updated monthly and the latter daily.

76. *Mechanical Engineering Abstracts.* The leading reference for its field, it provides worldwide coverage of mechanical engineering, engineering manage-

ment, and production engineering. Started in 1981, it has some 200,000 records. Updated monthly, with about 10,000 records added annually.

77. *Medical and Pharmaceutical Biotechnology Abstracts*. Covers medical biotechnology worldwide, including molecular biology, genetics, immunology, pharmaceutical science, public health, and related fields. Started in 1993, it has 25,000 records. Updated bimonthly, with about 4,000 records added annually.

78. *Medline*. Covers biomedical concerns based on some 3,900 journals in medicine, nursing, dentistry, veterinary medicine, the health care system, and the preclinical sciences. Started in 1965, it is updated monthly.

79. *METADEX*. File 32 on Dialog, this database covers metals and alloys. Started in 1966, it has 1.2 million records. Updated monthly, with about 40,000 records added annually.

80. *Meteorological and Geoastrophysical Abstracts*. File 29 on Dialog, this database covers meteorology and geoastrophysics worldwide based on more than 200 sources. Related coverage extends to physical oceanography, hydrosphere and hydrology, environmental sciences, and glaciology. Coverage from 1970, with 225,000 records, updated monthly. Abstracts are included for 1972–1973, and from 1976 to the present.

81. *Microbiology Abstracts*. Covers microbiological aspects of biochemistry, genetics, immunology, ecology of micro-organisms, bacteriology, and related fields. Started in 1982, it has 450,000 records. Updated monthly, with about 30,000 records added annually.

82. *NTIS*. The National Technical Information Service indexes and abstracts unclassified U.S. government-sponsored research and worldwide scientific, technical, engineering, and business-related information. Started in 1964, it has more than 2 million records. It is updated biweekly, with about 40,000 records added annually.

83. *Nuclear Science Abstracts*. File 109 on Dialog, NSA covers nuclear science and technology worldwide.Includes technical reports from the U.S. Atomic Energy Commission, U.S. Energy Research and Development Administration. This is a closed file with coverage from 1984 through 1976, with 944,000 records. Coverage of the literature since 1976 is provided by File 103, Energy Science & Technology.

84. *Nucleic Acids Abstracts*. This database covers genetic research, cloning, biosynthesis, immunology, and many related fields. Started in 1982, it has about 180,000 records. Updated monthly, with about 12,000 records added annually.

85. *Oceanic Abstracts*. File 28 on Dialog, this is the leading reference on oceanography, including related aspects of marine biology and physical oceanography, fisheries, aquaculture, nonliving resources, meteorology and geology, plus environmental, technological, and legislative topics. Coverage from 1964, with about 300,000 records, updated monthly.

86. *Oceanographic and Marine Resources.* This reference indexes and abstracts worldwide literature on marine and oceanographic resources literature, focusing on North American waterways and coastlines. The print versions are the *Oceanographic Literature Review* and *Deep-Sea Research, Part B*, and features the *Sea Grants Abstracts* database, supplemented by U.S. National Oceanic and Atmospheric Administration (NOAA) files. Covers since 1960.

87. *Oncogenes and Growth Factors Abstracts.* This reference database pertains to the study of cancer, with applications to molecular biology, immunology, virology, bacteriology, genetics, and related fields. Started in 1981, it has some 150,000 records.

88. *PaperChem.* This resource abstracts literature pertaining to pulp, paper, and allied technologies. The print equivalent is the latest 5 years of the *Abstract Bulletin of the Institute of Paper Science and Technology*. Started in 1967.

89. *PASCAL.* File 144 on Dialog, PASCAL is a bibliographic service from the Institut de l'Information Scientifique et Technique (INIST) of the French National Research Council (CNRS). It covers worldwide scientific and technical literature. The print version is the *Bibliographie internationale* (previously *Bulletin signaletique*). In addition to the original language title, there is a French translated title, and since 1973, an English-translated title. Most abstracts are in French. Coverage from 1973, with 12 million records, updated monthly, except August.

90. *Physics Abstracts*—see *INSPEC*.

91. *Pollution Abstracts.* File 41 on Dialog, this is an environmentally oriented database on pollution-related aspects of atmospheric science, mathematical modeling, and policy aspects of environmental action worldwide. Coverage from 1980, with about 250,000 records, updated monthly.

92. *Science.* File 370 on Dialog, this database from the American Association for the Advancement of Science (AAAS), covers the advancement of science, especially governmental policy and social aspects of science and technology. Does cover social science also. Coverage from 1996; about 4,000 records, updated weekly.

93. *Science Citation Index (SciSearch).* Files 34 (current) and 434 (pre-1990) on Dialog, this is a "must use" multidisciplinary index to scientific journal literature, covering some 3,300 journals in 100 disciplines. It enables the researcher to find who has cited whom and to trace chains of citations as well as search author abstracts. *Science Citation Index Expanded* is an enhanced online version that covers more than 5,300 journals in the sciences from 1987 to the present. *Web of Science* is a packaged online service that contains *Science Citation Index Expanded* as well as the *Social Science Citation Index* and the *Arts & Humanities Citation Index*. Coverage from 1974, with 16 million records, updated weekly.

94. *Science's NextWave.* This service from the American Association for the Advancement of Science provides weekly online coverage of scientific training, career development, and the science job market. Started in 1992, it is updated monthly.

95. *Solid State and Superconductivity Abstracts.* This database covers phase, crystal, and mechanical properties of solids, optical and dielectric properties, conductive and magnetic properties, exotic electronic structure and energy gaps, SQUIDs, impurity effects, flux structures and critical current, ceramics, twinning phenomena, and more. Started in 1981, it has about 160,000 records. Updated bimonthly, adding about 9,000 records annually.

96. *SPIN.* File 62 on Dialog, this database is the ''Searchable Physics Information Notices,'' covering physics research in the United States, Russia, and the Ukraine. Produced by the American Institute of Physics. Coverage from 1975, with more than 800,000 records, updated biweekly.

97. *TOXLINE.* File 156 on Dialog, this reference covers toxicology, providing bibliographic citations and abstracts from journal articles, monographs, technical reports, theses, letters, meeting abstracts, papers and reports. It is sponsored by the U.S. National Library of Medicine. Incorporates listings from 17 sources, with selected coverage as early as the 1930s and full coverage from 1992. It has 2.5 million records, updated monthly.

98. *Toxicology Abstracts.* This is the most comprehensive toxicology database, started in 1981 and having about 150,000 records. Updated monthly, with about 12,000 new records annually.

99. *WasteInfo.* File 110 on Dialog, this database covers nonnuclear technical, policy, and economic aspects of waste management. Coverage from 1974, with about 125,000 records, updated monthly.

100. *WaterNet.* File 245 on Dialog, this database indexes publications of the American Water Works Association and the AWWA Research Foundation, with worldwide coverage. Coverage from 1971, with 50,000 records, updated quarterly.

101. *Water Resources Abstracts.* File 117 on Dialog, this reference covers water resources, including supply, conservation, management, protection, law, engineering, planning and pollution; water-related aspects of natural, physical, and social sciences. Coverage from 1968, with about 300,000 records, updated monthly.

102. *Wildlife Worldwide.* This reference indexes world literature on mammals, birds, reptiles, and amphibians. It includes the U.S. Fish and Wildlife Service's Wildlife Review databases and others. Full coverage is since 1971, with selective coverage since 1935.

103. *Wilson Applied Science & Technology Abstracts.* File 99 on Dialog, this database abstracts more than 400 periodicals in a wide variety of industrial,

engineering, and technical fields. Coverage from 1993, with 1 million records, updated weekly.

104. *Wilson Biological & Agricultural Index.* File 143 on Dialog, this database indexes about 250 periodicals in biology and agriculture, with roughly equal coverage since 1983, with three-quarter million records, updated monthly.

105. *World Translations Index.* File 295 on Dialog, this unique database gave access to translations of scientific and technological literature sponsored by the International Translations Centre (ITC) and the Centre National de la Recherche Scientifique et Technique (CNRS/INIST). More than half the English translations were from Russian and an additional 30% from Japanese and German. No longer published, coverage is from 1979 to 1997, with nearly half a million records.

106. *Zoological Record.* File 185 on Dialog, this database covers some 6,500 journals, technical reports, books, conference proceedings, theses, and review annuals covering zoology, animal behavior, habitat, ecology, evolution, biochemistry, genetics, taxonomy, systematics, parasitology, zoogeography, reproduction, and paleontology. Coverage is since 1978, with 1.2 million records, updated monthly.

B. Checklist

1. Is your literature review thorough with regard to your hypotheses? Consider paring it to about 100 references most directly related to your hypotheses. Remember to repeat your literature search for breaking new reports by others in the course of your own investigations.
2. Have you clearly articulated how your research will contribute to solution of gaps, problems, or contradictions found in the literature?
3. Is it clear on the one hand how you are relating to the work of previous researchers, and on the other how your research is original and important?
4. Have you sought the advice of other members of the scientific community who are also doing work in your area, seeking to advance the state of the art and not duplicate existing work?
5. Have you fulfilled all ethical guidelines, including securing clearance as necessary from your university's Institutional Review Board?
6. Have you kept meticulous lab notes, documenting all steps of your investigation, such that it may be replicated?
7. Are you using the American Psychological Association or other style guide prescribed by your department?
8. Where possible, have you used instrumentation already validated by others, not only for validation but also to increase the comparability of your results?

9. Have you sought to expose your work to the critique of fellow students, your dissertation committee, and researchers in the field before your dissertation defense or publication?

BIBLIOGRAPHY

A. General

Briscoe, M. H. (1996). Preparing Scientific Illustrations: A Guide to Better Posters, Presentations and Publications. NY: Springer.

Brusaw, C. T., Alfred, G. J., and Oliu, W. E. (1976). Handbook of Technical Writing. New York: St. Martin's Press, 1976.

Day, R. A. (1998). How to Write and Publish a Scientific Paper. Phoenix: Oryx Press.

Feibelman, P. J. (1993). A Ph.D. is Not Enough! A Guide to Survival in Science. Reading, MA: Addison-Wesley.

Katz, M. J. (1985). Elements of the Scientific Paper: A Step-by-Step Guide for Students and Professionals. New Haven: Yale University Press.

Rubens, P., ed. (1992). Science and Technical Writing: A Manual of Style. New York: Henry Holt & Co.

White, J. H. (1997). From Research to Printout: Creating Effective Technical Documents. New York: American Society of Mechanical Engineers Press.

Yang, J. T. (1995). An Outline of Scientific Writing: for Researchers with English as a Foreign Language. Singapore, New Jersey, and Hong Kong: World Scientific.

B. Scientific Method

Beach, D. P., and Alvager, T. K. E. (1992). Handbook for Scientific and Technical Research. Englewood Cliffs, NJ: Prentice Hall.

Carey, S. S. (1998). A Beginner's Guide to Scientific Method. Belmont, CA: Wadsworth Publishing.

Kuhn, T. (1970a). The Structure of Scientific Revolutions. Chicago: University of Chicago Press.

Kuhn, T. (1970b). Reflections on my critics. In: Lakatos, I., and Musgrave, A., eds., Criticism and the Growth of Knowledge. New York: Cambridge University Press, pp 231–278.

McCuen, R. H., ed. (1996). The Elements of Academic Research. New York: American Society of Civil Engineers Press.

Polanyi, M. (1946). Science, Faith and Society. Chicago: The University of Chicago Press.

Polanyi, M. (1951). The Logic of Liberty: Reflections and Rejoinders. Chicago: The University of Chicago Press.

Polanyi, M. (1957). Personal Knowledge. Chicago: University of Chicago Press.

Popper, K. (1946). The Open Society and Its Enemies. Princeton, NJ: Princeton University Press.

Popper, K. (1968). The Logic of Scientific Discovery. New York: Harper Torchbooks.

Popper, K. (1979). Objective Knowledge: An Evolutional Approach. Revised edition. Oxford, UK: Clarendon Press.

Tice, T. N., and Slavens, C. T. (1983). Research Guide to Philosophy. Chicago: American Library Association.

C. Natural Sciences

Behling, O. (1980). The case for the natural science model for research in organizational behavior and organization theory. Academy of Management Review 5(4):483–490.

D. Biology

Aaron, D. K. (1996). Writing across the curriculum: Putting theory into practice in animal science courses. Journal of Animal Science 74(11):2810–2828.

Cannon, R. E. (1990). Experiments in writing to teach microbiology. The American Biology Teacher 52:156–158.

Cothron, J. H. (1989). How-to-do-it: Writing results and conclusions. American Biology Teacher 51:239–242.

Cooley, A. P. (1980). Writing in science—an innovation. The American Biology Teacher 42:534–536.

Council of Biology Editors Style Manual Committee. (1994). Scientific Style and Format: The CBE Manual for Authors, Editors and Publishers. Cambridge, UK: University of Cambridge Press.

Franz, C. J., and Soven, M. (1996). Writing in biology: The senior project. Journal of College Science Teaching 26(2):111–114.

Grant, M. C., and Pirrto, J. (1994). Darwin, dogs, and DNA: Freshman writing about biology. Journal of Science Education and Technology 3:259–262.

Haug, M. (1996). How to incorporate and evaluate writing skills in animal science and dairy science courses. Journal of Animal Science 74(11):2835–2843.

Hotchkiss, S. K., and Nelles, M. K. (1988). Writing across the curriculum: Team teaching the review article in biology. Journal of College Science Teaching 18:45–47.

House, K. (1983). Improving student writing in biology. The American Biology Teacher 45:267–270.

Iverson, C. (1998). American Medical Association Manual of Style: A Guide for Authors and Editors. Baltimore: Williams & Wilkins.

Leeper, F. (1984). Integrating Biology and English. The American Biology Teacher 46: 280.

Moore, R. (1994). Writing to learn biology. Journal of College Science Teaching 23:289–295.

Reynolds, F. E., and Pickett, I. (1989). Read! Think! Write! The reading response journal in the biology classroom. The American Biology Teacher 51:435–437.

Squitieri, L. (1988). Cue: How to get started writing in anatomy and physiology. Journal of College Science Teaching 17(3):279–280.

Trombulak, S., and Sheldon, S. (1989). The real value of writing to learn in biology. Journal of College Science Teaching 18:384–386.

Zeegers, P., and Giles, L. (1996). Essay writing in biology: An example of effective student learning. Research in Science Education 26(4):437–459.

E. Chemistry

Adams, R. C. (1990). Writing in science: It's all in how you say it. Writing Notebook: Creative Word Processing in the Classroom 7(4):33.

Atkinson, G. F. (1986). Writing among other skills. Journal of Chemical Education 63(1986):337–338.

Beall, H., and John, T. (1993). Writing in chemistry: Keys to student underlife. College Teaching 41:50–54.

Dodd, J. S., and Brogan, M. C. eds. (1986). The ACS Style Guide: A Manual for Authors and Editors. Washington, DC: American Chemical Society.

Labianca, D. A., and Reeves, W. J. (1985). Writing across the curriculum: The science segment. Journal of Chemical Education 62:400–402.

Meislich, E. K. (1987). Requiring good writing in chemistry courses. Journal of Chemical Education 64:505–506.

Rosenthal, L. C. (1987). Writing across the curriculum: Chemistry lab reports. Journal of Chemical Education 64:996–998.

Stanislawski, D. A. (1990). Writing assignments? But this is chemistry not English! Journal of Chemical Education 67:575–576.

Van Orden, N. (1987). Critical thinking writing assignments in general chemistry. Journal of Chemical Education 64:506–507.

F. Computer Science

Zobel, J. (1997). Writing for Computer Science: The Art of Effective Communication. Singapore: Springer Verlag.

G. Engineering

McCuen, R. H. (1996). The Elements of Academic Research. New York: American Society of Civil Engineers. Covers the entire research process, including finding advisors, selecting topics, defense of the dissertation, and publication.

Michaelson, H. B. (1990). How to Write and Publish Engineering Papers and Reports. Phoenix: Oryx Press. 1990.

H. Mathematics

Swanson, E. (1979). Mathematics into Type: Copyediting and Proofreading of Mathematics for Editorial Assistants and Authors. Providence, RI: American Mathematical Society.

I. Physics

American Institute of Physics Publication Board. (1990). AIP Style Manual for Guidance in Writing, Editing, and Preparing Physics Manuscripts for Publication. New York: American Institute of Physics.

Mullin, W. J. (1989). Writing in physics. The Physics Teacher 27:342–347.

Kirkpatrick, L. D., and Pettendrigh, A. S. (1984). A writing teacher in the physics classroom. The Physics Teacher 22:159–164.
Soriano, J. R. (1989). Thinking through writing. Science Teacher 56(3):70–73.

J. Searching Patents

Gordon, T. T., and Cookfair, A. S. (1995). Patent Fundamentals for Scientists and Engineers. Boca Raton, FL: CRC Press.
Lechter, M. A. (1995). Successful Patents and Patenting for Engineers and Scientists. New York: IEEE.
Walker, R. D. (1995). Patents as Scientific and Technical Literature. Metuchen, NJ: Scarecrow Press.

25

Dissertation Grant Programs

I. INTRODUCTION

Dissertation grants vary in scope from those that merely assist you in seeking other funding to those that will pay your full living expenses as well as all research costs. However, even small grants add to the researcher's prestige and constitute an important listing on the researcher's vita, because they are evidence that the researcher's project has been peer-reviewed in a competitive process. Writing a grant is a very worthwhile endeavor in its own right, forcing the researcher to clarify his or her theories and hypotheses, have a good literature review, and be able to articulate and defend his or her research design and methodology.

Each dissertation grant program will have its own set of requirements. Requirements may include citizenship, minority status, gender, student status (e.g., post-comprehensive examination status), intended career commitment, and others. Not infrequently, a dissertation proposal will require a letter of support from a faculty member who has agreed to supervise the dissertation. Often this faculty member will be the nominal ''principal investigator,'' even though actual research is to be done by the student. Corporate research programs, for instance, rarely fund graduate students directly. Other requirements may have to do with proposal length (going over may actually lead to your proposal being eliminated sheerly on this technical ground!), manner of delivery (e.g., express rather than postal mail), and, of course, deadline date.

The most important portion of the dissertation proposal will be the substantive dissertation topic. It must fall clearly within the priorities of the funding agency, which will normally have a printed mission statement or research agenda, which may change annually. It is the objective of the student seeking the dissertation grant to show that his or her topic fits within funding agency priorities and that it will make a significant contribution to the field. Importance may be demonstrated by discussion of gaps in the literature, needs reflected in statements from policy agencies, and letters from scholars in the area.

The budget is also a key part of the dissertation funding proposal. Each item will need justification. Often a university research office will provide assistance on breaking down and costing each element of the budget, from the stipend to travel costs to equipment to overhead costs. All cost estimates should be verifiable through a cited reference, such as a reference to federally negotiated overhead rates for overhead costs or a reference to *Wall Street Journal* page listings of exchange rates for costs of changing money to a foreign currency. The university research office assistant will bring to light costs of which the student may be unaware or prohibitions on asking for certain items (e.g., that the agency will not fund computer purchases). The student is well advised to take advantage of research office experience and to not prepare his or her budget in isolation.

The reference section of your library will have a selection of print resources relevant to funding your dissertation. Some of the most used are the *Annual Register of Grant Support* (R. R. Bowker Data Publishing Group), *Catalog of Federal Domestic Assistance* (to locate government agencies receiving grants and contracts on topics relevant to one's dissertation), the *Directory of Research Grants* (Oryx Press), the *Directory of Grants in the Humanities* (Oryx Press), *The Foundation Directory* (nongovernmental funding sources; see also the *Foundation Grants Index* and the *Source Book Profiles* from the Foundation Center), *Grants and Fellowships of Interest to Historians* (American Historical Association), the *Grants Register* (St. Martin's Press), *Guide for Grants and Contracts* (National Institutes of Health), the *National Directory of Grants and Aid to Individuals in the Arts* (Washington International Arts Letter), and the periodical *National Science Foundation Bulletin* (*NSF*).

A number of online sources exist to aid in locating dissertation grants. An excellent starting point is the Illinois Researcher Information Service (IRIS), located at http://www.library.uiuc.edu/IRIS/. This service allows the researcher to search for funding opportunities in every field from agriculture to zoology or view upcoming deadlines in 25 subject areas. The Foundation Center, located at http://fdncenter.org/grantmaker/gws_priv/priv.html, provides a "grantmaker search" facility for seeking grants from private foundations. A similar search service for corporate funding is provided at http://fdncenter.org/grantmaker/gws_corp/corp.html. Also note that many professional association home pages have discipline-specific pages listing dissertation funding in their respective areas. For instance, the one for the American Psychology Association is at http://www.apa.org/science/bulletin.html.

For those with Dialog Information Services access (online but fee-based), Dialog File 85 is Grants, produced by The Oryx Press, which provides information on more than 8,500 available grants offered by federal, state, and local governments, commercial organizations, associations, and private foundations. Each entry includes full description, qualifications, money available, and renewability. Full name, address, and telephone number for each sponsoring organization, if available, are also included. The Grants database corresponds to the print publications *Directory of Research Grants*, *Directory of Biomedical and Health Care Grants*, *Directory of Grants in the Humanities*, *Funding Sources for Community and Economic Development*, and the forthcoming *Funding Sources for K-12 Schools and Educational Organizations*. Through Dialog, among other methods, one can also access the National Technical Information Service (NTIS) online. The NTIS database gives access to information on all federal research grants and contracts.

For those with access to the fee-based Community of Science (COS) online grants and contracts information service at http://login.cos.com/, COS is the leading online network for research professionals, providing weekly notification of funding opportunities tailored to the individual based on the researcher filling out a form revealing his or her interests. With detailed user profiles, COS gives researchers personalized access via the web and email to relevant funding information, contact information, and related data, covering all fields of research.

A. Selected Dissertation Grant Programs

A wide variety of government agencies and foundations support doctoral dissertation research. A selection of these programs is listed below, organized by their respective deadline months (as of 2000, subject to change). Note that campus deadlines may be earlier. In general, the grant application effort should begin many months before the actual grant deadline. Note that most funding organizations welcome contact with applicants. You can often get a much clearer idea of funding agency priorities and requirements from a direct phone call to a program officer or, better yet, a personal visit. Direct discussion with program officers can alert you to additional funding opportunities you may not have noticed and will let you know the criteria by which your proposal will be ranked and judged.

1. January

American Educational Research Association Dissertation Grants (also March and September)
Decision, Risk, & Management Science, National Science Foundation
Economics, National Science Foundation
Law and Social Sciences, National Science Foundation
Minority Summer Dissertation Workshop, Social Science Research Council

Morris K. Udall and Excellence in National Environmental Policy Program, in environmental policy and conflict resolution
Political Science, National Science Foundation

2. February

Berlin Program for Advanced German and European Studies, Social Science Research Council, covering dissertation research on German or European affairs
Ethics and Values Studies, National Science Foundation
Harry Frank Guggenheim Foundation Dissertation Grants, covering the study of violence and aggression, any discipline
Institute of International Education (IIE) Professional Development Fellowships, for business and economics, law, journalism, public administration and international relations in relation to East Central European, Baltic, and CIS studies
IREX developmental fellowships for research in Azarbaijan, the Baltics, eastern Europe, Georgia, and nations of the former Soviet Union, covering archaeology, anthropology, business, demography, economics, geography, law, musicology, political science, psychology, and sociology (also in June)
Science and Technology Studies, National Science Foundation

3. March

American Foundation for Pharmaceutical Education
Hubert Humphrey Doctoral Fellowships in Arms Control, Nonproliferation and Disarmament
Lerner-Gray Fund for Marine Research, American Museum of Natural History

4. May

Agency for Health Care Policy and Research
Archaeology and Archaeometry, National Science Foundation
Cultural Anthropology, National Science Foundation
Linguistics, National Science Foundation
Physical Anthropology, National Science Foundation

5. June

IREX developmental fellowships

6. July

HUD (Department of Housing and Urban Development) Dissertation Grants

7. August

   Decision, Risk, and Management Science, National Science Foundation
   Economics, National Science Foundation
   Ethics and Values Studies, National Science Foundation
   Law and Social Sciences, National Science Foundation
   Political Science, National Science Foundation
   Science and Technology Studies, National Science Foundation

8. September

   American Psychological Association dissertation awards
   See http://www.apa.org/science/diss.html
   Doctoral Dissertation Awards for Arthritis Health Professionals

9. October

   American Lung Association, Behavioral Science Dissertation Grants
   Biological Instrumentation Resources, National Science Foundation
   DAAD-Fulbright: dissertation research in Germany, U.S. citizens
   Environmental Biology, National Science Foundation
   Fulbright-Hays Dissertation Awards, focusing on economics, geography, or sociology
   Not covering western Europe
   Health Care Finance Administration, Dissertation Fellowship Grants for social science
   Integrative Biology and Neuroscience, National Science Foundation
   Japan Dissertation Workshop, Social Science Research Council
   Sociology, National Science Foundation
   Spencer Dissertation Fellowships Program, in education research

10. November

   Agency for Health Care Policy and Research
   American Association of University Women Educational Foundation
   American Council of Learned Societies, Fellowships for East European Studies
   American Educational Research Association, Minority Fellowships; also Spencer Fellowships in educational research; also Dissertation Fellowships in conjunction with the National Science Foundation and the National Center for Education Statistics
   Dunbarton Oaks Junior Fellowships in Byzantine, Pre-Columbian, and Landscape Architecture Studies
   Environmental Protection Agency, Science to Achieve Results Program (STAR). Funds 100 fellowships at masters' and Ph.D. levels in environment-related fields

Ford Foundation Dissertation Fellowships for Minorities, covering behavioral and social sciences, biological sciences, engineering, humanities, mathematics, physical sciences, and selected interdisciplinary areas
Getty Center for Education in the Arts, covering art education
Henry Luce Foundation/ACLS Dissertation Fellowship Program in American Art covering U.S. art history
National Endowment for the Humanities Dissertation Grants
Social Science Research Council Dissertation Research Fellowships, Underrepresented Disciplines in Middle Eastern Studies. Focus on social sciences, philosophy, and fine arts
Social Science Research Council Dissertation Fellowships, Middle East, covering social science and humanities
Social Science Research Council Dissertation Fellowships, South Asia
Social Science Research Council—MacArthur Dissertation Fellowships on Peace and Security in a Changing World
United States Institute of Peace, Jennings Randolph Program for International Peace
Woodrow Wilson National Fellowship Foundation, Women's Studies Dissertation Grants, and Charlotte Newcomb Dissertation Grants in Ethical Studies

11. December

American Planning Association Congressional Fellowship Program, covering urban planning and public policy, working with a member of Congress
Charlotte W. Newcombe Doctoral Dissertation Fellowships, in ethics
Geography and Regional Science, National Science Foundation
Social Science Research Council Dissertation Fellowships for Soviet Union and Its Successor States. Covering social science and humanities disciplines
Social Science Research Council Dissertation Fellowship in Sexuality Research

12. All Year

Carnegie Institution of Washington, Predoctoral Fellows

B. Selected Dissertation Funding Agencies and Organizations

Contact information for selected dissertation funding organizations is listed below.

American Association of University Women (AAUW) Educational Foundation, P. O. Box 4030, Iowa City, IA 52243–1204; (319) 337–1716; e-mail: fellows@access.digix.net.

American Council of Learned Societies, Office of Fellowships and Grants, 228 East 45th Street, New York, NY 10017–3398; fax: (212) 949-8058. http://www.acls.org/; e-mail: grants@acls.org.

American Educational Research Association Minority Fellowships, 1230 17th Street, NW, Washington, DC 20036–3078; (202) 233-9485; http://www.aera.ucsb.edu/index.html

American Planning Association Congressional Fellowship Program; http://www.planning.org/govt/fellowship.htm.

Canadian Studies Association Enders Endowment, ACSUS, 1317 F Street, NW, Suite 920, Washington, DC 20004–1105; (202) 393-2580; e-mail: acsus@nicom.com.

Charlotte W. Newcombe Doctoral Dissertation Fellowships, The Woodrow Wilson National Fellowship Foundation, CN 5281, Princeton, NJ 08543-5281; e-mail: charlotte@woodrow.org; http://www.woodrow.org/newcombe/.

Environmental Protection Agency STAR Program, http://es.epa.gov/ncerqa/rfa/gradfellows01.html.

Ford Foundation Dissertation Fellowships, National Research Council Fellowship Office, 2101 Constitution Avenue, Washington, DC 20418; (202) 334-2872; e-mail: infofell@nas.edu.

Fulbright-Hays Doctoral Dissertation Research Abroad Program, U.S. Department of Education, 600 Independence Avenue SW, Washington, DC 20202–5331; (202) 401-9774.

Fulbright Grants for Graduate Study Abroad, Institute of International Education, U.S. Student Programs Division, 809 United Nations Plaza, New York, NY 10017. http://www.iie.org/fulbright.

Harry Frank Guggenheim Foundation, 527 Madison Avenue, New York, NY 10022–4304; (212) 644-4907; http://www.hfg.org.

Health Care Finance Administration, Attn. Marilyn Lewis-Taylor, Office of Internal Customer Support, 7500 Security Boulevard, C2-21-5, Baltimore, MD 21244–1850; (410) 786-6644; e-mail: Mlewistaylor@hfca.gov.

Henry J. Kaiser Family Foundation, Quadrus, 2400 Sand Hill Road, Menlo Park, CA 94025; 415–854-9400. Funds dissertations in health research.

Henry Luce Foundation/ACLS Dissertation Fellowships in American Art, American Council of Learned Societies, 228 East 45th Street, New York, NY 10017–3398; fax: (212) 949-8058; http://www.acls.org/jshome.htm; e-mail: grants@acls.org.

Hubert Humphrey Doctoral Fellowships in Arms Control, Nonproliferation and Disarmament, Office of Chief Science Advisor, Room 5643, U.S. Arms Control and Disarmament Agency, 320 21st Street, NW, Washington DC 20451; (202) 647-8090; http://www.acda.gov/.

HUD Dissertation Grants, http://www.oup.org/funding/add_ddrg.html.

Institute of International Education (IIE) Professional Development Fellowships, U.S. Student Programs, Professional Development Fellowship, IIE, 809 U.N. Plaza, New York, NY 10017–3580; (212) 984-5330; fax: 212-984-5325.

Inter-American Foundation, Fellowship Programs, Fellowship Office, Inter-American Foundation, P.O. Box 9486, Rosslyn, VA 22209; (703) 841-3800.

Inter-American Foundation Fellowship Programs for Grassroots Development Program-Dept. 555, 901 N. Stuart Street, 10th Floor, Arlington, VA 22203; http://www.iaf.gov.

IREX (International Research and Exchanges Board), 1616 H Street, NW, Washington, DC 20006; (202) 628-8188; fax: (202) 628-8189; e-mail: irex@irex.org; http://www.irex.org/programs/stg/index.

Link Foundation Energy Fellowship Program, Dr. Brian Thompson, Secretary, 200 Administration Building, University of Rochester, Rochester, NY 14627; (716) 275-5931.

Logistics Education Foundation, http://www.telebyte.com/htdocs/sole/lef.html#dissertation.

Morris K. Udall and Excellence in National Environmental Policy Program, 2201 N. Dodge Street, P.O. Box 4030, Iowa City, IA 52243; (319) 337-1650; fax: (319) 337-1204.

National Institute of Mental Health. Dissertation Research Grants in Child and Adolescent Developmental Psychopathology, HIV/AIDS Research, or Mental Health Services Research/Minority Dissertation Research Grants in Mental Health http://tigger.oslc.org/Ecpn/grantch1.html.

National Endowment for the Humanities Dissertation Grants, http://aicgs.org/gardinet/prog016.htm and http://www.neh.fed.us/grants/index.html.

National Science Foundation. Guide to Programs, http://stis.NSF.gov/NSF/NSFpubs/guide/start.htm. See also the NSF Social, Behavioral, and Economic Research (SBER): Program Announcement, the Minority Dissertation Research Grants in Mental Health, and other grant booklets.

National Science Foundation Grants for Improving Doctoral Dissertation Research (especially Anthropology; Decision, Risk and Management Science; Environmental Biology; Integrative Biology and Neuroscience; Geography and Regional Science; Linguistics; Law and Social Sciences; Political Science; Sociology; and Studies in Science, Technology and Society). Contact one of these programs at National Science Foundation, 4202 Wilson Boulevard, Arlington, VA 22230; http://www.fastlane.nsf.gov/aO/flcontacts.htm.

National Security Education Program (NSEP) Fellowships, Academy for Educational Development, Universal North Building, 1875 Connecticut Avenue, NW, Suite 900, Washington DC 20009–1202.

Social Science Research Council, 810 Seventh Avenue, New York, NY 10019; (212) 337-2700; fax: (212) 377-2727; http://www.src.org.

Spencer Dissertation Fellowships Program, 900 North Michigan Avenue, Suite 2800, Chicago, IL 60611–1542; (312) 337-7000.

United States Air Force Office of Scientific Research; 202-767-5021/5022; e-mail: collins@afosr.af.mil. Focus on the life sciences.

United States Institute of Peace, Jennings Randolph Program for International Peace, 1200 17th Street NW, Suite 200, Washington, DC 20036–3011; (202) 457-1700; fax: (202) 429–6063; e-mail: jprogram@usip.org; http://www.usip.org/fellows.html.

Woodrow Wilson National Fellowship Foundation, CN 5281, Princeton, NJ 08543–5281; (609) 452-7007; fax: (609) 452-0066; http://www.woodrow.org.

BIBLIOGRAPHY

Bauer, G. D. (1988). The 'How To' Grants Manual. 2nd ed. New York: Macmillan.

Lauffer, A. Grantsmanship. Thousand Oaks, CA: Sage Publications. A classic in the field.

Leskes, A., ed. (1986). Guide for Grants for Graduate Students. Princeton, NJ: Peterson's Guides, Inc.

Locke, L. F., Spriduso, W. W., and Silverman, S. J. (1993). Proposals That Work: A Guide for Planning Dissertations and Grant Proposals. Thousand Oaks, CA: Sage Publications. Chapter 8 deals with funding dissertation proposals, including an example from the National Institutes of Health. The last 100 pages of the book contain a wide variety of examples of funding proposals.

Schumacher, D. (1992). Get Funded! Thousand Oaks, CA: Sage Publications.

Index

Milton Keynes UK
Ingram Content Group UK Ltd.
UKHW021632071024
449327UK00020BA/1280